In Search of Self

A Personal Journey to Understanding and Acceptance

GAIL GILLINGHAM

In Search of Self

Copyright © 2018 by Gail Gillingham

No part of this publication may be reproduced, distributed, or transmitted in any form or by any means, including photocopying, recording, or other electronic or mechanical methods, without the prior written permission of the author, except in the case of brief quotations embodied in critical reviews and certain other non-commercial uses permitted by copyright law.

Tellwell Talent

www.tellwell.ca

ISBN

978-1-77370-710-5 (Hardcover)

978-1-77370-709-9 (Paperback)

978-1-77370-711-2 (eBook)

Table of Contents

This book is dedicated to my mother
Johanna Pearson
With whom I have shared so much of this journey.
Thanks for being there through thick and thin Mom!

In Search of Self
Preface

I sit at my computer, hands on the keys, feeling very humble, my mind overwhelmed with uncertainty. I know that the time has come for me to write this book, probably the most important thing that I have written in my life. I am not certain that I can do it justice. I know the material. I know how important this is. I know how to fit the model into anyone's life. I am concerned that my words will not be able to convey the importance of this model without having readers reject it because of its simplicity, or because it places them in a situation in which they become defensive. It is not an easy task, but I know that I must try and that the time is right.

On September 11, 2001 a group of men chose to use plane loads of men, women and children to state their message to the world. In the days, months and years that have followed this massacre, people all around the world tried to come to terms with what happened that day and to make sense of their own personal reactions. It was not an easy task. As I watched and listened, I knew that one of the reasons that we were having so much trouble is because we are trying to deal with a situation, using only bits and pieces of what "is", rather than looking at the whole picture. On September 11, 2001, most of us experienced a major shift in our 'self'. Unless we fully understand what the 'self' is, we will have problems dealing with all of the implications of the changes we are experiencing.

The purpose of this book is to outline a model of the self which will allow us to understand how the horror of a day like September 11 resulted in these feelings of uncertainty. It will provide a model of the self which is so vast that it covers every facet of each of us and yet, at the same time, so simple that anyone can understand it. This model will allow us to look at a human being in a new way, by describing the intricate connections between each of us and the world around us, so that we can clearly understand our reactions and our feelings.

The search of self is an individual journey that we each embark on, in our own time, and in our own way. Since we can only take ownership of our own personal journey in life, much of what I share will be of a personal nature. During my journey through life, I have had the opportunity to concentrate much of my energy and learning on two different groups of people who are at the extreme as human beings: those who fall within the spectrum of autism and those who were sexually abused as children. Their stories will also be included as we can learn so much from them.

I do not offer this personal information as a claim that I am an expert on the self, have done anything right, or as a road map for anyone else to follow, but only as examples of how everything fits within the model. I humbly hope that these portions of my story and theirs will provide the impetus for you to explore further and allow you to discover your own "true self" in your own way.

As you read through this book, pay attention to your reactions to the words that are written. It's not the words that reveal your 'self'; it is your personal reactions to those words. Our reactions tell us far more about ourselves than anything coming from the outside does. You may feel uncomfortable. You may nod your head in agreement. You may get angry. You may have an "ah ha" moment. You may want to stop reading. Each and every reaction you experience exposes more about your 'self': your beliefs, your coping skills, your fears, your dreams, your barriers. This is what the journey to self is all about.

CHAPTER ONE
THE MODEL OF THE SELF

A picture is worth a thousand words.

THE TIME IS JANUARY 1993. I AM SITTING AT THE KITCHEN TABLE OF A FRIEND IN HER home in a small town in the Northwest Territories of Canada. Her eyes darken with concern as she looks at me.

" I'm worried about you, Gail. Ever since I met you, I thought that you were the strongest woman I had ever encountered. But this morning the strength is missing. You appear as fragile as a butterfly. I feel like I could destroy you completely with one swat of my hand. And yet," she paused for a moment as the concern in her eyes intensified, "deep within, your core continues shining brightly. Unbreakable. Unbending. I've never experienced anything like this before."

Her words surprise me because they so vividly describe how I have been feeling for the last few months. My strength was gone. I was falling to pieces. I knew that I was not dealing with my life very well, but I didn't think that anyone else would be able to see it. In October, I had reached the point of suicide, an absolutely terrifying place to be. I had reached out to my husband for help, only to be told to do whatever I had to do, as he turned and walked away from me. I managed to pull myself back from the brink of death that morning, but in doing so, realized that my marriage of twenty-four years was over. Till death do us part. Through the following months, I knew that I could no longer stay in my marriage, but was torn by the reality that walking away meant giving up my job, my home, and the connections that I had with family members and friends. In the midst of the struggle to make these decisions, I had written to a friend to explain why I was asking to be touched so often. "It's like pieces of me are flying off in all directions. Your hands help me to feel whole again." And now, at this table, this friend could somehow see everything that I was experiencing.

I meet this description time and again through the following years. A woman describes feeling shattered, with whole pieces of her self missing, after her husband leaves her for his gay lover and admits that he has been involved in homosexual relationships throughout their marriage. Mia Farrow describes her feelings of "flying off in all directions at once" to Oprah, as her initial reaction to the realization that her husband, Woody Allen, was having a sexual relationship with their adopted child. My brother-in-law admits his confusion: searching for pieces of himself and trying to make sense of his life, after he loses a leg and his eyesight in a hit and run accident. And finally, in September of 2001, as the whole world copes with the reality of the terrorists using planes filled with people as weapons of destruction, these phrases are used by many to explain the personal experience of coping with this trauma.

At this point in time, September 11th, 2001 stands out for many of us as the day the world changed. Our sense of security and entitlement were shattered as surely as the planes hit their targets, leaving thousands dead and the core of a city in shambles. As we struggled to deal with the shock of the attack the word "surreal" was used time and again to describe how we were feeling.

We were lost for a time, unsure of exactly where we are and how we now fit into this world we call home. As the days and weeks went by, we struggled to understand, to grieve our losses and to prepare ourselves for whatever was coming next by listening to the stories of those who survived. Each different and poignant it their own way, these stories touched our hearts and eased the pain we were feeling. As the words flowed and as time passed, we began to feel whole again.

In the midst of the stories, a common element appeared over and over again: the feeling of being lost, of being adrift, of not knowing oneself. It's as if each and every one of us became a new person within the scope that of that day. How can we explain this shift in a way that makes sense? If one looks around one's world, or into one's reflection in the mirror, all appears to be the same. But yet, we know we are different. We have all changed in a major way. The changes are unique to each of us as individuals, but they are present in each of us. We have each experienced a major shift in our 'self'.

As we look back over our individual lives, we can all find other instances when our life changed in a moment and we felt like a different person completely. The terrorist atrocities on September 11th, 2001 were not unique in their power to totally change the life of an individual in an instant, but by the vast number of people who were affected all at once. This particular shift in the 'self' happened to almost every person in the world on the same day.

Searching the current literature on the 'self' does little to make sense of these feelings. Many wise words are written about accepting change, nourishing one's soul, acknowledging our feelings, taking responsibility for our own actions, reaching out to the inner child, making conscious choices rather than using automatic reactions, going through the grief process and finding our true selves, but all come up short when it comes to making sense of the experience of having one's self "flying off in all directions". In much the same way as the tale of the six blind men who come across an elephant and try to describe it by touching the trunk, legs, tail and so on, these many elements of being human are limited by dwelling on a specific part, rather than the whole picture. It's like trying to set a jigsaw puzzle with only a handful of its pieces. We may get to know a facet of the self very well, but are not able to create a whole picture. How can we construct a meaningful picture of the whole?

During the tumultuous weeks and months after I left my marriage, various pieces of advice from caring friends and relatives helped me understand some of what I was experiencing, but until I found something that represented the whole picture, I continued to live in turmoil. Each counselor I approached had a different focus for therapy. They all left me aching for more: for the whole picture, not just pieces. In fact, many of them listened to me describe my life and stated that my ability to see it from so many different angles meant that I was already in good shape. But I knew that I was not, and so I kept searching. As I listened to people throughout our world describe their uncertainty and discomfort with what happened on September 11th, I recognized myself, dealing with the chaos of my life in the early nineties, in each and every one of them.

In 1994, I came across a model of the 'self' which helped me to visualize a compete picture of who I am as a person, and in time, to explain fully what I was experiencing, not only for myself but for every member of my family, as they were also dealing with the breakup of my marriage in their own individual ways. In 1907, Dr. William James developed a 'model of self' which met my needs. Sadly, his work was ignored by the psychological community of that time as they focused on the theories of Sigmund Freud. Today this model is largely unknown in the psychological community. And yet, it makes complete sense of my feelings in 1993 and of the experiences of others that I have mentioned above. This model became the map on which I found my 'self' during the nineteen nineties, and made sense of what was happening around me and to me. Over the years I have adjusted some of the terminology and added a compass point which makes this model more powerful in providing a direction on which to steer my course of life. It also provides a visual example to my clients, during our therapy sessions, which helps them make sense of their journey. It gives meaning to their feelings and reactions and provides us with definite goals to work towards.

Human beings have a biological body consisting of cells, tissues, bones, muscles and organs, complete with a control centre in the brain, which connects to all parts of the body through the nervous system. However, being human is much more than being a biological entity. Throughout history mankind has tried to discover, to measure and to define the 'self' in ways that include the whole being beyond biology. Religion, philosophy, psychology, and medicine have all focused their efforts on this goal, in many different ways. The early Greeks, Romans and Egyptians all found ways to explain physical symptoms for which no organic cause could be found, which connected one's body to the rest of the world. Hippocrates assumed that four humors in the body: blood, black bile, yellow bile and phlegm affected the normal functioning of the brain. Environmental conditions of heat, dryness, moisture and cold could be used to treat the balance level of these humors. The Roman physician Galen and his associates developed these theories into a powerful and influential school of thought which extended well into the nineteenth century. Over time the focus moved on to theories that psychological differences in humans are caused by chemical imbalances with little understanding of how these imbalances occur. Brain development research throughout the last ten years has revealed new exciting information on how our brains are developed over time and opened the doors to further understanding. Attempts to classify and measure the various effects of genes, the environment, relationships, and of outside forces such as the events of September 11 are a source of continuous scientific research. Pulling this all into one package is not an easy task, but yet we must admit that it is reality. Each of us exists as a demonstration that the whole package is real and vital.

In his book, The Principles of Psychology Volume I, William James describes a theory of self which includes all the facets of humanity. James states:

> *A man's self is the total of all that he can call his, not only his body and his psychic powers, but also his clothes, his home, his wife, his children, his ancestors and friends, his reputation and works, his lands and horses and yacht and bank account. All these things give him the same emotions. If they wax and prosper he feels triumphant; if they dwindle and die away, he feels cast down - not necessarily in the same degree for each thing but much in the same way for all.[1]*

James goes onto describe the model of self as a series of four different levels, each circling the next, which incorporate everything that makes up each individual person. He named these levels as the pure ego, the spiritual self, the social self and the material self.

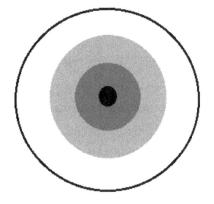

A simple diagram of the self would appear like this: with the pure ego in the centre, the spiritual self as the dark grey circle the social self as light grey and the material self as the white ring

Although this diagram looks very simple at this point, it is actually something that is impossible to draw in full detail. However, it can provide a good representation of the whole 'self' when one understands how everything is included.

This model of the self makes sense of the description my friend gave of me back in 1993 for I was indeed in a battle in which I losing pieces of my 'self' in all of my levels except for my spirit. This diagram can also be used to demonstrate the effect that something as traumatic as September 11, 2001 can have on each of us as individuals, as, again, we experienced loss in all the levels: our spiritual self, our social self and our material self. By incorporating all of the levels of the 'self' into a whole, we can come to a true understanding and acceptance of who we are as individual human beings, how we are unique in this world and how we can learn to truly accept others as they are.

---

1   William James (1890). *The Principles of Psychology Volume I*, Harvard University Press (*p. 291-292*)

THE SPIRIT

The centre core of our being is termed the "pure ego" by James, which likely has much to do with the psychological vocabulary of the late eighteen hundreds and the focus of the time on the work of Sigmund Freud. He states that the pure ego is the central point of the human being: the centre of life, the centre of feeling. This core is recognized in all cultures and has acquired many different labels throughout history. Soul, spirit, life force, heart, psyche, anima and animus, ego, and essence of life are but a few of the labels that have been assigned by different people and throughout different times. Ancient psychologists taught that our cores are inseparable from that of the world and yet separate, in that each core is on its own unique journey throughout life. As we search for meaning in our current world, many writers, psychologists and teachers are bringing the emphasis back onto this core as technology, science and individualism fail to meet our needs.

I prefer to call this central core the 'spirit' which fits better into the vocabulary of our age and is more easily understood in a multicultural, multiracial and multi religious world. Ego is limited by its association to specific theories and practices in the psychological community. Soul has religious connotations for many, with connections to heaven and hell, which may limit some people's willingness to respond positively to this model. For a diagram of the 'self' to be truly worthwhile it must be able to be used to describe every human being on this planet. Although spirit also has some religious connotations, it is more widely acceptable throughout different cultures and religions. Those of you who feel uncomfortable with any of my labels are certainly free to change them to anything you wish in your own diagram of self.

The spirit of each human being is the centre of one's individuality. It is a solid, unchanging force which comes to us in conception and lives on after the death of the body. It has no shape, no size, no weight and yet its presence or absence can be seen as one looks into the eyes of a living or dead person. Scientific research has yet to isolate, identify or measure just exactly what the spirit is, but scientists cannot explain life without it. Throughout history, in every culture and religion, the presence of the spirit is recognized in one way or another. Many who have been in the presence of others at the time of death claim to have seen the exodus of the spirit in that moment. Many who have been at death's door and recovered claim to have been surrounded by the spirits of loved ones who have gone before. Others claim to have experienced their spirit as being outside of their physical body. Some claim that the spirits of the dead are with us in our world as ghosts, or are able to communicate with them through psychic powers. I do not claim to have any exact answers as to what the spirit is, how it comes to us, and where it is before birth and after death. In the process of understanding oneself, these answers are not necessary and can vary widely from one person to the next. However, acceptance of one's unique spirit is the first step in discovering the self.

Defining the sprit is a difficult process for most of us as it is very difficult to separate what "is" from what we have learned throughout our lifetimes. I personally believe that the spirit comes complete with the knowledge of who we are as individuals, and what our journey on this world should be. It recognizes the forces of good and evil and knows the importance of honoring our creator, taking care of our world, and loving ourselves and others. It cries out with longing from deep within when we are not meeting its needs. It fills us with a joy beyond description when we are. It speaks to us with a voice that is known as intuition, which we may choose to listen to or to ignore. If we listen, it will guide us on our journey, protect us from danger, and help us reach our full potential. If we ignore it, we will suffer the consequences in many different ways including unhappiness, dissatisfaction, anger, and physical or psychological aliments. Listening to our own personal spirit and filling its needs is our ultimate task here on earth. This task is fundamentally different for each and every one of us.

Perhaps you, as a reader, are not able to accept this description of the spirit. This is okay. Coming to a complete understanding of yourself does not mean that you have to agree with or accept everything that I have written in this book. The ability to know and understand one's own spirit is an individual journey. I admit that this definition is closely connected to my various experiences here on earth and that my view has developed over time. Defining the spirit as the vital force of life within living beings as a starting point should allow you to work within this model in a way that is comfortable for you as an individual.

THE MIND

Surrounding the spirit we find a circle which James terms as our spiritual self. Since I have already chosen to use that term for the core, I call this circle the "mind". The mind is our thinking self, the inner subjective being which contains all our values and beliefs, our faculties and dispositions, our abilities and talents, our moral sensibility and conscience, our memories and our reactions. The mind is again made up of much that cannot be isolated, seen, or measured in a concrete manner. Most of the activity of the mind is hidden and revealed only through one's behavior.

The mind is divided into two areas: that which is conscious and that which is unconscious. The conscious mind is that which we are aware of such as our current thoughts and actions. The unconscious mind is that which is hidden, but which is also constantly on the alert as a source of protection for the body. In times of stress or danger, the unconscious mind often reacts automatically through the limbic system using responses that one has learned in the past or the automatic responses of flight, fight or freeze that ensure our survival.

As we will learn in the following chapters, the creation of the mind is dependent on the experiences that a person has after birth. From the time we are born, we learn how to 'be' in our world from our family, our friends and from a variety of institutions in society such as churches, schools and businesses. Our definitions of the world are those which we personally develop through experience from the time we are infants. Our reactions to any situation are dependent on similar experiences from the past and will often match those from our childhood. The more an experience is repeated, the stronger are the connections in the mind. The more traumatic the experience, the stronger the impact on the mind. A person who was raised in a home surrounded by love and gentleness will react totally differently when compared to someone who was raised in the midst of violence and neglect because of the individual mind that was created through those experiences. A person who has had a religious upbringing will react much differently to my choice of the word spirit than a person who was never brought to a church as a child, whether they have chosen to continue living in the lifestyle of their childhood or rejected it. The mind is the storehouse of everything that has been taught to us, of all that we have experienced, of the customs and traditions of one's cultural heritage and the religious beliefs that we have been exposed to. Every action and reaction that we partake in is dependent on this storehouse as its source.

THE SOCIAL SELF

The next layer of the self is called the social self, which consists of the recognition an individual receives from others. There are as many social selves for each individual as there are other individuals in the world who recognize him or her and who carry who an image of him or her in their mind. When you consider the incredible number of people that this includes for a typical person, you can visualize how big the 'self' actually is, and how impossible it would be to draw a detailed diagram of it. It's even more mind boggling to consider the dynamics of the social self of a major celebrity. This ring will include hundreds, thousands or even millions of different images as each person you have ever met or who knows of you has a spot within this ring.

These images do not necessarily match who we are as a person for they are based on the perceptions of the individual holding them. If we spend our energy trying to match all of these images, we will burn out. Our responsibility to ourselves and to others is to live as our true self and to accept others as they really are. However, most of us don't know this and spend our time trying to either be what others want or what we think they want.

In order to explain the impact of the social self on who we are as people, the more important a person in one's life, the bigger the space they will take up in the social ring, but even those you have only had contact with for a short time will have a space. These images change as one gets to know someone better and increase or decrease in size due to the degree that one is involved with a person at a particular time. As we age, the ring continues to grow with the number of new people we meet, keeping intact the images from the past. Death creates holes and destroys the symmetry of the social self as one loses the recognition of the person who has died, and yet retains the past image of this person in their memory, which is now in the mind. Only time and interactions with others will fill in that hole and decrease the space allotted to that image.

The position of the social self in the model of self as an inner ring emphasizes the importance of interpersonal relations to mankind. The preservation of one's positive social self is one of life's ongoing tasks. If we fail, we are in trouble. The most severe pathological symptoms show up in those who have been forced to dwell on the outskirts of the life of their community. Their condition likely indicates the lack of positive interpersonal relationships, not pathology. The power of our social self has been recognized throughout history in many cultures, as exile was deemed the ultimate punishment that a person could receive.

A major part of reaching our ultimate potential in life includes how we, as individuals, choose to interact with other people. The most important factor in building positive relationships is being accepted as one really is, and having the ability to accept another person as they are, in the same way that one needs to accept oneself. The images found within our social self are what determine whether this acceptance is occurring or not.

THE MATERIAL SELF

The outer circle of the model of self represents the material self, which is made up of all we have. This includes everything we can call our own and so, like the social self, is impossible to diagram in complete detail. It begins with our body which must be recognized part by part, function by function. We own our hair, our skin, our arms and legs, our stomachs, our heart and lungs and our muscles and bones. We own the nose on our face and our earlobes. We also own our height, our weight, and our ability to walk, to talk, to see and to think. We own our unique genetic code. We may be satisfied with each part of our body, obsessed with changing it or ignore it completely. Some parts may cause us pain, frustration or discomfort, which has an impact on our anxiety level and our ability to do what we want to do. Some parts change as we age or as we put more effort into them. Some parts are damaged in accidents, lost forever, or were missing when we started. All of this must be taken into account when one considers the 'self'.

The material self also includes the people in our lives. Those that hold the biggest spaces in our material self are those who are the closest to us: for many, our parents, our mates, our children and our siblings. We also have teachers and coaches, friends and neighbors, a boss at work and coworkers to work alongside. We have doctors, lawyers and bankers to deal with, policeman, fireman and paramedics to keep us safe, postmen, store clerks and waiters to serve us. These people take up space in our material self in a different way than they make up our social self as we own role that they play in our lives, not how they actually think about us or relate with us. In other words, the fact that I have a mother fills a space in my material self of 'mother', while her view of me is found in my social self. My view of her is not found within my 'self' at all, but in her social self, which is one way in which all our selves are interconnected. Some of the people in these roles last a lifetime and are never replaced if they are gone, such as our parents. Other roles are far more flexible. A person may replace one person for another who has held this role in the past, such as a next-door-neighbor or a coach. Other roles are held by many different people simultaneously such as a friend, a cousin, or a neighbor.

The material self is also made up of all the roles that we personally hold in our own lives. Each of us holds numerous roles simultaneously. As a woman I hold the roles of wife, lover, mother, grandmother, daughter, sister, niece, sister-in-law, mother-in-law, aunt, cousin, daughter-in-law, ex-wife, business owner, cook, friend, mentor, neighbor, Canadian, customer, patient, renter, homemaker, author, driver, therapist, photographer, musician, Lutheran, student, Baby Boomer, Scandinavian, female, and member of several different organizations, and many more, all at the same time. I also retain roles from the past which I do not actually fill at this present moment such as farmer's daughter, basketball player, hockey mother, and resident of the North West Territories. These roles from the past not only have affected my development as a self, but also will determine those who I relate well with in the present because of similar experiences in the past.

Our roles are all different in their make-up, expectations and level of importance from one moment to the next. They may conflict with one another in the amount of time or energy that they require, or in the picture that they portray to those we are interacting with. Juggling these roles becomes a major factor in our lives. Again, as the roles of others in our lives are part of our material selves, so are our roles part of the material selves of those we hold a role with. So as a mother in my material self, I also appear in the mother role in the material self of my four sons. As a patient, I have a position in my doctor's material self, and am also found in my landlord's material self as a renter. This means that we are all interconnected with each other in a very personal way, whether we want to admit it or not.

The material self also contains all of our material possessions such as our home, our jobs, the clothes that we wear, our pets, the vehicles we drive, our furniture, money, stocks and bonds, jewelry, artwork, books, computers, land, businesses and so on. Some of these things we own ourselves, others we share with other people such as family members, which means that they appear in more than one material self at a time. The material self also includes those things that we claim an ownership of, that we do not actually own, such as the communities we live in, the type of music or art that we enjoy, the sport teams that we support, our heritage, our school, our bank, our peer group, our country, and the planet earth. The choices that we make about the possessions we choose to acquire, to keep and to look after, defines each of us in certain unique ways as individuals.

The acquisition of certain possessions creates new roles for us to fill. For example, buying a house gives us the role of homeowner, which in turn leads to the requirement that one spend one's time, money and energy in different ways. The new role forces us to readjust other roles and the possessions within the circle of our material self. This fact really struck home to me back in the early eighties when my husband and I chose to buy a farm and move our children 'back to the land'. Suddenly my focus moved from buying new household appliances to acquiring rolls of barbed wire fencing, a necessity for keeping our cows at home. The energy that my 'self' expended had shifted completely with the acquisition of the farm and its animals. Every possession we choose to add or subtract from our material self affects the construction of the whole self and the energy we dispense.

Certain components of the material self are necessary for survival. If we do not have enough food to eat, clean water to drink, adequate shelter and clothing to protect us from the cold or the heat and clean air to breathe, we destroy the biological body. For certain people in our world today, every ounce of their energy and every minute of their time are spent on filling these biological needs. Sadly their human potential is wasted on providing these necessities for the material self instead of the other levels, which are so much more important in the long run. Even more upsetting is the fact that these situations exist because of the decisions of other human beings who concentrate their energies on enlarging their material self with little thought or concern of how their actions and greed impact others.

As one begins to focus on of all of the different facets which make up the self we may feel overwhelmed by how vast and interconnected it is. However, each of us is able to deal with all of this quite calmly and comfortably every day of our lives, moving effortlessly from one role to another, looking after our material possessions without much thought, and incorporating the various levels of the self with each other without being aware that it is even happening. It is only when we step back to look at the whole picture that we realize how big the self really is and how amazing it is that we are all capable of incorporating these different facets and levels together to become the one individual person that we are. This makes being human truly unique and incredible.

PULLING IT ALL TOGETHER

Although it is impossible to draw a complete diagram of the self, it is wise to practice thinking of what is included in the self through actual drawings to see how this formation pulls together to make a complete whole. This will give you the opportunity to grasp what is happening to you because of the connections that you are personally experiencing between these levels and to understand why you are reacting as you do. Although the process we will go through in the next few pages is simplified by limiting our examples to only a few concepts, it will give you the tools to work within the model. At no time is it necessary to deal with every facet of the self at once. In fact, it's impossible. Placing them in the model individually gives you the opportunity to picture how they impact the whole and whether you want to accept them as they are or make changes. In this diagram, I have used letters to differentiate between the different factors, placing each one in the level where one would find it. I am the using the concept of my 'self' to simplify the writing process, not because these levels and factors are actual descriptions of my own self.

In the first diagram, the mind holds my values of honesty (h) and commitment (c), my ability to paint (a), and my reaction of silence (s). My social self contains the images of me that my mother (m), my brother (b), my grandson (g), my neighbor (n), my banker (b), my landlord (l), my pastor (p), and my cousin (f) hold of me. The material level contains my house (H), my car (V), my weight (W), my roles as a wife (S), consultant (F) and friend (P), my diamond earrings (E), my cat (Z), and a symbol for each of my children (M D T G). These are only limited examples of what makes up each level, but they allow us to contemplate where the different factors fit in each level of the 'self'. Be aware that all my images of those individuals mentioned as contributing to my social self (my mother,

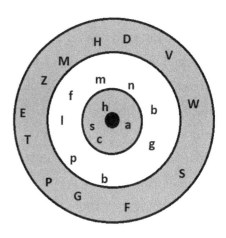

brother, grandson, pastor and so on) are also found in their individual models of self at the social level. Much of my material self is also found on the material selves of others.

By drawing out the four levels and then inserting different concepts and items to fit in each level we quickly realize that, although we can place an item in one level, each of these factors take up a space, in some way, in every level. For example if we place my mother and my job on the model, they will appear in all three levels, but in a different way in each. My ideal of what a mother is appears in the mind, her image of me as a person appears in the social self, while the fact that I have a mother is part of my material self. My concept of work, my different abilities, and my feelings about my present job are found in my mind. The impact that this job may have on the images that others have of me colors my social self, while the job itself is found in my material self. If we added my health to this diagram we would complicate it even further as we now have the way I am choosing to live in regards of my health to the model.

To clarify the model even further we can use size and position to understand how important we feel these items are to us and how much energy and time we are currently expending on each item. The importance of each item or concept may be indicated by how close it is to the centre of the circle while its size may demonstrate the actual amount of time and energy we expend on it. When I put my mother, my job and my health in the model honestly I can quickly recognize that, although I place my health as the most important in my mind, the time and effort I place on exercise and a healthy diet in my material level indicates something else. Both my job and my mother take far more of my time and energy. This is a choice that I, personally, am making for one reason or another, and am totally responsible for. It is also a choice that may or may not change over time.

Once we have determined the difference between how we believe, compared to how we actually live we will be able to pinpoint major causes of stress that we are creating for ourselves on a day to day basis. As we have stated before, our model of self is constantly changing, which affects the amount of time and energy that we have for our different factors and the satisfaction we experience. If we consider what might happen if one's mother got sick, we find that the time and energy needed expend on the role of 'child' may increase dramatically. One may no longer have the same time or energy to put into one's effort towards one's house or job. A person, who was quite content before, may now become discouraged and frustrated as these items no longer match each other on the different levels of the self. On the other hand, another person, who was discontented before, may find that they are happier now that they are spending their time with their mother. Each of us is unique in how we will respond to the changes that life brings us.

All of these examples are very limited because each level is made up of a huge number of factors which all interact with each other and which all take our time and energy in their own way. For many, juggling the various factors becomes overwhelming because of the amount of time and energy they take. Others get stuck focusing on certain factors which mean very little to them when it comes to what is important in their mind and spirit. This leads to discontent. Part of our life's journey is determining which factors we want to keep in our 'self' and which we need to let go of, but since no one talks about the self in this way, we are unaware that we are actually in charge of this. Most of the time we get so caught up in what we are doing that we don't know how to move on.

THE LIFE LINE AND COMPASS POINT.

The last concept which can help us determine how the levels of self all fit together in our model is to use the idea of a compass to measure how the different factors are interrelated between the levels. A life line, which resembles the line towards the magnetic north pole on our regular compasses, can be drawn directly from the spirit to the outer edge of the material self.

This connects all four levels of the self: the spirit, the mind, the social self and the material self.

The long line is called "our life line" because it indicates how to reach our full potential or "purpose" in life. This line is solid and unmoving throughout our whole life. When all of the factors within every level of the self lie on the line we have reached our "true potential". However, it's not easy to reach this point and so we spend our lives living on the line of our compass point, which is indicated by the shorter line. The compass point is constantly moving to point to the position of the different factors in the different levels of self. The further the compass point has to move away from the life line, the 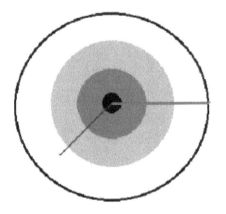 more energy we expend without even being aware of what we are doing. The more time that we spend living with our compass point away from our life line, the more difficulties we will have, both physically and psychologically.

In order to demonstrate the impact of these lines, I will use a relationship with a fictional friend. The V (mind) represents my value of honesty, which is part of my true self, so it lies directly on my life line. The M represents my value of friendship (mind), my image of this friend (her social self), and the role I am holding as a friend in my material self. The F represents my friend's image of and relationship with me (social self), as well as the role of friend that she plays in my life (material self). To make this example a little more powerful, we will assume that I have just moved into a new city and therefore have not had the opportunity to make many new friends, so this relationship has more impact than it might have in my home town. Also, this relationship is not as important to her as it is to me, so I am putting more time and effort into it, which is indicated by size.

This new friend is not honest. She is a shoplifter. She believes that I am just like her, which places her image of me directly opposite to who I really am, which is found on my life line: honest. My image of her is slightly closer to who she is on her life line as I have accepted that she is a shoplifter. However, everything else I believe about her is based on my own reality, not hers, and so my image of her is also a long ways off base. Don't forget that my image of her as a person is located in her social self in her model of self so you won't see it on this model. Our roles of what it means to be friend are also the opposite of what my "ideal" of a friend is in my mind. In order to continue my relationship with her in attempt to ensure that I am not lonely, I pretend that I also shoplift. In my pretense, my compass point has to move almost as far away from my life line as possible, expending an incredible amount of my psychic energy. The longer I stay in this relationship and continue this pretense, the more discomfort and dissatisfaction I will experience.

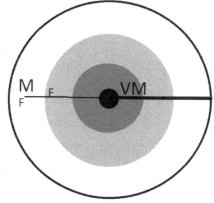

As we look at this example, I am sure that you can recognize that very few of us live on our life line. Most of us don't even make the effort to try to understand exactly what our values and beliefs are, much less attempt to explain our choices of behavior with them in mind. Many of us choose to deny that we have a spirit at all, or that we are all interconnected with each other and the world we live in. We get so wrapped up in our material possessions or relationships that we ignore everything else. And then when things fall to pieces we throw up our hands and move on to something new, in hopes of finding what we are looking for there. We blame our problems on anyone but ourselves, and turn to chemical means to ignore the messages that our body is giving us. Gradually the whole world suffers.

HOW OTHERS DESCRIBE THIS PROCESS

Attempts to describe this concept of living on one's life line have happened in many different ways by many different people, over time. For example, Abraham Maslow[2] used the concept of levels of

---

2   Maslow, A. H., (1970). Motivation and personality (rev. ed.). New York: Harper and Row.

human motivation as the basis for describing how people achieve their full potential. He described a hierarchy of needs which must be met if we are to succeed. The opportunity to become the best we can be is based directly whether or not the needs of each level are met. According to Maslow, the basic biological needs such as hunger, thirst, sleep and protection from the forces of nature (the material self), and the psycho social needs such as self esteem, affection and a sense of belonging (the social self) must be satisfied before one has the energy to concentrate on the next levels.

The final levels of this hierarchy are transcendence and self actualization. Transcendence is the highest state of consciousness, one in which one realizes their spiritual needs for cosmic identification, and accepts and acknowledges their individual role and the unique role of every other person in the whole picture of life. This level closely matches the final stage of moral reasoning developed by Lawrence Kohlberg[3] called the universal ethical principle orientation. To be true to the universal principles, one must feel oneself as a part of the cosmic direction in a way that transcends social norms. Right is defined by the decision of conscience in accord with self-chosen ethical principles appealing to logical comprehensiveness, universality and consistency. Maslow claims that these principles are abstract and ethical and are not concrete moral rules like the Ten Commandments. The basis of the universal principles followed during transcendence and self-actualization are justice, reciprocity and equality of human rights, and respect for the dignity of human beings as individual persons. In other words, transcendence is the point in which one is able to accept being part of a whole universe.

Self-actualization is the stage in which a person is able to accept themselves and others for what they are instead of trying to change either themselves or others into something else. In other words, self actualization describes people who are living on their life line and are able to allow all others to live on theirs. They are free to recognize and differentiate the needs and desires of others as separate from their own and allow others to journey through life without demanding that the fit into the same pattern as anyone else. They make rational choices of reaction in response to the uniqueness of each situation they are dealing with rather than responding with the automatic reactions they learned in childhood. They can form profoundly intimate relationships with at least a few special people but don't need to have others support them in everything they do. They are okay when they are all alone. They can stand on their own taking clear responsibility for themselves and own their thoughts, their beliefs and their behavior without apology. This is the gift they also give others, expecting them to stand on their own. They are spontaneous and creative, sharing their talents and abilities with the world without being overly concerned on how much they will gain from their efforts or how others in the world will react to what they are doing, resist conformity, and assert themselves when responding to the demands of reality.

---

3   Kohlberg, Lawrence, Levine, Charles and Hewer, Alexandra (1983). *Moral Stages: a current formulation and a response to critics*. Basel, NY: Karger.

Kohlberg, Maslow and other theorists who developed these models of life, based on stages, started with the assumption that people strive to move up through the levels of their models in much the same way as one moves up through a growth chart. This suggests that once you have achieved a certain level or stage you will remain there for the rest of your life. The experience of being human proves to be less structured than these models describe. Young children are at the level of self-actualization and gradually move away from it over time. As adults we all experience times when we feel we have reached our potential, and other times when it seems to have slipped away. Maslow recognized this error before he died and wrote a paper in which he described the experience of self-actualization to be an intermittent experience that few achieve and that no one stays at forever. One person he describes as reaching the point of self actualization was William James, who developed the model of self.

The model of self and the concept of a life line are more realistic as the whole self constantly exists from the time of conception. Awareness and/or acknowledgment of the different levels of the self may not always be present but this doesn't mean the levels don't exist. Our ability to meet our material and social needs will fluctuate throughout our lives. Our social self depends upon the people who are around us. We learn new reactions throughout our lives, but are not always able to access those that are most appropriate, depending on the circumstances we are in. The tendency of any human being to cry out to the creator in times of extreme distress indicates the connection with one's spiritual core is always there, but often neglected or ignored. In the midst of all of this, we do exist as a complete whole. Reaching our full potential becomes a choice of acknowledgment and understanding, something that we are all capable of.

Another theory resembles the journey towards living on the life line was developed by family therapist Murray Bowen[4]. He called this process self differentiation. He claimed that we each have a basic level of differentiation, which is developed through childhood and remains constant. However, we also have functional levels of self-differentiation, which fluctuate depending on one's level of anxiety. Although much of an individual's level of self differentiation is set during childhood, the development of the individual brain as a direct result of the interactive dance between genetic make-up and life's experience means that change can and does occur throughout one's lifetime. Maturity, life experience and therapy may all provide the impetus to change the way that we react, thereby increasing the functional level of self differentiation. However, during situations of intense anxiety individuals will have the tendency to return to reacting at their basic level as revealed during crisis situations. In order to increase one's functional level of differentiation, one must begin to recognize and understand these concepts, to desire change, and be willing to make the effort it takes to change. These are the same requirements that must be met if we are to live on our life line. High levels of self differentiation would indicate a situation in which a person is living close to his life line.

---

4   Bowen, Murray, (1992). Family therapy in clinical practice. Northvale, NJ: Jason Aronson.

As we compare this theory to the model of self, we can see that differentiation as described by Bowen is much like the compass point of our model, moving from place to place on our self to meet the specific conditions that we are dealing with in the movement. The basic level of differentiation is what was developed in childhood, reactions that are stored in our mind for the rest of our lives. We will be discussing how this happens in the following chapters. Bowen claims that the more differentiated a person is, the more they can be an individual in the midst an emotional group. In other words, the higher level of differentiation you are at allows you to live closer to your life line and let others live on theirs. This closely matches Maslow's level of self-actualization and Kohlberg's sixth step of moral reasoning. Since the life line begins with the core of the self, the spirit, and connects all of the different levels of self, the final goal in the search for self differentiation in Bowen's model would be to live directly on one's life line.

For most of us, the amount of discomfort that we experience during each day is not enough to make us pay much attention to what is going on in the self. However, the rising dependence on counselors, therapists, psychologists and medication indicates that our society does have a problem. As teens go on a shooting spree in our schools, we wring our hands and wonder what we are doing wrong for a time and then retreat to our comfortable lives without an answer. It is when we are faced with the extreme cases in our world, like the events of September 11, we finally may admit that we have hit a wall and need some answers. It is at that point that a complete understanding of the whole is so important.

A CASE STUDY

A woman sits on a talk show, trying to explain what has happened in a coherent manner. We listen in horror as she describes how her adopted sister was first sexually abused by her father, mistreated and neglected by her mother, and finally murdered. As she recounts knowing that this was happening for years, she explains her reasons for not calling the police were simple. These were her parents. One couldn't turn them in. One simply turned away and ignored what was happening.

She recounts the night of the murder in graphic detail. How she sees her sister throwing up a mixture of laundry bluing and heart medicine, which she had watched her mother mixing together. How she becomes hysterical, screaming wildly, and escapes to the bathroom, not knowing what to do when she realizes what her parents are doing. There she hears her father screaming at her sister, and the sickening thuds of his boots kicking her. She watches from the bathroom window as he stomps her to death in the back yard, and describes the sounds of her bones being crushed. At one point, she begs her husband to step in and do something, but instead he rushes to his children to make certain that they are all right. She runs down to hold her dying sister in her arms as her parents leave to buy gasoline. They return and dump the body into a hole, pour gas over it, cover it with logs and burn it through the whole night, adding more logs as needed. She packs up her husband

and children and goes home, wiping this whole scene from her memory. It is far too much for the mind and spirit to bear. In order to protect the self, this memory is sealed within the unconscious.

Years later she watches her children wrestling in the back yard. Her son picks up his foot and pretends that he is going to stomp on his sister who is lying on the ground. Instantly, the pictures from the past come back into her conscious memory and she remembers every detail clearly. At the time of the airing of the show, her parents have been arrested and charged with murder. She is the key witness.

The questions come, hard and fast. Why didn't she do anything? Why didn't she say anything? How is she dealing with the present, facing her parents in court? She has no other answers than that these people are her parents and she loves them. The host describes the high level of dysfunction in the home, citing several examples and suggests that this might be a factor in her silence. A psychologist steps in to state that this is a family secret, and family secrets are well kept secrets. But it doesn't convince the audience, who cannot comprehend how anyone can deal with this level of horror by keeping it quiet. And it doesn't give any clear answers to what happens now, once the secret is out in the open. The psychologist tells the woman that these people are not worth loving, even if they are her parents. She has to let them go. But he doesn't have any answers on how she is supposed to do this.

If one applies this story to the model of self, one not only can come to an understanding of what has happened with this woman, within this family, but also how to help her. First of all, one must realize that all levels of self are being affected. In the material self, the woman is living on the far side of the compass in her role as a daughter. Her social self contains the view that each of her parents have of her, which are also far from her life line self, as they expect her to accept that whatever they do is all right, and that she will keep the secret. We know that this does not fit on her life line because of her high levels of distress when she sees what her parents are doing to her sister. The true self is screaming out in the midst of the horror, but no one is listening. Her mind contains her values and beliefs of an ideal mother, father and daughter. Although, these beliefs may be close to her life line, in the fact that parents are supposed to be kind, loving and honest, it is the actual reality of her own parents that she has to deal with. Their behavior is so extreme that she cannot connect it with that of the parental ideal and so she chooses to look at her parents as she wants them to be, not as they really are. Since their behavior to this adopted sister does not match her ideal view of a father and mother, she cannot accept that the behavior is real and so does not report it. The final of act of murder is so far beyond anything her mind can deal with, it is blocked out of her consciousness. However, as our brain connections are formed through sensory experience, the sights and sounds of that murder are present in the brain and are released when a similar sensory experience occurs. At this point she can no longer block out the memory. Removed from the actual situation by time and space, she is able to choose different reactions than when she was in the midst of the anxiety of being part of such a horrific situation. She has to say something, to turn her parents in, and to become a witness, in order to respond to her true self. In the midst of all these actions, she continues to cling to the false pictures she holds of her parents. She doesn't want to give them up.

Helping a person in this state means helping them realize that they are not doing the self of their mother or their father any good at all by hanging on to a false image of them. Both her father and mother are murderers. They chose to destroy the young girl that they had taken into their home, first as a foster child and then adopted. Exactly why they did this, we may never know. But the reality is that they did it.

If one looks further into the life of this woman, one will likely find many more examples of how her parents destroyed others. These are the choices that they made in their lives. This is who they are as people. As one examines their reality, the image that the woman holds of her mother and father can gradually be moved towards that of their true selves. One can explore the positive traits and abilities as well as the negative factors. Perhaps her mother was a terrific cook who loved to serve her guests, or her father was a hard worker who brought his paycheque home to the family every Friday instead of spending it on himself. We don't hear any of this on the show, but it is important to focus on the positive as well as the negative when we form the social view of another person.

The true picture of the self will include everything about a person. Once it is put together the woman will discover that there are parts of the picture that make it possible for her to continue to love her parents and parts that are, in this case, revolting. As the picture reflects the actual person one is dealing with, the woman can accept her parents as they are: people, who made an incredible, horrendous mistake, and who have to face the responsibility of that choice. The woman no longer has to cover up for them, waste energy projecting a reality that does not exist, or twist herself to fit into their behaviors. She is free to look at them as they really are and decide how she wants to respond to them in the future.

As she goes through this process, she will experience grief. She is losing the parents that she built up in her mind. She must come to the realization that her ideal of parenthood was not lived out by her own parents. This does not mean that she needs to give up her belief of who and what parents are, but only accept the fact that her own parents failed to meet these standards. As humans, we all fail in many ways and accepting that reality for ourselves and for others is a major part of the understanding and acceptance of the self. She will respond with all the stages of grief as will be outlined in the following chapter. She may need help recognizing that these emotions are an important part of this step in the development of self. She may also need permission to allow herself to feel these emotions, and express these feelings.

Another major part of this process will be forgiving oneself for making the decisions that one did in the past. On her way to discovering her true self, this woman will have to admit that she did things and kept things quiet that were totally against her beliefs and values, and the opposite of what her true self would choose to do. She must forgive herself, admitting that she did the best she could at the time with the resources that she had, and make a conscious decision to move away from the behaviors that do not fit within her true self. She will also experience the whole process of grief as she makes these steps.

In times of high anxiety she must be aware that she will automatically respond in the ways she learned so well in her childhood family. She may run and hide as she did to the bathroom when she saw her sister throwing up. She may beg someone else to step in because she does not feel strong enough herself to intercede. She may not be able to speak up when she sees something unacceptable happening in her world. She can be prepared for this to happen. She can forgive herself when it does. This is how her brain was wired as a child, through no fault of her own. It is part of her "mind" and it is not going to go away. By accepting her automatic reactions and preparing herself, she can gradually choose to react in new and different ways in spite of the feelings of anxiety that threaten to overwhelm her. As this process goes on, she can finally face discomfort with confidence that she will be okay while being true to herself.

CHAPTER TWO
THE POWER OF CHANGE

Old Shakespeare got it wrong methinks
In Hamlet's tragic fall
T"is not conscience friends but comfort
Doth make cowards of us all

DEMI WALKER

I AM A LITTLE GIRL OF FIVE, LIVING ON A FARM IN NORTHERN ALBERTA. IT IS THRESHING season and our neighbors are working together on our farm, gathering the sheaves of wheat and bringing them to the threshing machine where the grain is separated from the straw. It's a very exciting time for a young child. My father and grandfather are busy with the threshing crew while my mother and grandmother work full time to provide hot steaming meals for the men, leaving us children free to roam where we may. During meals, teams of huge horses take over the stalls in the barn normally occupied by the milk cows. We walk cautiously behind them, feeling overwhelmed by the power they exude. At times we watch the threshing machine itself; so noisy, so complicated. The sweat pours down the faces of the men tossing the bundles of grain from the hayracks into its hungry maw and streams of gold pour out the other end. One fills the granary with the precious kernels of grain, our livelihood. The other forms the huge golden straw stack by its side. We are lowered into the granary and help shovel the grain into the far corners, often losing our shoes in the process and shivering with delight as our feet and lower legs are gradually sucked down into the grain. We revel in the noise, the dust, the nonstop activity. And then we head out into the field where it's so much quieter and peaceful. We hitch a ride on the backs of the hayracks, fully aware of the differences in our neighbors: those who will allow us to ride, those who truly enjoy our presence, and those who will outright refuse. Melvin Berg was our favorite. Two children could easily sit on one beam on the back of his hayrack and he always welcomed our presence with a smile and a joke. We stayed as far away from Albert Hanson as possible. His beams were cut off even with the rack, matching his demeanor, a clear message to each of us that we were not welcome.

This year something is different. Our neighbor, Talbert Velve, has acquired a front-end loader for his tractor. Instead of his team and hayrack, he brings the tractor for the threshing and heads out to the field, replacing the men who toss the bundles up into the hayrack by hand. On the last day of harvest, we ride out to the field on the back of a hayrack, as we always had, but this time, instead of going back in like manner, we wait for the last bundles to be picked up. Then Talbert allows us to climb into the bucket of the front-end loader. As we hang on tightly, he lifts the loader up into the air, as high as it will go. The metal bar, warmed by the sun, feels hot in my hands. I spread my legs and bend my knees to balance myself in the swinging bucket. I gaze out over the surrounding countryside from this vast height: the miniature farm buildings with the clouds of dust rising behind them, where threshing was in full progress; our cows, brown and white dots against the green, grazing in the pasture; the sky, gradually reddening with the coming of night; and finally the line of teams and hayracks moving slowly away from us.   Different feelings sweep through me as I stand there. Excitement, awe, and a sense of power as I look out over our land from this height. And then, as I watch the hayracks lumber away, a sudden overwhelming sense of sadness as I realize that this tractor, which is bringing me so much pleasure, is also a symbol of the end. New farming techniques are moving in. The old ways are disappearing. I know, in that moment, that I am experiencing the end of an era. And I was. The next year, threshing crews had been replaced by combines.

Once we have come to an understanding of the model of self and have taken the time to come to an acceptance of who we are as a 'self', we must also accept that this 'self' is not and never will be a solid unit which can be drawn, accepted and understood for all time. Only the spirit remains constant, the same from minute to minute, day to day, year after year. Everything else is formed over time and can be modified, discarded, lost, or rejected. The levels of the self, which encircle the solid core of the spirit, are a fluid, moving and ever changing bundle which encircles the central core. Certain parts may appear to remain static for a time, but everything in the self except the spirit is constantly evolving. Adjusting to these changes in the self is an ongoing process throughout each of our lives.

THE PROCESS OF CHANGE

There are many different factors that are important to take into consideration when one is considering the process of change. The first, of course, is to accept the fact that change is inevitable. As human beings, we are a part of a whole system that is constantly evolving into something new. Why should we, as a self, be any different?

Our whole world is constantly in a state of flux. The cycle of birth and death affects every living thing on the planet. Seeds sprout, plants grow, produce more seeds, die and decompose into the soil. Predators hunt for their prey in order to survive, only to become the meal of another predator. The inorganic world is also always changing. Water and air are joined by the living world to break down materials and transport them from one location to another. The deserts shift; the mountains erode; the ocean wears away at the shoreline. Weather patterns vary from one day to the next, with bands of high and low pressure moving constantly across the land and water. The minutes tick by on the clock as the seasons come and go, each leaving something new and different in their wake. The earth is part of a universe that is also always changing, forever expanding. Stars are born, burn and then die. Black holes are formed. Meteor showers collide with planets, dotting their landscapes with craters and hills. The light of our sun is actually a fire; slowly, gradually, reducing its size. Although it is hard to imagine, at some point in time, it too will be gone.

I am reminded on a daily basis of this constant evolution of our world as I walk in a ravine near my home. After years of drought, we are now experiencing a summer of rain and each day the ravine reveals a different aspect as the elements of plant and animal life, weather conditions, and human impact constantly modify the environment that I hike through. Much of this change is gradual. The leaves turn green, the flowers bloom, the squirrels harvest the spruce and pine cones, the tires of the bikes cut a groove into the pathway. However, on the mornings after the torrential rainfalls we are experiencing this summer, we are struck by the transformation that occurred overnight. The rushing water, making its way down into the creek, has gouged deep ruts into the gravel roadways. Huge logs have been carried along by the water and deposited in new locations. In places the actual banks of the creek have collapsed down into the water, taking trees, grass and other vegetation with them. Even the pavement isn't safe as the water works its way underneath through a small crack and erodes the base bit by bit. Without a firm base, the asphalt cracks and breaks. The rushing waters carry hunks of this asphalt down the slope and leave them scattered on the road at the bottom of the hill. These daily changes are a constant reminder of the strength of nature and how man's meager efforts in this world can be obliterated over time.

In the midst of all of this, we exist, each as an individual self, a solid spirit surrounded by an unstable form. Like the ravine, most of the changes in the self happen slowly and gradually, allowing us to incorporate them without too much stress and anxiety, but each and every one of them have an impact on the 'self' which leads to discomfort. On the other hand, abrupt and extreme changes may happen to our "selves" much like the impact of the rains on the ravine. These changes will take much more time, energy and effort to integrate into the whole.

Changes occur at all levels of the self except the spirit. We are born with a body that grows and evolves throughout our whole life span. We acquire possessions and roles that may stay with us for years, or perhaps only minutes or days. A flow of different people passes through our presence, each creating a different image of ourselves in our social self. Again, some may last for years and others for only minutes. The social images of long term will evolve over time as each person gets to know us better. We develop our mind over time through our experiences in this world, and are often challenged to modify or to cast out beliefs, values, and reactions which no longer fit the person that we aspire to be.

Attempting to exist without change in order to maintain the status quo is attempting the impossible and yet it is often a goal we strive for unconsciously. Change is uncomfortable, so avoiding change appears to be desirable, a sensible goal to work towards. This is seen very clearly in the field of autism, in situations where parents and professionals have concentrated on ensuring that as little change as possible occurs in the life of the person with autism because of their extreme reaction to change. This only makes things worse for the person on the spectrum. Since change is inevitable, allowing someone to believe that life without change is possible is cheating them of reality. Students are placed in the same setting, with the same schedule, the same teacher's assistant and the same expectations year after year after year. Although this appears to be helpful in regards to the lack of extreme response by the person with autism, it does nothing to help them succeed in our real world. We limit their potential by protecting them from change. Yes, it is more difficult to work with them through change, but it is imperative that we do so. Otherwise we create people who are so terrified of anything new, and so unwilling to expose themselves to anything different that they go into meltdown with very little input. All of their energy is concentrated on keeping things exactly the same. When things finally have to change, and they always will, the result is complete chaos. It is far better to expose people with autism, as well as everyone else, to change carefully and gradually, and help them face the discomfort with respect and pride. Then they can take their rightful place in our society.

In the midst of the inevitability of change we come face to face with the second factor of change. All change results in discomfort to the self, and is thus resisted by the self. One of the characteristics noted about people who fall within the spectrum of autism is their resistance to change. Many professionals talk about this resistance as if it is a deficiency, which is only displayed by those with autism, and is therefore a notable symptom of this syndrome. But that's not true. Everyone resists change to one degree or another. All you have to do is attend a university class to see this resistance occurring. Students choose a seat for the first class of the term and rarely move to another seat throughout the semester, although no one has made any effort to assign particular seats to each student. Occasionally someone will sit in a different seat, causing consternation to the student who typically sits there, up until that point. They are then forced to choose another seat, which typically is used by another student. One can feel the difference in the energy level as the whole room is forced to deal with this simple change. There will be individual differences directly based on one's level of discomfort and one's own unique make-up in the actual reaction by each student whose seat has been taken by another, but everyone reacts in one way or another.

A seat in a university classroom is a simple example of the how the discomfort of change impacts the reactions we choose. Life is far more complex than that. Attempting to keep one's environment the same will result in reactions that appear to be very bizarre to people who have not grown up in the same environment. Many people find it more comfortable to live in the midst of chaos, because it is all one has ever known. When their lives become too calm and satisfying, they will unconsciously do something that places them right back in chaos in order to feel normal. Some people will sabotage themselves whenever they experience success in order to satisfy their beliefs that they are a failure. The change of experiencing success is far too uncomfortable for them to deal with. A person who has a chronic illness or a developmental disability may resort to staying ill or disabled in order to maintain the same reaction from his family members over time. This is why the journey to understanding one's 'self' is an individual journey that we must each take on our own, and not rely on another to orchestrate. No one else totally understands the world that you have experienced in your particular body. The discomfort level you feel and the reactions you engage in are yours alone and may not make any sense at all to another person. They are based completely on your 'self'.

Part of the reaction of discomfort to change in the self is due to the amount of energy that is needed for change to occur. The rest is due to actual growth, modification or loss that happens to the particular level or levels of the self. If you can imagine the different levels as circles which are constantly in motion, stretching themselves to fit new components and developing holes when losses occur, which must be mended over time, you can see why it takes so much energy and often feels so uncomfortable to change.

The amount of energy required and the amount of discomfort felt is dependent upon the type and amount of change that occurs. Some of the changes that occur affect all levels of the self; some only one level. The impact of the multi level changes and the energy that we require to make these changes will be much higher than changes that only affect one level of self. Changes that occur at the level of the mind will have more repercussions and will be harder to deal with than those that occur on the material level because it is closer to the spirit. In other words, major changes to one's beliefs, values or reactions which are found in the mind are much more upsetting to the self than buying a new car or acquiring a different job as they are part of the material self. The more change that we experience at once, the more extreme its impact on our 'self'. Moving to a new home in the city you live in is much easier for the self than moving to a different city where you will have to adjust to a new home, a new job, and new neighbors creating the situation where you need to learn all sorts of new information. Change which affects factors that take up more space in your self and are closer to the center of each level will affect you more than those which are smaller and more distant. For example: the death of your child or a current lover will affect you far more than that of an old school chum who you haven't had any contact with for years. However, both will be felt, and both will change the self in their own way.

As a foster mother, I witnessed the amount of energy it takes to adjust to change every time one of our foster children would visit their natural families. About a week before the visit was to occur their behavior would begin to change. They would become whiny, irritable and often disobedient. By the time they were picked up for the visit we were usually happy to see them go, as it took so much more energy to deal with them in this state of flux. When they returned to our home, the process of modifying themselves to fit back into our environment began in earnest as they checked out everything they owned and all of the activities they enjoyed, one after another, as fast as they could go. Out would come all their toys and the board games to be touched, checked over and perhaps played with for a few minutes and then they would be out the door and over to the neighborhood park to swing and slide and then back to the house to touch base with the book they were reading, turn on the television to see a few moments of their favorite show and then on to cat or the dog or to make a phone call to their best buddy from school. The first few times I witnessed this frantic activity, I was very concerned and tried to install some sense of order to the process, which of course only made things worse as I was interfering with what the child had to do to feel complete in my home. Over time, as I watched each of the children rush wildly around our home, I learned to relax and let them be. Only when everything had been checked out and incorporated back into their self could they relax and be part of our family again.

For the majority of us, this extreme change in the self, from not only one home to another, but also from one family to another is not a reality. The example of foster children is that of the extreme as there was a serious reason that these children were living with me. They had been removed from their homes because it was not safe to live there and returning home meant returning to a threat of one type or another. This led to the heightened level of anxiety before the visit, which was evident in the change in their behavior towards us. Coming back to our home gave them the safety they longed for, and yet deep in their hearts they knew that this was not where they truly belonged. Their frantic activity signaled their attempts to become one with this environment again. Although we are not faced with this level of discord, each of us go through this process of adjustment whenever we move from one environment to another. My current job involves a lot of travel and I find myself spending a lot of time in a variety of hotels and motels. I am always uncomfortable on the first day. The more days I stay in one spot, the better I feel. And when I come home again, I find myself walking from room to room, reclaiming my house, my possessions, my self, and thinking back over the years to those little boys wildly rushing through our home doing the same thing.

In our current world, many children go through this change of homes on a regular basis as their parents have chosen to separate and live apart. Some deal with it better than others, and, of course, some situations are better than others. We must be aware that all of them are using an incredible amount of energy to incorporate these changes to the self every time they are expected to change homes. The amount of energy expended will lead to heightened levels of anxiety, which in turn will lead to using higher levels of coping skills, which are often recognized as inappropriate behaviors in children. A clear understanding of the model of self and how important consistency in our material and social levels is to each of us will allow us to be more patient and accepting of the stress we are placing on these children. By sharing this information with them, we can also allow them to understand the process of change in their lives, how it will affect them, and how to accept their own responses in a happy and healthy way. This moves us away from having something wrong with us, to just being human and all right.

In spite of the discomfort of change, which leads to the tendency to resist change, human beings are remarkably flexible and adaptable in their ability to deal with change, even extreme levels of change when necessary. This is because of the primary position of the spirit, which remains unchanged, no matter what, and its ability to survive. Extreme weather such as hurricanes, tornadoes and floods can wipe out most of the material self. Accidents and illnesses can destroy parts of the body. Wars and devastation can eradicate all the members of your family in an instant, obliterating your social self for a time, and yet one will survive. In fact, when faced with tribulations such as these, one often recognizes most clearly what is really important. The significance of each of the different levels of the self is revealed dramatically. The reactions of your mind keep you going in spite of anything that happens around you. The lives of those you love become far more important than any material possession. The body will heal and rejuvenate in spite of massive amounts of damage, or adapt to what has been lost. The self continues on in new and different ways. Each of us has this power within. It's not comfortable, but it is what life is about.

The third factor of change is that the only person that you can change and that you have the responsibility of changing is yourself. This is probably the most difficult factor to accept. It seems to be easy for us to recognize how others need to change in the midst of being blind to our own discrepancies. We often are unwilling to even attempt to change ourselves, claiming self righteously that "ALL would be WELL, if only the other person in the particular situation would make effort to change themselves." Far too often we hear these types of statements from men and or women in the therapy room: "I could be happy if HE were more romantic." or "I wouldn't spend so much time with the boys, if SHE didn't nag me so much." Neither statement is true. She can only be happy if she, herself, chooses to react with happiness. Her mood has absolutely nothing to do with his romantic efforts. He has freely chosen to hang out with the boys, knowing full well that the consequence of his absence will be hearing her nag. By refusing to accept the responsibility to make the effort to change ourselves, we create a world in which we continue living in a state we claim is not to our liking. In reality it is often more comfortable to demand the other change because we know it is not going to happen and it does not require us to use the energy and face the discomfort of change. The sad thing about this is that in doing so, we limit ourselves and those we care about, and never allow ourselves the joy of reaching our full potential.

Once we take the responsibility of changing ourselves we discover that we have indeed also changed the other person. Change cannot happen to one 'self' without having an impact on the selves of other people because all of our selves are interconnected at the different levels. Although we may think that our resolution to change is an individual decision and action, it does not take long for the change of one 'self' to spread to others. This became very apparent to me during the process of my divorce. In the beginning, I fully believed that since my sons were all grown, I was only making a decision that affected my ex-husband and my self. Our relationship was over. That was all there was to it. As time passed, I began to realize that leaving my husband was far more than the end of one relationship and that everyone I knew was being impacted in one way or another. Discovering James's model of self put it all in perspective for me. My leaving had not only dramatically changed all the levels of my self, and of those of my ex-husband, but it also had affected the selves of my sons, my grandchildren, my siblings, my parents, my friends and so on. The change I had wrought was immense and it shook not only the whole family to its very core, but also the community we were part of at the time. What's more, I, and only I, was responsible for this change. I was the one who had taken the steps to walk away instead of continuing to put up with a situation I could not stand any longer. In doing so I had altered the 'selves' of everyone I knew. No wonder divorce has such a massive impact on the world. No wonder it is often easier to stay. No wonder it takes so long to get over it.

When I work as a family and marital therapist I am often faced with situations in which one or the other of the couple chooses not to be part of the therapeutic process. The remaining mate often wants to give up in despair, fully believing that if their mate is not part of therapy, nothing good will happen. This is not true. I inform them that they, as an individual, can choose to do the work themselves to become the person that they want to be, and in the midst of this change, they will also evoke change in the person to whom they are married. Relationships do not always survive the process, but in many circumstances, they become stronger as the person who is doing the work begins to feel better about themselves. Their mate responds to these feelings in a positive way and the process of change gradually takes place in both selves. Other relationships crumble as the person doing the work realizes that they cannot continue to respond to the actions of the other in the same way. Again, once one person changes a single common reaction, the whole process is changed.

During my first marriage, I came to the realization, at a certain point, that I was being blamed for situations that my husband was creating in his imagination. It was a shock to realize that for years I had been reacting with guilt and shame for things that had not even existed in the real world. Over the years I had learned how to react to him to keep myself and my children safe in our world and I did it well. Once I realized that the situations weren't real, I quit accepting the blame, and stopped reacting in the same way. It was a positive step for me and for my self-esteem, but it certainly did nothing for our relationship. In fact, my decision to stop taking the blame for his fantasy world was the beginning of the end. We could not continue to live together because we were no longer safe with one another.

As time passed after the separation, and my whole family gradually evolved due to this situation, I was constantly frustrated by the assumption of one family member or another that I would continue to take responsibility for controlling my ex-husband's behavior during family gatherings. My refusal to do so led to a lot of conflict, as family members had to face the reality of his rage in different ways; a rage they had rarely been exposed to because of my efforts throughout the years to keep it in check. Over time I realized that I also had to accept the responsibility for creating this situation, as well as taking the responsibility for breaking up our family unit because I had done the job so well and, in doing so, taught everyone else that it was acceptable for me to take this role. This didn't mean that I was willing to step back into my previous behavior patterns, but that I became far more tolerant and accepting of their expectations of me. It was a long and difficult journey for each of us, which took years to work out, and will likely still affect us in the future. Ten years after I left, I finally had lunch with my ex-husband in an effort to see if we could be together peacefully to celebrate with our grandson. It was fascinating for me to observe how easily and unconsciously we both slipped back into our old behavior patterns and how comfortable it was for me to react in the ways I knew would keep him calm, in spite of my resolve not to do so. The lesson that I want to share with you about this is not to allow people to walk all over you, but that in the midst of every interaction you have with another, you are responsible for your own reaction. If you genuinely want things to be different, you can make it so by changing yourself. However, you must also accept the cost of doing so. Sometimes the change that occurs is for the better for all concerned.

As I came to the end of the process of writing this book I realized that I needed to have someone read it to determine if it was too much about me as an individual. I picked three readers: a close friend, a fellow therapist and a teller at my bank, who I didn't know very well but with whom I had formed a connection while I did my banking. All agreed to read the book for me.

Each time I walked into the bank the teller greeted me enthusiastically, claiming to really enjoying the book. At one point I asked her if it was too much about me. She looked at me in surprise. "About you, it's not about you. It's about me." I knew at that point that my words were having the impact I wanted them to.

One day I walked into the bank and she gestured to me to come to her window and said she had something to share with me. I waited until she was free to serve me and approached her. She whispered: "I have something to show you" and leaned forward pushing down her neckline slightly to reveal a small angel tattooed on her breast. "It's all because of your book. I have always wanted a tattoo and your book gave me the impetus to follow through on my desire." I am sure I had a strange look on my face as I certainly hadn't written this book to convince anyone to get a tattoo.

"But's that's not everything" she said. "You have to hear the rest of the story."

She then on to describe how she had decided to get a tattoo and the process that she followed to find the best tattoo artist in the city. Once she had determined who she wanted to work on her, she went into his shop and asked for a tattoo of an angel. This artist was a very angry hurt young man who had gone through the type of childhood that no child should face and who turned his back on all that is good in this world. His tattoos focused on death and blood, on pain and anger. He looked at her and said "I don't do angels. This is what I do. You can choose anything you want from here."

She was adamant about her choice. "I want an angel, and I want you to do it. I have done my research and I know you are the best tattoo artist in this city. I want you to tattoo an angel on my breast."

"I don't do angels" he repeated thrusting his artwork toward her.

"I'm sure you can find a picture of an angel somewhere" she replied reaching for his books of generic tattoo patterns. "Here" she said, "look here's an angel. You can do this one. And I am not leaving until you do it."

And so he gave in and put the angel on her breast. It was small. It was simple and she was delighted with it, but she wasn't finished with him yet. When the angel was complete she paid him and then said" okay, now I have assignment for you. I want you to design a special tattoo just for me. This is my number. Call me when you are ready with it."

"Certainly," he replied, and again pushed his artwork towards her. "Can you give me an idea of what you want?"

"I want a butterfly."

"But I don't do butterflies. This is what I do"

"Oh you can do a butterfly. You said you didn't do angels, and look, you did a beautiful angel. I am sure you can do an even better butterfly. Call me when it is ready"

She had the butterfly tattooed on her ankle and I have never seen a tattoo quite like it. The butterfly was at a unique angle it looked so real you expected it to flutter away. She said that after he was finished putting it on her he looked at her with tears in his eyes and said "I want you to know that you have changed my life completely. I had turned my back on everyone and everything because of my horrible childhood. You came into my shop and treated me like I was someone special. I won't be able to stay in that dark world anymore."

I don't have any contact with the bank teller anymore. She quit her job and the last I heard was planning to go into social work where she can have a positive influence on the people she works with. I wish her the best as she continues to live as her true self, tattoos and all.

Accepting the fact that one can only change oneself leads directly to the need to give up trying to change other people. This is not, and never has been, our job here on earth. It takes a lot of effort and practice to stop trying to change others and instead concentrate on oneself, but once one gets into the habit, it's a great place to be. I remember sitting on the floor one day sorting through the recycle box taking out all the odds and ends that my husband had thrown into it and grumbling about the fact that he was making me go to all this effort. This was back in the days when the recycle bins were all divided into many different levels. The box I was sorting was for newspapers: not magazines, not plastic, not letters. They each had their own separate bins. My husband told me that I was wasting my time. He claimed that this really didn't matter. I responded that it did matter to me. I only put the items into the particular bins that had the label for each item. This statement led to my realization that my sorting had far more to do with me than with him. If I chose to refuse to put anything else into the bin with the particular label, then I chose this job. It had absolutely nothing to do with him. My choice was whether I was willing to sort the material or not. I chose to do it as I felt good when I put the stuff into each bin as labeled. At this point in time, all this effort seems ridiculous, as the bins now take all of the paper products at once, but at that time, it was important enough for me to argue about. The question I had to finally face was whether it was important enough for me to allow it to strain our relationship.

As human beings we face these types of situations all the time in our interactions with others. The truth of the matter is that as long as we insist on trying to change others we usually make things worse. Although we may think (claim) we are doing things for their own good or ours, what we will be creating is a heightened level of resistance and anxiety in their lives, as well as interfering in their own personal journey through life. We will have a more positive impact by becoming the person that we were meant to be and succeeding in reaching our own potential as a model for others, rather than by attempting to help them or make them change. The only positive control that we have in this world is that which we have over ourselves. Let us learn to use it wisely.

However, once we have changed, as I have already mentioned, our transformation will automatically impact the 'self' of others in your life and they too will begin to change. In the midst of this process we must continue to be aware of the second factor of change: any change will lead to discomfort. This is why people so often resist the changes that other people make in their lives even if they are a good move in the long run. For example, a person who has lost a lot of weight will often discover that the people, who were pushing her to make this move in the beginning, do not react in a positive manner when he or she is successful. Parents often strive to make their children act maturely, only to resist treating them like adults when they do. This resistance is due to the change that is happening in their own self as a direct result of the change in the other and the discomfort that they are feeling because of this. When we make the effort to make positive changes in our lives, we must learn to ignore this resistance and not take it personally. As time goes by, the resistance to the change will fade as this discomfort of change in the other person declines.

The reality that we can only change ourselves is one of the most important factors to consider when one approaches professionals to help with this search of self. Professionals can help one on the journey in many ways, but one must cautious not to hand the responsibility of one's journey over to them. It is our personal journey. We have to own it ourselves. Be cautious of anyone who has determined the pattern of your journey in advance or who defines your reactions through their eyes and experiences or some theory or model that has nothing to do with you, rather than allowing you to discover the answers yourself. Be even more cautious of those who take credit for your success or regard your failure as a personal insult to their efforts or who imply that you cannot do this without them. This is your journey and each of us is capable of making it ourselves.

A fourth factor in the process of change is that the changes to the self affect each of us in very logical ways. Change that occurs slowly and gradually over time is more comfortable than any change that happens suddenly. Change that is anticipated is easier to deal with than change that happens without any warning. Change that is desired is more comfortable than change that is unwanted or resisted. Changes that one feels safe with are easier than those that put a person into a setting in which they feel threatened or in the unknown. Changes we choose or feel in control of are easier than those that are forced upon us. A person's individual reaction to change will be influenced by all of these factors as well as one's genetic make-up and past experience. In spite of all this, in the long run, human beings are very adaptable, and once we have accepted the change, we can go on almost as if nothing has happened.

The next important factor in the process of change is what I call a pendulum factor. This is especially strong in changes that happen at the level of the mind, but may play a part in all levels of self. The pendulum factor occurs when we make the decision that we want to make a change in our self and begin to do so. The effort we put out in that moment will be our best and the result will likely exceed our actual goal. So we begin a diet by cutting our calorie intake drastically. We stop smoking cold turkey. We start a study habit by poring over the books for hours at a time. We go to the gym and work out to the point that every muscle in our body aches. All of this leads to major discomfort,

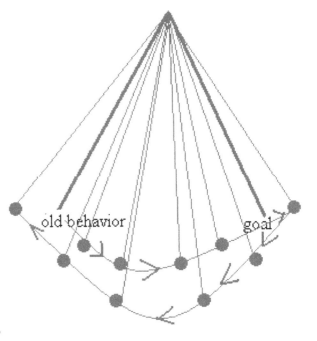

which often sends us scrambling back to what feels comfortable. We may actually find our selves responding to the change with behavior that is more extreme than what we were doing before we decided to change. We binge on high caloric foods. We chain smoke. We sleep during study time or have difficulty pulling ourselves away from the television screen. In turn, these reactions make us feel like failures and we either respond in the extreme again, or give up in despair.

Once we understand that this is part of the pendulum effect of change, one can relax, forgive oneself and keep on trying. We must accept the fact that any change we choose to embark on will lead to discomfort and anxiety. This discomfort will lead to the use of our individual coping skills, which may be the very factor in our lives that we are trying to change. When we choose to change and anticipate that it will lead to discomfort, we can expect that we may lapse and truly forgive ourselves when it happens. Gradually, over time, the reactions we respond with will not be as extreme. The reactionary force of the pendulum will diminish. The feelings of discomfort will decrease. We will become closer to the person that we are striving to be.

The last factor that we must consider in the process of change is that it takes time. Nothing that I talk about in this book can happen overnight for anyone. It took a long time to become the person you are. It may take as long to move on to something new. There are many programs out there that claim to be able help people change in a set amount of time whether it be a week, a month, six weeks, five months or whatever. I recently heard about a professional who claimed to be able to change a person dramatically in twenty-four hours. Attempting such a program is setting your self up for failure. We have to be ready as an individual to initiate the change. We have to be in control of the journey we are on. We often have to allow ourselves time to adjust to the changes we have made before we move on to something else, and we have to realize that the level of anxiety we are currently experiencing, as described in an upcoming chapter, may lead to what appears to be regression. As you will learn, it is not, but we have to be prepared for it.

I first truly learned this as I went through a support group for abused wives that went on for several years. I had already left my husband and had done a lot of healing on my own by the time I attended the group, but many of the women I was with were still living in the midst of abuse. As they recounted the abuse that they were experiencing week after week at our meetings, it was easy to wonder why on earth they were insisting on staying in their situation. But they weren't ready to leave and we had to learn to support them in their present, not in ours. As the weeks and months passed, more and more of them chose to leave their husbands, all in their own time and in their own way. As I watched this process happen to so many different women, in their own unique way, I learned to appreciate the message found in Ecclesiastes which tells us that "there is a time for everything and a season for every activity under heaven." In the same way that you must take responsibility to change yourself and only yourself, you must also take responsibility for the timing of the journey. Listen to your inner voice, not to other people and you will know when the time is right.

People who depend on others to determine when and how they will go through the process of change are people who miss the chance to achieve their full potential. If you try to rush this process, you will likely find that you are not making the gains you desire as quickly as you want, and that you often appear to backslide instead of moving forward. In an environment in which our coping skills are regarded as weakness, as illness, or as inappropriate, the protective reactions we use lead to a sense of failure, which often creates a feeling of futility and a belief that it is truly impossible for you to be anything else than what you are right now. You begin to feel that this is the way you are and that's all there's to it. Taking charge of your life, recognizing and accepting your coping skills for the role they play in your life, and making the changes in your own time will allow you to gradually work toward living on your life line and achieving goals that may seem impossible at this point.

DEALING WITH CHANGE

There are four types of change that happen to the self. One is a modification of what there was before, one is the addition of something new to the self, another is the actual loss of something that we once had, and the last is the replacement of something we have with something else. All these types of changes happen at all levels of the self, except for the spirit, which is unchanging, and many of them affect more than one level of the self at the same time. They all produce a sense of discomfort, but actual loss is felt more deeply, and lasts far longer than either the modification of the self or the addition of something new. As time goes by, these changes gradually refine and modify who you are as a self without anyone taking much notice. Major changes in one's material self such as getting married, having a child or changing one's job are generally apparent and even celebrated. Other changes such as paradigm shift in one's beliefs or understanding of the world may not be obvious to the rest of the world, but may affect you deeply and make you feel like a totally different person. The rest of this book will describe the process of change at each level in detail. But first we must understand the process of dealing with loss.

Loss creates holes in the self. A piece of the self is missing, gone forever, not to be replaced. The resulting hole takes time to heal over, up to two years or more, depending on the size and location of the hole in the self or, in other words, the importance of whatever was lost to the individual, as well as how the individual deals with the loss. I have a friend, on the autism spectrum, who was devastated by the loss of the dining room table in her home. Her foster parents had chosen to sell it to a family down the street without consulting her. The typical impact of the replacement of a dining room table is minimal in the lives of many, but this was not true for my friend. The table had served as a place of refuge. Overwhelmed by the stimulation she experienced in the home and the lack of understanding she lived with she retreated to the table for comfort. Over time she bonded with this table because of the sense of safety that it provided for her in the midst of a world that was not safe. Losing the table was just like losing her best friend. The lack of understanding of autism and of her reactions by family members meant that there was no one with whom to share her grief. The fact that the table was accessible, in a house just down the street, and that she was not allowed to go and visit it, compounded her feelings of loss. It appeared "silly" to her foster parents to "visit" a table. Now that we understand how the sensory system is heightened for people on the autism spectrum, her response to this table makes complete sense. Only now, as an adult, forty years later, is she able to bring her grief out into the open and go through the process outlined below.

There is a whole process involved in healing these holes of loss, a process which is known as grief. Although we typically associate the process of grief with the loss of a person in our lives, it is not limited to those situations. If we return to Dr. James's description of the model of the self, we realize that loss is experienced whenever something is modified or replaced in the self, as well as when a material item, a person or a factor in the mind (belief, value, ability, reaction, etc.) is gone for good. The same process of grief will be experienced in all of these situations, perhaps not to the same extent, but to some degree.

In the past, grief was assumed to be an intense emotional state which was experienced when a person lost something or someone with whom they had an emotional bond of some sort or other. However, research has determined that grief is not, and never has been, one specific state or feeling. Instead it is a whole process, through which an individual travels when experiencing loss. Elisabeth Kubler-Ross first documented this process in her book *On Death and Dying*[5] where she outlined six different stages of grief, stages which she observed during her work with terminally ill patients. Since that time, other stages have been added to her list, and it has been determined that these stages occur not only for the people who are dying, but for all of the family members and friends who are also facing their loss of this individual in their lives.

For many, grief continues to be regarded as a process that revolves around death. It was my experience of divorce, with its loss of the family unit, the commitment to another, the roles, the material possessions and so on, that opened my eyes to how powerful this process is in each of our lives in all situations of loss. Part of coming to a clear understanding of one's self using the model of the self means accepting that this process of grief occurs through all types of loss, not just death.

Although grief is not a pathological condition, and should never be considered as such, it certainly feels as though it might be as one goes through it. Our lack of knowledge of this process in our lives, our lack of understanding of how it all fits together, and our lack of acceptance of it as "normal" human experience often places us in situations in which we feel that we need psychological help in dealing with its effects. In turn, a psychological and psychiatric community, who do not ask the right questions at the right time, may allow these misunderstandings to continue. Instead of openly dealing with the impact and the stages of grief in the individual's life, one may focus on a specific stage as if it were the problem. A label is attached, such as depression, and treatment is administered for that specific condition with little thought of how it all fits into the current life of the individual or the whole picture of the self. The issue of loss is never resolved and the process of grief is halted in mid stride. At that point, we have moved from a normal human situation to the diagnosis of mental illness. This is a horrendous mistake.

---

5   Elisabeth Kubler-Ross, (1969). *On Death and Dying*. New York, The MacMillan Company.

On the other hand, when we begin to understand and accept the stages of grief as an integral part of our lives as human beings, we can allow ourselves and others the understanding and time needed to go through each of the stages; feeling the feelings that we have to go through in order to move on to the next stage. This is not an easy process. It does feel uncomfortable and the feelings do not always appear to be associated with the loss we have experienced. The message of society that we must quickly move on with our lives creates a belief that once the funeral is over, it's time to forget. We can convince ourselves that we have dealt with our loss quite well, and that our current condition is proof that there is something else seriously wrong with us. However, if we examine the situation in light of the loss, we will often discover that all we are feeling is true grief. One client came to me because she had come to the conclusion that she was a failure as a mother. She couldn't see anything positive happening in her life and she believed that her negative reactions to her children were destroying the relationships she had with them. Every day she wept in frustration over what was going on in her home. When I suggested that her tears had far more to do with the loss of her mother, six months previously, than her ability as a mother or the actions of her children, not only she, but also her children were released from the power of her grief. No longer did they have to feel the guilt and shame of having a bad relationship. Instead they could share the pain of the loss of their mother and grandmother. The mother's anxiety level decreased as she allowed herself to feel the sadness that she was experiencing and the children's behavior improved.

This is a lesson that often has to be learned over and over again. As we go through each day, experiencing the various facets of life that we each face, we tend to assume that our current emotional state can be attributed to what is currently happening during that day, rather than a result of being in the midst of the grieving process. Losing something or someone hurts for a long time. Months later the same mother phones again to share that she is at a breaking point because of her son's behavior. She has to be reminded again of the grief process and of the normalcy of all that she is experiencing.

The discomfort we are feeling leads to heightened levels of anxiety, especially if we are in the midst of a society in which the grieving process is not understood, accepted as normal and openly discussed. Heightened levels of anxiety lead directly to a decrease in the availability of our different responses, as we will learn in future chapters. Since loss is not usually an individual event, but one that occurs in groups such as families, everyone is going through this grief process at the same time. The discomfort affects each person at different levels and in different ways so the individual responses to this grief vary widely from one person to the next. The only certainty I can convey to you is that you usually won't experience the "best" behavior from yourself, or from others who are in the midst of this process. Give yourself, and those who share the loss with you, a minimum of two years for the whole process to work its way through. Be patient with yourself and others, recognize the coping skills that you and they are using to get through the pain. Be tolerant, accepting, forgiving. It will pass in time.

THE PROCESS OF GRIEF

The first stage of grief is denial and isolation. In this stage a person denies that what is happening or has happened is occurring, in an attempt to protect the 'self' from the discomfort of change that is happening. A person may deny that they have a terminal illness, as was documented by Kubler-Ross. The same thing may happen to family members, who either refuse to believe the diagnosis, or who refuse to tell the person who is terminally ill the truth about their condition. A close friend shared the denial of death that our society often clings to as she vented her anger at the doctors who were treating a family member. They had told her she only had a few days to live. "How dare they," my friend fumed. "They had no right to say that to her. They had no right to take away her hope for recovery." The day after I heard this disclosure, the woman died. Did she appreciate the very short time she had been given to prepare for her death? Did she listen to the doctors and make the effort to make certain that her affairs were in order and take the time to say good bye to the people she loved? I don't know. Perhaps she, like my friend chose to stay in the stage of denial. Perhaps not.

Another friend did make the effort to prepare for his death when his doctors told him that he had a very short time to live. His children and grandchildren were called in to visit. He met with his lawyer to draw up all the necessary papers. He phoned his friends and told them how much they had meant to him. Again the doctor's diagnosis proved to be inadequate. This man died within a week, instead of the month or two that had been predicted. However, his swift reaction to the news allowed his family and friends the opportunity to say their good byes. Such a gift in the midst of such a loss!

Denial happens in all other types of loss too. A man who is separated from his wife may deny that the marriage has any problems and may create all sorts of reasons for his wife's absence from the home. A young woman may make all sorts of excuses and accommodations for her friend's behavior in an attempt to remain part of the popular clique in her school. The horrifying knowledge that human beings were actually capable of an atrocity like flying the planes into the Twin Towers may be rejected, and then not thought about again, in order to protect one's image of humanity in one's mind. Of course, the constant portrayal of that day's events on the television in 2001 made this act of denial for most of us harder to accomplish. Perhaps a more accurate description of the impact of the stage of denial on our beliefs would be found in those people who heard about the atrocities being played out in the concentration camps during the second world war and chose to close their minds to the possibility that anything like that could be actually going on. Denial allows us not to experience the discomfort of change for some time. However, it cannot go on forever. At some point we must face reality.

Isolation accompanies denial as it is one way we can continue to lie to ourselves. By cutting ourselves off from those who would insist on our exposure and acceptance of reality, such as the doctors who told the patient of her upcoming demise, we can avoid the discomfort of change. If we pretend we don't have cancer, perhaps it will go away. If we turn off the television, we do not have to face the reality of the news. If we don't talk about something, it might not be real. I will never forget the pain in my aunt's eyes as she lay in the Cancer Institute and admitted that she had known there was something seriously wrong in her body for a long time. She didn't want to face it, so she didn't say a word to anyone. And now, it was too late. The cancer had taken over her whole body.

Isolation goes both ways. If I don't allow others to see my loss, I don't have to admit that it is real. If we cut ourselves off from those who are suffering a loss, we can also pretend that it is not happening. When I left my husband, my whole family chose not to visit me in my new home. At the time, it hurt very deeply, and I couldn't quite figure out why it was happening. The model of the self taught me that they were dealing with changes in their "selves" in much the same way that I was dealing with mine. It was uncomfortable for them to accept my new life. It was easier to pretend it wasn't happening. It was easier to refuse to engage themselves in my new life than spend their time with me, as they would have had to admit that change had occurred, and then they would have had to allow themselves to feel the discomfort of that change. Isolation, likely chosen without any conscious thought or comprehension of what they were doing, was the answer.

The second stage of grief is anger. The focus of one's anger can vary from one thing to another. Sometimes it is focused on others: the person who is dying or has died. How dare they leave you! To the husband who not has lived up to the commitments you made together in marriage. Towards God for letting this happen to you at this moment. Towards life, for being so difficult. Or perhaps it is focused on oneself. How could I let this happen to my body? Why didn't I take care of myself better? What a worthless, weak person I am if I couldn't stick with my commitment to the marriage. How come I stayed so long and worked so hard for something that was so worthless? Sometimes the anger is focused on people, objects or events that have nothing to do with the loss: your children, your job, the car. And sometimes the anger is just there, taking over your whole being, with no apparent logical basis. It makes you question your sanity. It makes you wonder if life is worth living.

Acting out one's anger is not necessary. One effectively moves through the stage of anger by openly and honestly acknowledges the it and allowing one's 'self' to feel it. Had I acted out my actual feelings of anger during my divorce, I would now be in jail for assault. However, allowing myself to act it out in my mind and feel how overwhelming the anger actually was, allowed it to be released and gradually diminish over time. It is okay to be angry at others, at God, or at oneself in the midst of the pain of the loss. It is okay to admit that one is angry and to feel that anger to the very depths of one's being. It is okay to tell others that you are angry, to bring it out into the open and discuss it. It is not okay to quash it, to deny it, to stuff it back down into oneself in order not to feel it. Often people are tempted to do this because it feels so uncomfortable. They will move back into the state of denial and isolation to do so. This will not allow you to heal.

It is also not okay to take your anger out on others, especially your children, your spouse or other family members. Yes, this may provide a release for a time, but again it will not do anything towards the healing of your pain. If you focus the anger on them, you will negatively affect your relationships with them, and may lose them too. People will tiptoe around you, trying to protect themselves from the fallout. You will also be living far from your life line which, as we already know, will lead to physical and psychological difficulties for the self. It takes a while to learn this, but if you are going to move on, you have to learn the lesson.

Anger will keep coming back until you reconcile yourself to its presence and allow yourself to express it openly and honestly. Admit that the loss you have experienced is painful. Admit that makes you mad. Think about the ways that you would like things to be and mourn the fact that they are not that way. Talk to others about your anger, sharing the pain of your loss instead of directing the anger at them. They still may want to avoid you, as the reminder of your loss brings with it discomfort, as they too have experienced the loss in their own way; but facing that discomfort together will allow the healing to take place. Ask forgiveness of others for the anger you have directed at them, and apologize for misplacing it. Ask forgiveness of yourself for all of the things you would have done differently had you known how this was going to turn out. Be willing to face the fact that life isn't fair and you don't like that. It makes you mad, and that is okay.

The third stage documented by Kubler-Ross is the stage of bargaining. This is a stage that is not talked about much, but is helpful as the 'self' attempts to postpone the reality of one's loss. Bargaining consists of making some sort of agreement, usually with God, that if "I" do this then the loss does not have to take place, or has not really happened. During my time of grief for my father, I found that much of this bargaining phase took place in my dreams. It was as if, although I knew that he was gone and could not be resurrected in this life, my mind was unwilling to let him go. Night after night I dreamed of family celebrations in which my father was present: healthier, younger and more outgoing than he had been in the last ten years of his life. These dreams brought a sense of peace and joy that lasted throughout the whole day. But I didn't get to stay there.

Bargaining usually occurs before the loss happens in an attempt protect the status quo. One may promise to stop smoking in order to have God cure whatever ailment has appeared in one's body. One may promise to make drastic changes in one's life if one is not forced to face the consequences of some action or another. A husband may promise his wife that he will never drink again if she will only stay by his side. A mother may promise to turn her life over to God if only her child can come through an illness safely. It is interesting to note how often God is involved in the process of bargaining even with those who do not usually admit that he exists. This is an indication of how we are forced to face the truth in times of trial, and how real this model of the self is. The spiritual core will pull you to its creator, no matter what you believe or how you have developed throughout life.

Sometimes the loss is avoided for a time, at least. We have the choice then to keep our promise. Since so many of these promises are based directly on the coping skills we use to deal with anxiety, they become very difficult to keep, especially in times of stress. We fail. We are ashamed. We retreat into a place in which we believe we are not worth the effort: that we cannot change, that everything that happens to us is inevitable and is not worth striving through. We move on to the next stage of grief: guilt.

At other times the loss happens anyway and one reacts to that loss with a sense that they have been rejected by God or by whomever the bargain was made. Instead of focusing on ourselves we may point the finger of blame at another. This too isn't very helpful. In the midst of this blame we often lose our connection to our beliefs. Now we are struggling with a higher level of grief, as it is not at the level of the mind, the closest part of our self to our spirit. We have to go through the whole process again at a grief level, and still have to deal with the process of the original loss. We may begin to believe that the bargaining we did was futile. We didn't do it right. We didn't believe hard enough. We didn't make the right bargain, and so again the process of grief takes its inevitable step to the next level.

On we move to guilt: the stage in which we assume personal responsibility for the loss that has occurred in our lives. A majority of this guilt may not be logical, but reveals a very natural human egotistical tendency. Our tendency to centre everything on ourselves means that we often assume we are responsible for whatever happens in our life, either directly, by causing something to happen, or indirectly, by not doing something which allows something else to happen. A friend felt guilty over the death of her brother for over twenty years. She was just a little girl when her mother had a miscarriage and this brother was lost to the family. That morning she had messed up the living room and her mother had been very upset with her, yelling at her about how messy and inconsiderate she was, as she cleaned up the toys for her. Shortly thereafter, the mother went into labor and the brother was born dead. The child assumed that it was the stress of having to clean up her mess which had led to the early labor. Of course, it had nothing at all to do with her brother's death, but no one took the time to share this with the child. She carried her guilt for years: guilt that was demonstrated in a need for perfectionism in everything that she did.

Guilt is a common stage for children to become stuck in as they assume responsibility for things over which they have no control. A lot of this guilt comes through the way that we, as adults, react in times of anxiety, often blaming others for trivial matters in the midst of trying to cover up our concern for other problems or situations. As we attack our children, they assume that they deserve our anger and our blame. This leads to an acceptance of responsibility for whatever has happened, be it divorce, a death, or whatever. As we try to avoid our own feelings of discomfort, we tend to isolate ourselves and not talk about the losses we are experiencing. In response, our children learn not to share their feelings openly, and carry them deep within for decades. Only when the energy to continue carrying this guilt becomes too heavy, does the child, who is now an adult, reach the point where it must be dealt with. This usually does not happen until one is in their late thirties or early forties. The stress is usually revealed as depression, uneasiness, and a lack of satisfaction in one's life, one's job, or with one's partner.

The guilt of not meeting the expectations of the person who has passed on can often keep us stuck in a situation of not living as one's true self for some time. This is a place in which we can become stuck by keeping a promise, choosing a career, trying to live the dream that another didn't accomplish, didn't have the chance to even try, or perhaps started but didn't finish. When we do this, we are moving away from living on our own life line as we concentrate on that of the other. It is better to grieve the loss of all these dreams than to try and take them over for someone else.

The only way that we can get through the stage of guilt is to accept the reality of what has happened and forgive ourselves for our part in the situation. In our first story, where the child accepted the guilt of her brother's death, a clarification of what actually happened was all that was needed for the woman to let go of this guilt. However, she also had to consider how she had reacted over the years because of this guilt, and how her life might have been different if she hadn't been immersed in the guilt. These reactions and their consequences must also be accepted and taken responsibility for. The act of forgiving herself has far more to do with her lifetime of reactions that were based on the belief that she held that she was responsible for her brother's death, and the loss of that belief, than for the "guilt" she bore.

One of the highest levels of discomfort that we face in life is dealing with guilt in which we have to face taking responsibility for something that we have actually done, whether our actions were done on purpose or by accident. This level of discomfort leads to an incredible array of difficulty in the lives of everyone involved as they try to avoid the pain. The person who has made the mistake will often resort to the use of coping skills to deaden their pain in order to carry on with their life as best they can. Everyone else who is interacting with this person will likely try to avoid any mention of the situation in order to protect themselves and to protect the person they care for. The more serious the result, the higher the level of coping skills needed to reduce the discomfort. Over time whole families, and actually all of society, suffer, as energy is spent on coping skills, not achieving one's full potential

A friend started to smoke as a teenager, an action that was not acceptable in her home. In her attempts to hide this habit she accidentally set the house on fire. Her younger sister tragically died in the fire, in spite of her father's frantic attempts to rescue her. The father was not able to forgive himself for failing to rescue his daughter and never was the same again. He died within two years, most likely of a broken heart. My friend never openly admitted what she had done to anyone and carried her guilt in silence. Her family suspected that she might have been involved but never said anything about it to her, afraid that it would upset her too much. She struggled on through life, using alcohol to dull her pain, never dealing openly with burden of guilt she carried. This led to problems in her ability to sustain relationships and to mother her children.

The truth finally came to light for me when child protection services moved in to remove the children from the home because of her inability to care for them in her state of intoxication. In the midst of the chaos of that night, I found her weeping over the flowers she had saved from her sister's and her father's funerals. Only then was I able to realize how this guilt had taken over her whole life. But it didn't help me to know this as I had no idea at the time what to do with this information. She fled to the streets to dull her pain. Now she was not only guilty for the deaths of her family members but also a failure as a mother. I have never been able to find her again. I only hope that somewhere, somehow, she has been able to bring the truth out into the open and deal with it. I hope that she can truly forgive herself for the mistake that she made. And in the midst of my thoughts of her, I wonder how many others who are living on the streets are stuck in similar situations.

I believe that the origins of our justice systems throughout the world are based on the innate knowledge that we all have that one must move on from guilt. Bringing the truth out into the open and taking responsibility for whatever has happened allows everyone involved to move on. Asking and giving forgiveness are a huge part of this process, both of others and of your self. Hiding the action, holding the guilt close to your heart, leads not only to heartache and disaster for yourself, but also for those you hold most dear. Sadly, many of our current justice systems have moved away from directly making a person admit their guilt to focusing on society taking the responsibility to prove they are guilty. Publicly acknowledging one's reality is too uncomfortable for everyone involved. Our whole society suffers.

The next stage in the process of grief is depression. During a grief process which is allowed to be felt, this depression is likely connected to the realization that one is not in control and cannot stop the loss from occurring, or create a situation in which what is lost can be returned in some way or another. Depression is a feeling of worthlessness, both of oneself, and of one's life. One feels empty, disconnected to anything or anyone, and alone. Typically the feelings of depression experienced during the grief process are temporary, lasting for about two weeks or less. However, this is not true for all people or all situations. During the process of grief, which is unresolved, the issues of denial, anger and guilt over time, will finally create a state of depression which appears to come out of nowhere. Few people, including many in the professional psychological community make the effort to associate depression with the loss that has occurred in the past and truly believe that there is something clinically wrong with the individual.

The common symptoms of depression include the loss of interest or pleasure in daily hobbies or activities, including sex; a persistent sad or depressed mood, often described as an empty feeling; a change in appetite with either a weight loss or gain; difficulty in concentrating or in making decisions; a change in one's normal sleep patterns; the feelings of fatigue or a lack of energy; the feelings of sluggishness or restlessness; increased feelings of guilt, worthlessness or lack of hope; unexplained crying or a sense of not having any emotions at all; and thoughts of death or suicide. More extreme depression can present itself through physical symptoms such as headaches, abdominal pain or other general aches. Some deeply depressed people also experience anxiety attacks.

The typical clinical treatment for depression combines pharmacology with psychology. The message that comes with this treatment is that there is something wrong with you as a person usually through the biochemical reactions in your brain, if you have reached the point of depression. Depression currently has the distinction of being the illness which is the leading cause of disability worldwide. As I watch all of the advertisements on our television, promoting one anti-depressant or another, I have a tendency to wonder if this "illness" is not indeed created by a society which is unwilling to face discomfort of any kind, in the midst of a world that is changing so quickly that the typical person cannot keep up with the changes that are happening to the self. It is even more scary to realize that the medical community is currently coming to the realization that these medications are not as effective as once was thought and can even lead to more extreme problems such as aggression or suicide.

When we look at depression through the model of the self, we can recognize the problem is not living on one's life line and thus not being able to reach one's full potential. Most of the time, this is missed, because people do not understand how the whole self is connected. Labels are administered and chemical means are suggested as solutions to the discomfort the person is experiencing. Being fully aware of the role of depression in the grief process and working with a person to understand their feelings as they go through this process and striving to really understand the self and live on one's own life line is usually more effective.

In the midst of experiencing the different reactions that follow a loss to the 'self': denial, isolation, anger, bargaining, guilt and depression, we will also feel sadness. This sadness will occur throughout all of the different stages and may be one of the reasons that we have problems relating the other emotions to the process of grief. The level of pain felt through this sadness will be based directly on how big a hole in the self was created through the loss. At times the pain of sadness will feel as if one has actually been cut by a knife. Many people choose not to allow themselves to actually feel the pain and will do anything to avoid it. But the pain must be felt in order for healing to occur. As the actual healing takes place, the level of pain gradually decreases over time to the point that it is finally gone. This doesn't mean that you have stopped caring for that which you lost. This doesn't mean that you have forgotten that which was lost. It only means that the hole in the 'self' has healed and you are whole again. The loss has moved from your material and social level to your mind where it will be stored as memory until you die.

The last two stages of grief are acceptance and hope. When we reach the point of acceptance, we have allowed ourselves to feel all of the other emotions and have connected these feelings directly to the loss that has occurred. A major part of acceptance is admitting that the impact of what has happened is not always what we wanted or believed and we must take the time to forgive ourselves for whatever reactions we have had during this time of grief. Forgiveness is a giant step in being able to allow ourselves to hope for the future.

With hope comes the end of the pain. At this stage we know that we can continue living without whatever it was that we have lost. Although we may prefer not to have experienced the loss, we do know that we are okay. The stage of hope gives us the opportunity to be thankful for the gift that we lost and the pleasure of the memories of the good times in our past with whatever, or whomever, we no longer have in our lives. We can and we will go on, reaching forth in joy to our fellow man as we continue our journey.

The process of grief for a particular loss may reappear from time to time during one's life, especially for those things that are very important to the individual. One may experience the emotions of anger, or guilt or depression again, when one is reminded of the loss in a particular way. A child may grieve the loss of a parent as they go through the milestones of their lives such as a graduation or a wedding. The parent of a disabled child may re-experience the grieving process every time their child's peers reach a level their child is incapable of, such as getting one's driving license, or leaving for university. Anniversaries, times of celebration and similar experiences can bring back the pain of loss. Sensory information that matches that of your interaction with the person who has died, or the item that was lost, may resurrect the feelings of grief. About three years after my father passed away, I had the opportunity to attend a concert in which a singer paid tribute to my father's favorite country and western artist. He walked onto the stage dressed like the singer from the past. Part of his costume was a pair of leather wrist guards, which were worn by cowboys to protect their wrists. The only other pair of these I remember seeing, belonged to my father as a young man. We often played with them as children. The sight of those wristbands, combined with the sound of the music that my father loved, released tears of sadness that flowed silently down my cheeks for the remainder of the concert. Our mind is a storage container for all of the connections of a lifetime, and is constructed to react through sensory input. Loss is uncomfortable and will be felt. The body will react. Our feelings must be expected, accepted and allowed to be felt. It's what life is all about. It's what being a 'self' is. It is okay.

It is time to accept the fact that grief is a very real and normal part of being human. No one can go through life without experiencing grief. Trying to avoid or ignore the process will only magnify the amount of discomfort one will face in the future. It is also time to acknowledge that there is not a "proper" way to grieve. Grief is a totally unique and individual process for each of us, which will be different for every loss we experience during life. The process that is outlined above is not a set formula of rigid steps that we each follow, but only a journey each of us takes in our own individual ways.

We are beginning to see this acceptance happening in society as grief counselors become readily available whenever crisis situations erupt in our world. However, it is also very important to accept the fact that grief takes time and energy. Getting things over with quickly is not the answer. Those who are grieving may need help for weeks, months and even years, not just a couple of days after the loss. Or they may just need to be left alone to sort out their feelings without any deadlines or expectation levels. Respecting the whole grieving process, and allowing people the time and space they each need to go through it all, is far more important than supplying a counselor for a couple of hours or days. We each must be free to grieve if we are to become the people that we are meant to be. Loss of portions of the 'self' does not mean loss of full potential. It only means that we will hurt for a time.

The Act of Forgiveness

A major step in the process of change which will be mentioned time and again throughout this book is the importance of forgiving others and oneself in order to let go of the pain and reactions of the past. This process appears to be simple for some people and some circumstances as they are able bring the situation out into the open, say the words of forgiveness and let go, but it is not that easy for the majority of us. Yes we may say the words. Yes, we may want to let go completely, but it doesn't seem to happen.

In the past I suggested that clients write statements of forgiveness in letters to share with those they were forgiving, or to bring to the grave of those who are no longer here to forgive in person. Some found that the process of writing the words was a powerful release and all they needed. Others claimed the burning the words brought resolution. But some were still stuck, wanting to forgive, trying to forgive, but finding that they were continuing to cling to the pain of the past. Recently I have found a new way to work through this.

In Matthew 18:21-22 Peter asked "Lord, how many time should I forgive my brother when he sins against me? And Jesus replies "I tell you, not seven times, but seventy-seven times." I have always been taught that this is a symbolic number which indicates that we are to continue forgiving as many times as needed. Dr. Bill Nelson, the creator of the biofeedback system I currently work with, questioned what would happen if we took this number literally instead of symbolically. He suggested that his clients use a process of writing out their act of forgiveness 77 times. In other words write out a line of forgiveness 10 times every day for 10 days plus 7 times on the 11th day. It is something that I now do myself and also suggest to my clients who find themselves hanging on to the past in spite of their desire to let go.

The process of writing out the line of forgiveness on a daily basis like this is fascinating as it allows one to look at the complete picture over time in ways that one had not been conscious of. One starts with a premise of what one needs to forgive. For example I began my first experiment with the line "I forgive my husband for lying to me". As I was writing out this line, thoughts of the lies of his brothers, sisters and parents kept popping into my mind. I realized that they had blocked our family as much as his lies had. The line changed to "I forgive all of the members of the Gillingham family for lying to me." Once they were added into the process it was time to face myself. I realized that I, too, was a member of the family and had followed suit in so many ways. By the end of the eleven days I felt completely washed clean of all the lies. It was an amazing process.

A friend now uses this process to work through the relationships of her past, one by one. It started as a way of saying good bye to her mother after her death. As the weeks passed different interactions with her mother came up that she had long forgotten, but was now carrying as negative messages to herself. "You will always be fat. You have your grandmother's hips." Together we are learning that it is not always the big traumas that are blocking our ability to truly forgive, but all the little slights that happen throughout childhood that may not have appeared to be important in the moment, but create the person we become. The time it takes to write out the line 77 times allows the doors to open one by one and the release to be complete.

There are a couple of factors to be aware of if you decide to follow through on this process. First of all: keep you statement short and to the point as you will lose your initiative if you have to write too many words in each sentence. Secondly, it is very important to pay attention to what you are writing while you go through this process. You may have a clear idea in the beginning, but as time goes by you may find that you are unconsciously writing something else. Pay attention to what comes up. The words may open new doors for you in your journey to understand yourself.

Forgiveness is such an important element in freeing yourself to live on your life line. The feelings you cling to, because of whatever the other person did to you, are your response, not theirs. Letting go is a process of freeing yourself, not the other person, no matter what they did. However, this process also allows you to put them on their life line in at their social self as you accept them for the person they truly are. Once we understand and accept this interconnection between all of us, we are truly free to change the whole world.

A CASE STUDY

She was born in a remote northern community in Canada. Her father died shortly after her birth. Her mother died from tuberculosis when she was six years old. She contracted tuberculosis from the same source as her mother, along with her sister and brother. They were all hospitalized near home until the death of her mother. Then the three children were transported to a sanitarium, far from their home community. There her brother and sister were cured of the tuberculosis and returned home. She was weaker and ended up spending 17 years of her life in this hospital. During this time she was assigned to a foster family for short periods, when she was well enough to be out in the world, but she never had the opportunity to return to her home community.

Due to her illness, she missed out on everything that a normal child does, which included playing outside in the fresh air. She did not receive an education. She never saw anyone from her family or her home community. She wasn't allowed to play with other children. She had little to do with anyone but nurses and doctors.

At age 23, it appeared that the tuberculosis was defeated, so she was sent out into the community to live. She moved into an apartment in the city where the hospital was located. She met other young women from the north and began to go to parties with them. One night she met a young man, who took her home and raped her. At this point in her life, she knew absolutely nothing at all about sex, having not been told anything by anyone during her years in the hospital or during the time she spent with her foster parents. She got pregnant from that one sexual encounter. As she did not understand what was happening to her body, she went back to the hospital for help. Her doctor confirmed the pregnancy. He decided that an abortion was necessary as she was still in a weak condition because of her illness. He also decided to do a tubal ligation in order to protect her from further pregnancies. She willingly signed the papers for both surgical procedures with very little understanding of what was happening to her.

She carried this secret for 30 some years. When she got married and had difficulty becoming pregnant she went to a doctor who told her that she could not have children due to the tubal ligation. This was the first time that she fully understood what had happened to her. Her husband told her that it was okay with him, because what the doctors had done for her meant that she had lived, and that he was able to love her.

Throughout the years since she learned about the tubal libation, she was able to ignore it by not thinking about it. However, this had gotten much more difficult as time passed and she no longer could put the thoughts out of her mind. She kept thinking about the fact that no one had taken the time to tell her about sexuality while she was in the hospital and with her foster parents. She could not believe that they did not protect her by giving her the information. She was upset with the death of her baby as it was against both her religious and cultural beliefs to have an abortion. She was upset because having a tubal libation is also against her religious and cultural beliefs. The thoughts of "how could they do this to me" and "how much she I had missed out on in life" swirled around in her mind constantly. She could not sleep. She could not eat. The medical community diagnosed her with depression and prescribed antidepressants. She refused to take the medication because of her cultural beliefs.

I was the first person, except for her husband and doctor, with whom she had shared the whole story. Throughout the first session with me, she cried continuously, expressing her failure to understand why anyone would do this to a helpless child. She expressed great sorrow at the loss of her childhood, her family, her home in the north, and her ability to have children. She claimed that she was unworthy of the love of her husband because she could not give him children. By the end of the session she said she felt as if a huge weight had been lifted off her shoulders and that she felt much better having shared her story.

We began the treatment process by looking at each of the stages of grief: denial, anger, guilt, depression, sadness, acceptance and hope. She listed all of the areas of grief she has not dealt with throughout the years of her life:

1. The deaths of people she cared about: Her father, mother, two sisters, a brother and her foster parents.

2. The loss of her childhood because of her disease. This also includes the loss of her closeness to her family, her culture, and her land. It also includes the loss of all the experiences that children have growing up, as well as the loss of education.

3. The loss of her baby through the abortion, and the loss of her ability to have any more children through the tubal ligation.

She easily recognized her ability, throughout the years, to forget about what had happened in the past, as denial. She wondered at her inability to carry on in denial at this point in her life. Although we understand that it is likely connected to the reality that one uses a lot of psychic energy to keep the denial going, and that she no longer has that amount of energy available, we chose not to concentrate on the "whys" of this question. Instead we continued on to examine the rest of her emotional reactions as found in process of grief, to acknowledge them and to let them go. She wrote statements of her feelings, read them out loud and then destroyed the paper they were written on. Some she shared with me in the therapy room and others were dealt with at home when the feelings of the past overwhelmed her. We talked about burning the written words, but she found that ripping them up and putting them in the garbage was enough. An example of an anger statement she used was:

> *Mom (foster mother), I am angry that you did not take the time to tell me about sexuality.*
> *I am angry because you robbed me of my ability to protect myself, by keeping this information*
> *from me.*

The statements of feeling were directed at various people in the past and covered a wide range of topics. Anger was the toughest stage to work through, as she did not feel she had the right to be angry with these people because they had looked after her throughout the years. Expressing the anger was stepping over a cultural and social boundary that was firmly etched in her mind; a boundary that she also had to let go of.

Once we reached the point of acceptance in the process of grief, we began to look at new ways for her to allow herself to feel the emotions she was experiencing, to accept them for herself, and to share them with others. She recognized that she had developed a strong pattern of behavior of not feeling free to share her feelings openly with anyone. She also had a tendency to sit and imagine the inner reaction of others, such as her husband, rather than asking him directly what was happening for him. We examined how these patterns had worked for her positively as a child in the hospital and the foster home in many ways, but she admitted that they were not effective for her at this point in life. Did she want to keep them or discard them? What did she want to replace them with?

As we looked at the model of self, we considered how her definition of a woman and her strong beliefs that one needs to have children to be a "real" woman were impacting her life at this time. We discussed how the role of motherhood fit within her cultural context. We began to look at different ways she could find fulfillment in her life without having a child of her own.

The loss of her culture was also examined and she realized it was not necessarily gone for good. We reframed the fear that she was forgetting her language, to that of taking pride in being bilingual. The fact she retains her native language, learned as a small child, in a world of English since the time she was eight, is something to take great pride in. Reframing brought another revelation for her as she remembered that she is also able to understand two other native languages, and would often act as a translator as a child in the hospital when people arrived from the north who could not speak English. She is not only bilingual; she is multilingual. In these ways we concentrated on the strengths she has as a woman, on the positives instead of negatives. She was pleased to report that she began to take pleasure in the things she did in the past, has a good appetite, and when she can't sleep because of her memories chooses to read a book instead of rolling the negative memories and "what' ifs" around in her mind all night. She is looking forward to getting involved in crafts again.

Each of these steps led her closer to living on her life line. Although changes were happening at all levels of self throughout the process, these changes were easier to deal with because they brought her in line with her spirit, not away from it. She still cannot have children. She was robbed of this gift by decisions made by others for her. It was not right. It was not fair. But it is, and it cannot be changed. The tubal ligation is as much a part of her 'self' at this point as any other part of her. It is okay.

CHAPTER THREE
THE DEVELOPMENT OF THE SELF

The Lord called me before I was born,
while I was in my mother's womb he named me.

ISAIAH 49:2

IN THE CORNER OF MY OFFICE STANDS A PORCELAIN DOLL. SHE HAS LONG BLOND CURLY hair and wears an off-white dress with ruffles and beads. White socks, shiny patent shoes, pantaloons and a crinoline complete her costume. To the doll collector she may represent a certain value, but to most people she is only a piece of decoration. However, in this office, she is a representation of the importance of the different factors which influence the development of the self.

As a young child, I was a thumb sucker. I am not certain how my family or the community reacted to this habit as I don't remember a negative or positive response of any kind. I do have memories of sitting with two other boys my age as a preschooler, who obviously also sucked their thumbs. We were comparing the different ways in which one could position their hand, thumb and nose in the process of sucking one's thumb and trying out the methods used by each other. At that moment, anyway, it was definitely not an issue.

As the time for me to attend school approached, my mother must have worried about this habit as she promised me a certain doll if I quit sucking my thumb. This doll was advertised in a weekly farming newspaper. We cut the page out of the paper and came to an agreement that if I did not suck my thumb, she would order this doll for me for Christmas. It must have been very important for me because I have clear memories of lying on the couch, holding the picture of the doll in my hand, wanting desperately to suck my thumb, but not doing so. I knew that if I did, it would mean no doll. Christmas arrived and she was mine. Sadly, she was dependent on beauty, not quality, so she did not last very long. Within a short time all I had left of her was a bald head. I kept this head with my other special possessions for years.

Just before my 50th birthday, I was walking through a mall and suddenly came face to face with the doll I have in my office. I stopped abruptly, my eyes riveted on her face in the store window. She looked just like the picture of the doll that I had carried all those years ago. Her hair, her dress, even her shoes looked the same. I had to have her. I rewarded myself by buying her as my 50th birthday gift.

The model of the self illustrates the self as four levels: the spirit, the mind, the social self and the material self. Although the spirit is a constant throughout our lives, the rest of the levels develop over time to produce the individuals that we now are. This process of development begins at our conception and carries on throughout our whole lives. I share this doll with you because for she represents two major factors in my life which are a force in the development of the self: nature and nurture.

NATURE

The concept of nature is determined by our biological make-up. When we are conceived, the development of the 'self' is dependent on the genetic code that we receive directly from our parents. The combination of their separate sets of genes creates a totally unique genetic code for each of us. Neither we, nor our parents, have any control at all of our personal genetic make-up. Our body is dependent on its genetic code for its size, its appearance, and its ability to survive in this world. It determines everything from the outward visible features of our bodies such as our sex, the color of our skin, the shape and color of our eyes, and the texture of our hair, to a variety of factors within our bodies such as our level of sensitivity, our ability to metabolize foods, and how well our immune system works. Genetic evidence suggests that we are more similar to whom we are related and to those who come from the same racial and cultural backgrounds as we do, but we are all connected. In the midst of this connection, each of us is totally unique, for our genetic code is specific to us, and to no one else, unless we have an identical twin and even then there are differences.

In spite of our knowledge of the differences in each of our genetic codes, current medical, psychological, and educational practices are based directly on a scientific method that concentrates on similarities rather than differences. Instead of celebrating our diversity and trying to understand and accept how each of us is unique and can use our individual talents and abilities to contribute to the world, we concentrate our efforts on making everyone the same. This is most apparent and terrifying in current genetic research in which scientists are concentrating on discovering the "defective" genes with a future goal of replacing them and with cloning the perfect genetic example of a species.

One of the major current beliefs we face is that information only has value if it has been scientifically validated. Individuality does not play an important role in a society which holds this belief nor with a scientific community focused on similarities and retaining the status quo. The importance of being "the same" is a major feature of research studies, which use the scientific method based on control groups, random sampling, validity, reliability and significance. The only research that is acceptable is that which meets these rigid standards and is statistically significant, which means of course, that it fits the majority of the human population. Being the same becomes far more important than reaching our own individual potential. Differences are something to be feared, to be hidden, to be labeled and disposed of.

However, a world with no differences would be an impossible world to live in. If all of us became exactly the same, our civilization would collapse within minutes, as we would be missing so many different vital components of humanity which keep us alive. We all could be doctors, entertainers, accountants, or perhaps engineers. I have no idea what might be determined as the ideal example of humanity. However, if we were all doctors, there would be no entertainers, no accountants, and no engineers. And of course, there would be no need for doctors as each of us could doctor ourselves. In the meantime, we would starve without food, die of exposure without clothes or shelter, and lose our connections with the past and with each other without educators, writers and so on.

That each of us is unique is what makes humanity so vibrant and exciting. Because of others in this world, who have interests and talents very different from my own, I am able to sit at this computer and type out these words to share with you, completely dependent on the designer of my software, the engineers who made my computer, the electricians who make certain that the electricity keeps flowing to my electrical outlets and the publisher who arranges access to this book for you. My needs for sustenance are met by the grocery store across the street as well as through a number of restaurants in the area, which are in turn supplied by a variety of farmers from all over the world. A janitor, whom I have never met, cleans my office space, which allows me more time to write. The landlord arranges for the plumbers and other service people to come in to make certain that I have heat, water and working bathroom facilities. If these people were not in my world it would be impossible for you to be reading this book at this time. I would have to concentrate my energy on meeting my needs for survival instead of these words.

The willingness of those in charge to rely on that which is the same, instead of celebrating all that makes us unique, is terrifying. It puts each of us in a situation in which our differences are discounted or belittled, while our similarities are placed on a pedestal. It gives rise to the belief that there is a certain "normal" way for a person to be, which does not meld with the reality of genetic difference. It leads to the use of "labels" to fit those who do fit a certain "standard": labels that are used to derogate and to discriminate. However, it is not how we are the same that is going to allow us to have a beneficial impact on the world. It was not the people who chose to be the same who made the great discoveries in our world, such as electricity, penicillin, and air travel, on which we rely today. It was those people who were not only willing to be different, but who had learned to celebrate their differences. Our unique talents and abilities, which allow us to fill our role in this world in a meaningful way, are being eroded by this false belief of the power of sameness.

I am a sensitive person. My sensitivities showed up very early in my life, as my skin was so sensitive to perfume when I was born that my mother could not even use baby soap on me without causing a rash. I don't do well in crowds. I tire quickly in noisy or visually active spaces and also have a tough time concentrating when there is an extremely high level of stimulation. I cry easily and have trouble interacting in some social situations. These all may appear to be negative attributes, but being sensitive also means that I pick up the emotional feelings of others very easily, which allows me to be effective as a therapist. It gives me the ability to pay attention, so that I can recognize and accept differences in others. It also provides an ability to be aware of small details, which help in the planning and organization of projects and events. However, my level of sensitivity caused a lot of problems for me in the past, mainly because I had no idea of how I was unique and how I could use my abilities. In a world where the emphasis is on everybody not only being the same, but also competing on what is assumed to be a level playing field, a sensitive person like me has a lot of difficulty.

As a child I was told that I was shy, and that this was a not a good thing to be. As a teenager and young adult, I continued to hear this message and to berate myself for it. Shyness was a 'weakness" that had to be eliminated. I was not as "good" as anyone else because of it.

In my mid thirties I returned to university to study psychology. At this point I focused a lot of effort on understanding the concept of "shyness" and discovered the work of Jerome Kagan.[6] Years of research on the differences between what he terms inhibited and uninhibited people have revealed that there are biological and physiological differences between those who fit in these two groups. These include such factors as a difference in the heart rate acceleration, in blood pressure levels, in pupillary dilations, in muscle tension and in cortical activity in the right frontal area of the brain when exposed to stressful situations. In other words, the biological responses of the inhibited (or shy) person are vastly different that those of the uninhibited when they experience identical situations. This is directly dependent on their genetic code, over which, as we have already stated, we have no control at all.

So, when I, as a shy or inhibited person, enter a room full of people, who are laughing and talking loudly, my body responds to the impact of the noise and chaos in a different way than does the body of the uninhibited person, who is by my side. My heart rate goes up. My production of sweat and salvia increases. My brain goes on alert, while his basically remains calm. This leads to an increase in anxiety for both of us, as he cannot feel or understand my responses any more than I can feel or understand his. My anxiety level, as a direct response to the physiological changes in my body, and based directly on the amount of sensory input I am receiving, will begin to increase and be demonstrated in noticeable responses, such as my voice going higher, my verbal responses becoming stilted and so on. These responses do not make sense to those who are not inhibited because their body is not responding in the same way. And since I wasn't aware that this is how I am different, I accepted the fact that it was something I was responsible for changing through will power. I was rejected by others and by myself, because my behavior was different than that of the rest of the group

6   Kagan, Jerome (1994). Galen's Prophecy: Temperament in Human Nature. Basic Books.

which is considered "normal". However, when you take my personal genetic code into account, my behavior is completely "normal" and adaptive for my particular body and has nothing at all to do with learning or not learning social skills, being "good" or "bad" at something, a weakness, or my individual level of will power.

Since I have come to understand and accept my individual physiological responses, I am able to feel them happening and to attribute them to the stimulation that is occurring around me. This lessens my anxiety level because I know what is happening and accept the fact that this is okay. A lower anxiety level results in the obvious outward signs becoming less noticeable, to the point that others are no longer aware of what I am feeling. This makes social situations so much more comfortable for me, not because my physiological responses have changed, but because I am reacting to them differently. It's come to the point that very few people I meet believe that I once was considered shy. The lack of understanding of this genetic reality for much of our world is evident in schools where children are mocked, punished, and even drugged for their biological responses, which differ from what is considered the norm, or acceptable. It is also demonstrated on a new "reality" television show in which the producers plan to measure the heart rate of the contestants to determine who can do the "best" in facing stressful situations. What the developers of this type of show don't understand is that the level of the heart rate may have nothing at all to do with the ability of the person to withstand stress. Instead they will be measuring how the genetic code has determined that this particular person will react to the stressful input. The "winners" will be those who fit within the group which has been termed "uninhibited" because of their genetic make-up, not because of any talent or ability they have.

The genetic make-up of the sensory system for each individual determines the individual level of response to the same amount of sensory input from the time of birth on. *Every individual has a personal version of the world of sensations, and that version is the one that counts. If loud noises or bright lights or soft touches irritate a child, it makes no difference that you find them pleasurable. If an infant cannot organize what she sees well enough to make out her mother's smile, it makes no difference that another child can. Every child comprehends and reacts to each type of sensation in a particular and characteristic way.*[7]

During the late eighties I met a group of people who live on the extreme outskirts of our society. They have what is termed the developmental disability of autism. People with extreme cases of autism do not learn to speak, appear to withdraw into themselves, having as little interaction with other people as possible, and engage in extreme repetitive and stereotypic behaviors which may range from rocking, pacing, or flapping their hands to head banging or self mutilation through pinching or biting themselves. However, there is a whole continuum of people who fit within the spectrum

---

7   Greenspan, Stanley and Benderly, Beryl (1997). *The Growth of the Mind and the Endangered Origins of Intelligence*. Perseus Books. p. 48.

of autism, people who experience the triad symptoms on which this diagnosis is based: a qualitative impairment in communication, a qualitative impairment in social interaction, and the use of restricted repetitive and stereotypic patterns of behavior, routines, and interests at different degrees.

When I first began to work with these people, I was very confused and frustrated by their behavior, as I had no idea of what was going on with them. Nothing that I read, at that point, helped me to understand or to know how to help them. The program I was involved with seemed to only make their responses more extreme. However, as time passed, I began to recognize that many of their behavioral outbursts were a direct response to a sudden increase in sensory input of some kind. For example, one child began head banging fiercely after an electric saw was turned on near him. I determined that perhaps their response to sensory input had something to do with their condition of autism.

After the movie *Rainman* was released, Oprah Winfrey invited people with autism onto her talk show to share how it felt to be autistic. Temple Grandin, one of the guests on this show, confirmed my assumptions about sensory response when she stated:

> Now the reason that children withdraw is because of sensory problems. Loud noises just hurt my ears. When a loud noise goes off, I put my hands over my ears. It hurts. People touched me. It was like a tidal wave of stimulation. On an autistic child a scratchy petticoat will feel like sandpaper, just scratching her raw. Her skin is over sensitive, and my hearing - certain sounds will just blast through my ears. You're so overwhelmed by the defect in the sensory system that all you want to do is withdraw because it just hurts. How can I be thinking of emotions when I'm just trying to protect myself from this terrible noise onslaught.[8]

In the years that have followed I have come to know people who fit within the autism spectrum from all over the world. Their extreme response to sensory stimulation is a constant factor in each of their lives. It's so different than what I experience in the same space. They speak of their skin burning from the texture of clothing which is new, too tight or of a certain fabric. Of feeling the imprint of my hand on their arm for more than two hours after I touched them. Of hearing every sound in a building, from the dialing on a phone call in an office down the hall, to the conversation at the other end of the building and being driven to distraction by paper rustling, pencils scraping along the paper and the constant ticking of the clock and humming of the fluorescent lights. Of not eating certain foods because the sound of chewing roars through their ears, or the taste is too strong, or the texture revolting. Of smelling someone's perfume from an office on the floor below

---

8   Temple Grandin on Debra Dimaio and Jim McPharlin *"Autistic savants"*. *The Oprah Winfrey Show* transcript. Chicago: Harpo Productions, January 10, 1989) p. 11.

or gagging from the odor of a coworker's menstrual pads. Of seeing each hair on my head as an individual stand, or the whole world in fragments.

In order to teach others about the reality of autism from a sensory viewpoint, I designed a workshop in which we would increase the level of sensory input in a classroom situation and teach a lesson to the participants in the midst of this stimulation. The response of the participants has been very interesting as two results were achieved. In the first place, the participants are unable to learn the new material and fail the exam at the end of the class. Secondly, they all resort to one type of coping skill or another, some very obvious and others more covert, to deal with level of stimulation they are experiencing. Most of these coping skills could be referred to as "autistic-like behaviors" which indicates that autism is the direct result of the human body dealing with too much sensory stimulation. This reaction of resorting to autistic-like behaviors has also been noted by other researchers, who have exposed so called "normal" subjects to high levels of stimulation.

These results led me to conclude that human beings are all on a continuum of sensitivity in which those with autism fit on the extreme end of the sensitivity to stimulation axis. If we place the whole human population on a bell curve graph, there will be one "normal" human being in the exact centre of this graph and each of us will fit somewhere else within that space. I have no idea of who this one person is, but I am certain that it is not me. I actually place myself on the inhibited side of the graph about halfway between the "normal" person and those within the autism spectrum.

The impact of sharing this graph with others has been very positive, especially in school classrooms where I carry out environmental assessments for children with autism. Part of my service includes a presentation to the other children in the classroom so that they can understand how their classmate is different, how to move away from concentrating on his disability and focus in on his abilities, and how they, as his fellow classmates and friends, can interact with him in a way that is most beneficial. I draw a bell curve graph on the board and use it to explain how all people are different and how we all fit into a multitude of these graphs as human beings. I use the difficulties the child has and the areas of ability as names for the graphs, such as mathematical ability, musical aptitude, sports ability, and so on. I tell them that we all have our distinct place on each of these graphs and that there hundreds of different graphs like this that we could create. In some of the graphs we, as an individual, may place on the high end, which indicates that we are talented, on others in the low end, and on still others, close to the middle. I tell them that no one is on the high end of every graph, or only on the low end. Our talents and abilities are spread throughout all of the different things that man can do and be.

Then I introduce the sensitivity to stimulation graph, telling the students that this graph is for an area which has a great impact on the life of their classmate as he fits on the extreme of this graph. I share the same things about this graph that I have with all the other graphs. There is one normal person who fits in the very centre of the graph. We all fit somewhere on this graph. I show them where I think I might fit. I tell them about how inhibited people have bodies that react to stimulation at a much higher level than that of the normal person and so these people are the ones who like things to be quiet and organized, who prefer to spend a lot of time alone or with just one friend rather than attend big parties, who like to read books, and perhaps play on the computer all by themselves. Then I go on to the uninhibited side where we find the people who like big parties, and lots of noise and excitement. They often choose to do extreme sports and enjoy things like riding roller coasters, bungie jumping, sky diving and mountain climbing. They like lots of people around them and are seldom alone. At this point most of the children in the classroom have the tendency to put their hands up in the air and say "that's me, that's me!"

Next I show them where their autistic classmate fits on the graph, on the very extreme on the sensitive side, explaining that you can see that there are not a lot of other people like him as the graph shows less numbers here, and that is why they don't know anyone else like him. I tell them that he can hear, see, smell, taste and feel at a higher level than they can. This means that he will hear a helicopter flying towards us before the rest of us can hear it, that his clothes may feel scratchy on his skin, and that odors are stronger to him. This means that living in our world is more difficult for him. But it doesn't mean that he doesn't have abilities too. He is very musical and can keep a rhythm and stay on tune as well as anyone in the class, that he is pretty good at counting, adding, and subtracting, and can read the same books as they do when he is in a quiet room. However, when our voices are loud, he gets very upset because it is very, very loud for him since he hears better than we do.

The typical response from the children at this point is "How do you know these things?" and "How can we help?" I begin by sharing how I have come to my conclusions. I ask them to think about the boy's behavior when there is a lot of noise and activity going on in the room and they reply that he is running back and forth and flapping his hands. Then I ask them to consider another situation: "What happens when he is alone in the room with just one of you?"

They stop and think and then reply, "He's quietly sitting in his desk, looking at a book."

"And this is how I know," I reply. "He is different when the room is noisy or quiet. When it's noisy he has to calm himself by running and flapping his hands. So if you really want to help him, you do not try to stop him by touching him as that will only add to his discomfort. Instead you become quiet and still and he will calm down on his own. And that's why we take him out of the classroom at certain times, because it is easier for him to learn and to finish his work where it is very quiet."

I go on to explain that when the teacher is asking them to be quiet, she isn't doing this because she is mean, but because she wants to make the classroom a safe place for everyone to do their work, including the boy with autism. If the children are quiet, they will not only help the boy with autism, but also anyone else in the room who is on the sensitive side of the graph. Perhaps the students on the uninhibited side of the graph can do their work in the midst of any situation without too much difficulty, but a lot of noise and chaos is going to make things harder for those who are sensitive, which includes me.

This is where the presentation suddenly changes and becomes meaningful to everyone in the room as an individual. I have never been in classroom where I haven't seen certain students getting in trouble because they haven't been able to keep up with their classmates in some way or another. As they look at the graph and think about what is happening to them, a light dawns. Their faces change and they slowly and carefully put their hand up into the air and state with confidence "I am a sensitive person." They won't have to wait until they are in their mid thirties to figure it out like I did.

By teaching children this way, we can make a huge impact on the amount of bullying and teasing that goes on in our schools. If we move away from concentrating on "the same" to celebrating our diversity, our children will not need to go through the system feeling as if they don't fit in and that there is something wrong with them. Perhaps it would decrease the number of children who become so desperate that they finally snap and use guns in an attempt to destroy in a system that is causing them so much pain. Perhaps it would lower the number of teenagers who get so desperate they commit suicide. Perhaps it would lower the number of cases of depression that psychologists face. If we began this process in the preschool or elementary school years the tension of being a teenager would be greatly diminished. It's going to take a major effort on the part of society, but I believe that we are beginning to take the steps to do it. It's not been that many years since children's arms were tied down in an attempt to break them from the habit of using their left hands to write. It's been even less time since schools were segregated by race. The inclusion of those with disabilities is a current battle in which great strides are being made. We are beginning to learn that being different is not a threat. The next step is to begin to make the most of our differences instead of trying to change them or hide them because we are ashamed of them.

Our unique levels of response to sensory stimulation are only one way in which we respond differently because of our genetic code. Each of us is a combination of hundreds of different factors that are not the same in every human being. Coming to an understanding of who we are as a 'self' means discovering and accepting the individual differences which are built into one's individual genetic code and working with them instead of against them. One factor that I have had to deal with is the way that my individual body metabolizes and stores the food I eat. I come from a family in which one parent could eat anything and not gain an ounce, while the other appears to have the ability to gain weight by just thinking about food. To my frustration I inherited the metabolism of the second rather than the first and have had to learn to accept the fact that I have a body which appears to be capable of gleaning every nutritional particle it can from whatever passes my lips. Dieting only leads to an increase in weight, as my body goes into starvation alert and becomes even more efficient at breaking down the food. For me, being healthy means giving up on the desire to be willowy thin, and concentrating on eating healthy foods and exercising regularly instead of dieting.

Other people experience different metabolic reactions, which are dependent on their genetic code. The tendency for North American Aboriginal people to develop diabetes is linked directly to their inability to metabolize carbohydrates and sugars in the same way as the rest of us. Allergies or intolerance to certain foods or chemicals such as salicylate, which is found in aspirin, tomatoes and broccoli, may also have a genetic component. Because these allergies happen on an individual basis, scientific research based on "normal" or "typical" responses and random sampling appears to be insignificant. The medical community, which is relying on empirically validated research, denies that these problems exist. Various individuals suffer for years due to this lack of understanding and acceptance of what is happening to them.

Another important area, which will affect the development of the "self," and which is determined by our genetic make-up is our individual learning style. At this point we know of seven different kinds of intelligence: linguistic, logical-mathematical, spatial, musical, bodily-kinesthetic, interpersonal (the ability to understand others), and intrapersonal, (the ability to understand one's own self). Everyone has all these kinds of intelligence, but in different proportions. One person may be very good at sports, reading, and interacting with others, but not be able to sing on tune, or understand algebra easily. On the other hand, another person may be a mathematical whiz but not be able to recognize faces of people they have met before or remember where they have stored something. Again, each of us is very unique in the proportions that we have of each of these learning styles, which makes the way we learn best and store our memories very different from one another.

A retired teacher and I sit next to each other in the dining room of a hotel. Both alone, we cautiously inspect each other and begin a tentative conversation, eager for an interaction, and yet not wanting to intrude into each other's private meal. Within a few seconds we both realize we are open for conversation and spend the next hour sharing together. She tells me that she is at the hotel for a wedding of a family member. I tell her I am here to work with children with autism. She tells me that she is a retired teacher and that autism is a fascinating subject for her. I mention full inclusion of all students. She tells me that this is impossible because those with the disabilities make learning impossible for the typical children who are already having trouble in the classroom. I share my belief that it is not the disabled child that is a problem for these students. They are already in trouble because their learning needs are not being met by the regular type of teaching. I begin to describe my ideas of changing classrooms so that they are open to all learning modalities so that every child in the classroom will have their needs met, and where differences are celebrated, not a threat. She begins to share stories of unique children she has met and how much she yearns to know how to help them.

"I should tell you about my daughter," the woman states. "She has a learning disability, but she also has this unusual talent. She had a lot of trouble in school when she was young. She couldn't hear all the time because she had problems with her ears. When they were bad it was like she was deaf, but when they were okay, she could hear fine. Her hearing came and went without any control on her part. After we had tubes inserted, she was fine."

She goes on to describe her daughter's unique talent. Because of her learning disability, she worked in the school office during high school. She kept record of the students' attendance. In doing so, she had access to all of the birthdays of every student in the school. Without any effort at all, she memorized those 2000 plus birthdays and remembers each of them, even though many years have passed. She also knows the birthdays of all of the family members.

"So what is the learning disability?" I ask. If she could not hear the information that was being shared, she had a hearing problem, not a learning disability. How is she going know that which she did not hear? How can she access that what she did not hear? There is no way for her to have any idea what she has missed. How could those around her know exactly when she was able to hear and when she was not? This is not a "learning" disability. Why has she been shackled with this label? Had her teachers fully understood about the hearing loss, she could have had all information shared visually as well as auditorily. It's not that difficult when one knows about it. Had she been labeled "deaf" it would have been an automatic response. Instead she got the label of "learning disability". She was given the message that she was not good enough to learn as other children did. She was denied the right to the same education as her peers because of this label.

Temple Grandin, a professor at Fort Collins University and advocate for people with autism, also had problems in a typical classroom because she is a visual learner. She has devised a simple test which can help you come to an understanding of your own strengths and weaknesses in this area. She tells you to picture one church steeple in your mind, a second and then a third. She claims that how these steeples appear will indicate your strongest learning style, which for her is visual because she "sees" an actual view of the steeple she chooses. When I took this test with her, I focused on the steeple of the church I had grown up in, the elaborate spire of a church I had just visited in England, and the square steeples of an Episcopal church I attended with a friend in the States. As I analyzed what I was experiencing, I realized that I could not actually "picture" any of these steeples but found that I was swept over with the emotions that I had felt when being in the presence of these steeples in the past. It was then I came to realize that my most accessible memories are primarily stored as emotions, and that this is why I rely so completely on photos to remember my past. I have a very limited visual memory and find it difficult to even picture what my children look like in my mind. However, I must store visual memories as I do recognize something by its appearance if I have seen it before. For example, I cannot describe to you what the cat food box looks like or even form a picture of it in my mind but will be able to pick it out in the store as soon as I see it. Since I have taken this test and shared it with others, I have come across people who see the steeples only as words, as geometrical forms, and as the pictures that Temple describes.

Our differences in learning styles will impact how well we will do in educational systems which are developed primarily through the use of auditory activities. Children who do not flourish within our regular school systems are likely children who are not auditory learners and whose gifts and abilities are actually being ignored or discouraged by an educational system in which differences are labeled as disabilities. These children, who do fit the norm, are given a label, discriminated against, and treated as a category instead of a unique human being. As we continue to explore the development of the 'self' through nurture, we will see how horrifying and destructive this whole process can be to the 'self' of a child.

The journey to understanding one's 'self' includes coming to a clear understanding and acceptance of your own genetic make-up. We are not going to be able to change the genetic make-up of our bodies, but we certainly can learn how to understand what is happening to us because of our genetic make-up and change the way we react to what is happening to us. My body is still very sensitive, but it no longer has the negative impact on me that it had in the past because I now know what is going on. My understanding of the need for kinetic input (touch) in my learning process means that I now rely on taking notes while reading information that I have to remember. The adaptations that you will need may be very different. This is okay, because they will fit you as an individual.

NURTURE

Biology sets the stage for human development by providing the genetic blueprint, but it does not take long for the environment to begin to influence the final outcome of the 'self'. The development of the fetus is first affected by the environment of the womb. Environmental factors such as alcohol, smoking and drugs while in the womb are known to have a negative impact on the size and the health of the child. The levels of stress experienced by the mother during certain periods of the pregnancy may change how the child develops. A pregnant woman can feel the fetus respond when she gets into a hot bath or walks into a room in which loud rock music is being played, which indicates that the fetus has experienced the change in temperature or noise level and is responding to it. An infant who has had classical music played or stories read, while in the womb, reacts differently to these experiences after birth than one who has not. However, this input is limited when compared to the onslaught of environmental stimulation on the brain of an infant after birth.

At birth, a baby's brain contains 100 billion neurons, virtually all the nerve cells it will ever have. It also contains a trillion glial cells, which form a kind of honeycomb which protects and nourishes these neurons. However, the stabilization of the pattern of wiring between the neurons in the brain has yet to occur for most of these cells. The brain has laid out a network of what is required for the basic operation of the body's organs so that the infant will survive. It is neural activity, driven by a flood of sensory experiences coming directly to the child from the environment, which takes this rough blueprint and progressively refines it.

During the first years of life, the brain undergoes a series of extraordinary changes based directly on experience from the environment. When a baby is born, it can see, hear, smell and respond to touch, but only dimly. The wiring for vital life functions such as heart rhythm and breathing are in place in the brain stem, but all of the other connections between neurons in the brain are limited. Within the first few months of life, the brain's higher centers create millions of new synapses. By the age of two, a child's brain contains twice as many synapses and consumes as much energy as the brain of a normal adult.

Each time a child listens to a sound, looks at an object or reaches out to touch something, tiny bursts of electricity shoot through the brain, knitting the neurons into circuits. Again genes come into play. As we consider the individual development of the self, the factors such as level of one's sensitivity to stimulation play an important role. When we combine our knowledge that sensory stimulation from the environment is the method through which our brain is wired after birth with the fact that the level of sensitivity to sensory stimulation from one child to the next is going to differ due to their genetic make-up, we open a whole new concept in our understanding of the development of the self. The specific sensory input that an infant is exposed to from birth on will affect the wiring of his/her brain. The specific genetic code of that particular child will determine the level of response to the sensory stimulation, which will also determine the wiring of the brain. This means that every brain will have its own unique wiring. The process of wiring the brain continues on through the preschool years of the child. Everything that happens to this child during that time will have an impact on the actual make-up of his/her brain.

So we have a child who is born into a home in which he is held and cuddled by his mother most of his waking hours. His brain will develop differently from that of the child who is left in her crib, baby seat or baby swing to entertain her self when awake. Whether the holding and cuddling is a positive experience or not will be determined by the level of sensitivity of that particular infant. Some children may feel constrained in the arms of their mothers because their tactile and/or olfactory response is higher than that of another child who may experience only comfort and love. The child who is on the extreme end of the sensitivity response may scream and become rigid every time that anyone tries to hold them because the experience is so overwhelming it becomes unbearable. Their mother's arms are not a safe haven because of their genetic code. The differences in these children's responses has nothing at all to do with the mother's actions or reactions, but rather is based directly on their own biological reality. However, the choices that we make as parents to provide sensory stimulation and to respect the response that we get back from our infants will play a major role in the final brain that is produced.

For experience is the chief architect of the brain. Deprivation of any kind for a child, whether it be nutrition or stimulation, means that the actual brain suffers. Typical children, who are not touched or who do not play, produce brains that are 20% to 30% smaller than those normal for their age.

Children who are abused or experience high levels of trauma early in life develop brains which are tuned to danger. At the slightest threat their hearts race, stress hormones surge, and they anxiously track the nonverbal cues that might signal the next attack. Children born to mothers who suffer from depression show markedly reduced activity in their left frontal lobe, which serves as the center for joy and other light hearted emotions. Infants who are exposed to early pain and stress react more strongly to pain as toddlers, while premature infants who were exposed to multiple painful stimuli in neonatal intensive care units exhibit hyperaglesic responses to subsequent pain, an increased level of sensitivity that outlasts the initial pain by hours and even days. Autistic children, with their higher response to sensory input develop larger, denser, and heavier brains than their peers. High levels of magnification reveal that their brains have more minicolumns than a typical brain and that these minicolumns are smaller than normal. The direct result of this construction is that these brains are overwhelmed by information coming in from the environment which would not affect most people. This reveals a double-edged sword in the midst of brain development. A heightened level of response to sensory input creates a brain that reacts at a higher level to sensory input. Once this brain is constructed, we can do little to change it.

The growth of a child's brain drives children to actively construct their own learning, which in turn, creates further growth. If one takes the time to closely observe our babies, one can see this process in action. Their eyes survey all that a room has to offer. Their hands reach out to grasp anything that is within their reach. Items that can be lifted are brought to their mouths to be further explored. They twist and turn and roll their bodies in an attempt to get as much information in as possible. On the other hand, children who are not safe, whether because of their unique biological make-up, physical pain due to medical difficulties, or unsafe environments, construct a different type of learning, which focuses on developing coping skills which either limit the amount of stimulation that the brain receives or protects them from what is happening in the environment. They may choose to use repetitive behaviors such as rocking or sucking one's thumb to produce endorphins which block the reactions to sensory input in the brain. Or perhaps they may choose to be quiet so as to not draw attention to one self so that they are not picked up, or exposed to abuse of any kind. These processes take place automatically, with little acknowledgment on our part. However, we will deal with their input on our self for the rest of our lives because of the construction process of the brain.

It is repeated experience that strengthens the connections in the child's brain so that actions and reactions become unconscious, or in other words, done without actual thought. This gives us the opportunity to do without the input of energy that thought requires. We write effortlessly without thinking about the shape of the actual letter or the direction that the pen is going. We type without looking at the keys. We drive without being conscious of what our hands and feet are doing.

One of the places I notice this unconscious reaction is on a hillside as I drive home from work. In order to get from home to the office and back again, I have to cross a river which has numerous bridges throughout the city. The easiest for me to use is called the Low Level bridge which means that I drive down into the river valley and then up again as the bridge just goes from the actual river bank to the other side. A certain section of this road has three lanes, one of which is used for different directions at different times of the day. Most of the time the centre lane brings us up out of the river valley, but during rush hour in the afternoon and evening the control lights change. When one is driving down during the morning and early afternoon two lanes of traffic merge at the top of the hill to flow into the one lane used to go down. The road has been constructed so that this merge happens very easily. When the control lights change, one has to turn slightly left to go into the centre lane to continue down the hill. It is at this point that my unconscious takes over, time and again. There is no need to use signal lights at this point, for although one is turning slightly left, one is continuing on in the centre lane. In fact, turning on one's signal lights may cause a problem, as there actually is a road to the left one can turn into, so that other drivers may surmise that this is what the signal indicates and react accordingly. But as soon as my body begins to turn to the left, I automatically turn on the signal light. Once it is on, I am oblivious to it until I get about halfway down the hill and hear it ticking. I have to consciously tell myself not to use the turn signal, which of course, is not how most of us drive, especially on roads we drive on often.

Our little ones seem to know that repetition is necessary as they repeat the same actions over and over again until they have them mastered. They are content to listen to the same bedtime story every night for weeks on end, or watch a video repeatedly. They will climb up on the arm of the couch and jump down only to run back to the arm and do it all over again. They ask the same questions over and over again, no matter how many times we give them an identical answer. It's an incredible process that we each do automatically, on our own, as toddlers. As adults, we experience the power that repetitious action has in our lives as we find ourselves at work with no memory of the drive or complete several different tasks simultaneously with our mind on one. It's only when we do something that is totally new to us that we have to consciously think of each movement. The more we do this new activity, the more unconscious it becomes.

Knowing that repetition wires the brain gives us an insight to ourselves as we look back into our childhood to discover what happened over and over again to make us the people that we are today. A child who is given any message repeatedly will carry that message throughout their life. So when we tell our children that they are "lazy," competent," "cute," or "bad," they take these messages with them, even if we are joking or not paying any attention to what we are saying. Reactions to stressful situations develop through the situations that we experience repeatedly as children. A child who has experienced the drunken rage of his father will learn to copy his mother's reactions to this anger or develop his own unique coping skills to keep himself safe. The religious values that we carry today were developed through the repetition of lessons at Sunday school and church or the lack of this repetition. This process carries on throughout our lives. Repetition is used to change one's habitual reactions as one learns to automatically respond in a different way through practice.

When we realize that the brain is not something that we acquire at birth as a solid entity and cannot change, but is instead an organ which is developed through the actual experience of our lives, the unique differences in each of us as a 'self' become even more profound as does the importance of understanding and accepting our own "inner child". Much of our development, so instrumental in forming our self, happened to us as infants and toddlers, of which we have no conscious memory. As a newborn I was taken home from the hospital to a small house on a farm in Northern Alberta. There I spent my early years with a limited number of people, wide-open fields, and a variety of farm animals. The type and amount of sensory stimulation that I experienced in that rural setting as a toddler was far different from that which was experienced by my grandchildren, who started their lives in large cities during the 1990's with the television as a constant companion. This means that our brains are wired differently. This development of the brain through actual experience likely explains much of the evolutionary process that mankind has undergone over time.

As the brain develops, the mind of the self is created through the storage of information that the child is exposed to and experiences. Our family, our community, and our culture become a part of the self during this process. We learn how to live, how to interact with each other, how to protect ourselves from pain, and how to define and accept ourselves, by the way that we are treated and through the information that we are given as small children. The basic element of thinking requires lived experience, which is sensation filtered by an emotional structure that allows us to understand both what comes through the senses and what we feel and think about it as well as what we might do about it. Much of this information is gathered through the experience of watching our family members interact with one another. More is added through actual experience with our peers.

The title of the book "*All I Needed to Know I Learned in Kindergarten*" is a good synopsis of this process because most of the connections in our brain are have been created by the time we reach grade one. For the next five to seven years, the brain enters a new phase in which the neural connections are strengthened and consolidated through experience and repetition and in which excess cells, which are not being used or are damaged, are pruned. During this period the brain also rests as it prepares itself for the next big struggle. For the brain is not complete at this point.

At the beginning of puberty (approximately age 11 for girls and 13 for boys) the brain suddenly produces a whole flood of gray brain matter in the frontal cortex, and the process of building neural connections begins all over again. Those who comment that teenagers appear to be brainless at times aren't as far from the truth as one would think, except for the fact that it is not that they don't have a brain, it's that their brain is not completely connected. Again actual sensory experience is the architect of these new connections, and again the process takes a number of years to complete. In many ways, the level of difficulty and frustration experienced by our toddlers is mirrored during adolescence as the years of 13 for girls and 15 for boys resemble the "terrible twos". These years are the most difficult to go through, both for the teens themselves and for their parents. By age 17 this building process draws to a close and the brain begins again to strengthen and consolidate those connections which are used the most often, and prune those that are not needed.

At this point in time, brain researchers have stated that the process of brain development is complete by the early thirties. I don't believe that this is true. I predict that further research will determine that major changes of some sort occur in the brain during the mid life crisis period, as well as during pregnancy, birth and menopause for women.

By the early twenties, the brain is no longer as malleable as it was in the earlier years but has increased in power. Talents and latent tendencies which have been nurtured throughout childhood and adolescence are ready to blossom in the new adult. Potential for greatness may be encoded in the genes but whether and how that potential is realized depends directly on experience in the critical early years. Through repetition, new synapses will continue to form and strengthen throughout life, but never again at the same rate as they did in childhood. Adults may continue to improve their brains through reading and experiencing. The brain, however will not be able to master new skills as readily, or rebuild connections after trauma, as easily as it did during childhood.

The wiring that occurred in one's early years does not disintegrate. This was demonstrated my instant recognition of my doll that I described at the beginning of this chapter, even though I had not thought of her for at least 45 years. The celebration of my success in giving up a habit that I had relied on since I was born was as sweet in my memory that day in the mall as it was at Christmas, when I finally held her so long ago. She is a strong part of my 'self'. The doll of my past has her place in my 'mind', as a symbol of what I accomplished so many years ago. The doll of the present holds her spot in my material self, a visual reminder of all that has gone before. The same is true for you, based directly on the experiences of your lifetime.

PUTTING IT BACK TOGETHER: A CASE STUDY

She was 16 the day her life changed forever. Life was pretty good, back then. She was a typical teenager: an above average student who had a few problems with math and science, an avid soccer player who worked part time in a jewelry store and taught children about God at her community church. She had a group of about 20 girlfriends, who were very close and spent their weekends together. She was known to be the "happy-go-lucky" one in the gang, the kind of person everyone wanted to spend their time. This resulted in an overactive social life which often led to disagreements with her parents but they weren't severe enough to worry about.

She describes the day that everything came to an abrupt halt. "Four friends and I decided to jump into a car and go for a ride. We were in grade eleven that year. I wish I could forget the semi-truck staring me in the face as I looked out of the passenger window of my friend's car. The thought "It's only going to tap us crept through my mind and then I screamed as the front fender of the truck came crashing into my body." In that split second she lost her current self. All of her levels were ripped to pieces, never to be regained in the same form.

The loss of the material self was the most noticeable at first. Her broken and bleeding body was rushed to a nearby hospital where she lay for a week in the safety of a coma. When she awoke she found it was far too difficult to be present in her body because of the level of pain and trauma. She dissociated to protect herself and spent the next nine years in a zombie like haze. She was so removed from herself that she couldn't even see her face when she looked in the mirror.

He body works differently now. She has become more self-aware and realizes that she no longer deals with the stress of life as easily as she did in the past. She knows now that the fatigue she suffers is more debilitating than all of her physical injuries. Her sensory responses are heightened so that it takes more energy just to be in the world today. She has to be aware of the people around her. If they are too needy, they drain her of her supply of energy. She gets upset and flies off the handle over minor incidents when she is overly stressed. She wants to be as organized as she was before this all happened, but finds that things can get out of control so fast. Then she is overwhelmed and has a hard time helping herself out of the disorganization.

The material self is also made up of the roles and the possessions that we hold, and in that brief second she lost all that she held before the accident. She was no longer a confident student, a soccer player, a teacher, or a friend. She was a patient, lying in a hospital bed, whose time was spent with doctors and specialists. Her best friend Kim, sitting right behind her in the car, took the brunt of the impact and died at the scene of the accident. She lost her other friends as they returned to their lives as students, once their minor injuries had healed. They thought she would be like this forever. They were all so young and so naive. They couldn't wait for her to catch up with them. She also lost her joy and comfort in possessions as she realized how insignificant they were in the midst of the pain.

After her body healed, she returned to high school to fail almost all of her courses and came face to face with the destruction of her mind. She found she couldn't remember things from one day to the next. Even a tutor couldn't help her. It took a while for it to dawn on everyone, but there were even greater obstacles to be faced. Eight months after the accident she arrived at a brain injury unit. She had to deal with the damage that one cannot see. Here they had to re-teach her everything that she had known in the past: how to tell time, how to subtract and carry the numbers, how to write essays and how to complete other basic skills. Things that she had been doing for years. Things that she had excelled at. Important information. Some was lost forever. Some just needed to be found again. Everything she learned had to be taught in a very concrete way, almost like teaching a child with pictures or hands on. The abstract was so frustrating. She had such a difficult time grasping it. Relearning everything that she had at 16 is a long journey that isn't over yet. Her steps were very slow.

She says the brain injury changed her in so many ways that it is hard to imagine. Her easy-going nature disappeared as she dealt with so much pain on every level imaginable. She developed new reactions to the world. She couldn't trust her ability to speak and act any more. Sometimes she would want to say something to someone but her brain could not register it and she would lose her words. At other times the wrong words would come out and she would be embarrassed. She couldn't trust her emotions either. When something sad would come up, like a funeral, she couldn't find her tears or feel any sadness.

She learned to forgive herself for the times of thinking indecisively. It was as if the piece of her brain that allowed her to think things through and problem solve didn't exist any longer. For a while she felt as if she could never make up her mind for fear of making the wrong decisions. At other times, she acted impulsively. Many wrong decisions were made. Many harmful situations were created. She had to learn to lean on others when she couldn't trust herself to decide correctly. To be open about her injury and the effect it has on her. To ask for help and support when she needs it.

She has lost her sense of safety in the world. She is also doing EMDR (eye movement desensitization reprocessing) to help her deal with the vividness of her memories of the accident, so they don't pop intrusively into her head when she doesn't want them to. So they aren't triggered so often, by seeing another accident, or having a close call herself. She tries to protect herself by not putting herself in these situations, but it isn't always possible. The flashbacks drain her of all her energy for days.

The changes in her material self and her mind led directly to the destruction of her social self. Her family and friends tried to stick with her, keeping their view of her from the past alive but it was an impossible task. She wasn't that person any more. They didn't know how to interact with her. They couldn't understand her. Her injuries weren't compatible with living the life of a teenager. She processed information much more slowly than she had in the past. Before the accident she was overly confident, as most teens tend to be. Now she couldn't look anyone in the eye. She was bowed down, hiding from the world. She became serious. No one can make her laugh because nothing is funny any more. In the midst of all of this, no one knew quite how to view her as she really was. No matter what they did, they didn't seem to be able to get it right.

Although the spirit itself is unchanging, the connection with her spirit was likely one of biggest shifts in the self she went through that day. She had two near death experiences at the time of the accident. She describes these as so many others do: the tunnel, the light, and the overwhelming feelings of love and acceptance. They changed her as dramatically as anything else did. She knows what life is about now. She recognizes the importance of love. She knows how we are all connected with each other and with our creator. She no longer worries about speaking bluntly and honestly and tells it like it is when she is faced with injustice, abuse, or neglect. This doesn't make her popular with anyone, but she knows what is right and what is wrong. She cannot tolerate the falsity of people living as pseudo selves. She is distressed by the materialistic attitudes of many in the world.

She wishes at times that she could recreate her self from the past, could go back to being that carefree teenager and start all over again. As the truck tore through her body, all the levels of her self changed dramatically. It's impossible for her to be who she once was, but then, none of us can step back in time and erase the changes that happen each day. We have to accept that we are only the particular self we are, in this present moment. We are formed by our experience. This is what life is all about.

As she looks back to this event in her life she is proud of her accomplishments. They told her that she may never walk again, but she persevered and not only walks but runs. She passed her grade 12 equivalency, graduated from college, traveled around the world, learned a foreign language, held a full time job and redeveloped relationships with a number of different people including family members. Throughout the years she has learned about the strength she has through her absolute faith in God. She has a deep sense of compassion that she knows she wouldn't have without her loss. In the midst of being the same person she was before the accident, she is completely different on all levels of the self. She has to accept it. There is no other way to be.

Chapter Four
The Development of the Mind
Beliefs and Values

I believe in God the Father
I believe in God the Son
I believe in God the Spirit
One in three, and three in one

So go the words to a chorus that I learned as a small child. A chorus that comforts and sustains me as an adult. A chorus that describes some of my deepest beliefs. Beliefs that I am very aware are not shared by all who will read this book. Each of you would likely choose a completely different opening for this chapter, and that is okay. This is my opening, because this is part of what I believe.

The beliefs and values that we have stored within our minds are unique and individual to each of us based on our own personal experience in this world. The words of this chorus became part of me in the world in which I was raised: the world of a Lutheran Church in a Lutheran community. I was first brought to this church as a very young baby to be baptized. It was a miserably cold day, near the end of December. Temperatures hung around minus 40 degrees and very few ventured out to the service. The Pastor was leaving at the end of the month, and no one knew for certain when we would get another, so my parents were determined to bring me there and have me baptized, no matter how bad the weather was. We traveled to the church with the team of horses and the cutter, more commonly known as a one horse open sleigh. We picked up the next-door neighbors to take the role as my godparents. I became a member of the church, and a child in God's family.

This, of course, was only the beginning of my journey in developing values and beliefs. Exactly what happens through baptism, and what are the long-term results, I cannot say. I do know that I have always felt like a member of the family of God, no matter where I am, or who I am with. Is this because of my baptism, my upbringing or the fact that we are all children of God? I can't say for certain. What I am certain of is that my involvement in the church, from that first day and on, has shaped who I am as a person, what I am willing to accept and believe, and what I reject unconditionally. It's not the sole source of my belief system, but it definitely is the foundation.

You are going to have a completely different belief system from mine, based on your experience as a child. Your beliefs are as right for you as mine are for me. As I outline my beliefs in the upcoming paragraphs, I am not doing this as a claim that what I believe is what everyone should believe or as an attempt to make you believe as I do. These descriptions are only an example of how to determine which of your own beliefs are controlling the way you live. You need to know where they come from and why you are holding on to them. This is the only way you can come a clear decision of which beliefs you want to keep, and which you want to discard. If you don't know where they came from and you don't know why you hang on to them you will continue to live under their influence.

The beliefs that I have now were learned through direct teaching in Sunday School, Vacation Bible School, Bible Camp, Sunday morning sermons and Catechism classes as well as through reading and studying the Bible on my own. They were learned through the modeling of my elders, both positive and negative, in the church, in my home and in the community. They became part of me through direct experience and through the experiences that were shared with me by others.

I believe in God the father, Creator of heaven and earth because there is absolutely no way that I can look at the intricacy of a new baby's hand and think that it's perfection has happened through some kind of chance. I believe in Jesus Christ, my Savior, not only because I was taught about him from my earliest years, but also because of the direct experience that I had when I welcomed him into my heart. In an instant I was changed. It is very difficult to put into words but suddenly the world was a warmer, brighter, more wonderful place. I was no longer torn between my feelings. I was no longer searching. I had come home. I believe in the Holy Spirit who lives within me because of my choice to accept Christ as my personal savior who supplies the gifts of the spirit that I do not have myself: gifts of love, joy, peace, patience, kindness, goodness, trustfulness, gentleness, and self-control. I'll never forget the time, that as a young mother, I was joking with friends about the lack of patience I was experiencing with my children. One of them bought me a poster which said: "Grant me patience, Lord. But hurry!" Another friend reminded me of the verse in Galatians, which describes the gifts of the spirit. I already had been given patience by God. I was neglecting to choose to use it. From then on, actively choosing to use these virtues has been a big part of my life. And yes, there are days that it doesn't happen. Those are the days I chose not to access these gifts. Those are the days of shame, of guilt, of failure. Those are days in which I beg for forgiveness.

I believe that I am a sinner. That there is no way that I can be a perfect person, no matter how hard I try. But this is okay because of the power of grace. I believe that heaven awaits me after death. Although I am not perfect, I am loved by my Father in heaven, and I have been saved through grace, by the death of his son on the cross. I may not understand the whole process at this moment, but

I have faith it is there and that is all the understanding I need at this point. And I do believe that forgiveness and the gifts of the spirit are there for everyone to access.

I believe in the power of prayer, because time after time, it has made a big difference in my life. I am driving down an icy highway, early in the morning on my way to college. A line of traffic is coming towards me. A truck pulls out of the line and swings into my lane. I am not worried. There is plenty of time for him to get back into the other lane. Suddenly this truck begins spinning in circles right in front of me. It has hit black ice. The driver no longer has any control. I freeze momentarily, thinking to myself `"I don't know what to do!" and then automatically begin to pray. "God, I don't know what to do. Please take over." I loosen my hands on the steering wheel. I wait for the coming motorists to pass by and then swing the wheel, trying to get into their lane without hitting the spinning truck. I, too, hit black ice and lose control of my car. I let go of the wheel and let the car plow into the ditch. About 10 feet away the truck joins me. I breathe a sigh of thanks for the protection that God has provided.

When some people listen to this story, they don't believe that prayer had anything at all to do with the situation, but I know that it did. I had been taught all my life to go for the ditch in this sort of situation. Had I followed that advice; had I followed my own learned reaction, I would have been in the exact same spot as the truck. We would have collided as the driver pulled out of the spin. At the speeds we were traveling we would have likely died or been seriously injured. Instead, something made me wait for the oncoming traffic and turn into the opposite lane. This meant that, although I also lost control and landed in the ditch, I was beyond the truck at that point. Our lives were all saved.

In another situation I have been asked by my Pastor to visit a couple who were experiencing marital problems. I was rather gullible at the time and had difficulty saying no to anyone. So there I was, sitting in the living room of two people I had never met before. The man was on some type of drugs. He was very angry and had gone into the kitchen and picked out a butcher knife with which to kill his wife. I had arrived in this moment, and she invited me into the room, hoping I would divert his attention. All of the time I talked with that couple, I was also constantly praying to God to keep us calm, to give me the words that this couple needed to hear and to keep us safe. The moments passed so slowly. The man's emotional state rose and fell. At times he collapsed on the couch, weeping with frustration. At other times he stood upright, brandishing the knife, screaming that he needed to kill her. Throughout his reactions my voice went on: calmly, quietly. Gradually his calm periods became longer than those filled with rage. Gradually he began to agree with his wife and me. Gradually he opened up and shared his real feelings. Finally he handed me the knife and got a few things together and left the home. He knew it wasn't safe for him to stay there at this time. He knew that he needed help. He went to find it. There was no way, at all, I could have done this on my own. I depend on the power of prayer.

And in the midst of all this I also believe in the power of evolution. It may not quite look like the typical view of evolution as depicted in science textbooks, but I do know that it does exist. Why? Because change is inevitable and evolution is the continuing record of change over time.

In the months and years after I left my first husband, I was forced to deal directly with my beliefs and values in a way that I had never done before. Leaving my family meant going against many of the beliefs that I held dear. I had no idea at the time how much this would affect me. There wasn't a single therapist I approached who seemed at all interested in what role my beliefs played in how I was dealing with the marital breakup. Only after I discovered James's model of self, did I realize why I was having such a negative reaction to these beliefs and how much power they held over who I was, or was not, as a person. It felt as though leaving my husband meant giving up these beliefs. This wasn't true, of course, but I did have to face the reality that I had not lived up to my own beliefs. I had failed in ways that were very important to me.

Our beliefs and values are part of our mind, the inner circle of the self, the part of the self that is the closest to the spirit. Any change that happens in the mind is going to have a much bigger impact on the whole self than change that happens in the social or material self. Any time one is living off of the life-line in one's mind, one will have more difficulty than if one lives off the life line in the material or social self. Leaving my husband meant making a decision and taking steps that were in many ways completely opposite to what I actually believed. Staying with him, in spite of the years of abuse, and in spite of the danger that I was in, felt easier than giving up these beliefs. But in truth, the whole picture was pretty muddy.

I believe in monogamy. This belief is tied closely to my belief that a sexual union is a spiritual union and is sanctified by God. I don't know exactly why or how I developed this very strong belief in this area, but I never saw marriage in the church or by the state as being "the marriage". To me, marriage occurred when two people came together sexually. Part of this is based on the descriptions of "marriage" in the Old Testament, but I believe as much came from the novels and such that I read throughout my childhood and teenage years. So, when my first husband refused to take "no" as an answer, and pressured me to the point of sexual union, I fully believed that we were married in God's eyes and that this was where we would stay.

In the midst of this belief, there was a conflicting belief. I also believed that there is a "perfect" mate for each of us and that the goal before marriage is to ensure that one finds this mate. I knew very well that my first husband and I did not have this type of relationship. In the midst of this "knowing" I also knew that I was being cheated out of something that was very important in my life. At one point I attended a party, which went far into the night. So far, in fact, that it was not the safest place to be, as too much alcohol had been consumed and people were becoming too tired to control their emotions and behaviors. The women were sitting around a kitchen table and one of them began talking about her husband. He was a man with a drinking problem and had a lot of medical problems throughout their life together. At this point in time, he was unemployed due to back injuries and she had been forced to take a job as a cleaning lady in order to support the family. As she described her love for this man she made the statement: "No matter what is happening in our family, when I see him coming up the walk towards the door, I still feel like the luckiest woman on this earth because he is mine." How I envied her that evening. I was stuck in a marriage that had me on the life line with my beliefs about monogamy and as far away as possible from my life line when it came to my "soul" mate.

And then there was my belief about commitment, which played a major role in my marriage but also extended far beyond my marriage to all other areas of my life. Once I made a commitment, I kept it, no matter what. As I stood before the altar on my marriage day and recited the marriage vows I realized that I was saying the most important words I would ever say in my life. But this was only one level of commitment for me. When I sign up for a course, I attend all classes, I read all the textbooks, I hand in all assignments on time and I do the best I can on all exams in order to meet my commitment to the education facility I am attending. When I take on a job, or sign a contract, I do the same thing. Commitment is very important to me.

I believe in the family unit. I believe in the importance of being one's mother, one's father, and that parents need to work together as a team. I believe that children should be raised by both of their natural biological parents if at all possible. I believe that raising our children is the most important task that any of us will ever do during our lives, and that we give our all in order to ensure that this job is done well. As my marriage drew near to its end and I confronted the reality of the danger I was facing, the importance of being grandparents kept me from moving on. As I took on this new role in my life I realized that I believed that grandparents had to be there together for their grandchildren, as much as parents. And so, to a point, I stayed much longer in my marriage than I would have, had not my grandson been born

In the midst of all of this I believe in honesty. And yet, I lived a life that was mostly a lie. The more I learned about the sexual abuse that had happened to my husband, the more I had to lie and cover up what I was feeling. The more he blamed me for what was happening in our relationship, the more I had to lie and cover up the truth. This was not as serious when I was living in a state of denial myself, (which you will learn more about in chapter 6), but once I opened my eyes to what was actually going on and refused to accept the blame any longer, honesty was compromised beyond its limits.

Although these are only a very small sample of my beliefs, they were the ones that had the greatest impact on my life during the months and weeks that led up to the point where I finally fled my home and broke up my family unit for good. They were the forces that bound me in my marriage, and the forces that kept me in upheaval. And when I felt like I was drifting off in pieces in all directions, it was these beliefs in my mind which were flying off the furthest. Although I wasn't aware of it at the time, it was beliefs that had me experiencing the deepest levels of grief, the greatest shifts in myself. Once I found the model of self, I could finally figure out what was happening. I could examine each of my beliefs and see how they were impacted by leaving my husband. I had to decide if I wanted to keep these beliefs or to give them up and replace them with others. I had to allow myself the various stages of grief for each of the beliefs as I went through this process. I had to forgive myself for having the belief and sticking to it, or for not living up to it. This process took years.

I had to give up my belief of marriage and monogamy to a degree. I still believe in monogamy as being an important part of a marriage, but I no longer believe that someone has to stay with another person just because a sexual union has occurred. I am very aware that many of these unions are not consensual. Many are the result of bad judgment in the moment. Having sex with a person should not make you a slave to that person for the rest of your life. Of course, I still believe it is wise to limit yourself sexually; to make certain that you know what you are doing when you give yourself to another. I still believe that there are spiritual connections within the sexual act whether you want them to be there or not. Does God bless and sanctify each sexual union? I believe he does. Is he disappointed when they do not work out to be permanent? I am certain he is. Does he forgive us when we fail? Most certainly!

In leaving my first husband I got to embrace my belief in a "soul mate" to the full degree. I am now married to the man I fully believe was meant only for me, and I was meant for him. The joy that the wife talked about during that party so many years ago is now mine and when I look at him I do feel like the luckiest woman alive. In the midst of this joy there is a sense of pain and sadness. Why? We knew each other before my first marriage. We recognized our connection to each other at that time. We spent wonderful times together. But we were both so young, so naive, and so low in self-confidence. Instead of standing up for ourselves, we gave in to others. Instead of sticking by my belief in the importance of finding one's soul mate, I gave into the demands of another and then stuck to the monogamy belief. Instead of following my own intuition, I followed the sanctions of the society I was part of. This robbed of us 24 years of life that we could have spent together. This robbed us of the chance to have a child together. This robbed us of the chance to parent together. We can never get it back. And yet, we can and do make the most of the time we have left. And in the midst of that time we also celebrate five very special gifts, our five children who would not be the same wonderful people they are, had we not made the choices we did when we were younger. They are definitely worth those years apart.

The belief in keeping a commitment affected me in quite a different way. Although I had made a commitment to my ex-husband through our marriage vows, I fully believed that this vow had come to an end with his walking out on me when I was at the point of suicide. I had promised to stay "until death do us part" and in my mind, death had been there and he had turned his back on me. However, there was another major commitment that held me back for a long time. We, as a couple had signed a contract to provide services to an organization for a year as house parents for a student residence. The first contract had been fulfilled the year before. Near the end of that contract, I realized that we were in big trouble as a couple. However, we were also experiencing a lot of positive growth in the work we were doing. I ignored my intuition and signed another contract for the following year in spite of my uncertainty. This was a major mistake. Within a couple of months I knew we were not going to make it through in one piece. I tried to continue as a couple but that proved too dangerous. I tried to continue on my own, but he would not stay away. And so, in the end, I was the one who was forced to flee. This devastated me as much as anything else did. Failing to live up to that contract was failing to be true to myself as a person.

I don't suppose that I will ever forget the day I left. I was working at my desk when the phone rang. It was for a young man in the house and I called out for someone to let him know he was wanted on the phone. I left the phone lying off the hook as I continued to work on the computer. When he picked it up in another room, he could hear that it was off the hook and began making accusations that I was listening in on his phone call. I could hear him yelling and quickly put the phone back in place. I hadn't had a good night's sleep in months. I was living in danger every moment as I never knew when my husband's rage would break out and how extreme it would be. I had far too much work to do and too many people to be responsible for. This young man was accusing me of doing something that I would not ever do. He was telling everyone else in the house that I was someone I was not. I snapped and went screaming down the hall after him.

I knew in that moment that I could not stay any longer. I packed up quickly and headed for the airport. My last view of the house was one of the young men standing in the front window waving good-bye. I still can't think about that moment without crying. I didn't stop shaking for months.

In leaving that day, I was the one who broke up our family unit. I was the one who split the team of Mom and Dad. I was the one who shattered not only the family unit of my husband and children but also that of our parents and their siblings. Separation and divorce was not a common element in my family. I was the one who had brought this reality into our midst. I was the failure.

Twenty-one years earlier I had reached a point of decision. At that time I had three young sons and was expecting my fourth. Some of the secrets of my husband's childhood had been brought to light and I had hoped that this knowledge would make a difference in our relationship. It hadn't. This makes sense when one realizes that I had only encountered the tip of the iceberg at that point, but I didn't know there was more to come. I thought I understood him better, which should have made a difference. We had had a rough day and by nightfall I realized that things were never going to change. He was going to continue on in the same manner for the rest of his life. I was never going to be able to have the relationship with him that I wanted.

That night I left him and the children. I spent the whole night walking and thinking, trying to decide what to do. I could pack up the boys and leave. I had all of our money in my pocket at the moment. It wasn't much, but it would get me out of the city at least. How would he react? Since he was violent in our home, I could only expect it to get worse. Was it worth it? Is that what I wanted for my children? No, I wanted them to have a family. I wanted them to know their father. By daylight I had come to a decision. I would stay in my home. I would stay in my marriage. I would make the best of it for the sake of my sons. I would make certain they got to know the best of their father. I would make certain they would be safe and secure. I would make certain that would experience a home life like I had. And so I returned to my home and kept my promises. I was the stay-at-home mother he insisted on, because he didn't trust me to be around other men. I learned to scrape by on very little and do without myself, so my children would have the chance to take part in sports, music and drama. I accepted the responsibility for keeping his rage in control and modified my actions, my personality, and my wishes to meet his needs. I never said a word of this to anyone. I was a success. But at what cost?

The last of my beliefs that left me reeling through my separation was my belief in honesty. Although I would never have admitted to giving up honesty to keep my marriage intact, it is exactly what had happened. My husband lived in a world of fantasy, created solely to cover up the pain of his past. I allowed his fantasy to continue. I accepted the blame for his anger. I changed my behavior to meet his needs. He was smart enough never to attack me in front of others. I was the one who explained away the bruises with lies. I was the one who never admitted a word to anyone of what was going on. I could have stood up for myself. I could have charged him with assault. I could have been honest with my family. But I wasn't. I was living a life as far away as I could from my belief of honesty.

When I took my Master's Degree in Family and Marital Therapy, I decided to carry out a research project on the impact of childhood sexual abuse on the wives of men who had been abused. It was an incredible eye opener as I faced wall after wall in trying to carry out this research. It was then I realized that the partner of a person who has been sexually abused loses all of their rights. The "secrecy" that shrouds childhood sexual abuse and the insistence in confidentiality means that the "partners" have no right to say anything about their experience. As soon as they open their mouths, they have overstepped the boundaries of confidentiality. No wonder the pain and horror of this perversion goes on and on across the generations.

With a lot of perseverance I did manage to come up with enough subjects to meet my needs. The study revealed that the experience of the "wives" was the same across all the different relationships regardless whether the husband had been assaulted as a young child, a teenager, or by a member of either sex. Each wife confided that they spent their lives "walking on eggshells, not knowing exactly when the next blowup would occur. They changed their own behavior to ensure that the rage was controlled. They accepted responsibility for being the troublemaker in the relationship. The level of rage intensified once the secret was in the open. They kept the secret for their mate after they had learned it. By the end of the study I had named it *"Maintaining the facade"* as the role adopted by each of us, as wives, was exactly that. In my mind I saw myself standing holding a long curtain rod in my outstretched arms. Heavy drapes cascaded down to the floor, covering up all of the aspects of our family life that I did not want anyone to know about. For years I had held the role of holding up the rod so that no one could see the truth. Finally I was too weak. I couldn't do it any longer. I collapsed and in the midst of my collapse, the truth was revealed. I was the failure.

Throughout the months and years following my separation, I had to go through a very painful process of facing each of these beliefs, admitting that I had failed in one way or another in meeting them as I should. There were days that I never stopped crying as I allowed that pain to wash over me. I had to prune and modify my behavior to fit what I actually believed. I had to forgive myself for failing, for dropping the curtain rod and allowing the world to see the reality of my family life. For being too successful as a liar, so that my parents, siblings and their families did not believe me, once I actually started telling the truth. How could have this been going on for 24 years without them noticing anything? It doesn't make any sense to them. I had to ask for forgiveness for the many ways I failed. I had to forgive others for their lack of support, because I knew it was based completely on my willingness to lie in the past.

And what's more I had to face the reality that the family that I created was not the family that I believed it to be. My children did not get to know the real me. The energy that I put out to take responsibility for his rage was not there for me to use to mother my children. I verbally taught them about love, honesty, faith and respect in the midst of modeling the exact opposite. In the midst of my lies, I claimed to be honest and lost their ability to trust me. It's been a long uneasy journey, one that continues to this day but it is getting better all the time. The more I live on the life line of my beliefs, the more joy and peace I experience.

As you travel through your search for self, it is important to examine your beliefs in order to come to a clear understanding on the impact they are having on your life in the present. Beliefs guide what we see when we look at the world and how we respond to what we have seen. They determine how we think, feel, act and define situations we experience. They can strengthen our resolve to stand and fight, or make us turn and walk away from others.

Each of us creates the world we live in through that which we believe. In other words, if I believe that I, as a woman, will not have the same opportunities as a man, I will create my world with that view in mind. However, if I fully believe that women are self-reliant and can do anything that men do, my world will look very different. Having been raised as a Scandinavian, in a world where women were expected to be able to do everything that men do and expected to be self-reliant, I do not believe that I have ever felt that the obstacles in my way in life had anything to do with me being a woman. As a baby boomer, I have been surrounded by women who held the opposite view as they fought for liberation. Their battle made little sense to me, believing as I did that my limitations had more to do with lack of finances, with choices limited by geography, and through the limitation of choice. Once a certain choice has been made and followed through, other choices have either been eliminated or modified. Although I chose to become a stay-at-home Mom in my marriage, this choice was made to satisfy my husband's needs, not because I, myself, felt that I was limited as a woman. My older sister chose to study computer technology in 1966, a choice that was not considered viable for men at that time, much less women. She has used this education in many different ways, throughout the years: programming computers, teaching at a University and currently working with a large company that specializes in upgrading computer education for business executives. However, she also chose to spend part of her life at home, raising her daughters and pursuing what might be considered be a more feminine lifestyle. She quilts, and also was very involved in organizing quilting organizations for years. None of these choices were based on her need to be a woman, or to compete in a male world. They were the choices that fit her as an individual and met her own particular needs.

The choices I made were very different, and yet in their own way, also very satisfying. I believe that when we concentrate on specific gender roles, we often lock ourselves into a certain way of thinking, and then limit the life that we have to live. For me, this was not an option, but for many women it became a self-defeating belief. Facing your own beliefs will allow you to measure the choices you are making and determine whether you are willing to hang on to a belief that may well stand in your way. I believe the choice to follow through on one's own interests and talents are far more important than locking ourselves into any rigid belief system.

Assumptions, based directly on our beliefs, may also limit us. Through my work in the field of autism, I had the opportunity to meet two different people, in two different parts of the world. Both of them returned to university as adults, and both of them had a lot of difficulty concentrating and learning from lectures. Both of them discovered that the visual aids used during the lectures were all that they were able to understand and remember. Both resorted to memorizing their textbooks in order to pass their exams.

One of these people was a man from Ghana who had immigrated to Canada as a young man. His grandparents had originated in India, but he had spent his childhood in Africa. When he was at the university, he attributed his problem understanding the lectures to the fact that he was dealing with a very new and different culture in a newly learned language. The other student was a woman in Virginia who had grown up in the Southern States, and who had been involved in the feminist movement since the early 1970's. This woman had concentrated much of her study effort on women's studies and fully believed that her problems at the university stemmed from the patriarchal structure of the university system. Both of these students developed their own unique coping methods to deal with their problem, and both of them graduated from university.

I met them several years later when they were involved with autism, one as a parent and the other as a counselor. It was at this time they both discovered something about themselves, which they had never known before. Both of them are highly sensitive to sound. Their hearing is very acute. The problems that they had in the lecture theaters had far more to do with the distortion of verbal language due to this level of acuity, than it did to either his culture or to a patriarchal structure of learning.

False beliefs have been a common problem for mankind throughout the ages. There are many examples of different beliefs that have been discarded over time. There are likely many more beliefs commonly accepted today that may be added to this list in the future. Columbus sailed towards the west directly challenging the beliefs about the shape of the world. The discovery of germs as a source of illness totally changed medical practices in the nineteenth century. Most of our current beliefs are based directly on what we claim is scientific research but even then we may be wrong. An important factor to understand about the dependence on scientific research is that publication is contingent on peer review. Peer review means that the research is read and accepted by other people working in the same field as the researchers before publication. Understanding the human tendency to resist change opens our eyes to the reality that peer review is an instrument to protect ourselves from change. Ideas which are new and different are rejected by a community which is trying to protect the status quo. A review of important discoveries from the past provides a clear picture of what happens to anyone who is striving for change, especially at the mind level of beliefs and values. Galileo was thrown into jail for suggesting that the earth traveled around the sun. Pasteur was laughed at for suggesting that doctors wash their hands before delivering newborns. The doctors who discovered the link between mosquitoes and yellow fever had to fight for years and put their own bodies and those of a group of subjects in danger before the medical community would publish their findings. New information is a threat to the self of every person who accepts old theories as truth. It takes years before it is accepted by one's peers. Thus, what is published is not necessarily relevant, as much as it is non threatening.

The first step in determining which beliefs you wish to keep is to recognize that all of the values and beliefs you depend on were developed through your experience as a child. This doesn't mean that truth does not exist. This also does not mean that your spirit does not know the truth. In fact, every spirit is totally aware of the truth. But our mind is created through the life we live. The "truth" is corrupted through what we have been taught and exposed to over these years.

The material, social and mind levels of self speak louder than the spirit, demanding our attention. If we are not taught to keep in touch with the spirit as children, we will learn to ignore it. I cannot determine what level of self you are in the habit of listening to at this moment. This is your responsibility. However, reaching our full potential depends on accessing the truth through our spirits, not through our mind or other levels of self. We may have to learn to turn off the tape recorder of the mind which repeats the lessons of the past in order to focus in on our spirit. We may have to learn to be still and listen, which is not something that is common in this world of technological stimulation. We may have to relax and allow ourselves to feel discomfort, rather than automatically using coping skills to numb our feelings. We may have to learn to ignore the social view of others in order to hear our own voice. It all takes effort. It all takes time. But we are capable of sorting it out.

So how do you know when a belief needs to be modified or discarded? Your spirit will tell you in many different ways. Make the effort to listen to the voice. As we learned in the first chapter, the spirit comes complete with the knowledge of who we are as individuals, and what our journey on this world should be. It recognizes the forces of good and evil and knows the importance of honoring our creator, taking care of our world, and loving ourselves and others. It cries out with longing from deep within when we are not meeting its needs. It fills us with a joy beyond description when we are. It speaks to us with a voice that is known as intuition, which we may choose to listen to or to ignore. If we listen, it will guide us on our journey, protect us from danger, and help us reach our full potential. If we ignore it, we will suffer the consequences in many different ways including unhappiness, dissatisfaction, anger, and physical or psychological aliments.

There are two major reactions that allow you to determine whether the belief system you are living with is compatible with your spirit or not. The first is a sense of dissatisfaction with one's life, the need to search for new and different answers at a spiritual level. If you are experiencing this sense of discontent, you have not arrived at the answer. So many of my friends are on what they call a spiritual quest, searching the world over for their own particular fulfillment through different spiritual guides and religions. Most of these people were hurt as children by the church in one way or another and so they have turned their back on Christianity. As they describe their excitement in finding a new guru who will provide the answer, I think back on that feeling I had for so many years before I turned my life over to God and accepted the gift of salvation through Jesus Christ. This choice provided the peace that I was looking for, and I have never felt that dissatisfaction since. My spiritual quest came to an end. This choice is available to everyone in the whole world.

This is not to say that I believe that the Christian Church is a perfect place. The Church is a human institution, which makes as many mistakes as any individual human being does throughout their lives. Horrendous decisions have been made through the Church over the years that have nothing at all to do with Christianity. Millions of people have been hurt in one way or another through people who call themselves Christians, but who are not living or interacting in a Christian way. The Church is human, and as human it is imperfect. Christianity, on the other hand, is perfect. Becoming a Christian is the choice of accepting Christ as one's Savior and living through grace. It's an individual response, an individual choice, an individual way of life. It doesn't make you perfect. You are still human, but it allows you to access to the gifts of the Holy Spirit: love, joy, peace, patience, kindness, goodness, trustfulness, gentleness, and self-control. Through these gifts you are able to love anyone and everyone, which is the true goal of the spirit. It puts us on our life line in a way I have not found any where else

Will your sense of dissatisfaction lead you to Christianity? I don't know. One of the continuing mysteries of the Bible is that it clearly states that there are not only those who are chosen to follow Christ but also those who are destined not to believe[9]. I do know that as long as you are searching, you have yet to find the answer to your own particular journey. The sense of dissatisfaction comes directly from the spirit. It's telling you to pay attention. It's telling you that there is far more to this life than you are living in the moment.

The second way to measure whether you want to keep a belief or not is how you react to the beliefs of others. If you feel uncomfortable in any way when you are confronted with the belief of another that is in direct contrast to your own, pay very close attention to those feelings. Your discomfort is likely an indication that something about this belief is not meeting the needs of your spirit. All of your responses are your own, not those of the other person. Defensiveness, fear, pain, and anger are all clear messages to you that you are either hanging on to a belief that is worthless, or that you are not living up to your own true beliefs in the moment. For example if you believe in pro choice and an ad fighting for the rights of the fetus makes you uncomfortable, the feelings you have are your feelings. They say nothing at all about another person or their beliefs. You are not responsible for fixing them. You are not responsible for changing their beliefs. You are only responsible for yourself. Examine each of your beliefs closely through your emotional reactions to understand whether they are worth keeping or not.

If we get stuck in a belief that is not true, we limit our potential. If we have a belief we do not live up to, we drain our energy levels. If we assume things, based on false beliefs, we may be off track. If we reach the point that we have to give up a belief, the grief will affect us far more than losing any person, any role or any possession. This is especially true for beliefs that have done more harm to the self than good such as: "Smoking does not harm the body" or "I do not deserve success", or "It's a woman's role to be subservient". If you come to the point where you realize that you have to give up such a belief, you must also be prepared to deal with the pain of holding on to it so long, the realization of what you have lost or destroyed because of this belief in the past and the acceptance of the guilt and the anger you are feeling. You will go through the whole process of grief for the loss of this belief as well as the loss of time and opportunity that hanging on to the belief cost you. Once the grieving process is over you must forgive yourself. You did the best you could with the knowledge you had at the time.

BELIEVING IN ONESELF: A CASE STUDY

He was four years old when he first realized that he had to depend on himself in this world. He had been outside, playing on the top of the doghouse when he dropped a rock. It hit another rock on the ground. As they struck each other, a spark of light flew out into the darkness of the night. He

---

9   1 Peter 2:8

rushed into the house to share this experience with his father and was told it was impossible. He returned to the doghouse to drop one rock after another to see if he could make a spark fly again. He did. In that moment he learned to trust only that which he could test himself. It's a lesson he wishes he had stuck with throughout the years. It's the lesson that he depends on as he faces the present, moment by moment.

He grew up in a family with an abusive, alcoholic father and a quiet, submissive mother. His paternal family was locked into a fanatical religion, one which focused on shame and punishment rather than love and redemption through grace. He grew to fear his family, his community and his creator. It's taken him over fifty years to walk away from this past and celebrate who he really is as a person.

His lesson as a child served him well throughout the years. In spite of the aggression and hostility he experienced in the world, he refused to partake in the violence. He stepped back and went his own way to become known as a person who accomplished his goals. He excelled in technical areas such as electronics and welding, and worked at a variety of jobs throughout the years. He met a young woman who came from a background much like his own. They were married and began to build a home together. Everything seemed to be going along fine until an accident at work led to a slight back injury. The pain of this injury took him to a doctor, who prescribed antidepressants to help cope with the pain. This medication changed the chemical make-up of his body and he began to act differently. He knows now that he was experiencing the effects of serotonin overload: alternate feelings of hot and cold, sweating and nausea but at the time had no clue what was going on. It was the first step on the long road into depression, anxiety, progressive cognitive scrambling and a vast array of other symptoms and general craziness. He claims that he has no better way to describe this.

As the years passed he gradually lost the ability to depend on himself as his body continued to react negatively to the antidepressants he was taking. In 1993 his whole world came crashing down. The combination of anxiety developed through problems with employment, problems with his wife culminating in divorce, and the increasing impact of the antidepressants on his body brought him to a breaking point. He was institutionalized in a mental hospital and began a journey through hell, as more and more medications were administered, each making him feel worse than before. He spiraled deeper and deeper into despair in the midst of fighting a growing battle against an ever-increasing array of physical symptoms and mental degeneration.

In time he began to refuse to take certain medications and recognized a sharp reduction in the symptoms he was experiencing, but was always ordered onto more. He went through many medication changes, each leading to the disappearance of some symptoms and the beginning of others. These included severe feelings of scalding, freezing, sweating, nausea, anxiety, manic behavior, a deep detachment from reality, an inability to make his body do what he wanted it to, diarrhea and urinary incontinence, suicidal urges, blackouts, panic, arthritic pain, stomach cramping, loss of emotional content, cognitive collapse, obsessive-compulsive thoughts and behaviors and phobic responses to any activity, effort or exertion, which led to a total withdrawal from reality. After six years he finally said "Stop" and walked away from the psychiatric community. He describes his condition at the time as little different from someone awakened from general anesthesia for a significant surgery, minus the surgery. Recovery from this state has taken years.

He returned to the lesson he had learned as a four year old and started searching for answers that fit his own body in his own way. He cared for his dying mother until she was hospitalized. He began researching diet, vitamin and herbal remedies that work for him. He began to go to a counselor and used EMDR (eye movement desensitization reaction) to release the various phobic responses that accumulated over the years. He attended a lecture offered by Dr. Temple Grandin and discovered a kinship that he had never felt before. He discovered he was on the autism spectrum. His life began to make sense.

He still lives with the aftermath of all the decisions that were made for him by a medical community that had no idea or interest in treating the actual person he was. He has undergone surgery to repair the locking of one finger, identified as "trigger finger", the direct result of one of the medications. He has also undergone small gum surgery to help correct the damage to his upper gun from the massive tooth grinding he did while on other medications. He continues to suffer with tardive dyskenesia, a movement disorder caused directly by some of the medication he took in the past. The flinches grow gradually worse, year after year. He fears that the intensity of these flinches will kill him in time. There is no treatment available to reduce their impact on his body. He also suffers from type II diabetes, the direct result of another one the medications he was given. He is gradually regaining his memory, his energy, his cognitive function and an improvement in his general health, but the progress is slow.

. He feels totally and completely alone in his community. He carries the scars of the abuse that he experienced as a child from his father and the abuse of a psychiatric community that relied on scientific research that didn't take account of his particular body. There are no medications at all that been scientifically validated for people on the autism spectrum and yet they gave him one after another. He is still looking for help, but no one has answers that work for him. No one will take responsibility for the damage that has occurred over the years. No one wants to deal with his concerns openly. Everyone seems more concerned with protecting their own self image, protecting the medical community at large, protecting the pharmaceutical companies that produce these medications and protecting their own bank accounts than they are about him. He's trying to find answers for himself. He's trying to protect others from suffering as he suffers now. He isn't having much luck, but he won't stop. What else can he do?

CHAPTER FIVE
THE DEVELOPMENT OF THE MIND AUTOMATIC, UNCONSCIOUS AND RATIONAL RESPONSES

"The individual sees the world that he wills to see"

KIERKEGAARD

I AM STANDING ON THE VERANDAH OF MY GRANDMOTHER'S HOUSE. MY NOSE IS PUSHED up against the window as I stare in at the group sitting around her dining room table. My aunt, uncle and two cousins are eating supper with my grandparents. My heart is heavy. I want to be in there, included in this meal, instead of standing out on the verandah. But I haven't been invited and so I find myself on the outside, looking in with deep longing.

I have no idea at all why I was not invited to join that meal. I do know that my interest lay only in my cousin Trudy, who was my kindred spirit at the time. We were inseparable when we were together, which was certainly not as often as I wished. And here she was, within reach and I couldn't be with her. Perhaps I had already eaten my supper. Perhaps no one thought that I would even be interested in coming in. Perhaps my grandparents wanted to spend some time with Trudy without having me glued to her side, as we had a tendency to ignore everyone else when we were together. At this point in time, I am only certain that I was not standing on that verandah because I was being punished or purposely being excluded because they knew how much it would hurt me. And yet, it's almost fifty years later and I still cannot think about that scene without feeling pain.

As we look at the development of the self through our genetics and the wiring of our brain, it may feel futile to try to change that which is already in place. However, change is not only possible, it is inevitable. All of the levels of the self are continuously changing. There isn't a single part of us that is static except for our spirit. In fact, resistance to change is likely a bigger problem than change itself.

However, we cannot understand the process of change without understanding where we have come from, how this has affected us, and how it has created the person that we are at this moment. We are often given the message that all we need to do is to use our will power and the change will occur, but it's not that simple. The discomfort of change, the pendulum effect, our current level of anxiety and the pressure from our social self will impact our efforts and often lead to a sense of failure. Then we are ashamed for our weakness and are convinced that if only we tried harder, or perhaps cared more, we would be able to succeed. And so we fail time and again, each time feeling worse about who we are as an individual. This is why it is so important to understand all of the concepts shared throughout this book.

The search for the true self continues on with an understanding of the difference between automatic, unconscious and rational reactions in our body. This takes us back to the construction and the processes of our brain. As the brain grows in the human embryo, it begins with a minimal nervous system, the brain stem, surrounding the top of the spinal cord. This regulates basic life functions like breathing, metabolism, heart rate, stereotyped reactions and movement. This brain does not think or learn, but is a set of regulators which ensure survival. From this primitive root emerge the emotional centers which began with the olfactory lobe, which encircles the top of the brain stem. One layer takes in information from what we sense and sorts it out. The second sends messages throughout the nervous system, telling the body how to respond to this information.

Key layers of the emotional brain build up over this layer. Together they are called the limbic system. The limbic system refines two powerful tools, learning and memory, which allow humans to make choices in survival and fine-tune their responses to adapt to changing conditions. The neocortex forms as the top layer. This region plans, comprehends what is sensed, and coordinates movements while the bottom layer acts as a sentinel and responds automatically (instinctively) in times of danger.

The neocortex is the section of the brain that makes Homo Sapiens distinctly human. No longer do we only feel and respond to sensory input, we also are able to think about our feelings, and even more, have feelings about our thoughts. The neocortex allows a survival edge over other species with its ability to face adversity and to use long-term planning. It is also the seat of art, civilization and culture. However, this higher center does not govern all of our emotional lives. In times of crisis and emotional emergencies, we switch back to using our limbic system.

A key role in this process is played by the amygdala, which is our emotional centre and acts as the storehouse of our emotional memory. If our amygdala is removed or its connections to the rest of the brain are severed, we are no longer able to gauge the emotional significance of events and become totally uninterested in other people. The affection we feel for others, our urge to compete or cooperate and our place in our social order are all stored within the amygdala. It triggers our tears and our need to reach out to others. It also acts as our emotional sentinel. In times of emotional stress, the amygdala can take control over the thinking brain by hijacking the limbic system, which then responds automatically. The actual construction of the brain allows this to happen.

Our brain discerns what is happening around us through the messages that it receives through the sensory system. Research has shown that sensory signals from our eyes, ears, and so on travel first in the brain to the thalamus, and then across a single synapse to the amygdala. A second signal from the thalamus is routed to the neocortex, the thinking brain, through a longer circuit. This branching allows the amygdala to respond to the stimulus before the neocortex receives it.

The amygdala is the storehouse of all of our past emotional experiences. Each sensory stimulus that arrives from the thalamus is measured against that which is stored in the amygdala. If this message is "safe", based directly on past experience with the same input, the amygdala does nothing. The stimulus then reaches the neocortex, the information storage centre of our brain.

All of the various responses we have learned throughout our lifetime are stored in the neocortex. In ideal situations the neocortex is able to access all of these responses to initiate the best response specific to the particular stimulation received. Unconscious responses are those which have been stored in the neocortex and happen with very little thought. Different factors, such as time and level of anxiety, affect the ability of the neocortex to access all the choices available. The less time we allow ourselves to develop a response, the more likely we will react unconsciously without perceived thought. The level of stress or anxiety we are experiencing will affect the ability of the neocortex to access all of the information, thus limiting our choices of response. The responses we have had the longest (since early childhood) or those which have been repeated the most often, are the most accessible in the neocortex so they will happen automatically. New responses we are trying to cultivate, such as replacing a habitual pattern, are more difficult to access and need more time and thought to carry out. However, all of these responses are formed in the neocortex.

As a simple description of this process I will share my reactions to cherry pie. Many people will have wonderful responses to the sight, smell and taste of cherry pie based directly on their experiences as children. Mine aren't so good. The only time I had anything to do with cherry pie was on a trip to the city when I was about eight years old. We went to a restaurant for supper and I decided to have cherry pie for desert. At this point, I don't know if I was coming down with the flu before I ate that meal, or if there was something that I ate which disagreed with my stomach, or if it actually was the cherry pie that made me sick, but I spent that whole night throwing up. Since the sight and smell of cherry pie evokes memories of that night, I have a tendency to avoid it at all costs. My neocortex has not had the opportunity to store any other kind of response to cherry pie. I expect that I could "train" myself to enjoy it if I made the choice, but so far I haven't.

One could compare this singular reaction to cherry pie with the multiple reactions I currently have with the computers I use. Although I have had many different negative experiences with computers over time, I am determined to continue to use them and so am building up a lot of different responses to various computer problems in my neocortex. The more time and effort I spend on the computer, the more options I am able to access when I am forced to deal with a difficulty. However, times of anxiety will limit my responses, and often lead to more serious situations as I automatically respond without taking the time and effort to make a conscious choice. The more the conscious choice is repeated the more it becomes hard wired into the neocortex, and the more it becomes the "automatic" choice during times of certain stimulus input. A new computer means these responses may need to be replaced. Again it takes time before the new "automatic" response is in place. This whole process will be affected by the level of "threat" that one experiences as well as the reward one receives for interacting with whatever stimulus we are talking about. My determination to continue to try to work with a computer has a greater reward than my determination to enjoy cherry pie, which was a threat to my physical body the first time I ate it.

If the amygdala perceives the stimulus as a threat, it immediately alerts the limbic system, which automatically reacts to protect the body. There are three major forms of response: fight, flight and freeze, which are used to ensure the survival of the individual. The intensity of the stimulus as well as the individual make-up of the person will determine which of these responses is used. In these circumstances, the body acts without thought, and usually has no memory at all of what happened.

A friend went through an experience like this recently. She has a daughter who was perceived to be deaf from birth and who has recently been diagnosed with autism. It had been discovered that certain people in the child's school were tying her down to a chair in an attempt to control her behavior. A meeting was called to discuss these incidents. The teacher, who had reported the use of restraints and who the mother trusted, got up to speak. Instead of focusing on the importance of protecting the child, this teacher began to rationalize why the child was restrained. Within seconds the mother had cleared the table, grabbed onto the corduroy jumper the teacher was wearing and had ripped it completely off her body. The mother has no memory of how she got up from her chair or across the table. She has no memory of ripping off the clothes. She does remember being held by another teacher with the pieces of cloth in her hands.

The mother, naturally, was horrified at this response. This is not how adults are expected to react in our society. And yet, when one considers the reality that she had found out her child was suffering for years without anyone stepping in, and then to have the only person she trusted in the school turn against her, it does make sense. The survival of her child was paramount. The limbic system swung into action. Whenever a human being is pushed to certain level, instinct takes over and the body reacts automatically. This is how we survive.

As an adult I can recount at least two personal instances of this type of automatic response. The first came when I was in my early twenties. I was a young mother at that time and had decided to enroll my sons in music lessons. They were very young, and I was required to attend each group session with them. As the weeks went by I found that I was growing increasingly agitated during these music lessons. My muscles tensed, my hands sweated and my teeth clenched. I would glare at the teacher, willing her to understand and to obey without being at all aware of what I wanted of her. My anger grew through each session. I began to clutch my hands together, imagining them encircling her throat; squeezing, squeezing and squeezing. I was horrified as I realized that I actually wanted to kill her! I was locked in the limbic response of fight.

Twenty years later I attended a reunion in the small town in which I live. As newspaper editor, I was deeply involved in the planning, organization and documentation of this reunion. Everything went off without a hitch, and I finally had time to relax and enjoy myself at the closing dance in the community skating arena. As I walked in I felt the load of the week's responsibilities slipping away and looked forward to just having fun. Within a few minutes I found myself in the center of the building, my back up against the boards, frozen in fear. I couldn't move, I couldn't reach out to my husband who was chatting with friends nearby. I couldn't speak. I shook with terror.

Both of these experiences came on without warning and did not seem to make any sense at all in the context in which they were experienced. I felt good sharing my love of music with my young sons. I liked the teacher and felt that she was doing a great job. In the second example, I felt great because the reunion had gone so well, and I love to dance. The unexpected intensity of anger and fear in both these situations was terrifying. As a very analytical person, I took the time to look back into my past for an explanation.

Music class for my sons included singing, learning to play the organ and playing various instruments in a rhythm band. As I watched the band portion of the classes I was swept back into my own past, remembering the rhythm bands I had played in during grades one and two and the performances we gave at the annual Christmas concerts. They were good memories, but they were also laced with emotional pain, for the rhythm band was one way in which my grade one/two teacher controlled our classroom.

My first teacher was an angry, violent woman, who took out her unhappiness on certain children in the classroom including me. As a child I was hurt and confused by her behavior. As an adult I recognize her behavior as an indication of her problems, not mine. However, as an adult, I continue to live with the aftereffects of her behaviors and my need, as a child, to develop coping skills to protect myself from her. The long-term effects of her treatment to me have surfaced during times of high levels of stress throughout my life.

The rhythm band had a hierarchy involved in it. The lowest members of the class got to play the sticks, the next the blocks, then the bells, and finally at the top were the triangles. As a child I very quickly noticed and understood this hierarchy, which might not have been apparent to others. I can remember the cold look in my teacher's eyes as she handed me the sticks time and time again. How I ached to play the triangles! But only her chosen pets got that privilege. Even in the few instances when she allowed us to choose our own instruments, and I got my hands on a triangle, she would take it away from me and give it to someone else. I never had the chance to play one during that time.

So here it was twenty years later, and unbeknownst to my sons' teacher, I am watching and waiting for them to be allowed to play the triangle, and (as I perceived) they never have the chance. This teacher is treating them exactly as I was treated. My mother instinct rises within me. I am going to protect my children from the pain that I have suffered for so many years. And so I reach the point of contemplating murder!!

Once I realized what was going on, I approached the teacher and asked that she make sure both my sons have the opportunity to play the triangle. When she heard my story, she was very happy to comply. After they had been given that opportunity, I was able to relax and enjoy the rest of the year of classes. I never again felt that anger. In closing this example, I might mention that my sons did not really appreciate my efforts on their behalf. They both thought that if I had to ask for something special, at least I could have made sure that they got to play the drums! But it was my self that we were dealing with, not theirs.

The second experience involves my past with a dirty old man. I never actually had any physical contact with him, but he haunted my life, constantly making suggestive comments to me at public gatherings at church and in the community. The harassment began when I was in preschool and continued on throughout my life, even when I was a wife and mother. It only stopped with his death.

Over the years I developed strong measures to protect myself against this man. Whenever I was out in public, I would always position myself where I could see the door, just in case he came into the room. I would stay close to a group of people, but never actually allowed myself the freedom to be part of that group. I had to be aware. I had to keep watch. I could not even concentrate on conversations, just in case he appeared.

As an adult I had begun to recognize these behaviors and to deal with them. He was dead. I did not have to worry about him any more. I could stop watching and waiting. I chose to sit with my back to the door, even if it felt very uncomfortable. I forced myself to partake in conversations with those who were around me. As time went by, I thought I was making great progress.

The reunion was a unique and disturbing reminder of this man's influence on my life. In the first place, it was the type of gathering that he enjoyed, and had he been alive, he would likely have been there. I was tired and had been under a lot of stress, so my defenses were likely low. The arena was a terrible place in which to protect myself. There were several doors, in all four directions, so it was impossible to face them all. It was dark, dusty, smoky and crowded. One could hardly make out the features of those who were close, much less have any ability to watch everyone in the room. My protective behaviors were of no use to me. I froze against the wall in fear.

That night, an absolutely wonderful man came to my rescue. He had noticed my strange behavior and personally came over to invite my husband and me to his table. He took my arm and drew me close to him as he escorted me to my seat. He sat close to me all night physically touching me time and again, reassuring me that everything was all right. In time I was able to quit shaking, to enjoy the conversation that was flowing at the table, and even began take part in it. As I gradually relaxed, I realized what had happened. Mr. J. still had power over me, even from the grave!

As I look at these two experiences in my life, I am very conscious of how we must be aware of the experiences we have had in childhood, and of the protective behaviors that go along with them. Details, which appear to be trivial, may jog our memory, releasing the pain of the past. The sensory message is picked up by our amygdala and flashed directly to the limbic system as DANGER. As a woman, wife and mother, I thought I had gone far beyond the influence of Mrs. S. and Mr. J. I now have to accept that fact that they, and the pain they caused me as a child, will be with me for the rest of my life.

Once we understand how the limbic system affects our own personal responses we can also make the effort to recognize how it is affecting the behavior of others. Throughout this book I have mentioned the abuse I experienced in my marriage. As I look back over the years, I now realize that the physical abuse I experienced was a direct result of the limbic system protecting my husband from his past. He was abandoned time and again as a child, first by his father, and then by his mother, when she suffered a nervous breakdown, and finally by his whole extended family. He was separated from his sisters and forced to live in a Catholic orphanage with his brothers. There he was physically and sexually assaulted by the so-called christian brothers who were supposed to be looking after him. Not only was he helpless against these assaults to his own body, but he also could not protect his younger brothers. None of this was his fault. He had absolutely no control over any of it. He was a child, surviving in a world no child should ever have to face.

The biggest fear this man faces is that he will be abandoned again. Throughout our marriage, I was the person he was most afraid of losing? The sense of abandonment, stored in his amygdala, was triggered by a variety of different stimuli. Whenever he felt that I was about to abandon him, in one way or another, he would reach a point where he would react at a limbic level. His response was fight, and I was the one he was fighting. Now that I understand how this all works, I can forgive him for his actions. This forgiveness extends, not only to the physical abuse, but also to his refusal to admit that ever happened. Does he even remember how many times he hit me? I don't know. Limbic response is not remembered. How can I fault him for a response over which he had no control and does not remember?

Sadly, we knew none of this during the time that we lived together. Sadly, even a degree in psychology did not give me the information I needed to understand it all. Sadly, our society does not provide us with this knowledge we so desperately need in order to understand ourselves and others. Sadly, our society makes no effort to protect children from the life this man was forced to endure as a child. And so the inevitable happened. He was abandoned again, this time by me. I couldn't continue living in the situation I was in. I couldn't continue to experience the abuse. And so I had to leave in order to survive myself. His worst fears came true again.

As we grow and develop as children, we learn how to respond to various situations in many different ways. The direct experiences, which are stored in our brain circuits, will determine whether we as adults will react with our emotional memory or our rational mind. Although we may be given messages that those who react emotionally are weak, while those who are rational are strong, it is not that simple. It is the sensory input we receive in our brain and the actual experiences we had as children which govern whether we will react rationally or automatically.

One of the dangerous assumptions the psychological community has presented over the years is that as human beings we are in complete control of our reactions and responses at all times. A young mother is confronted with the question: "At what point do you give yourself permission to respond in this manner?" by a television psychologist as she describes her extreme reactions to her young daughter's behavior. Although I am not suggesting that one is not responsible for one's actions, we must realize that we can only react with the various patterns of behavior we have accumulated throughout our life time and that the higher our level of anxiety, the more limited these responses become. Extreme situations will result in the use of the automatic responses of the limbic system. Anxiety will gradually decrease the number of different reactions we can access from our neocortex. The higher the level of anxiety, the more and more limited are the reactions we can access, to the point that all one has left is that which was learned during our earliest years as modeled by our parents. We are not giving ourselves "permission" to "do" anything. We are simply dealing with the situation with a very limited number of options. Focusing in on the negative behavior and the apparent inability to have control over it will only heighten the level of anxiety and make things worse. The solution to this young mother's behavior, which is likely the exact same kind of treatment she received from her parents as a young child in times of stress, is to reduce the level of anxiety. Part of this process is to accept that high anxiety will result in certain behaviors which are hard wired into the 'self' and forgive ourselves for our reactions.

Our responses to sensory input are based directly on previous experience, which will be different for each of us. This means that whenever I am in a situation in which I feel left out for whatever reason, my emotional memory taps into my experience on that verandah so many years ago, feeling pain, which raises my anxiety level and triggers the protective reactions I have developed over time. Only, after I had looked back into my past to discover what event had led to this response, could I rationally begin to understand what happens to me, and how I can move beyond the automatic response to a more rational one.

At this point in time, whenever I experience feelings of being left out, I know that my first reaction will be that of pain. I also recognize that I often resort to some extreme behaviors so that I do not experience the pain of being left out. Accepting that this is who I am as a person, makes it all okay. I don't have to berate myself for my lack of will power. I don't have to feel weak or worthless. I can just accept the fact that when I feel the pain of being "left out," it is coming from my past, not the present. How I react to this pain, at any point, is my choice. The more I face it, the less it hurts, because repetition creates stronger brain connections. It is in facing this pain and finding new ways to respond that I gradually can overcome that particular memory stored in my amygdala.

However, whenever I am in a situation in which the emotional pain is extreme, I will react automatically with my typical response, which is to freeze. This process of freezing has a variety of different levels, the most extreme being unable to move or speak, to the least, in which I can no longer state what I think or feel, but am able to agree with what others are saying. I rarely notice this happening to me in the present moment. However, when I think back over what has happened I can recognize exactly when it started, when it ended and what happened because of my inability to speak. Knowing this about myself allows me to accept and forgive myself for behavior that I do not rationally control.

Understanding one's responses begins with honestly exploring and accepting what happened to us as children. We are not responsible for any of this. We did not choose our parents. We did not set up the circumstances in which we were raised. We had no power to change what was happening to us. We played no role in the decisions that were made for us. We cannot change the past. It was, and in our mind it continues to be, and this is all right. In fact, because of the construction of our brains, it will "be" for the rest of our lives. However, our response to the past is totally dependent on our present. We can choose to make a conscious effort to develop new behaviors or continue to react with the responses we learned in early childhood. We can spend our time feeling sorry for ourselves, or blaming others for what happened, but it will not do anyone any good. And it certainly won't help one reach their full potential. Playing the role of the victim will only create a situation in which one appears to continue to be victimized. However, as adults, no one is the victim. A person may have chosen to live within that role but they have the power to reject it. Instead they are using their energy, not only to keep themselves from living to their full potential, but also holding back those they interact with through their choice

Acceptance of one's childhood includes the acceptance of your parents as they truly are. They did the best they could in the situation they were in. They based their parenting practices directly on what happened to them as children, as did their parents, and all parents before them. Very few people set out to traumatize or neglect a child on purpose. But situations happen and parents often react automatically or unconsciously, based on what happened to them as children, in the same way that you and I do. It's all stored in their brains in the same way. Patterns of behavior are passed on from one generation to the next through actual learned experience. Accepting this reality is a very vital step in reaching your true self. Only then can we truly begin to shift the process so that future generations can have more positive experiences.

As we grow and mature, our reactions evolve to a certain point because of the experiences and roles we take on over time. Being a parent oneself, often has an impact on reactions in ways we don't expect. Suddenly protective mothering instincts may take over our automatic reactions in defense of our children. Shortly after I had left my husband, I was in the midst of dealing with the incredible pain of knowing that I was responsible for breaking up our family unit. At this point in time, I had little contact with any members of my family and was seeped in loneliness. I had just come to the realization that the threat of this pain I was experiencing was the force I had avoided for so many years by staying with my husband in spite of the abuse. I was hiding out in my apartment, cut off from everyone in my life, and wallowing in the pain I was feeling. I had returned to the verandah, the outsider who was not welcome. In the midst of this pain, a phone call from my daughter-in-law stating that my son was in trouble was all that was needed to snap me out of these reactions and have me rushing to his side. As a mother, the safety of my child took precedence over my own survival. As I faced his difficulties by his side, the devastating pain of exclusion was totally forgotten in the midst of my concern. However, it returned time and time again over throughout the following years.

THE DEVELOPMENT OF OUR INDIVIDUAL RESPONSES

There are five different factors that we must take into consideration in understanding our childhood development. These will be completely different for every person and can only be understood in the context of each of us as an individual. They include actual experience, the specific environment one was raised in, one's cultural background, the transmission of familial patterns of behavior and sibling position. The responses that we store in our neocortex come directly from one of these factors or another.

DIRECT EXPERIENCE

As a small child, I lived in a relatively secure world. I feel blessed by my upbringing because I fully realize that many, many people did not have a home like I did. Although we were not wealthy by any means, I did have all the necessities of life: food, shelter, clothing, security, acceptance and safe relationships with my immediate and extended family. Not all children are lucky enough to have this. My brain was not wired through pain: the discomfort of hunger, the fear of a father's rage, or the sorrow of the death of a family member. However, none of us have perfect lives. In my search of self, I have to deal with my own circumstances just as you do yours.

There are two major experiences that impacted me in a negative way as a child which I have already mentioned: the presence of the dirty old man in my church community and the treatment of my grade one and two teacher towards me. My schoolmates copied the cruelty of the teacher, which spread her influence throughout all my years at school. As I write these words, I'm not certain how much their reaction had to do with what they learned from her or from the responses that I chose to use, but I do know I endured years of bullying and rejection.

The experiences with these two people robbed me of my ability to trust and accept myself as I was. Instead of being fully involved with whatever was going on whenever I was in a group situation, I retreated to the sidelines to protect myself. I became a watcher, not a participant. I lived in a fantasy of the future, instead of the present moment. I buried my feelings in books and food. I didn't expose the real Gail to anyone, not even myself. These responses took over my life to the point I almost missed living it. A video of my grandson's first birthday shows how extreme my withdrawal had become. As I watch the party, I find it hard to believe that I was even present. You don't see me. You don't hear me. But I was there.

Understanding one's individual responses is developed though revisiting one's childhood to discover the source of one's response, not to find someone or something to blame it on. For example, I once tried to figure out where my habit of self-destruction came from. It appeared that every time I told someone I was going to do something, I would then go to great lengths to make certain I was not successful. After mulling this over for days I found myself driving along a highway in tears. I could feel myself as a young child, sitting in my desk at school swearing that I would never let anyone know what I wanted again. As soon as the teacher knew I wanted something, she made sure I did not get it. I carried that promise for years without even being aware of it. There are still times I need to remind myself it isn't worth doing.

Only when you understand where the response comes from can you make a decision whether you want to continue responding in the same way, or change how you will react. Once you make this decision, it will take many situations before it becomes an automatic response. The more you repeat the new response, the more automatic it will become. Times of high anxiety may find you slipping back into responding with the past behavior. This is okay. It's actually something that you should expect to happen. Once you have acknowledged that you are under stress or anxiety and that this is why you responded automatically, you will find it is easy to move on to the new response. Forgive yourself. It's who you are.

All of our reactions are based on values and beliefs which were developed over time through lessons taught to us in ways that meant the most to us as an individual. One of the ways that this happens is through the stories that we were told as children to illustrate certain ways of thinking. Revisiting the family or community stories you were told may open your eyes to many of your personal responses to what is happening around you. A major story that has had an impact on my whole life was shared by my paternal grandfather. As a young man he immigrated to America from Sweden. Because of the timing of his departure from Sweden, he and his brother had the opportunity to travel on the Titanic on her maiden voyage. He described the experience of standing in line to buy tickets for the trip when the announcement came that there were no more tickets available. He described watching people cry because they could not go on the Titanic. A few days later he was back at the docks, waiting in line to get on the ship that would take him to America. The word came that the Titanic had gone down. Again he described watching the people in the line crying because they had not gone on the Titanic. As a small child I marveled over the different feelings that these tears represented. As I grew older I was struck by the realization that I would not exist if this story had a different ending. Had my grandfather been able to get the tickets for the Titanic as one of the Swedish immigrants, he would have been in the lower levels of the ship, where very few of the passengers survived. Grandpa would not have been alive to meet Grandma and father a son, who in time became my father. This provided such an incredible picture of the complexity of life and how the outcome of what may appear to be a minor incident can have a huge impact on generations to come. As an adult I realize that this story is the basis of my ability to accept whatever outcomes happen without too much anxiety. Although circumstances may not live up to my expectations at the time, they may well be a blessing in disguise. This lesson makes life easier in so many ways for me as setbacks and failures are not regarded as negative, but only a road to opportunities one may not have considered.

As with experience, the stories from our childhood come in many different forms. They may be stories of courage and success. They may be stories of disillusionment and distress. They will either make it easier for us to view life as positive or negative. Concentrating on our own individual stories may provide us with a clear picture of why we choose to react to different situations in our life as we do. Once we reach that understanding, we must make the effort to decide if we want to continue on in the same pattern. My lesson from the Titanic story has been a positive force in my life. In direct contrast, a friend, who finds himself constantly focusing on all the negative things that have happened to him in the past, needs to make a change in his behavior. He knows that he is copying the pattern that was set by his parents and grandparents as they dwelt on the negative aspects of their family history. This focus leads to heightened anxiety as he faces the present and future. Exposing this pattern of behavior and choosing to move away from it has a far more significant impact on his level of self-esteem and the depression he is feeling than any medication he has taken. Using the times that he slips back into his habit of negativity as indications of anxiety allows him to figure out what exactly in the present is leading to a heightened level of discomfort. Once that is in the open, he can deal directly with what is happening in the present instead of focusing on the past.

We can also choose to use our childhood experiences to make life easier in the present. As an adult I travel a lot and have discovered that I do not sleep well the first time I am in a particular bed. At one point I spent some time with friends in Pennsylvania. They live on a farm and are in the process of fixing up an old farmhouse. It was October and a chilly wind blew all the time I was there, coming in through the cracks around the windows, which had not yet been replaced. It was a sheep farm, and the products of the sheep were used by the family. This included wool batts in the quilts on the bed I slept in. On my first night there, I was amazed to find I slept like a baby. The same thing happened the next night, and throughout the rest of my visit. For a person who recognizes that a good night's sleep is one of the most important gifts one can experience, it was like a miracle. As I analyzed the situation, I realized that this bed was almost identical to the one I had grown up in. The house was cold. It was totally dark once night had fallen and the lights had been turned off. Even more significantly, the quilts on the bed matched those I had grown up with. The heaviness of the same type of woolen batts brought a comfort that polyester or down could not match.

After that trip, I used this information to create sleeping arrangements that match what I experienced as a child. The room is dark and as cold as possible. The sheets are flannel, and the blankets are heavy. In direct contrast, my husband grew up covered with light blankets, and so we have multiple covers on the bed to meet both of our needs. We sleep well.

At this point in time we have taken this information one step further. We are making the effort to change that which our bodies learned in childhood. The reality of my travel means that I do not sleep in cold farmhouses very often, but instead hotels and motels. We have purchased bedding which matches those which hotels and motels usually use to have up against our skin when sleeping. We have also purchased a mattress which comes close to those that are used in hotels. This allows our bodies to experience a similar tactile experience in both sleep settings. We are discovering that we have no problem sleeping in any hotel as long as we have control of the temperature and are able to make the room as cold as possible.

The impact of direct experience on our self means that our search must be an individual journey based on our own unique experiences. As soon as we become dependent on the theories or methods of others we lose our way. Although counselors or therapists may point us in a certain direction and offer suggestions that may apply to our particular situation, we must measure everything through our own experience if we want to truly understand. This is where the psychological community has come up against a wall in attempting to base their understanding of humanity on a scientific measurable method which depends completely on similarity instead of difference. Each of us has had an individual journey through life which creates a unique 'self'. Until we free ourselves of rigid standards, we will be in trouble.

In your own personal search of self, you must make the effort to understand the experiences you had in the past which impact the reactions that you use in the present. Recognizing where your reactions originate allows you to decide whether you are reacting to what happened to you in the past, or what is happening in the present moment. Although many of the reactions were developed in situations in which they were the best that you could do at the time, they may no longer be your best choice. This is especially true when you have had negative experiences such as bullying, abuse, or neglect. Behaviors, which were developed as a means of protection, may hinder your progress toward achieving full potential in a world in which protection is no longer an issue. However, you cannot decide whether you want to use them or replace them if you do not know how they developed. It takes energy and effort to figure this all out, but it is worth it in the long run.

ENVIRONMENT

The second factor to consider, when trying to understand our responses, is the specific environments in which we grew up. My responses were developed on a farm, near a very small village where everyone knew everyone else or at least assumed they did. These would be totally different from those who grew up in the high-rises or the slums of a city. I lived in the north with frigid winters and short summers, which has resulted in a deep delight in the four seasons and a thrill of excitement when facing a blizzard. I lived through a childhood devoid of telephones, running water, and television. We used horses for a lot of work on the farm and cooked and heated with wood. We raised most of the food we ate and sewed our own clothes. This means I am much more self-sufficient than many people I meet of my age, and can cheerfully go without many of the "necessities" of our modern world. None of this means I am better or worse than anyone else. It just makes me who I am.

During my childhood, I was surrounded by adults who were basically good, kind, honest and worthy of respect. This has resulted in a response in which I unconsciously expect the same of the people I meet today. Most of the time, this upbringing works well for me, but it doesn't help much when I am dealing with people who choose to do evil, destroy, lie, or are untrustworthy. My initial response to these behaviors is to assume I must be mistaken and that what I am seeing or experiencing can't actually be happening. In the past I had a tendency to blame myself for many things that occurred because I didn't want to believe that people could choose to act negatively. It took years to realize and accept that many people in the world are not like those I grew up with. It took years to accept that many of the behaviors I was dealing with were indications of dysfunction. It took me years to realize I had to assume the responsibility to protect myself from certain individuals and that people who are cautious and distrustful of others may be 'smarter' than I am. I guess it would be nice to live in a world in which everyone is as good as I would like them to be, but that is not reality. I have to learn to judge the actions of others and decide how I am going to respond.

Coming to an understanding and acceptance of oneself means one will also realize that one person's reactions will likely differ immensely from that of another, based on one's own childhood environment. The first time I experienced this head-on was late one night as a I joined a number of people leaving a community dance and heading to the home of one of the other couples for an after-party gathering. I was with a friend of aboriginal descent. We had come to know each other as we cheered on our sons, side by side, as they played hockey. Our relationship developed over time, based on similarity of thought and interests in many ways. The woman had grown up just a few miles away from the town I lived in and worked at the public school in this town. We had all enjoyed our time at the dance, and now were moving on to the next part of evening, a typical reaction of the group we spent our time with. As we walked towards the house, the woman began shaking and asked me to hold her arm in an attempt to calm her reaction. I asked her what was wrong and she admitted that this was the very first time she was entering the home of a white person. She was absolutely terrified. Both of us were in our mid-thirties. Both of us were raised near this community. Her experience, just miles from mine, was totally disparate. I held her arm as she fought her fear of entering the house. I held her arm, once we were inside, until she stopped shaking. Only then did I let go. Only then were we both able to enjoy ourselves in the way I had anticipated when we left the dance. She was okay. It was okay.

This reality was again experienced clearly on a visit to Philadelphia in 1997. A friend joined me at a conference and together we decided to explore parts of the city. The concierge at the hotel gave us directions to what he described as the best shopping mall in the city. When we arrived at the mall, we discovered that it was in the heart of Philadelphia and that it was used predominantly by African-Americans. The shopkeepers and the shoppers all had dark skin, and many of the shops concentrated on supplying items that would be part of the African American culture.

As a person who had been raised in northern Canada and had no exposure at all to these people as a child, I was absolutely thrilled to be in the midst of what I considered a new cultural experience. My friend's reaction was the exact opposite. She was terrified.

She was raised in Charleston, South Carolina in the days of total segregation. As a young girl she had been taught that black men were dangerous. Her reaction to this mall was one of overwhelming fear and I could actually feel her body trembling as we walked along together. The intensity of our different reactions made this shopping trip difficult. I wanted to explore, to check everything out. All she wanted to do was leave as quickly as possible.

Because we are close friends, and also both therapists, we were able to share our reactions with each other and to discuss them openly. Her reaction makes as much sense in the light of her life's experience as mine does. As a therapist she believed that she had managed to walk away from these lessons from childhood and had become comfortable interacting with African-Americans. In fact she had many friends and clients of colour. But that was in her home and her community where she felt safe. The heightened anxiety of this new environment pushed her back into her childhood reactions. Being exposed to my enthusiasm allowed her to take the time to face her fear and to stay in the mall for a short time, while my acknowledgment of her fear meant our shopping trip did not last as long as I would have preferred.

The journey towards self must include the realization that every person has their own individual story and that we cannot base our definitions of another's reactions on our own story, no matter how much we may believe that we "understand" and can "empathize." While I was growing up I attended school with the same group of children from grades one through twelve and felt that I really knew them and understood them. After all, they lived the same kind of life I did, didn't they? Twenty years after graduation a knock sounded on my door. I went to answer it and was surprised to find one of my former classmates standing there. She told she wanted to thank me for the positive influence I had had on her past. I was mystified by her presence and invited her in to hear her story.

I had first met her when we started grade one together. She had been part of my life for twelve years and I felt that I knew her well but I was wrong. That afternoon passed swiftly as she shared her story of life in a family in which anger, frustration and abuse were rampant. I listened in amazement to this woman describing horrors I did not believe possible. Horrors that she had faced everyday as she got off the bus after school. Horrors that she had fled on graduation from high school and refused to return to. She had not seen any member of her immediate family since graduation and she didn't intend to ever see them again.

In the midst of this story was another one. A story of appreciation of the impact my family had on this young girl as she was growing up in the midst of such abuse. Over our years of time together in the classroom, I had invited her to my home to stay on several occasions. She wanted me to know how much these visits had meant to her. How she watched my parents and my siblings interact together without the anger and the pain that was so prevalent in her own home. How she had taken these lessons she had learned with her into her own marriage and how she had tried to parent her children in the same way that she had watched my parents parent us.

I was flabbergasted with this revelation for I had never thought much about how my parents parented at that point in time. As she was speaking, I kept thinking that it wasn't very often that she was in our home. Had we known about her home life, would we not have made the attempt to include her more often? Had we not perhaps included her siblings in the invitations? And then the feelings of shame as I thought about her final visit to our home.

The last time she visited our home was when we were ten years old. It was my birthday and I had chosen her to be the friend who would stay over. She gave me a book of fairy tales that I still have today. As it was in the midst of winter, we spent our time playing in the upstairs of our house, creating plays and concerts that we performed using the clothes drying on the clothesline as our theater curtains. In our eagerness to show off, we opened the family trunks in which were stored a variety of family memorabilia. One item in the trunks was my mother's wedding dress. She was very excited to see this dress and asked to try it on. My sisters and I didn't care and so she wore it in the production of the play we were performing. The buttonholes were torn while she undressed and it was returned to the trunk in damaged condition. Weeks later my mother came across the damage and demanded to know what had happened. We told her that our visitor had worn it. She was banned from our home from that time on. What kind of an impact could we have continued to have on her life if we had placed her value above that of a wedding dress? But we had absolutely no idea at all of what we were dealing with at the time. We did the best we could with the knowledge we had.

Most of the time, we are totally unaware of how the responses of others depend on their specific childhood experience and how we judge these reactions based directly on our own experience. Instead of trying to discover why a person may react differently, we reject or ridicule them because they are not reacting as we do. Our assumptions are based on our own experience, and nothing more. Probably the best example I can use is the development of psychoanalytic theory by Dr. Sigmund Freud. He grew up in a home where childhood sexual abuse was rampant and so he developed theories about the human condition based directly on his childhood reality, assuming that his responses were because he was human, not because he was sexually abused as a child. He had no idea they were directly connected to his own past. The world accepted his theories for a long time before people began to realize they did not apply to everyone. Even so, many still do not recognize the connections between his theories and the childhood sexual abuse he experienced unless they have concentrated their energies on studying the long-term effects of these experiences on an individual.

In your own personal search of self, you must make the effort to understand the environment in which you were personally raised in order to understand the impact it continues to have on your reactions in the present. It doesn't matter if the world you lived in was a positive place or a negative one. They are both going to develop responses which will not be effective all the time. You must make the effort to figure out how the environment you are currently dealing with is different from what you are used to and how you should choose to react. This will take conscious thought and effort. Although the past continues to be part of us in our minds, it is far more effective to base our responses on the present moment. Responsible adults make the effort to make responsible choices. One can only do this if one makes the effort to understand the difference between the environment you are basing your reaction on: the past, and the environment you are part of: the present moment.

CULTURAL RESPONSES

The third important area to consider when exploring your childhood is to look at the impact your particular culture has on the development of your individual responses. Cultural responses are a direct result of the unspoken messages you receive from those around you on the "appropriate" way to behave. We adopt them, often without even being aware of their existence, and are very uncomfortable around those who do not respond in the acceptable way.

I grew up in a Norwegian community in Canada, surrounded by the language, the customs, the food, and the arts of Norway. Although I was always aware (and a little bit proud) of our connections to the old country, I never really took much notice of the lessons I was learning from unspoken rules around me. However, when one grows up surrounded by them, they become a major part of the 'self' that responds unconsciously.

One woman in our community was shunned. She was of particular interest to me as a child, as she had once been married to a distant relative, so had a family name. This gave me a link to her in a community in which we had few family links, as our relatives all lived in neighboring towns. I knew very little about her, other than she had left the man she was married to and was now living with another. A grown up daughter also lived in the community. The daughter's main attraction in my life was that she was engaged to be married to a family friend for years, but the marriage never did take place. As a child, I spent many hours mulling over how and why this would ever happen. I still haven't figured it out. On the other hand, the only time I ever remember seeing the mother was in parades where she appeared in incredible costumes on horseback. My female relatives seemed especially irritated by the fact that this woman would display herself in public. I remember often hearing such comments as "Doesn't she have any shame?" which also gave me something to wonder about as a child.

In time she passed away. A couple of years later, her daughter died and her belongings were offered for sale at a community auction. As the editor of our community paper at the time, I decided to attend this auction. As I walked around looking at the different sales items, I came across a woman who was holding an old wedding portrait in an ornate frame. She angrily thrust it at me, asking if I wanted it. Shocked, I replied "No" and asked who it was. She stated that this was her grandparents' wedding photo and she had no idea why people would ever think she wanted it. I asked who the people in the photo were. She gave our family name. Again, I was shocked as I had no idea there were people in our family I did not know, no matter how distant. She went on to tell a story that totally changed my picture of the woman in the previous paragraph.

This woman at the auction was the eldest daughter of the family mentioned above. There were three children in all, the other one a son, whom I also had never heard anything about. At the time this woman was four years old, her father had sexually abused her. The mother immediately packed up and left with the two children in order to protect them. She was newly pregnant with the third child, the one whom I had always known about and whose belongings were being sold. The whole community shunned the woman for leaving and looked after the husband who had been deserted. By the time I was aware of this family, the children were all grown and living on their own, the oldest daughter and son, as far away from our community as they could get, and the younger daughter, reunited with her father, having never been told what had happened.

As I listened to this woman share the story of her life, I began to appreciate the courage of the first woman. Here was someone who had stood up for her children and said "No" to her husband the first time he had touched his daughter. She had believed her daughter and did everything she could to protect her. It had meant giving up everything and yet she had done it. In many ways she became my hero as I dealt with the impact of childhood sexual abuse in my own life.

At the same time, I was repulsed by the actions of the community in which I had grown up. Not only had they made her life and the lives of her children hell, they had put the man on a pedestal, looking after him in many ways, which included giving him the job as the janitor of the school: a place he certainly should never have been. Did he touch any other children? I have no idea, and I certainly have not heard of any complaints of that nature, but he still was not the best candidate for the position he held. It took years for me to finally understand what had happened to this family.

When I took my Master's Program in family and marital therapy, one of our courses concentrated on the cultural differences one might come across in the therapy room. We had an excellent textbook, which outlined the different reactions one might find in particular cultural groups. The chapter on the Scandinavians explained to me exactly what had happened to this woman. She had broken some of the unspoken "laws" of the community in the midst of keeping others:

1. Be hardworking.

2. Be caring for other people.

3. Be strong: strong willed and strong on the outside.

4. Show that you can deal with things externally, even if you have feelings internally.

5. It is preferable if people get along.

6. Getting angry is not getting along.

7. Keep hurt, sadness, and so forth, way inside.

8. It is okay to show good feelings.

9. But showing good feelings in an obvious way is never done; it has to be done subtly.

Leaving her husband broke the fifth rule of getting along. However, in the midst of leaving she obviously kept rules number four and seven, not telling anyone exactly why she left. And, of course, the husband was not about to admit what he had done. For the rest of her life she lived on the outskirts of the community: silent, tough, indomitable and yet, I am sure, exceedingly lonely. What could I have learned from her had I known all this when she was still alive?

This chapter also opened my eyes to who I am as a person and explained so well the many decisions I had made throughout my life. Not telling my parents about the dirty old man, the school teacher or the treatment of my fellow students now made sense to me. My decision to stay in my marriage was a perfect picture of someone who is following these unspoken rules. It also explains my family's reaction to my choice to leave. Breaking the unspoken rules of the community was very uncomfortable for them. I became the threat in their lives, not my ex-husband, who was continuing on in the manner in which they felt comfortable. It explains the power of secrecy in our family, where not admitting one's pain was more important than telling the truth.

The unspoken rules of one's culture may determine gender relations; educational expectations; the importance of money, land, or possessions; pride or shame in one's heritage; and the coping skills one develops to cope with anxiety. These rules may determine whether a young person achieves success by choosing to hang on to family ties and supporting one's parents or by achieving self-sufficiency and independence at an early age. They are the force behind the question of which is more important: hard work or creative endeavors, sharing one's thoughts and feelings freely or keeping them to oneself, respecting authority or asserting one's own rights. Different cultures will have different responses to all sorts of factors in our day-to-day lives. Understanding your own culture and how you have absorbed or rejected its unspoken rules will allow you to make sense of many of the things that happen to you.

The actual society we live in provides the basis of these unspoken rules. For me, as an individual, my particular culture was a combination of the Scandinavian ancestry of my parents and my birth country of Canada. Since we lived in Northern Alberta, we were isolated from the rest of the world in many ways so that the influence of television, movies and magazines that others my age experienced was weaker. Thus the impact of the unspoken rules of my ancestors is likely stronger for me than for another woman my age, whose grandparents came from Norway, and who grew up in a large city surrounded by a variety of different cultures. My country of birth also makes a big difference.

As the world responds to the threat of terrorism in different ways, understanding the society in which we were raised gives us a clearer picture of how we are going to respond as individuals. As a Canadian, I am always amazed at the response of my American friends whose war-like actions appear to be at odds with the message of world peace toward which they claim to be working. It becomes very apparent that my view of how peace is achieved does not match theirs. I believe that another Canadian author has explained this difference well from a historical perspective. Pierre Berton compares the historical settling of the United States with that of Canada. In the United States the settlers arrived first and carved out their homesteads on their own, faced with the reality of protecting their homes and newly claimed land personally. The gun became their source of protection from wild animals, the aboriginal peoples whose land they were taking, and outlaws. They were forced to take the law into their own hands in order to survive. In direct contrast, the law arrived in the Canadian west before the settlers did in the form of the Royal Canadian Mounted Police, who set up outposts throughout the west. The government made the effort to sign the treaties with the aboriginal people before the land was opened to homesteading. Although this was also likely not the best way to do things, it was a very different way and affects the way that the two countries currently respond to crisis situations and to ordinary world events. I first learned this lesson in the 1980's, but it continues to help make sense of what is happening in our world today.

We were visiting friends who had moved to Alberta from the States. They had invited us over to meet family members who were visiting from California. Other families from the neighborhood were also present. A man drove into the yard and joined our group. He had just arrived home from overseas and the topic of conversation quickly turned the focus on him. He explained that he had just come in from Indonesia. The Americans, including those who had moved to Alberta, began talking about the need for a military presence in Indonesia. The man questioned why and the Americans stated they had assumed he was in Indonesia on a military base. The Canadians, including me, shook their heads in confusion. Why would anyone assume you were in Indonesia except to work in the oil field, which was what he had been doing. Our definitions of the situation were based directly on the countries we call home.

Problems occur in the 'self' when one's cultural upbringing and the responses one experiences in the world do not fit along one's life line. We can choose how we are going to respond to what is happening around us in many different ways. However, if we are going to truly reach our highest potential as human beings, these choices must respect our own individual beliefs and values, not those we have unconsciously adopted from the society around us. If we look at World War II as an example, we quickly realize there were many people in Germany who chose to deny what was happening in the concentration camps, to close their eyes to the plight of others and apparently to support that which they did not believe in. Why? In order to protect themselves, not only as a body but as a whole: their mind, their social self and their material self. It was only a few who stood up to the powers that were and followed their true "spirit" or life line. These people became the "heroes" of the war, the people who we choose to hold up as examples of extraordinary human beings. Other historical events produce other heroes such as Martin Luther King Jr. who refused to accept segregation for the African American people, Mother Theresa who gave up all worldly possessions to serve the destitute in India, or the many reformers who walked away from the man-made rules of the Catholic Church creating a vast array of Protestant churches.

The events of September 11 opened our eyes to the fact that our world is not quite the safe haven we thought it to be. Our personal reactions to this crisis and the world events that follow will determine our personal level of stress and anxiety as actions are taken by the various governments in the world. As I write this statement the government of the United States appears to be determined to go to war with Iraq, no matter how the rest of the world responds. By the time you read this, the outcome of this determination will be apparent and you will be feeling the effects of what has happened. The amount of energy you are expending will be affected by what has happened on a world level as this decision and your response to it matches your own personal life line. A world in which the claims are made that 'God' is in charge while humans send bombs is not a world in which actions match words. This discord will be experienced in each of us as a 'self'. How you personally react will define who you are as a person.

In your own personal search of self, you must make the effort to understand the culture in which you were raised in order to decide if the unspoken rules you have absorbed during your childhood are ones you wish to keep and respond to or not. Although I have been using the threat of the terrorists as an example, these messages cover all facets of life and affect your whole being. Unless you make the effort to define these for yourself and put them out into the open, you will respond automatically, and you will be stressed by your response if it is not on your own personal life line. How do you react personally to messages such as "Thin is beautiful", "There is a normal and appropriate way to react", or "It is important to keep up with the Jones's" in material possessions? You may have to stand tall and reject that which is happening all around you in order to meet your own potential.

Are you brave enough to do it, or are you willing to expend your energy living on the opposite side of your life line because of the unspoken rules of your culture?

TRANSMISSION OF FAMILIAL PATTERNS OF BEHAVIOR

We drive into the parking lot slowly, counting the cars, noting the RV's and the tents lined up against the far corner of the lot and the people grouped together in a variety of lawn chairs, deep in conversation. We park near the entrance of the building and choose to focus our efforts on the community hall instead of the campers. A murmur of voices greets us as we enter the door and face two stairways, one going up and one descending. We follow their lead and head down into the lower level of the hall. It's quiet and cool in contrast to the hot August sun outside. Tables and chairs line the length of the room. Over on the far side a couple of women sit at a registration table and a man hovers nearby. We cautiously approach, hoping to be in the right place, a little unsure of our presence in this moment.

Our mission at this place is two fold: We are here, first and foremost, to celebrate a family reunion with my husband's mother's family and attempt to get to know all these people he is related to. But we are also here to solve a mystery. We want to know why his family has been cut off from these many relatives for so many years. Our curiosity was piqued a number of years ago when we first heard that the Glenn family held a reunion every other year for the last 30 years. It grew stronger with the death of his Uncle Billy when we met a number of people attending the funeral who we did not even know existed. My studies in family therapy and his contact with members of his father's family increased our interest. We are determined to see if we can figure things out.

When we tell the women who we are, we are welcomed with much excitement, warm hugs and eager questions whether any one else in our family is coming. We sadly tell them "No". We tried, but couldn't talk anyone else into following our lead. Maybe at future reunions, but for now they would have to be satisfied with my husband, his wife, daughter and grandchildren. Hopefully this will break the ice for the rest of his immediate family. Our presence marks the first time a member of Clay's immediate family chose to be part of this celebration. It brings as many questions as it does pleasure for us and for the many who are gathered to celebrate their family connections.

By the end of the weekend, we have only cleared away some of the mist of the past. The family story is certainly not clearly written in black and white. As each person shares their version of the story, bits and pieces come together; some to clarify, others to contradict what we think we already know. We are very aware that the "truth" is somewhere in the middle of all this. A truth that is hard to pinpoint. A truth we will likely never be able to declare as fact.

It's a family story which is likely very typical of those of its time. A story of a family affected by poverty and riches, power and control, political differences, immigration, separation, the trauma of war, as well as love and marriage where babies were born outside wedlock as well as within, and where disease and accidents brought early and unexpected death. Secrets were created, held, and then exposed over time. These secrets led directly to feelings of acceptance or rejection which in turn created patterns of behavior that were passed on through the generations over time. We certainly cannot lay any guilt or shame for the continuation of these patterns, as they were developed by people who were trying to do the best they could in the midst of the circumstances in which they were living. We search for answers, not to blame or to reject those who have gone before us, but to try and understand why we do what we do. On this warm day in August we are awed by the realization that what happened in this family over a hundred years ago has such a strong impact on the current moment. The behavioral patterns of the past are in action in the present moment, determining which members of the family are enjoying the reunion as well as those who chose not to come.

The strongest behavioral patterns we recognize come directly from the members of Clay's immediate family. When we tell them we are attending the reunion and invite them to join us, their response is the same, whether it comes from his mother, his brothers or his sister. They all state that they would love to attend BUT. . . . . . . and then comes some weak excuse, which really doesn't make sense, but gives them a way to explain why they continue to chose to cut themselves off from the others. It is far more comfortable to remain static in one's behavior than step out into in an unknown world. I suppose this pattern is most apparent to us because it is the one we know we have used ourselves in the past. It's the one we are breaking at this moment.

Clay is not the only member of the family to be breaking his family's pattern of behavior. Another woman is also there for the first time. Rena comes from an offshoot of the family. Her grandmother married one of the original brothers, after divorcing her first husband and leaving her first three children, including Rena's mother, in the care of her mother. These children were raised as "uncles and aunt" to the rest of the children born to the brother and this woman. Rena shares the bitterness her mother felt in being rejected by her grandmother in this fashion. Like Clay, she had no contact at all with the many people gathered for the reunion. Although her family had also been invited throughout the years, none of them chose to come until this year. Her tears flow as she tells of the hole in her life and the lives of her siblings because of the separation from this family, enforced by her mother's pain. She speaks of the incredibly warm welcome she is experiencing and we cheer with pleasure when she wins the raffle for the family quilt which has been created especially for this reunion. She wishes her siblings could also experience this healing force.

The intergenerational transmission of familial patterns of behavior refers to patterns of behavior which are repeated one generation after the next with very little awareness that this process is occurring. This process was first described by Dr. Murray Bowen, a family and marital therapist and is used in his method of family therapy. When he went back over the history of the families with whom he was working, he discovered that there were certain patterns of behavior that could be traced from one generation to another or perhaps would skip a generation or two and then occur again.

The first time I encountered a clear picture of the transmission of a familial pattern of behavior over generations occurred with a young girl I knew. Shortly after we met her, I noticed that she was beginning to gain weight. I questioned her on the possibility of pregnancy. She admitted that she was.

About a month before the birth of this child, the young woman's mother came to see me claiming that she needed to talk privately with me. She said she had something to confess that she had never told anyone before and wanted to know how to share this with her daughter. Years ago, when she was the same age as her daughter is now she got pregnant. She went into hiding and had her child without anyone in her home community, including her whole family, knowing. She gave the child up for adoption and tried to go on living without thinking about this child. Of course, it didn't work. The child was always on her mind, but she did manage to keep her secret. She got married, had several other children, and raised them to adulthood. No one in her current life had any idea at all that this other child existed. I was the first person she had spoken to about this child, throughout the 25 years of its life.

The mother is well aware that keeping this secret has had a negative affect on her whole family. She knows that she does not have as close a relationship to her husband as she wants with this secret between them. She believes her children have been harmed by the presence of the secret in the home. Her oldest son committed suicide. She believes the secret had something to do with this. Her other children are not as close to her as she would like. She feels she is pushing them away because she cannot tell them about her first child. She wants all this to change but it is very difficult.

And now, unaware of her mother's past, the daughter has followed the exact same pattern as that of her mother. It's almost as if she has no control of the situation at all. Certain professionals insist that the girl give up the child for adoption in the same manner that her mother did years before. The daughter refuses. Her brother's death is far too recent for her to face giving up another family member. She chooses to keep the child and raise it herself in spite of the difficulty this will place on her.

The birth of the new baby led to an opening of the family. The secret was revealed, first to the father and then to the children in the family. The mother took the chance to go and visit with her first-born and see her for the first time since she was born. No one reacted to the news in a negative way. They believed the mother had done her best in circumstances that were not easy for her.

As I played my role in the midst of this family drama, I couldn't help but notice that there was a similarity in the behavior of the mother and daughter. Although I didn't have a name for it at the time and wasn't aware it was a common element in intergenerational families, I was struck by what had occurred. How could the daughter follow exactly in her mother's footsteps without having any knowledge at all of what had occurred in the past? In time I realized that the same had happened to me, though the pattern was completely different. This time it involved being comfortable in the midst of keeping a secret.

When I was seventeen, I met a young man, who claimed he was swept off his feet from the moment he first saw me, and that he couldn't live without me. We dated for a few months. Unlike any of the other young men I had dated, he was insistent on having sex with me, claiming it was the proof of how much he loved me. My family was entranced with him, but I soon recognized that the person who appeared in public was not the same as the one I was dealing with in private. However, I became pregnant and was forced to make decisions I was not prepared to deal with at such an early age. At the time I felt like I was too shy and awkward to stand up for my own feelings, but when I look back over the letters I wrote to my family during this period of my life, I do realize I was very clear in my position of not wanting to marry the father of my baby because I knew I would not be able to deal with our differences. However, I reacted to the crisis situation in much the same way I had learned from my father: to back away, be quiet and go with the flow of meeting the expectations of our society, rather than my own needs. The die was cast. I quit university, got married and began raising a family. Many years later I was to discover that this unplanned pregnancy linked directly to the multigenerational transmission process within our family as it played a major role in one of our biggest family secrets.

My paternal grandmother immigrated to Canada from Norway when she was a young woman. She met and married my grandfather in Edmonton. They homesteaded in northern Alberta and raised two children together: my father and my aunt Anna. Throughout our lives, little was said about my grandmother's past. We knew a lot about my grandfather and his many brothers and sisters, but little about Grandma. We did know that she came from the Hardanger Fjord in Norway. She did have a picture of the house she was born in and of relatives that she seldom mentioned? We did know that she had worked as a nanny in Edmonton and that her charge had gone on to become the Minister of Highways as an adult. But that was all. It wasn't a big deal as we were all so busy in our present lives. Grandma was respected by her neighbors. She was a hard worker. She was serious and like a typical Scandinavian, wasn't big on hugs or kisses for her grandchildren. But she made us sugar cookies and taught us how to count in Norwegian. What more could we want?

My grandmother died of leukemia when I was a teenager. After a few years, my grandfather followed her to the grave. With his death, my father and his sister had to go through the pile of official papers they had left. This is when the questions started. For in the safety deposit box, along with the wills, some stocks, bonds and other certificates, were three pieces of identification that had come to Canada with my grandmother: her birth certificate, her ticket from the ship that brought her here and her immigration papers. And on these three pieces of paper were three different last names: Knutson, which is how we had always known her, as well as two others we had never heard before. As we looked at the three names, we realized for the first time how little we actually knew about her. What did this mean? Who exactly was my grandmother? Why would she have different names? Had she been married before? Were there people in our family we had no knowledge of?

Around this time, my parents were planning to visit Norway and decided to see if they could solve this mystery while they were there. They placed advertisements in newspapers in the Hardanger Fjord looking for anyone who would know my grandmother, using relatives on my mother's side of the family as contact points. They sent along the picture of the house and included all three names as reference points. Since Grandma had not left any contact information to her relatives, it was our only choice. Mom and Dad left for Norway wondering what their efforts would reveal.

The advertisements did their job. When my parents arrived at Mom's cousin's home, they were greeted with letters from people who claimed to be cousins of my grandmother; people who were looking forward in great anticipation to meeting my parents. A journey to the Hardanger Fjord was added to the vacation itinerary. There they were welcomed into a home with great joy, by people who clearly loved my grandmother and knew far more about us than we did about them. For there on the walls were pictures of our whole family, my parents and their children, my aunt and her whole family, taken shortly before my grandmother's death. Again, Mom and Dad were perplexed. What did this mean? Why had these people been kept secret from all of us, when we were obviously not a secret to them? The answers came quickly.

As it turned out, my grandmother was the illegitimate child of a landowner and his servant. When you look at this fact from the point of 2005, it really doesn't appear to be a big deal, but to my grandmother, born over a century earlier, it was. Being illegitimate was shameful. She chose to come to Canada to hide that shame. She spent her whole life hiding her secret to the point that she refused to let anyone know anything about her past. One of her cousins came to Canada later and homesteaded near our community. She refused to acknowledge his presence or his connection to her in any way. Only when my parents visited her cousins in Norway did they realize that this man had been part of our family.

I am sure that my grandmother kept her secret in order to protect us all, her husband, her children and her grandchildren, from inheriting her shame. It likely wasn't easy, as she was loved by her family in Norway. They kept in touch with her throughout the years. It wasn't that she wasn't proud of us, which was evidenced by our pictures hanging the walls so far from home. But she felt her silence was necessary to protect each of us. A silence that hung over our family for years. A silence that affected each of us in our own way. A silence that allowed me to become comfortable with secrecy and be able to live in the midst of another secret for twenty years without any awareness of what was going on. And unbeknownst to us all, in 1968, we took part in the multigenerational transmission process of this shame when I was forced into marriage by my pregnancy. Her great-grandchild would not suffer the same fate.

Since I learned about the process of intergenerational transmission of familial patterns of behavior, I have been able to recognize it happening in many of the families I work with. It so often makes sense of situations that aren't really that logical. It allows people to look at their behavior from a different viewpoint, one that does not need to include guilt or shame. Following these patterns is usually an unconscious reaction. Making the decision to move away from it is a rational choice we can only make once we get to know who we really are. As we already know, changing the pattern will be more difficult as it leads to discomfort, so the unconscious choice happens more often.

I am sitting in a case conference surrounded by teachers, counselors, social workers and other professionals who have come together to formulate a plan of action for a young man with whom I am working. We are hoping he may return home to his family and attend the school in which we are currently meeting. His mother is in the midst of describing her expectations at home in regards to homework and her willingness to work closely with the school in hopes of maintaining a successful placement. As she describes her relationship with her son in glowing terms and shares her determination to make certain that he keep on top of his work, I watch the eyes of the professionals widen in disbelief. Finally someone speaks up and directly asks the mother "If this is the case, why is the child out of the home?" It's a question I wondered about myself, every time I talked to this woman. As she glibly states her stock reply, "It's for the protection of the other children in the home," I watch the other professionals, totally aware that the contrast between her words and his placement make no sense at all to them. The meeting continues on with the focus of the safety of the other children in the classroom taking precedence over what is happening in the home.

But her statement does make sense to me. It took a long discussion about the mother's past to make things clear. It makes sense to me because I am aware of the power of patterns of behavior in a family. The mother was the youngest child in her family. She had four older brothers. While she was in the womb, her third oldest brother died in a freak accident. The whole family was devastated, but none more than the second oldest brother. He and his younger brother were only a year apart and had been inseparable all their lives. The parents dealt with their grief and the grief of their children in the same way they had learned from their parents: through silence and withdrawal. The young boy was unable to match this behavior and became more and more vocal about his loss. Other negative behaviors began to appear, which he seemed unable to control. In response, the parents had him placed out of the home shortly after the birth of their daughter. This mother grew up never knowing any other family life than one in which a child had been given away because of his behavior. When she was faced with the increasing difficulty of life with a child with autism, she followed her parents' response and had him placed elsewhere. It was the natural thing for her to do, in spite of her love and her concern. I am sure if one traced further back into the family history one would find this pattern repeated more often. And I am sure the pattern may happen again, not in the child's own family, but in the future families of his brothers and sisters who have grown up without him in the family home.

Dr. Bowen recognized that physical illness also appeared to occur through intergenerational patterns. When I first studied his concepts, I didn't easily accept the theory that our bodies could also unconsciously follow patterns, but the following story convinced me that he might be correct. How else can you explain this family story considering the time and the connections involved?

My godmother was born in Norway. She was the second daughter in a small family of four, born four years after her older sister. When she was six, her ten-year-old sister walked into the house and said to her mother "Oh Mama dear, I believe my brain has broken." She lay down upon the couch and died. She had experienced an aneurysm in her brain.

My godmother's mother never got over the death of this precious daughter. She went into a deep depression and spent the rest of her life in bed, leaving my godmother to be raised by her father when he was present, and look after herself the rest of the time. It was not an easy time for this young girl, but she survived and grew up to be a tough young woman. In time she met a man and they married, had a child and decided to immigrate to Canada. They homesteaded in Northern Alberta and ended up as our next-door neighbors.

The years passed. My godparents raised five children, who went on to get married and raise families of their own. At one point their grandson got a girl pregnant while they were teenagers. The family was never told about this baby. The girl gave it up for adoption at birth. Years later, the baby got in touch with the family as she looked for her birth father as an adult. She was welcomed with open arms of love by the whole family and they got to hear the rest of the story. For this young girl, almost a hundred years after my godmother's sister had died, in an adopted family on the other side of the world, also experienced an aneurysm at age ten. Luckily medical intervention was available and she lived through the experience, although there was a little brain damage.

The transmission of patterns of behavior from one generation to the next will happen whether we want them to or not, as they are dependent on unconscious reactions, not conscious ones. A major step in understanding oneself is to make the effort to trace our families back as far as possible and to gather the details on how these families lived and worked together during their time. In the past, much of this information was passed down from one generation to the next through stories. One's history was something one needed to know. It was something one carried with pride.

As our ability to move around the world became more sophisticated and individualism began to take precedence in society, we lost much of our ability to know and gather this information. No longer is the typical child surrounded by a vast array of extended family members who can connect him to the past. No longer can a young person depend on the reminder from an elderly neighbor down the street that his interest in geology is just like that if his Aunt Betsy, who died before he was born. Our neighbors hardly know us, much less our relatives. The oral tradition of the past is lost in a milieu of television and movies that appear to be so much more entertaining than the lives of our relatives. Instead of rejoicing in the survival of our family over time, we focus in on constructed "survivor" shows that have nothing to do with reality. In the midst of our ignorance, the familial patterns will continue to be passed on from one generation to the past because we are unaware it is happening. It doesn't make much difference if they are worthwhile patterns with positive outcomes, or are destructive in one way or another. The secret the family carries drains the family of energy, which would be so much more useful if used for something else. A baby's birth is something to rejoice in, unless it is unplanned and comes far too early. The future choices of a teenage mother are very limited when she has a child to care for. The pattern of incest can and has totally destroyed one generation after another in families. Only when we are aware of these patterns can we protect ourselves from falling into them. In order to reach our full potential as a 'self' we need to obtain this knowledge in any way we can.

SIBLING POSITION

My family gathers at a hotel in an attempt to deal with the stress and uncertainty of the strange behavior of my father. His body is failing and he has completely withdrawn from the life he formerly lived. The decline has been a gradual one over the last five years, but it is now getting so severe that it can no longer be ignored. At this point father is sleeping almost twenty-four hours a day, getting up only to eat and to go to the bathroom. His legs are unsteady and he often falls unexpectedly. Although nothing serious has happened to date, my mother is deeply concerned, and refuses to leave him alone at any time. Due to this situation, both have become virtually house bound, cut off from the world they live in, except through the telephone. The family meeting is an attempt for all us to come to terms with what is happening and to have father checked out by a team of geriatric specialists. We plan to devise a strategy for the future based on the findings of the doctors.

The oldest child is absent, as she has been for most of our lives. Her job is far more important than anything that is happening in the family. The second child sits quietly in the background, listening to what is being said outwardly and measuring it against what she knows is not being discussed. The third child is constantly checking on both her mother's feelings and those of her father. She, alone, takes the initiative to ask the father directly how feels about what is happening and waits patiently for his answer. The fourth child fumes that the oldest is not present, claiming that he wants us all to be involved in what is going on, and openly worries that the impact of day-to-day care will fall directly on himself, his wife and his children. Throughout it all, my mother talks constantly, expressing both her feelings of fear and the inadequacies in Father that she is dealing with on a constant basis. Father sits quietly, surrounded by those he loves so dearly with a tear in his eye and a smile on his face. This is my family of origin dealing with a crisis situation in their own particular manner. It is also a clear picture of the different family members reacting in the typical manner of sibling position in a family.

The final factor one should consider in regards to the development of one's reactions and the understanding of oneself is one's placement in birth order in one's family. Sibling position research was first carried out by Walter Toman[10] and incorporated in family systems therapy by Murray Bowen[11] in the early 1960's. Further research in this area has been completed by Hoopes and Harper[12].

Toman based his work on a theoretical premise that certain fixed personality characteristics are determined by one's position in their original family configuration. Over time it has been discovered that each of us unconsciously adopts a certain function in the family when we are born according to our position in the sibling order. These functions are used to strengthen the family unit. Very few of us are aware that this process is happening, and yet we carry our roles quite well without any thought. The oldest child tends to be a leader, the one who works hard and takes responsibility to get the job done. The second child becomes the thermometer of the family, open to all of the unspoken messages and the undercurrents within the system and ready to expose them in order to make the family function at an optimum. The third child is in charge of relationships, making certain that each and every person in the family is interacting with each other in the healthiest way possible, and the fourth child is the keeper of the family unit itself, holding it together at all costs.

When I first read about these different functions for different sibling positions I was quite amused, thinking that the psychological community had far too little to do, to come up with such theories. That day in the hotel room completely changed my viewpoint as I saw myself and my siblings adopt the function that fit our own sibling position without any clear understanding of what we were doing. I began to observe other families and saw the same pattern appear.

As a second child I am an expert on reading the unspoken rules that are occurring in any situation. I have always known I was able to do this. No one ever pointed it out to me, or explained anything about it. I assumed, quite naturally, that it was something all people are capable of doing and I interacted with others, especially my siblings, on that premise. So it came as quite a shock to learn that each of our positions in the family had given us different functions in the family and that mine, as the "reader of the unspoken" was mine alone. But it did explain why it happens so often that my siblings have no idea what I am talking about when I try to bring the unspoken out into the open. It also explains why I often appear as a threat to others, those who are not as comfortable with the unspoken as I am. And it does explain why I have always gravitated to the second child in another family. We are on the same wavelength.

10   Walter Toman, (1961), *Family Constellation*. New York: Springer.

11   Michael Kerr & Murray Bowen (1988). Family Evaluation: An approach based on Bowen Theory. New York: W.W. Norton & Company, p. 314.

12   M. Hoopes & J. Harper (1992). *Birth Order Roles and Sibling Patterns in Individual and Family Therapy*. Provo, Utah: Brigham Young University, pp. 33-76.

Understanding my position in the family has opened up a new understanding of my siblings. I have been able to let go of much of the frustration I had with them in the past when they did not do what I expected them to do or react in the ways I thought they should react. It made no sense at all to me that they couldn't see what I can see. It does now. It has also allowed me to accept the different reactions of my children throughout the years with more patience and understanding. I don't expect them to react like each other. I know that it is impossible for them to react in the same way. It's a waste of time and energy to compare them with each other.

Understanding the impact of sibling position on one's behavior has also allowed me to be a better family and marital therapist as I pick out which sibling position one is born into through their reactions in the therapy room. Couples made up of a first-born and a second child are going to interact differently that those made up of two fourth-borns. A child's position in the family will determine much of the interaction between that child and his siblings or parents.

Determining your sibling position is easy. Just count down from the first born in your family of origin to your spot. Be aware that all children in the family are counted, even those who were lost at birth or through a miscarriage. When my boys were young we spent a lot of time with a family of three boys. At one point I mentioned that our families were so much alike and yet different. I said, "You have a son to match my second, my third and my fourth son. But you're missing the oldest one."

"Yes", She replied, "we are. We lost him in Holland. He died shortly after he was born."

Whenever a child dies, his space is left untended. After the fourth child, the cycle returns to the beginning and starts all over again. So a fifth child takes the same role as the first child; the sixth child, the role of the second; and so on. Small families lose the roles that do not have children to fill them. So a family of two children has no one to concentrate on relationships or the family unit. Perhaps this is one factor in the disintegration of the family system over time.

PULLING IT ALL TOGETHER

As we travel through our lives, our mind is created through the experiences we have in the environments in which we have been placed. In the same way that we do not choose our genetic code, we also have little choice in these experiences or in the environments when we are children. However, they mark us for a life. They create our 'selves' which are revealed through our actions and reactions in the world. Taking control over these reactions is a major step in allowing us to be who we were meant to be.

We won't ever get there if we don't make the effort to look back and recognize what has made us as we are. This doesn't mean we have to spend a lot of time recreating the past or wallowing in the pain. It means that we make the effort to understand where our reactions originated. Only then can we choose to stay as we are or to move on to new and more effective reactions that match our true selves.

There are those who talk about our life experiences as being lessons that our particular spirit has to learn on this journey through life. I do not believe that this is true, and I have reasons for my beliefs. I see our creator who as a father who wants the absolute best for his children --- a father who places us here on earth and willingly helps us throughout our journey through life. He does not place obstacles or barriers in our way, but he does give us the freedom to make our own choices, to take responsibility for ourselves.

These are the choices that impede us. The choices made by others in the past, which we take on through the transmission of intergenerational patterns of behavior. The choices made by others around us that end up as the cultural and societal lessons we learn, and the beliefs and values that we incorporate into ourselves which impact the choices we make in turn. The choices made by others when we were too young to make the choices ourselves; choices which led directly to the need for coping skills to deal with the pain that we experienced. Coping skills that developed through our direct experience in this world. Coping skills that are holding us back in the present moment. These aren't lessons. They are the direct result of the free will that God has given each of us

When we speak of our experiences as life lessons, we allow people to do anything they want to us and to others. This becomes a perfect excuse for a pedophile who places the value of his pleasure before the rights of a child. If one believes that everything that happens to us is a lesson we have to learn, then the pedophile is only the tool used to teach that lesson. What a horrendous way to see our world. The development of self is based directly on the experiences we have so we would not be the same person we are if we had not had a specific experience, but this does not make the experience necessary. This does not make the experience "right".

If we shift the paradigm from lessons learned to brain created, we realize how important it is for each of us to clearly understand the impact of experience on ourselves in the development of our self, and on everyone else in their self development. Our universe exists through natural laws which are constant in spite of man's attempts to claim control over everything. These natural laws include those that allow for the creation of our individual brains through experience. They also determine the different levels of the self, a self that is constantly changing. The discomfort of change leads to our attempts to keep everything the same, which in turn, appears to lead to "lessons" being repeated over and over again. However, it is not the lesson that is important as much as the fact that we must move from automatic responses to rational ones in order to effect change. As long as we allow ourselves to continue to react unconsciously, we place ourselves back into the same situations, feel the same emotions and resort to the same reactions. A cycle is created which repeats itself over and over again, as long as we refuse to make the effort to change.

I will never be able to return to that verandah and join in with the family around that dining room table. However, I am able to recognize the source of the pain of being left out. At this point I can make new decisions about my reactions. Will I retreat in pain and continue to look with longing from the outside, or will I knock on the door and ask whomever I am interacting with to include me? Like my family, so many years ago, those whom I feel are neglecting me are often so caught up in their own thoughts and actions, they have no idea of the impact their behavior has had on my feelings. I can reject my habitual response of withdrawal. By reaching out to them I avoid the pain that I have carried so many years.

As you go through your own search of self, you too can isolate your reactions and discover exactly where they have originated during your journey. Do they come from experience, from your culture, from your family, or are they part of your own particular genetic make-up? Once you have determined the source, you can recognize them and actively choose whether you will allow yourself to follow the unconscious behavior, or create a new response. There will be times when you don't have as much control as others. Understanding the source of your own reactions is the first step. Accepting the power of anxiety in your life is the next.

A CASE STUDY

IN FLANDERS' FIELDS

In Flanders' fields the poppies grow between the crosses row on row
That mark our space and in the sky, the larks, still bravely singing fly.
Scarce heard amidst the guns below.
We are the dead.
Short days ago we lived, felt dawn, saw sunset glow.
Loved and were loved and now we lie in Flanders Fields.
Take up our cause, to you we throw, the torch, be yours to hold it high
If ye break faith with we who die, we shall not sleep though poppies grow
In Flanders fields.

JOHN MCRAE

She sat in her desk and tried desperately to ignore the horrible feeling in her stomach. She knew where it was coming from, but she didn't know what to do about it. It came every year at this time. Every year when the teachers took this poem out of their desks and shared it with the class. Every year when she was expected to learn it by heart and smile as she recited it. Every year when they drew pictures and coloured poppies and wore them pinned to their shirts. A feeling of revulsion, a feeling of guilt, a feeling of shame, a feeling of fear and of pain. She wanted to get up and leave. She wanted to throw the poem back into the face of her teacher. She wanted to scream out her frustration. But she didn't. She hunched down into her desk and tried to become invisible. She gritted her teeth and concentrated on getting through the class without anyone recognizing her distress. She did this every November, every year of her life at school.

She was born in Germany. Her parents immigrated to Canada when she was a young child. She moved into an educational system which annually celebrated the triumphs of the Allied forces in the first and second World Wars through this poem. She grew up in a community which wore the poppy proudly to commemorate our victories and the loss of our young men. She moved from the environment of the enemy to that of the liberator. She couldn't leave her past behind.

Her discomfort with Flander's Fields continued on throughout her life until she finally faced that discomfort and wrote her own personal rebuttal. She dedicated these words in memory of her husband's grandfather who was gravely wounded and blinded in Flanders' Field in World War I. Of her maternal grandfather who died in training before arriving at the Eastern front and his two brothers who also died war-related deaths in World War II. Of her paternal grandfather, stepfather, uncle and cousin who all perished along the Eastern Front in WWII. Of her father-in-law who was interned and narrowly escaped death by starvation in a French POW camp in World War II. Of his four brothers who were executed in the Soviet Union for their pacifist and religious beliefs, not heeding their leader's call in the late 1930's. Of her father's horror as he joined the 13 million women, children and seniors in refugee treks in search of safety; leaving behind one out of five, frozen and unburied alongside the wagon trails or fallen through the Baltic Sea ice. Of their many friends and neighbours who also perished in one way or another because of these wars. These are her words:

FLANDERS' MUD

In Flanders' Fields you know
I know,
the poppies grow within row and row of crosses
so we know
and remember those
whose blood and bone
are left below.
No poppies grew that day,
those years,
as leaden boots squished and
slopped bloodied mud
beneath their feet
in bullet rain.
My grandfather lay,

cheek to mud,
draining blood from gaping holes
adding poppy blood to dirty mud
soles upturned slowly writhing
praying to God above comfort those he loved
sure he was
his bones would remain in the rain.
Cheek to pillow he awoke
and remained,
rescued from death but not from pain
face down he lay a year and a half
as stitched gut of swine
now his intestine
healed the holes yet he remained
forever blind through loss of blood
to the mud of Flander's Fields.
And every year,
as we hear,
the Flanders' poems and mournful tones
I recoil - unsure of self of how to remember
those young brave heroes
who followed the call
to defend us all and
fight for freedom
putting bullets and holes
Brave young men
who followed the call
to defend and fight
to set aright that which was wrong
who all paid heed to leaders' creeds
to pick up arms and harm another.
What is right
and what is wrong
what is freedom
who is hero
when leaders call

and young men follow

where is honor in this mud?

Could it be that when in November

you remember

your brave grandfathers

they stood eye to eye

and muddied foot to muddied foot

facing mine

whose bullet put whose blood in the mud?

Could it be when we remember

veterans and heroes

I remember victims and loss

the orphaned child my mother was

the empty lives

the silenced calling

forever falling

in despair.

Could it be when I remember

on this day in November

my German grandfather's blood in mud

my young uncles' bones in frozen soil

you recoil -

you recoil at my daring

accuse me of uncaring?

For all these years who hears

the silence of the children

who try in November to remember

but all across this land

painfully understand

their family heroes stood not on this

but on that the other side

of distant battle lines

young men following yonder call

no less naive no more compelled

than young men of Allied call

Today in November when I pause,

with my poppy
I pray we can ignore the rhetoric
and pay no heed to leader's calls
for setting wrongs
with arms and bullets
firing flowery slogans
like propaganda
words shoot and explode.
Let us use our poppies instead
to remember the dead
those in countries today
yesterday
tomorrow
and all throughout the many years
and let the sharp
poppy pins provoke us
to prod for peace.
Let's swallow the mud
and ensure no more blood

HANNAH NOERENBERG

NOVEMBER 11, 2000

CHAPTER SIX
THE POWER OF ANXIETY

What Matters Is Not The Size Of The Load You Carry,
But How You Carry The Load.

IT IS A HOT SUMMER DAY IN THE EARLY 1980'S AND MY FAMILY IS ACCOMPANYING MY sister and her family to the Calgary Stampede, touted as the biggest outdoor show in the world. I'm not sure if it meets this claim, but it is a big show, with many different types of attractions spread over several acres of land.

We are a party of ten in all: my sister, her husband, their two children ages two and five; my husband and I with our four sons, ages five through nine. We park our cars a long way from the entrance to Stampede Park. As we walk along the river and finally cross the bridge to the entrance, I realize that this distance makes our typical response to our sons getting lost (go to the car and we will find you there) almost impossible. I tell my children to stick close by us because going back to the car will not be feasible. I fully believe that they have all heard me and understand. We pay our entrance fees and enter the park.

It's not as crowded as I thought it would be and we have a good time visiting the different animal exhibitions and little trouble keeping an eye on everyone as they check out the sites they want to see. After playing tic–tac-toe with chickens, who are rewarded with grain when they pick the right squares, the children begin to clamor for a chance to go on the rides, so we gradually began to move in that direction, stopping to check out various displays on the way. For a moment my sister and I are distracted by the activity in a certain booth. When I turn back to look for the boys, everything has changed. It's 6 p.m. and the grounds, which had almost seemed deserted a few minutes before, were now teeming with people. In the midst of this discovery we all realize that Tim is gone. My six–year-old son is missing, and I have no idea where he is.

We search quickly, frantically, frustrated by our inability to see more than a foot ahead of us, all the time silently praying for his safe return. We lay blame on each other, each of us expecting that the other had their eye on Tim. We rush to the Lost Child Booth and talk to the security guards giving them a description of Tim and where we had last seen him. We focus on the grounds around us because we had told the children not to return to the car. All to no avail. Tim was gone, and we had no idea how to find him. Finally, my sister and I reach a point we never thought possible. There we stand, face to face, screaming at each other at the top of our lungs in the middle of the Calgary Stampede. We attack each other for the loss of Tim, as our husbands and other children try to pretend they have no idea of who we are.

In desperation I leave and head to the car. Perhaps he had not followed my directions and gone there. It was so far away. The route was difficult and confusing. There was little chance that he would be able to find it if he tried. But it is my only hope and so off I go.

It turns out to be false hope. Tim is not at the car. I begin walking back to the grounds with tears streaming down my face. Where was my little boy? How was I going to find him? I was overcome with grief and desperation.

Then I saw my sister and the children heading my way. They had Tim with him. It turns out that he had indeed returned to the car because he hadn't heard me tell everyone not to do that. He had waited there for us, while we were concentrating on searching the grounds and talking to the security guards. He finally gave up on us coming and had returned to the gate, but no one would let him in. The people at the entrance determined that he was just a child who was trying to slip in without paying. They didn't bother contacting the Lost Child Booth. And so he sat on the riverbank near the entrance and waited for us to show up. This is where my sister found him, safe and sound.

Anxiety is the direct result of a threat of some kind or another to the 'self". Since the self is made up of far more than the actual body and mind, anxiety will build when anything within the self is threatened. The threat can happen to any level of the self: mind, social or material, and may affect multiple levels at the same time. The closer the threat comes to the spirit, the more extreme the impact. The more important the part of the self that is threatened, the more extreme the impact. The more levels the threat affects, the more extreme the impact.

If we look at the above example, we can clearly see this process as the loss of my son at the Calgary Stampede threatened the self in multiple levels and multiple ways. As a mother, my child was very high on the list of what was important to my self. He and his three brothers were undoubtedly the most important people in my life and my role as their mother was the main thing I was living for at the time. His loss threatened all three levels of self: the material self---my son and my role as a mother; the social self---his relationship with me and my relationship with everyone else in my life based on the fact I was his mother; and the mind---my beliefs about the importance of keeping my children safe, of being there for them at all times, and so on.

Loss of control in the situation made things worse. The distance to the car made our usual plan unworkable. The sudden appearance of the crowds of people impeded our vision and our ability to move quickly. The child find people had no way of actually helping us and did not even take the time to let the gates know that a child was lost so that Tim could have been apprehended when he tried to come back into the grounds. Nothing I did made things better. No one I contacted managed to help.

On top of the loss of control came the effects of chronic anxiety. A cold fear based on the awareness of other situations, other children. The fear of evil: that someone may have stolen him away. Someone who would hurt him. Someone who may never bring him back. It had happened to others. It could happen to me.

The combination of all this anxiety led directly to our reaction of screaming at each other, a reaction that neither of us had ever thought we would reach, especially in public. Where was this reaction based? I don't know. But I do know that it is a place I may return to in the future because it did happen again, the day before my father's funeral. About twenty years later my sister and I find ourselves in the same position, screaming at each other at the top of our lungs. Our father has just died. My family insists that my ex-husband is to be present at the funeral and I am cannot deal with his presence in the midst of this pain. I am horrified to be reacting like this at such a time. And yet I am.

She leaves and I fight to retain control. I spend the rest of the afternoon trying to reduce my level of anxiety using repetitive games on my computer. Finally I reach a point where I feel that I can safely be with my family. I phone my brother and he tells me my ex-husband is there and I am not welcome. My thalamus relays the messages from my sensory system. The amygdala reacts with PAIN. The limbic system swings into action. I automatically flee and drive home: five hours on the highway without any thought or feeling. Thankfully I didn't have an accident.

It takes a long time to process what has happened. To figure out and to accept our reactions. To forgive myself and to forgive the rest of my family. To think of missing my father's funeral without crying for days. What we have just experienced is our own personal reactions to the highest level of anxiety that we have faced together. Throughout the months that follow I personally face the reality of how my 'self' deals with extreme levels of anxiety.

Each person will have their own unique reaction to anxiety. In fact, each of us has many different reactions that we automatically respond with or actively choose between. Anxiety is a very natural part of our lives as it is the result of a threat to the self. The self is threatened by change, and change is inevitable. Life is the process of dealing with change in the self on a constant basis. Learning to accept change and developing coping skills to lower the level of anxiety is our journey on this earth. Each of us faces this challenge in different ways. The choices we make will affect our ability to enjoy our life and reach our full potential. Sadly these concepts are the most misunderstood and mistreated in the field of psychology. Instead of allowing people to develop a clear understanding and acceptance of themselves and how they personally cope with anxiety, therapists focus on "fixing" what appears to be negative and inappropriate behavior with no interest in or idea of the reason for the behavior. Instead of understanding that the various coping skills we use to cope with anxiety are tools of survival, these skills or behaviors are often defined as "mental illnesses". Instead of building a true sense of self, individuals lose their self-esteem through messages of shame, guilt and weakness because of their reactions to anxiety. Hopefully this book will help change that process.

STAGES OF ANXIETY

I began to understand the importance of understanding the impact of anxiety, and the coping skills we develop to deal with it, when I began to work with a very special group of people: those within the autism spectrum. In the beginning I didn't have a clue what was happening, and the professionals in charge of our program were of no help, as neither did they. My first days on the job were spent in total frustration as I tried to make things happen according to the schedule that had been laid out for me, never knowing just when a "blow up" would occur and I would be face to face with extreme behavior in the form of head banging, self mutilation or aggression. I had my clothes ripped off my body. I came home from work with arms bloodied from scratches and pinches. Finally it reached a point where I found myself facing a man who was much bigger than I with a chair raised up over his head, ready to smash it down on mine. I was terrified. I didn't have a clue how to respond. It was in that moment I learned not to react to the behavior. To be calm. To control myself instead of trying to control him. To listen. To really listen to the messages they were giving me. To stop relying on verbal conversation and to focus in on the whole picture: the environment, the context, body language, behaviors. To stop following the advice of the psychologist and follow the lead of those I was caring for. Gradually peace came to our world and new positive reactions emerged as the anxiety level in that home began to decrease.

It's been 30 years since I met my first friends with autism. Since that time, the number I know personally has grown into the hundreds. The lives I have affected positively are in the thousands. They come to me in joy instead of fear or anger. They want to be with me, for they know they are totally safe in my presence. It's not because I do anything difficult. It's not that I am doing anything out of the ordinary. They choose to be with me because they know I accept them for the people they are, that I respect them as equal to anyone else on this earth, and I love them unconditionally, no matter what may happen in my presence.

Over the years, people with autism have taught me much about the impact of anxiety on their lives. Their extreme response to stimulation results in a much higher level of threat in environments that do not bother the typical person. People with autism are constantly bombarded with stimulation to the point that they are constantly dealing with anxiety.

When we are calm, we do not see as many of these kinds of visual exaggerations or defects as we do when we are having overloads to the nervous system. When we go to sleep, we are at rest, and then only, as we are upset most of our waking hours. When I am calm, I can concentrate on learning, but, when I have overloads, I can do little to function normally.[13]

For many, even sleep remains elusive as they react to the temperature of the room, the tactile reaction to the bedding, the ongoing noises in a home and a mind that never is still.

There are five basic levels of anxiety experienced by people on the autism spectrum. These are no stress or anxiety, buildup, survival level, shutdown and meltdown. Their exposure to the level of 'no stress or anxiety' is very rare due to the fact that their sensory system reacts at such a higher level than ours. However, it is the only time that we see people with autism at their full potential. In other words, we rarely get to know who they really are because of their level of anxiety.

Buildup is the stage in which the level of anxiety is building in the body due to input through the sensory system, the body or the mind. At this point the person is able to deal with what is coming in without too much of a problem and can appear to be calm and able to focus on information in the environment and interactions with other people. As the buildup continues the person will become more and more agitated until they reach the point of survival. In this stage the person has to choose between a variety of coping skills to deal with the anxiety.

There are two ways of dealing with anxiety: either through decreasing the input of stimulation or through blocking it out. The person with autism has different methods to accomplish these goals. They can either withdraw from the environment to decrease the impact of the stimulation on the body, or they can use repetitive and stereotypic behaviors to build up the level of endorphins in the brain and thus decrease their feelings of pain and discomfort. Withdrawal can be anything from leaving the room to turning off fluorescent lights or taking off one's clothing. Another type of withdrawal is retreating into one's imagination to the point that one is unaware of what is happening around them. Each of these choices will reduce the impact of the stimulation on the body and thus decrease the level of anxiety.

In direct contrast, repetitive behaviors produce endorphins, which provide a solution from the inside out. We all produce endorphins naturally in our bodies to reduce stress. This is why we pace or rock our bodies. The repetitive movements are the catalyst for the production of the endorphins, which were first isolated and understand through studies of caged animals. The longer these animals paced, the higher the level of endorphins in their bodies. A simple example of producing endorphins, which you may have experienced, is having a paper cut on the tip of your finger. When we feel the pain we automatically shake our finger (a repetitive behavior), which creates the endorphins. The pain of the cut disappears.

---

13   Charles Martel Hale, Jr. I Had No Means to Shout p.83, 1999. {**Not sure about this format**}

Withdrawal and/or the use of repetitive action lowers the anxiety level of the body to the point where it is able to continue on learning or doing in the environment without a problem. The process feels like this:

> *My lack of interest and involvement in the outside world did not protect my mind from the flood of unwanted information that continually assaulted my senses. The unmodulated sensory input often overwhelmed me, causing me mental torture, and I would begin feeling mentally confused and sluggish. My head would feel fogged so that I could not think. My vision would blur, and the speech of those around me would become gibberish. At this point, I would feel compelled to make certain repetitious movements. I had a constant fascination with objects anyway, particularly sticks, and if any were around I would pick them up and beat them together. If not, I would use my hands, flapping them rhythmically back and forth to a driving inward beat. Acting on my compulsion to stim brought relief. It allowed me to intently focus on an object of my choice. The noise in my head quieted. The fog cleared. Objects became clear again.[14]*

Once the body is calm, the person can return to the tasks or interactions they were engaged in without difficulty, but buildup from stimulation will continue. One will have to return to using their coping skills over and over again as time goes by and the buildup of sensory input to the body occurs again.

The person with autism may not choose to decrease the level of buildup, but instead block out the feelings in their body through shutdown. Shutdown is achieved by overloading the sensory system by putting in too much information, or by focusing completely on a task or object or an imaginary world. Coping skills that overload the system include looking directly into a bright light, watching a spinning object, screaming loudly, turning on loud music, drinking something like Tabasco sauce, smearing one's feces or self mutilation through biting, pinching or head banging.

When a person is in shutdown, there is no reaction at all to sensory input. They cannot see, hear, feel or smell. There is also no reaction to physiological reactions such as hunger, pain or the need to go to the bathroom. Shutdown feels like this:

> *Calmness or pleasantness is when I feel nothing except numbness and peacefulness. I like that feeling very much. It's like a sleepy feeling, I think. I try to keep numb and calm. I function best when I am this way. It may sound terrible, but trust me it's very good for me.[15]*

Although Scott claims that shutdown is very good for him in this quote, the honest truth is that is a very dangerous place to be. We have lost people on the autism spectrum as they walked out in front

---

14 Daniel Hawthorne, 1998, unpublished manuscript.

15 Scott McGifford, 1998, unpublished manuscript.

of moving traffic in shutdown and died as a result of neither seeing nor hearing cars approaching. In times of high anxiety, they may go without food for days on end as they do not feel their hunger. And, of course, they are ostracized by a society which believes they are incapable of being toilet trained because they are mentally retarded, not because it is impossible to feel the physiological urge to go to the bathroom while they are in shutdown. The lack of this urge may also lead to severe problems with constipation.

The last stage of anxiety for people with autism is meltdown. This is the extreme of the autistic experience and is a horrendous place for them to be. Each of them uses their own particular term to define this experience such as the "big black nothingness," or "falling off a cliff." Each person on the autism spectrum spends most of their energy each day trying to avoid meltdown. The coping skills they use, whether withdrawal, repetitive or overloading are vital in the avoidance of meltdown.

Meltdown is a total loss of control and can be best described as an extreme panic anxiety attack. From the outside it looks like a temper tantrum and can include aggression. From the inside it feels like this:

> *The walls went up and my ears hurt. I had to get out -out of the room, out of this thing stuck upon me, suffocating me inside like a shell of flesh. A scream rose in my throat. My four-year-old legs ran from one side of the room to the other moving ever and ever faster, my body hitting the wall like a sparrow flying at a window. My body was shaking. Here it was. Death was here. Don't want to die, don't want to die, don't want to die -the repetition of the words blended into a pattern with only one word standing out; the word die. My knees went to the floor. My hands ran down the mirror. My eyes frantically searched the eyes looking back, looking for some meaning, for something to connect. No one, nothing, nowhere. Silent screaming rose in my throat. My head seemed to explode. My chest heaved with each final breath at the gates of death. Dizziness and exhaustion began to take over the terror. It was amazing how many times a day I could be dying and still be alive.*[16]

Understanding autism means understanding these different stages of anxiety and the impact they have on the person within the spectrum. Being there for a person with autism means paying close attention to the level of stimulation coming in from the environment and closely listening to the body language of the person to understand at which stage they are. It means changing my own behavior and modifying the environment to cut down on the impact of stimulation, instead of trying to fix the person. It means respecting the behaviors which are used as coping skills, whether they are repetitive or overloading, and realizing that the outcome for each will be different and will need different interactions on my part. It means sharing all this information directly with the person

---

16 Donna Williams, 1994, Nobody Nowhere

with autism because they may not understand it any more than you understood the concepts in this book before you read it.

Sadly, this is not what has happened to the majority of the people within the autism spectrum in the past, and is not what is happening in our current treatment programs. Instead the focus lies in "fixing" the behavior of the person with autism to make them 'appear' normal. So called 'professionals' go to extreme lengths to carry out these treatments, including administering electric shock, psychotic medications, restraints, and hours and hours of intensive behavior therapy with no understanding at all that the behaviors used by those on the spectrum are there for protection. No wonder these people are so excited to meet someone like me.

Once I had recognized the importance of coping skills for those with autism, I realized that they are a constant factor in the lives of each and every one of us. Being autistic is not at any point being either sub human or alien. Instead, it is the extreme of human existence. Each of us is capable of going through the five stages of anxiety as outlined above. However, most of us never reach the points of shutdown or meltdown unless we have been placed in extreme circumstances. We fluctuate between buildup and survival and back again without paying much attention to, or being aware of, what is going on. During this time we use the same types of coping mechanisms used by people with autism. The only difference is our level of response. We are able to be less extreme because our brains are not responding at as high a level as theirs are.

Anxiety is the result of a threat to the self. A threat to the self constitutes change in some form or other. The anxiety is felt as discomfort in the body. The body reacts to this discomfort with some type of coping skill. The coping skill decreases the feelings of discomfort in one way or another so that the self can deal with the discomfort brought on by whatever change is occurring. The level of discomfort is directly related to the importance of what is changing to the individual; any connection to the past, especially to anything traumatic that happened in early childhood; and the amount of control the person has over the change that is occurring.

In other words, anxiety due to a child moving out of the home for the first time will be much higher for a parent than that of a neighbor relocating to another town. A child who was neglected as a small child and forced to go without food would react more strongly to an empty cupboard than someone who has never missed a meal. A person who chose to change jobs themselves will have less anxiety than if they were fired. The higher the level of anxiety the more one depends on their coping skills whether through quantity or quality.

An apparent contradiction that happens in this process is that feeling good about something is often as anxiety causing as the negative emotions such as sadness, fear and anger. This is because the anxiety is directly due to a change in the self. If we are dealing with a person who has never felt loved, has never felt successful, or has never felt beautiful, any situation in which they experience these emotions will create a change in the model of self, and thus a high level of discomfort. The automatic reaction to these positive feelings may be to return to a feeling to which they have become accustomed and do something that doesn't appear to make any sense to someone who has had access to such positive feelings all of their lives. They may do something mean to the person who is trying to love them to prove they are unlovable. They may purposely make mistakes in order to sabotage any feelings of success. They may cover up their beauty or choose clothing that is unbecoming in order to feel unattractive. All of these reactions have gradually built up during the life of the child. They are carried in the mind and will be used without conscious thought.

The process of understanding the self involves recognizing how the various levels of anxiety are present in one's body and then determining which coping skills one has a tendency to rely on. None of us uses only one type of coping skill and each of us is unique in the way we develop and use our coping skills. This is definitely an individual journey. However, we can use another's experience to begin the journey of recognizing our own patterns of behavior.

The major coping skill I relied on in the past was food. Discomfort in my body was recognized as hunger. Food was eaten to appease this hunger and deaden the feelings of discomfort. For the first 40 years of my life almost all anxiety was dealt with by eating: emotional pain, physical sickness, concerns about money, major changes in my life such as moving, and so on. Needless to say, my body has suffered and continues to suffer for it. At this point in time, I have reached the point where I am fully aware that what I am feeling is not hunger, but discomfort due to anxiety for one reason or another. I have succeeded in stopping the automatic response of eating whenever I feel uncomfortable, but I still respond to anxiety with feelings I call hunger. I have to consciously tell myself to figure out what the feeling means and deal directly with the anxiety or I find myself eating without thought. I haven't lost much weight, but at least I am not still gaining.

For years I was told that my habit of eating was bad. For years I was told that I had to change the way I ate. For years I was given the message that I was weak and had no self-control when I ate more than I should. For years I was overcome with shame because of my eating habits which, of course, led to a heightened level of discomfort and the need to resort to my coping skill again. It was a constant cycle of failure and shame every time I listened to those who were trying to "help" me. In the end, it only led to a greater and greater weight gain.

There were times during these years that I was completely aware of how I was using food to block my feelings: to deal with the life that I was living. I knew that much of the food I ate covered up the pain of the abuse I was dealing with on a day to day basis, blocking out the shame that I was feeling for living life as I was, and hiding my body behind layers of fat and large clothing so that no one would pay any attention to it. There were times that I wanted to exercise. There were times I wanted to stop eating. There were times I wanted to give my body the attention it deserved. I tried, and then something would happen; my self would be threatened in one way or another, and I would indulge in too much food all over again. Nothing could change until I took care of all the other problems in my life. It took a long time to do that.

The journey to understand my 'self' has led me to a place where I now can accept that eating is one of my coping skills for dealing with anxiety. I can recognize the discomfort I am feeling may not be hunger, and I can choose whether I am willing to face the feelings and go through them, or whether I will allow myself to resort to blocking them out with food. I have learned to tell myself that it is okay to feel pain. That it is okay to feel anxiety. That it is okay to be uncomfortable now and then. And that it is also okay to eat if I have to, even when I know that food is not the answer. I can forgive myself for not being perfect, because I know life is hard and when I am dealing with change in one way or another food may be the one way I can succeed in the moment. This is okay. Once I reached that point in life, it was interesting to find that I was no longer reaching for food as often as I did in the past.

Food is not the only coping skill people use to block their feelings of discomfort. It is the one I developed over time, but there are many others out there. There are a variety of different copings skills available at all the levels of the self. Denial, family secrets and projections are examples of those used at the level of the mind. Triangulation and over functioning are found at the social level of self. The use of cigarettes, alcohol, drugs, and caffeine all have the same affect on the body as food does and are thus used at the material level as this is where one finds the body. Exercise programs such as jogging or weight lifting develop endorphins in the body, which are as effective at blocking pain as any of these other substances and can become a method of coping. Others may choose to use repetitive behaviors in much the same way as those with autism do. Tapping a pencil, bouncing one's leg up and down, or twirling a piece of hair over and over again all reduce the impact of anxiety on our bodies through the development of endorphins. The lure of video and computer games is based directly on this reaction to repetition. Each person develops their own coping skills based on their personal history, their own body, what is available and the amount of pain they are feeling. Each person uses their own coping skills to the level they require to deal with the level of discomfort that they are currently experiencing. Each person will increase the level of use of a coping skill in times of increased stress or anxiety. Once we can accept this about ourselves and about others we can move on.

At this point I have chosen to use repetitive games on the computer such as free cell and solitaire to help me block out anxiety when it gets too high for me to cope without blocking it out. In times of extreme stress, such as the days after my father's funeral, I have spent whole days in front of the computer screen. I know this may not be the most effective way to deal with life's problems, but I believe it is better than eating at this point in time, and is necessary for me if I am going to calm myself enough to deal with the changes that are taking place. Thankfully, those days are few and far between.   There are a lot of times that we are not in full control of what is happening in our lives. There are times we have to wait for others to do whatever it is they have to do to allow us to get on with our lives. During those times I believe it is better for me to block out my feelings to keep the situation calm, rather than attack this person and cause a lot of damage to the social selves of both of us. And so, I pass the time, I play the games, and I wait until the change has occurred. I put the anxiety out into the open to decrease its power in my life. And I forgive myself for the time it is taking.

Like grief, anxiety is a very normal state for human beings and both have been labeled as a mental disorder by the medical community. Instead of affirming the reactions of anxiety as a normal human state in times of stress and change, the psychiatric community has determined that anxiety is a "disorder" and that there is something "wrong" with the person who is experiencing it. At this point they have broken anxiety down into 13 different disorders as outlined in the DSM IV. Treatment for anxiety again focuses on the use of medication and therapy which results in varied levels of outcome by those have been labeled.

The most extreme forms of anxiety are post-traumatic stress disorder (PTSD), dissociation and panic anxiety attacks. Although I don't believe there has been much research done in this area, I have come to believe that PTSD is the direct result of the self experiencing an extreme threat to another self. Since we are all connected closely to each other and to the source of life, anything that happens to another is going to affect us. The common thread found in experiences of people who have developed PTSD is the experience of living through the horrendous experience of pain, death or torture of other people. This is why so many soldiers suffer from PSTD after being involved in wars.

During the late seventies, my family had the opportunity to attend an air show at our local airport. A variety of demonstrations had been planned for this show. The day started out warm and sunny but as time passed a very cold blustery wind came up. This made standing out in the open space of the airport rather uncomfortable. However, everyone had paid their entrance fees and was looking forward to the show, so we all came up with means of staying warm such as huddling together or wrapping ourselves in a variety of blankets that we found in our cars. The wind hampered one act after another. The parachute team was unable to perform their planned sequence and ended up just jumping out of the plane and landing in front of us. An attempt to parachute a bulldozer out of a cargo plane ended up in a spectacular crash with pieces of the machine flying off in all directions. This didn't deter the producers of the show or the audience. We all gritted our teeth, determined to stay for the grand finale: a demonstration by the Snowbirds, the Canadian military synchronized jet plane team. As they roared above our heads in perfect formation, we responded with our own roar from the ground.

About halfway through their show, my sons decided they were far too cold to watch any longer. We started heading back to the car to go home. I glanced back at the planes flying overhead. There were two planes flying directly at each other, and then as they got to a certain point, veering away.

The silhouette of the one plane stood out clearly against the blue sky. With horror I realized one wing was missing. In seconds this plane had disappeared to the ground in a fiery crash. The realization that I had just witnessed the death of a pilot as a bizarre form of entertainment flashed through my mind. The whole area erupted into chaos as about one third of the spectators rushed forward, not wanting to miss out on a single detail, one third headed to their vehicles to leave and the other third, including me, stood still, in shock, not knowing what to do. What an example of the limbic responses of fight, flight and freeze! The rest of the evening passed in a blur as we searched for the boys we had lost track of in the melee, as we joined family members in my brother's home trying to make sense of the accident, and as we watched the plane tumble out of the sky, over and over again on the television news.

The image of the plane silhouetted against the blue sky with one wing missing was frozen into my brain and I couldn't stop thinking about it. I began to believe the whole show had been a warning for this pilot not to go up into the sky. The wind, the cold, the failure of the other demonstrations. Why wasn't it stopped? Why did we all insist on staying and watching? Why was I there? How could I have allowed myself to take part in such a scene? How could I have allowed my sons to witness it? I dreamed about the plane. I lay awake tossing and turning, thinking about the plane. I had trouble concentrating on any of my usual tasks as the picture would flash through my mind.

As weeks and months passed, the scene gradually began to move back out of my consciousness. But it wasn't gone for good. Simple little reminders would bring it back and days would be spent going over the circumstances again. Watching news on the television became a threat as the Snowbirds are a popular feature at many of our national celebrations and once the accident had been investigated, they were back up in the air, entertaining others. A fly-by during such events as a football game and over parliament hill Parliament Hill on Canada Day threw me right back into shock again. Their sudden unexpected presence at the Grey Cup took my breath away. It felt as if I had been slugged in the stomach. Each time this happened I would go through the whole process of horrifying dreams and sleepless nights all over again.

About two years after the accident occurred, the Snowbirds returned to our community. They were doing a show in a nearby area and flew to our city to honor the pilot who died. I sat out on my back step and watched them fly back and forth over the city with tears flowing down my face. I said good-bye to the pilot. I asked for forgiveness for my part as a spectator in his death. I allowed myself to completely feel the pain and the horror. As the planes soared and whirled above me, I felt a cleansing occur. The trauma was over. I could be at peace again.

This experience is the only example of PTSD that I can say I have experienced in my life time. I do realize that, compared to the experience of many others, it was not that severe. The fact that I was able to go through it all without psychological help is an indication the impact was low. However, my experience was very real, and allowed me to understand how something like witnessing the unnecessary death of another person can affect me as a whole. Reliving the scene in my brain and allowing myself to feel the pain and the guilt were what brought me to the end of this process. I still cannot watch the Snowbirds in comfort. I find myself holding my breath until they are safe on the ground again and praying that another accident will not happen in front of me.

In direct contrast to PTSD, dissociation is the extreme reaction to a threat to one's own physical body. The spirit actually leaves the body during the trauma and moves around the environment on its own. People who have experienced dissociation describe watching their body from a distance. They have clear memories of what happened to the body as they watched, but no memories at all of the feelings the body experienced. Dissociation appears to be the coping skill humans have developed to deal with the pain of an experience which would likely cripple the self forever, if it were allowed to be felt.

Dissociation is not actually an anxiety label, but instead a common reaction to extreme anxiety situations such as a near death experience whether in accidents, on the operating table, or through assault by another person. Again we have a number of different labels for dissociation in the DSM IV, creating the situation in which people are told there is something wrong with them, instead of acknowledging the fact that this is again a normal human reaction to severe situations. It appears that when the body reaches a certain point of pain or harm, the spirit leaves and watches from a distance. Perhaps this happens to all of us as we die. We don't have too many people who have actually died and stayed that way, coming back to tell us exactly what happened. People who have experienced dissociation of this type do tell us they did not feel any physical pain until their spirit is back in their body.

The other experience commonly resulting in dissociation is through sexual assault. Again personal descriptions of this experience state that the spirit leaves the body and watches the assault from a distance. People who have experienced dissociation during sexual assault rarely have repressed the memory of the assault and are able to describe what happened in detail. However, they do not have any feelings of the experience to describe and often are confused by this lack of feeling. They may assume that the experience is something they were watching happen to another person, not to themselves. Children who have been sexually assaulted often engage in dissociation to protect themselves from further pain and humiliation.

The extreme form of dissociation is called dissociate identity disorder by the American Psychiatric Association.[17] In the past this was known as multiple personality disorder. People with this disorder have two or more distinct identities or personality states, each with their own relatively enduring pattern of perceiving, relating to, and thinking about the environment and self. Individuals with this diagnosis frequently report having experienced severe physical and sexual abuse, especially in

---

17 American Psychiatric Association (1994). Diagnostic and Statistical Manual of Mental Disorders, Fourth Edition, p. 484-487.

childhood. The accuracy of such reports is questioned by the medical community, as they believe these people may be especially vulnerable to suggestive influences. However, the people responsible for the abuse cannot be trusted to report honestly either. Perhaps the absence of the spirit during dissociation allows other spirits access to the body. I don't know if there is any way for research to determine if this is true, especially in a scientific community, which is not even open to the fact that we have a spirit, but I do believe we can eliminate this problem if we care enough to ensure that no child is ever abused in this way again.

Panic anxiety attacks are periods of intense fear or discomfort accompanied by a number of physical and cognitive symptoms. These attacks appear to have a sudden onset and build rapidly, but they actually are created by the build up of anxiety over time. In the same way as "meltdowns" in autism signal the inability of the body to deal with the current level of input, panic anxiety attacks alert us to the fact that this body is no longer able to deal with the amount of anxiety it is experiencing. Such attacks are often accompanied by a sense of imminent danger or impending doom and an urge to flee. Physical symptoms may include palpitations, sweating, trembling, shaking, shortness of breath, chills, hot flushes, numbness, tingling sensations, chest pain or discomfort, nausea or abdominal distress, and dizziness. The cognitive symptoms may include fear of losing control, "going crazy", and/or dying, as well as derealization or depersonalization. People who have experienced panic attacks describe them as intense. They often result in withdrawal from social and community activities as the person worries they may recur in a similar setting.

Panic anxiety attacks usually occur in people who are either dealing with far too much change in their lives at one time or in people who are living completely opposite to their true self, or life line for too long a time. Recognizing and reducing the amount of anxiety in their lives, making changes which will allow one to live on their life line, and allowing oneself to openly grieve what one has lost will likely do far more to eliminate panic anxiety attacks, than medication ever will.

ACUTE VERSUS CHRONIC ANXIETY

There are two different types of anxiety in our lives: acute and chronic. Acute anxiety is "real"; a threat that is actually occurring to the self in the moment. One may not have any control over the change that is occurring in the moment, but acute anxiety is something that has to be dealt with in the real world. Examples of acute anxiety include the death of a family member, the loss of a job, the fact that one does not have the money one needs in the bank account to pay the bills one has accumulated, an actual illness one is dealing with, or an actual disaster such as a typhoon, earthquake or fire.

In direct contrast, chronic anxiety is that which is not real, but dwells in our minds and drains our energy, even if it doesn't exist. Chronic anxiety is reaction to a threat we have created in our imagination. When one is experiencing chronic anxiety, one is focusing on events or situations that may have occurred in the past or have the potential to occur in the future, not what is actually happening in the present moment. One might worry about contacting HIV, having a child abducted, losing one's job, facing a tornado, or getting in an accident instead of focusing on the reality of one's day to day existence. One might spend their energy concentrating on something that happened to them in the past, or to others such as their ancestors, either in fear it will happen again or as an excuse for the present circumstances in their lives. Although there is a possibility that these situations may occur, they are not real in the moment and thus the energy used on them is wasted energy. Chronic anxiety is also that which is created when we determine how others are feeling or reacting through our imagination, rather than asking them directly. When we spend our time and energy in chronic anxiety we eat away at our 'self' in much the same way a metal object is eaten away in an acid bath.

In the past, our ancestors faced life in an acute anxiety mode. The threat to the 'self' was very real, and one had to be continuously on the alert to protect oneself. The self was smaller as one had few possessions and one's social self was limited to the people within the village or clan, but threats to the body were many. Death from disease, wild animals, famine or disaster was common. This continues to be true in some parts of the world, but for most of us, it's something we rarely have to face.

The fascinating thing about human beings is how content we are to dwell in a state of anxiety. As we have moved to the point where we experience less acute anxiety due to the progress we have made making the world a safe place for our bodies, we immerse ourselves more and more in the state of chronic anxiety. Instead of protecting our own bodies, we concentrate our efforts on protecting the possessions we have accumulated. As our social self expands we spend our energy worrying about the impact or the impression that we make on others. And we concentrate on what has happened in the past or what might happen in the future rather than living in the present.

Whole industries now exist, based directly on our level of chronic anxiety, and we as humans are quite willing to fall into their traps. We go without today, in order to secure a future based on the money we have invested in the stock market or other financial activities. We spend our wages on insurance premiums in order to allow us not to have to deal with whatever might happen. It's supposed to make things easier for us but it only makes things worse as we now have to worry if we have the "correct" insurance; if we are "covered" for every and any eventuality that might occur, and of course, if we have enough income to pay for the premiums. All this for something that hasn't occurred and we hope doesn't occur.

The media heightens our concerns daily as it showers us with stories of how bad things are for us. The negative aspects of life are dwelt upon in all the gory detail: accidents, murders, crime, disease and disaster. A single death becomes an "epidemic". An approaching storm advances with minute-by-minute warnings on the weather channel. Newspapers report the dire consequences of the food we eat, the activities we do, or do not, partake in, based on one scientific study after another, only to print a contradictory story the next day. The government gets into the action with warnings of terrorist activity within and without our national boundaries. Alarmists predict the imminent collapse of society as we know it due to global warming, government debt, or a simple a glitch in computer programming.

All of this in the midst of a reality in which man is not in control of the universe, no matter how much he wants to be, claims to be or strives to be. A reality in which death is the inevitable end of life, no matter how well we prepare ourselves for the future or how careful we are to protect ourselves. A reality in which we only have a certain amount of time to live. The minutes fly by no matter what choices we make.

The choices we make do affect the quality of our lives, the joy and happiness we experience, the satisfaction we have when we look back at a life well lived, the love we share with others. These are the things that are important in the long run, which are discovered time and again by those who come face to face with death through disease or disaster. But most of us miss out on them as we allow chronic anxiety to rule our lives.

The direct result of anxiety is a decrease in our ability to live our lives to their full potential. Anxiety results in a decrease in the ability to choose our reactions to any situation, and thus we often get stuck reacting unconsciously with reactions that were learned in early childhood as protective behaviors. There is a decrease in the amount of energy that is available for doing, for growing, for loving, and for rejoicing. There is a decrease in the ability of the body to look after itself. Our immune system falters and we are less able to fend off the viruses and bacteria that may invade our systems.

Anxiety is an inevitable part of life, but our response to it is a choice. Acute anxiety is real and must be faced. Any attempt to cover it up, to avoid it, to deny it, is only going to make things worse. Chronic anxiety is totally unnecessary. It doesn't add anything positive to our lives, but we can fall into the trap of letting it rule our lives. We choose to indulge in chronic anxiety and we choose to live in a society in which fear mongering is a daily reality. We may not be aware of this choice, but it is a definite choice. It is only when we ask ourselves if the fear that is taking over our thoughts is actually real in the present moment or not, and if we want to waste our energy on it or not, that we are able to make a conscious choice whether it rules our lives or not. To be your true 'self' is to face the reality of acute anxiety by bringing it out in the open and to say "no" to the habit of wallowing in chronic anxiety.

THE POWER OF ANXIETY: THE POWER OF CHOICE

My husband and I are driving on the 401 near Toronto. We are looking for a hotel to stay in for the night so that we can fly back to Alberta first thing in the morning. The hotels we have stopped at are charging what we see as exorbitant rates. I have just completed a presentation on autism nearby and have no desire to spend all that I earned on one night in a hotel. It seems like such a waste of my effort. My concern about spending this much money grows more and more severe. In the meantime, my husband is also experiencing anxiety. He hates driving on the 401 as he believes that the worst drivers in the world are here. They follow so closely. He does not want to have an accident in a rental vehicle. The longer we stay on the road looking for a hotel, the more anxious he becomes.

As our anxiety rises, we begin to respond to each other in different ways. He retreats to what I call his "redneck male chauvinism statements" running me down as a woman, while I get more and more cruel and sarcastic. Both of these responses can be traced directly back to our families of origin and are not typical in our interactions with each other. However, as one's level of anxiety increases, the tendency to return to the automatic reactions based directly on actual childhood experience also increases. We both are hurt by the words of the other, but neither of us seems to know how to stop ourselves. Suddenly I remember the work I am doing on anxiety and I ask Clay what is causing him so much anxiety. He tells me about the tailgating he is experiencing and how fearful he is that an accident is about to happen. He doesn't want to drive on this road any longer. Then I share with him my feelings of frustration over the cost of the rooms and the little I will have left from my presentation just because I have to pay for a night's sleep. He acknowledges my feelings and admits that it frustrates him too. But we do have to find somewhere to stay. In the end we compromise by deciding to stay at the next hotel we see, no matter what the room rate is. Our cruel comments to each other have subsided. We are a loving couple again.

In this situation we are dealing with two different types of acute anxiety. The traffic on the highway and the amount of money to be spent are real. They must be faced in one way or another. Bringing the anxiety out into the open didn't stop the reality from occurring. We still had to find a hotel and we still had to pay for a room. Luckily, the next hotel we found was not quite as expensive as those we had already tried, but we still spent more than we had wanted to. However, putting our anxiety out in the open allowed us to move on from the responses of our childhood back to those which were more loving and kind. We didn't have to take the statements we were making to each other as personal. We knew they had far more to do with the anxiety we were feeling than how we actually felt about each other.

This is the true secret of decreasing anxiety. Once it is out in the open, it loses its power. By being openly honest about what is bothering us and how it is affecting us, we can return to a place in which all of the reactions we have learned through our lifetimes are accessible. The higher our level of anxiety, the more limited is our access to the information stored in our neocortex. It's as if there were a whole deck of cards with different reactions available when we are stress free, but as soon as anxiety begins to impact our 'self', the cards begin to disappear. Those that were learned the most recently are the first to go. Those that were learned in early childhood are the last. The higher the level of anxiety, the more limited our responses and the more these responses will mirror those that we learned while we were toddlers.

If you want to know what your own individual responses to high levels of anxiety will be, all you have to do is look closely at your parents, or whoever cared for you when you were a toddler, to figure out how they reacted to stress. You will see that same behavior coming out in yourself. In our home we have an interesting situation in which the behavior of our parents, while stressed, is similar and yet the opposite. My mother's comments become more and more cruel and sarcastic as her anxiety level increases. In direct contrast, my father became silent. In my husband's home, the father was the one who made disparaging comments about women and children, when anxious, while the mother withdrew in silence. At this point in time, both of us are aware that these behaviors in ourselves indicate high anxiety. It's taken a while for us to figure it out, but it sure makes life easier once you understand it.

This information can be used as a double-edged sword. In times of acute anxiety, in situations in which you have absolutely no control, you can forgive yourself for your response and expect that this response will continue until the situation is over. You can also do the same for your loved one, attributing his or her behavior to the level of anxiety instead of taking it as a personal insult. Or, when you are in the midst of using these behaviors, you have the opportunity to recognize that anxiety is occurring by their presence. You can measure the amount of anxiety you are experiencing by your responses, and you can make the effort to bring that anxiety out into the open to defuse it. This is especially powerful in times of chronic anxiety.

We have moved into a new home. There is a clothesline in the back with which I am delighted, as there are certain clothes I wear that have to be hung while drying. After I use it the first time, I discover it is rusty and my clothes are being marked. I choose to use plastic bags between the line and the clothing in order to rectify this situation.

My husband comes out one day as I am hanging out the clothes. He asks what the plastic bags are for and I tell him. He says that he will take down the line right away and we will replace it. I immediately get very angry and loudly tell him, "No, I am hanging out the clothes. I have control of this situation. I do not want you to take down the line." He, in turn, responds in anger and withdraws. Both of us have copied the behaviors we learned from our mothers as children.

While he is gone, I take the time to ponder on the intensity of my anger and my response. It doesn't make any sense at all in the midst of the life we are living. Why should a clothesline mean so much to me that I would get that angry and speak with such a cruel tone to him? I finally come up with an answer. My reaction is based on my past. In my previous marriage, my husband would decide to do things, start the project and then leave it unfinished, often because there was no money to complete it. In those circumstances, he would have removed the current clothesline and never gotten around to replacing it. This had happened to me time and time again over the years. Something that wasn't perfect, but was working for me, would be taken away and never replaced. My anger flared. I was not about to lose this clothesline.

This reaction made absolutely no sense in my present life. If my current husband started something like this, he would complete it. He would take down the clothesline, go directly to a store, buy a new one and install it. That was his way of doing things.

In this situation, it took a while for me to recognize both the anxiety and its source. As it was chronic anxiety, based on situations I had experienced in the past, it made absolutely no sense at all to my husband. He was not anxious himself but he was also not willing to put up with the way I was talking to him. When he returned, I explained and apologized and we smoothed things over. This wouldn't have happened had I not taken the time to bring the chronic anxiety out into the open.

Wallowing in chronic anxiety can become a habit that is difficult to break, especially if you come from a family in which chronic anxiety has been a major force. In these cases, bringing the chronic anxiety out into the open will reduce its power, but if one is in the habit of concentrating on the anxiety, one may need to take further steps to alleviate this pattern of behavior. The secret to reducing one's focus on chronic anxiety is to get into the habit of living in the present moment. This is a major feature of living on one's life line because we can only live in the present. We may want to look at the past in order to understand our reactions in the present. We may want to make some plans for the future in order to achieve a certain goal, but true life is that which is lived in the present moment. Chronic anxiety is not part of that present moment.

I am driving down the highway on my way to an out-of-town job and begin to think about the different things happening in my family that are causing me pain. The longer I do this, the more awful I feel. I am, in that moment, wallowing in chronic anxiety, and actually telling myself I have the right to do this because of what "they" are doing to me. I remember a client I have been working with and how I admonished her to live in the present moment instead of her mind during our last session together. If it was good enough advice to share with her, it should be good enough for me to try myself. I decide to move to the present moment.

But how to do this as I drive on this boring prairie highway? It is far too easy to drive unconsciously, especially with cruise control, and to ignore the monotonous scenery as it goes by. It all looks the same. I decide to concentrate my efforts on watching for hawks sitting on the fence posts or in trees along the highway. The ban on the use of DDT's has allowed the population of these birds to increase, and they are now a common sight along this highway.

As I drove along, watching for the hawks, I discovered how impossible it was to do two things at once. There was no way I could concentrate on the emotional pain I was feeling at the same time that I was looking for the hawks. I found myself stamping my feet on the floor of the car in frustration as I lost the feeling of pain I had conjured up and then realized how ridiculous this was. Everything was in my mind. My family wasn't setting out to hurt me. They weren't present. They weren't doing anything to me, or not doing anything to me. The pain was mine alone, created through chronic anxiety. I could choose to let go of it, or to wallow in it. It was absolutely impossible to stay in the pain if I chose to live in the present moment. I chose to enjoy the beauty of the hawks.

Living in the present is being fully aware of everything your body is taking in through its sensory system in the moment. It's paying attention to the visual details of the world around you, truly enjoying the colours, the textures, the shapes, the beauty. It's listening to the sounds of the world; the songs of the birds, the murmur of the wind, the purring of a cat, the hum of the furnace motor. It's smelling the individual scents. It's taking note of the fabrics against one's skin, the texture of the orange peel, and reaching out for physical contact with others. It takes effort to get into the habit of living in the present moment, but it is the best place to be. It's where we really learn to appreciate the lives we are living, the beauty that surrounds us, the joy of the moment. You cannot reach your potential by focusing on the past or the future. Living on your life line is living right now.

REDUCING ANXIETY THROUGH COPING SKILLS

Anxiety is an inevitable force in our lives. Our 'self' recognizes the destructive force of anxiety and develops a series of coping skills to decrease the anxiety we are experiencing. These coping skills are learned through direct experience from the time we are infants. Many of them are based on our individual bodily needs such as sucking a thumb. Others are based on the copings skills that have been modeled to us by others, especially our parents. Some of our coping skills have a biochemical basis, some are more psychological in nature and others depend on social interactions with other people. All of these coping skills have one goal: reducing the impact of anxiety on the self.

Psychological coping skills are carried out at the level of the mind. These were first described by Sigmund Freud as ego defense mechanisms. Freud's daughter Anna continued the work in this area and developed it further. At this point in time 15 different ego defense mechanisms have been described.

Freud developed a model of self in which two parts of the personality, the id and the super ego were moderated by the third aspect: the ego. He believed that the id was the primitive, unconscious part of the personality. The fundamental drives of life, sexual, physical and emotional pleasure, were stored in the id. Id acted irrationally, being governed by the pleasure principle without any consideration for reality.

The superego was considered the storehouse of an individual's values and moral attitudes. These were learned from society. A child internalized the oughts and should nots from their parents and other adults in society in their superego which then became the conscience of the individual. Within the superego, one also found the ego ideal, which was the view of the kind of person one should strive to be. Thus the id, which strove to do what feels good, operated in direct opposition to the superego, which insisted on doing what was right.

The ego was the reality-based aspect of the self, which arbitrated between the id impulses and the demands of the superego. The job of the ego was to choose actions that would gratify the impulses of id without any undesirable consequences. Freud believed that the ego was governed by the reality principle, which put reasonable choices before the demands of pleasure.

Dr. Freud claimed that ego defense mechanisms are how the extreme desires of id are controlled by the ego. The conflicts created by the impulses of id are dealt with through a variety of different psychological means in order to protect the self from conflicts experienced in the normal course of life. These mechanisms are vital to an individual's adaptation to the conflicting demands of the id and the superego. Freud believed that they are mental processes that allow the self to maintain a generally favorable self-image.

In Freud's terms, anxiety was the intense emotional response to the conflict between the id and the superego. If the defense mechanisms were not working, the conflict would be felt in the consciousness. In order to avoid feeling the conflict and keep the urges under control, other defense mechanisms would come into play. It is important to remember that Freud lived in an era when sexuality and aggression were considered to be the central aspects of personality development. The Victorian Era is one in which these basic drives were considered shameful.

Times have changed. Basic drives are now accepted. However, the ego defense mechanisms that were recognized by Freud and his daughter continue to play a major role in the lives of many people in spite of this acceptance. Why? Because these reactions are not and never were used to cover up the conflict between the id and superego. Instead they are coping skills which are used to block out the discomfort of anxiety from the body.

COPING SKILLS AT THE LEVEL OF THE MIND

Coping skills of the mind which are used to block the feelings of anxiety include: denial of reality, displacement, emotional isolation, fantasy, isolation, projection, rationalization, reaction formation, regression, repression, and undoing. Each of these defenses allows a person not to feel the actual anxiety their body is experiencing. They block out the feelings, in much the same way that people within the autism spectrum use overload of the sensory system to shut down themselves. I believe that most of these reactions are developed in childhood to block out pain of one sort or other. Although many of these defenses are modeled by parents and others, many also are an instinctual response that we are born with to protect the self.

Denial of reality is the practice of protecting oneself from unpleasant reality by the refusal to perceive it, or to admit it is real. This was a major coping skill used by my ex- husband's family. In many situations, denial is the only way the self has to deal with reality, because if one admits the truth, one's self would shatter. During the 24 years of my marriage I was so frustrated by this coping skill as I had no idea at all of what had happened in their past. Whenever my husband, his parents and/or his siblings would deny something that had so obviously happened right there before my eyes, I couldn't figure out what was happening. The last time my mother-in-law visited my home, I finally realized how significant denial was in this family.

In the summer of 1963, my mother-in-law had a nervous breakdown. Her husband had left four years earlier and she struggled in her efforts to raise six children on a limited income, with little help from her family or her community. Because of the nervous breakdown, the children were removed from her home and placed in two Catholic orphanages: one for the girls and one for the boys. They stayed there for four years. The parents were reunited and reclaimed their children. Twenty-two years later all hell broke loose as residents from the orphanage where the boys had been living charged a number of the Christian Brothers who ran the orphanage with sexual abuse. The trial was a featured item on our national and local television news, radios and newspapers for a full year. All of the brothers charged were convicted. During this time, my husband and one of my brothers-in-law admitted to me that they had been sexually abused when they were in the orphanage. The brother-in-law wanted to go to the authorities and report what had happened to him, but his mother talked him out of it.

We were sitting at our dining table one afternoon when another news story broke about the orphanage. I asked my mother-in-law how she felt about it. She stated that the brothers were wonderful men. They had never hurt anyone. Everything in the news had been fabricated by cruel and malicious people who just wanted money.

I stared at her in absolute shock. How she could she be so calm as she made these statements? Didn't she understand how desperately her children had been hurt? And then, in the next instance, I understood that she did know, but if she admitted it had happened, she would have to take responsibility for their presence in the orphanage. She was the one who had the nervous breakdown. She was the mother who had not lived up to her responsibilities. Her children had been damaged beyond belief. She couldn't face the reality of that pain and so she denied it existed. It was the only way her 'self' could remain whole.

Since that point I have come to the realization that there are thousands and thousands of parents out there who are in such a place. Parents who have acted in a certain way who are now dealing with unbearable things that have happened to their children over which they had absolutely no control. As a parent, they did the best with the information they had. Their children, the most precious things in their lives, were hurt. They cannot face that pain, and so they deny it exists. This is especially true in the field of autism where desperation plays such a huge role. The feeling of hopelessness felt by the parents leads to a desperate search for answers. In response, the professional community, with little understanding of the reality of autism, comes up with bizarre and inhumane treatments, which can only be described as torture when you consider the super sensitivity of this group of people. Many parents continue to support these treatments in spite of the fact that they have done nothing for their children. Their children, in fact, denounce them as inhumane. It doesn't make any sense until you look at the emotional pain that is involved. How you can admit making a mistake with something as precious as your own child? Your 'self' cannot deal with that much anxiety. And so you deny.

Denial becomes a habitual response to the discomfort of anxiety at all levels: individual, family, institutional, governmental and societal. The amount of denial going on in our world on a daily basis is staggering and is truly warping the world in which we live. It happens when we shrug our shoulders and say, "Kids will be kids" in response to alcohol and drug induced frenzy. It happens when evidence is not admitted into the courtroom because of a human mistake, which means that criminals do not have to take responsibility for their behavior. It happens when scientific research studies are not published by peer review journals because the evidence is contrary to what is currently accepted, or even worse, will negatively affect the financial picture of a company or government body. It happens when we attack an individual who has had the courage to stand up and say, "This is wrong" instead of joining in and making things right. It happens when we put friendship or financial standing before the safety of children. It happens when we turn our backs or close our eyes to what is happening like ostriches with our heads in the sand because we don't believe we can make a difference.

Denial makes it easy for us not to change all that needs changing. If we do not admit what is real, then we do not have to admit there is a problem. And if it is not a problem, then there is no need to use the energy one needs to make the changes. This is a major fallacy as the energy which would be used for change is actually spent on keeping the truth under wraps. It takes a lot of energy to keep denial going, energy that is forever lost in reaching your one's full potential.

Denial leads to the keeping of family secrets that can go on for generations. These secrets need energy in order to stay as secrets. The energy that family members use to continue the secret is then not available for anything else and this means that everyone in the family exists in a higher level of anxiety at all times. The bigger the secret, the more energy is wasted. Living up to one's full potential means bringing these secrets out into the open so that they do not have any power any longer.

Family secrets affect the self, not only one's own self, but all of the selves in that family. Opening the door to the secret will affect many. This means that anyone who chooses to make the effort to reveal the secret will likely deal with a lot of resistance in many different forms. Each person in the family will resort to using their strongest coping skills in order to keep the secret intact. Friends may also get involved, even if the particular secret has nothing to do with them, but in protection of their own family secrets. The revealing of family secrets is likely one of the biggest changes in the self that we undertake because it involves so many other selves. It is still worth the effort.

It is not necessary to insist that all family members follow your course of action in regards to secrets. I can accept the reality of my husband's past in the midst of interacting with a mother-in-law who is still in the midst of denial. I don't have to try to change her behavior in order to change myself. The impact of admitting this truth on my self is very weak as compared to what will happen to her as she faces the truth. However, having the truth out in the open allows her to gradually move towards accepting it in a way that will not shatter her self in the present. This is okay. We all do the best we can with the knowledge we have in the moment. She had no idea of where she was placing her children. She is not guilty of the crimes of the Christian brothers. Once she comes to that acceptance, she can let go of the secret and forgive herself for her part in this horrendous situation. In the meantime our gift to her is the unconditional love in the midst of understanding her reactions.

The second defense mechanism that is used as a coping skill is called <u>displacement</u>. This is a reaction in which one discharges their pent-up feelings, usually of hostility, on an object less dangerous than those which initially aroused the emotion. A man comes home from work, where he has been insulted by his superiors. He cannot hit back at them and so he takes his feelings out on his wife and his children. This may include anything from insulting them in turn, to actual physical assault on their bodies. In the midst of using displacement as a coping skill, the person will usually come up with reasons to blame the victim for his behavior, claiming that something they did instigated the response. The initial situation is never brought into the story. It's as if it never existed at all. Much of the violence in families can be traced directly to displacement. However displacement need not be as severe as family violence. Displacement occurs every time we focus our negative reactions on someone or something other than the actual anxiety we are facing. My negative comments to my husband and his negative comments to me on the highway near Toronto are as much an example of using displacement as the above example.

<u>Emotional isolation</u> is a defense mechanism in which a person withdraws into passivity to protect the self from being emotionally hurt. If you do not allow yourself to feel anything, nothing will hurt you. A close friend began to use this as a child and continues to use it whenever emotions are too uncomfortable for him to face. He talks about the day this all started. He was about eight years old. The family was sitting around the kitchen table having supper. His father had come home from work in a drunken state, and was following his usual pattern of behavior when drunk, which, if you read the above paragraph, may well have been displacement. He was going around the table, focusing on each person, saying cruel and obnoxious things to them until he made them cry. Only then would he move on to the next person. He didn't appear satisfied until everyone at the table was crying. As my friend watched this happening, knowing full well that his turn was coming, he suddenly realized he didn't have to cry. The response of crying belonged to him alone. In that moment he swore that no matter what his father said or did, he would not cry. He kept this promise that night. His father realized that something had changed in him. He never picked on him in the same way again, but they also never developed a close father/son relationship. Emotional isolation may protect one from emotional pain, but it comes with a huge cost to the social self.

Fantasy is likely the most common defense mechanism we use. It can range from a simple daydream when we are bored, to creating a whole imaginary world where we can escape whenever we cannot deal with our reality. In fantasy we gratify our frustrated desires through imaginary achievements. For many, fantasy can be a trip to a movie where we can forget about our lives as we follow the action on the screen, or perhaps a novel in which we pursue the romance or excitement that we don't find in our real world. Fantasy in this form is not a problem as long as we are aware of what we are doing and if we do not let it take over our whole lives. It becomes a problem when one becomes so saturated by the imaginary world that one misses out completely on the present moment. Scott is one of my friends with autism who used fantasy as a coping skill as a child.

> *I wanted to escape from myself and spent most of my life retreated in an autistic bubble of fantasy inside myself to the extent that I today only have memories of the inside world and fragments of the outside. Why? Very simple, the internal world inside me was completely filtered, totally controllable, and offered no sensory overload of any kind. It was also a very visual action (imagination) of the most incredible detail. The outside world offered me just the opposite; lack of structure, no control and a never-ending series of sensory overloads from varying factors.*[18]

Fantasy was the coping skill I personally used over the years to deal with the pain of feeling left out as a child and as an adult. I would spend my time fantasizing about whatever was coming up on my calendar, interacting with the people in the way I wanted to, with myself as the center of attention. And then, when the event was taking place, there I was, fantasizing about the next event, instead of being in the present moment. There were times I would catch myself doing it, and wonder what on earth was wrong with me. It didn't make sense that next week's bus trip would be so great, if this one was like this, but then I'd slip back into the fantasy world where I was safe, and where I was being entertained. I missed out of a lot of my life in that manner. At this point in time, it's a place I rarely go.

Fantasy is often developed by children to escape the horror of their home life. A friend talks of the Beatrice Potter world she created based on the wallpaper on her bedroom walls. As this woman works on defining her 'self' she has come to the realization that she has very few concrete memories of childhood. When she speaks with her siblings, she is amazed that she cannot remember any of the horror they describe. Where was she? And then she remembers her escape to the world of Beatrice Potter, where her imagination took her to a place of peace, of joy, of serenity. These are the memories she carries to this day. No wonder it was where she preferred to be.

---

18 Scott McGifford, 1999, unpublished manuscript.

The advent of motion pictures, television and computers has created a world in which many of us spend more time in the midst of fantasy than in the present moment. Its lure is clearly indicated by the extravagant salaries paid to those who create the fantasies we live in and the influence we allow the actors and the actresses to have in our lives. Many people know the characters of soap operas much better than they do their next-door neighbours, or even family members. Some hang on to the words of a popular rock star/actress as she describes her parenting skills as if they were coming from the top expert in the world, not someone who has chosen to expose our young people to filth and garbage for years. Others spend most of their time and energy in a world of fantasy games on computers, video machines or in game stores. Dungeons and Dragons became a popular way for teens to escape into fantasy during the 1980's. This has led to the creation of a huge variety of different fantasy games on which one can focus. Many people are so caught up in this world of fantasy games that they spend all of their energy keeping these games going: their time, their money, their physical energy, their social interactions. They have very little life outside the games room. Occasionally the world of reality is able to break through to our consciousness: the Olympics, the Gulf War, the trials of O.J. Simpson and Anita Hill, the horror of 911. But all too soon the novelty is over; we lose interest and prefer to return to our world of fantasy.

A young boy came home from school in the early 1990's and excitedly announced to his mother, "The war is over!" She was perplexed and asked him why he thought the war was over. "We get to watch the Flintstones when we eat our lunch again." No, the war wasn't over. It had just lost our interest.

And now, 15 years later we create "reality shows" in order to pretend we are indeed living in the present moment. It is a lie. We are still in the midst of fantasy. We have chosen to lose ourselves, and lose each other in our search for something to dull our anxiety. In doing so we have managed to create a world in which we are blind to the anxiety we are feeling and the effect it is having on us. This is not to say that movies, novels, games etc. are necessarily a bad thing. However, we must understand how they fit in our individual picture of self, how they are a method of running away from what is real, and how they can keep us from living on our life line. Meaningful life is a life that includes real people to interact with at a personal level in the present moment, not those who are portrayed on a screen before us.

Compartmentalization is the extreme form of emotional isolation. Through this defense mechanism one cuts off one's emotional reactions by placing them into logic-tight compartments in one's mind. Through this coping skill, one is not only isolating themselves from others, or from specific environments, in order to avoid being hurt, but one is also isolating their thought process so that they cannot even be hurt by their own thoughts. One consciously refuses to think about the hurtful situations or put themselves into situations in which they may be reminded of the pain.

In 1993, a movie called *The Boys of St. Vincent* was released in Canada. It was based on the orphanage in which my ex-husband spent four years of his life. At that time, I watched the movie with my ex-husband by my side. I realize now that I must have been at a point of shutdown as I had very little response to what I was seeing, other than recognizing specific behaviors I had experienced in my own home during the 24 years of our marriage. Finally I was able to understand where he had learned these behaviors and how they had developed through a need for protection. They were not an indication that he was a "bad" man. He was a man who had learned to protect himself as a child in the midst of an environment that no child should be subject to. My husband's reaction to the movie was much stronger. He spent a good part of it in the bathroom throwing up blood. During this time, I copied the movie with intentions of watching it again to understand my life further.

I have never been able to do so. As soon as the opening scene comes on the television screen, I am overcome with horror and have to turn it off. This reaction has extended to all movies featuring scenes of family violence or child sexual abuse. Allowing the sensory input of such activity into my brain triggers emotional experiences in my amygdala and brings back all the horrendous memories of my past and his. It's not a place I want to be. In fact, it's not a place I feel I can afford to be. It takes far too much of my psychic energy to deal with it. And so it's shoved back into its little compartment with the lid screwed in place.

This doesn't mean I am able to be in full control of what comes in that might release that lid. Yes I can stay away from the movies, the books, the television talk shows if I choose, but at times, life throws you a curve you don't expect. A couple of times recently I have been staying in a motel with my husband when a fight has broken out between the couple in the next room. As I hear the anger and the terror in their voices, the insults, the crashes and banging of furniture, I am swept back into the anguish of my past. It takes days to come out of it. This is called a flashback. It takes days to come out of it. I am completely drained of energy during that time. Sinking into one's feelings, no matter how horrible they are, allows the body to release the emotions from where they have been stored. This has made things better for me but I continue to react from time to time. Thus the defense of compartmentalization continues to protect me. It may be a necessary component in the life of any adult who has lived through trauma. We must be tender with ourselves and with others who use compartmentalization, especially during the times when they haven't been able to keep the lids on their compartments secure.

Projection is the defense mechanism in which we project our feelings and our difficulties onto another person and then blame them for creating the feelings in ourselves. Projection lets us off the hook for not living up to our full potential. I don't have to take responsibility for the outcomes in my life because "they" or "he" or "she" is to blame. I don't have to take responsibility for my decisions or my actions because "they made me do it". I don't have to take responsibility for my feelings because someone else is causing them. I am the victim. I am blameless. It is a crutch that will hold one back the rest of their life unless it is released.

Projection plays an interesting role in our society. Not only do we use projection to avoid taking responsibility for our own feelings, but we teach our children they have to be careful not to "hurt" someone else's feelings. They have to be careful what they say. They have to be careful what they do. In response we have all reached the point where it is okay to blame others when our feelings are "hurt" and believe there is something wrong with anyone who dares to speak the truth about us. We have moved away from each of us taking responsibility for ourselves to a point where we are expected to ensure that nothing we do or say has a negative impact on another person. We are striving to do the impossible by attempting to take responsibility for all of the feelings of everyone else, instead of focusing on our own. We don't even dare to try to feel our own much less express them.

One day I sat and watched an older native women on television as she described the sexual abuse she had suffered as a child in a residential school. As hard as she tried, she couldn't express herself without tears flowing down her cheeks and her voice growing high and tight with emotion. She kept trying to keep the tears back so the interview could continue. She apologized for crying and explained that she thought she had worked out all the pain and anger so she didn't have to cry any more. The reporter, who was talking to her, obviously was very uncomfortable with the tears. As I watched the interview, I could see that this woman felt she was less of a person because she could not describe her abuse without crying.

But why shouldn't she be allowed to cry? Why shouldn't she have the freedom to express the pain freely, no matter how long it takes? Why do we expect her to sit calmly and describe such horror? What on earth is wrong with us? This person was destroyed as a little child. The tears should be flowing from all of us, for the pain, the humiliation and the loss of self she had endured at the hands of very evil people. Instead we worry about the impact her feelings have on the reporter and all those who will ultimately watch this program who were not hurt as children. We expect those who are in pain to protect us from our response to their pain. This is projection at its worst! Those who have been violated need to be allowed to feel their pain and to know we feel it too

Projection is a problem that is constantly faced by people on the autism spectrum. As very logical and honest people, they are continuously being reprimanded for saying and doing the wrong things because they say exactly what is on their minds in the moment without making any effort to worry about the effect that the truth has on others. The question that begs an answer is "Whose problem is this?" Have we created a world in which we portray a twisted view of ourselves and of others by claiming that human beings are too weak to face their real emotions? How is this going to help us reach our full potential?

A friend of mine is married to a man who has Asperger's Syndrome. As she dealt with weight she had gained through the birth of her three sons, she began to feel her husband was very cruel and was purposely trying to hurt her. Every time she asked him how she looked in an outfit, he would say something like, "Those pants make your hips look wide." She complained to me that she already knew that her hips were wide and that his reminder about her hips was meant to hurt her. Of course, when we look at the impact of sensory input on our reactions, we should expect such pain to occur. The phrase about the hips is a reminder that she is not feeling good about her body, but is this because he is cruel? Is this a message about him, or about her unwillingness to accept herself as she truly is? Is she celebrating her womanhood or caught up in the fallacies about the human body fed to us by the media?

Instead of focusing on trying to fix her husband, we considered how she could respond to this comment other than by feeling hurt. Was it possible he was just answering her question directly as she asked it, without any thought of being cruel? Was it possible he was just telling her the truth, that some pants made her hips look bigger than others? Was it possible he was trying to protect her because he knew she was upset by the size of her hips, by pointing out the pants that made the situation worse? By looking at his responses in this way, she was able to move to using the information to create a wardrobe that effectively hid the size of her hips, rather than wallowing in the pain of the picture of cruelty she had created in her mind as chronic anxiety. Instead of blaming him for her feelings, she began to take responsibility for her own. This is the step we all need to take.

Projection is a major problem in situations where secrecy is paramount. If one cannot admit the secret, then one must have another reason for feeling as one does. Since secrecy ruled my first marriage, projection became the defense mechanism my husband used to make sense of the feelings of rage that consume his body at all times. Every time he got angry, it was my fault. I was the troublemaker. I was the slut, throwing myself at other men, so that he couldn't control his jealousy. I was the one who was never satisfied with anything he did. Of course, I was none of those things, though I certainly was willing to take on the role in order to maintain peace and keep our family together.

Projection in long-term relationships requires cooperation from the person who is being projected upon. This partner must be willing to take the blame and play the role or the relationship will not survive. The tears flowed down my face as I knelt on the floor, cleaning up the broken shards of glass from the television set he had just smashed. The linoleum was new, installed the previous week. And now, it was already slashed in places. As I worked I was overwhelmed with the sense of "I don't even deserve a floor that looks new for more than a week." This type of thinking became my pattern of reaction after every major blowup.

Twenty years after our marriage I was traveling with my two younger sons. We were coming home from my oldest son's wedding. My husband had returned home right after the wedding, leaving us to take a short vacation together before school started. After driving for hours we came upon a mall where a carnival was set up in the parking lot. Needing a break from the car, we decided to stop, and the boys rushed off to enjoy the rides. I chose instead to go into the mall where an antique show and sale was taking place. As I browsed through the merchandise, I came upon a teapot that matched my china pattern. I was shocked to see that the price on the teapot was $350.00, ten times more than I had paid for an identical teapot during the early 1970's. When the boys came into the mall, I showed them the teapot and told them how much I had paid for mine.

Once we were back on the road the topic of the teapot was resumed with a question from one of the boys. "What happened to your teapot?"

"It was smashed along with everything else when your father destroyed the kitchen in Manitoba," I calmly replied.

"Oh." A pause, and then another question. "Why was he so angry that day?"

My answer was spontaneous. "Because I....." and then I came to a sudden stop. Because I what? I hadn't done anything to cause his rage that day. Of course, he did try to blame it on me. I have no memory of how I responded at the time, but now, a number of years later I was fully aware that I had done nothing. And for the first time I realized how convoluted our lives had become. His rage, a product of the sexual assault of the Christian brothers, dominated our home. Keeping his anger in check took most of our energy. His secret, which could not be safely revealed, meant he had to project his feelings elsewhere. I became the target. My feelings of worthlessness, built up through the years because of my shyness and my earlier relationships with Mr. J and Mrs. S, allowed me to accept the blame. His fantasies created situations in which I was a troublemaker, a slut, or unsatisfied. I had spent the last 20 years taking blame for something that wasn't real, for situations he was creating in his imagination. It was an impossible situation. There was no way I could make things better, no matter how hard I tried, because none of it was real.

I came back from that trip a different person. No longer was I willing to take the blame for his anger, no matter what. In the weeks that followed, our relationship deteriorated to the point of no return. He needed someone on whom to project his feelings. I was no longer willing to be that person. No longer was I safe in his presence. In the months that followed he finally revealed the secret of the abuse and spent hours recounting the horrors that had happened to him. It wasn't a good situation for either of us but it was how we coped. In some ways things were better, because the anxiety was now out in the open, but reliving the past was not a worthy journey for him nor for me. And in the midst of this, I became a bigger threat, because I now knew the secret. Could he trust me?

As you can see from this example, projection can and does work both ways. A person who is feeling worthless, or willing to take the blame for anything that happens, may get into the habit of defining any situation or any comment from another person as their fault, no matter what is going on. A person who uses this type of projection may take the simplest comment or action made by another; turn it into a negative thought and then determine that this person doesn't "like" them or "thinks" they aren't any good based on that thought and react accordingly. Many times the comment or action has nothing at all to do with the original person, but the habit of taking things personally controls their life. Although I originally began this pattern by accepting the blame when my husband accused me directly, I went on to develop a habit of taking the blame on myself in all sorts of situations having nothing to do with me. People who project non-existent feelings on themselves are as difficult to have a relationship with as are those who blame you for their feelings. You have to be so careful of what you say or do, for they will take it personally and react negatively, no matter what is really going on.

In Freud's terms projection was the process in which what is internal is projected out onto that which is external. For example. rather than recognizing hostility in oneself, one sees others as hostile. Again this is a process that can go both ways. During the time I was married to my first husband, he projected his feelings of lack of trust on me, claiming that I was constantly cheating on him and acting like a slut. In direct contrast, throughout our marriage I projected my feelings of trust on him, based directly on my own beliefs, feelings and behavior. It was only after I left the marriage that people shared his infidelity with me and I became aware that his lack of trust was based directly on the fact that he was not trustworthy.

This is one of the reasons we need to make the effort to understand ourselves and our reactions as an individual person, rather than measuring how we respond by some type of acceptable societal picture. A man is cheating on his wife. She remains oblivious to this situation for a number of years. When it finally comes to light through one way or another, she is devastated. No one can understand how she could have missed the obvious clues he was leaving. The guilt and the shame may be overwhelming. But if she is a person who does not triangulate, who does not even consider cheating on her husband herself, there would be no reason to be looking at their life through anything but her own reactions. We live in our individual bodies. We measure other people by our individual responses, not by theirs, nor by those of society. Our minds are constructed through our personal experience and our minds do the job they were constructed to do. It takes a lot of work to realize just who we are so that we can step out of ourselves and measure another. Most of us don't do it. How we measure others says far more about ourselves than it does about anyone else.

Rationalization is the defense mechanism in which one attempts to prove that one's behavior is rational and justifiable no matter what one does. This is an area that is rather gray when it comes to the world of psychology, because what is clear and rational to one person may not make any sense at to another. What's more, the professionals in the field of psychology have a tendency at times to act as if they "own" the definition of rational, so one may claim that his arguments about the problems of his client are clear according to his rational way of thinking, based on his own experiences and in direct contrast use the "rationalization" of his or the patient as the basis of negative thinking or as a criteria for a diagnosis. I run into this situation time and again in the field of autism, in which my friends have been diagnosed as schizophrenic, based on their answer to a very simple question.

The psychiatrist/psychologist asks: "Do you hear voices?" The person with autism listens for a moment and replies, "Yes," an answer based directly on the fact that their hearing is so acute that they are hearing real voices from other rooms in the building.

The professional may diagnose schizophrenia from that simple statement, as he, with his "typical" level of hearing, cannot hear the voices. However, some may go on to ask another question such as, "Are these voices telling you what to do?" The person with autism listens again, and if the voices are actually telling someone what to do, which is as common as not, the person will again answer "Yes." The diagnosis is thus confirmed, based on the rational thought of the professional, not on the actual reality of the person with autism and of the world around him. Medications are prescribed, which do more harm than good if you do not have schizophrenia, and far too many of my friends begin a downward spiral from which it is very difficult to pull out of, due mainly to resistance from the psychological community.

As you may understand, rationalization has a huge impact on what we are talking about throughout this book. The automatic reactions we all develop throughout our lives make sense when one considers what has actually happened to us. However, to a person who has experienced the opposite type of lifestyle these rational responses make no sense at all. At one time I was involved in a situation in which a group of parents were very concerned about what was going on in our local school. Petitions were drawn up and signatures were collected. Meetings were called. The school board was challenged.

At that time our best friends in the community were a couple who had escaped from Hungary in 1956, as the Russian troops moved in. They absolutely refused to have anything at all to do with our group. Although they claimed to support our actions, they would not put their names down on the petitions. To the majority of our group, who had only known life in Canada and the United States, their behavior made no sense at all. However, the past of our friends from Hungary had taught them otherwise. We had to respect their reaction.

Rationalization as a defense mechanism is used to justify one's behavior or wishes, based on a rational argument rather than on what is actually happening. A young divorced mother does not want her son to have any contact with his father. The courts have ordered weekly visits. The mother devises a schedule for the child making any visit almost impossible. She uses her concerns about the child's health, his need for a regular pattern of sleep, and the amount of time required for the child to calm down after returning from the visit as an explanation for this schedule. Due to the inflexibility of the schedule, the father throws up his hands and gives up on trying to visit regularly. The mother has accomplished what she wanted. The son no longer sees his father.

Rationalization when used as a defense is very frustrating for people who are trying to intervene in any way. Since the argument appears to be rational, anyone questioning the motives or behavior of the person is suspect. Trying to prove the argument to be irrational may be futile, as the definition of "rational" is firmly built on the individual's experience in the past. A man was raised in an alcoholic home where loud voices and strong emotions led directly to fear and pain. He marries a woman who was raised in a very different environment. In her family, loud voices and high emotions were accepted as a common way of interacting with each other. When she gets loud, he gets scared. He withdraws into silence, which for her is like a death sentence, as she feels he is removing his image from her social self. He becomes more silent and withdrawn on the assumption that this will allow her to calm down. Once she is calm he is prepared to return to interacting. But it doesn't happen. The longer he is silent, the more upset she becomes. The cycle spirals out of control.

Each of these people is acting rationally according to their individual upbringing. Trying to convince either of them that the other is rational is not ever going to work. The only way peace will be achieved is if each of them begins to recognize that their own reaction is directly based on their individual upbringing and makes complete sense when one looks at it through actual experience. Developing one's own sense of self means one can also consider the model of self of another person and figure out what reactions are going to happen if a certain stimulus occurs based on that person's upbringing. Then we can stop taking the reaction personally as it has very little to do with the present situation. The man can learn to accept that the woman will become distressed when treated with silence. The woman can expect that a loud voice and high level of emotion will result in silence from the husband. Although they may never reach a point where these two reactions will not take place, they can choose their next reaction based on this knowledge. The cycle can be arrested at the beginning rather than having it spiral out of control.

Rationalization is another coping skill that is used at a societal level as well as at an individual level. Any decision that is made by a group can be rationalized in one way or another. If one is proved wrong, other rationalizations are brought in to decrease the level of discomfort. The current war in Iraq is a clear example. Certain governments chose to believe the information that Saddam Hussein had weapons of mass destruction hidden in Iraq. Other countries chose not to partake because they did not believe the information shared was sufficient to prove there were such weapons. Each rationalized their own reactions in their own ways. Now that these weapons have failed to appear, the British and American governments have chosen to rationalize their presence in Iraq was necessary for other reasons. The patterns of behavior go on.

Repression is the defense mechanism in which painful and dangerous memories are pushed out of consciousness. The person is no longer consciously aware of the memories and will tell you they never experienced anything like this. This is in direct contrast to compartmentalization in which the memories are stored in a conscious level and the person is fully aware they had the negative experience in the past.

Repression is the defense mechanism that is used when the 'self' is not strong enough to face the reality of what has actually happened to it. Memories that are repressed are extremely traumatic to the individual. Examples include watching the death of another person or being sexually assaulted as a young child. Memories may be completely gone, or portions of them may remain with the most traumatic moments missing.

As a young child in grade two I have a very vivid memory. I am sitting in my desk in our one room schoolhouse, watching my teacher beat her daughter with a yardstick. Horrible feelings of guilt, combined with a deep sense of gratitude, flow through me as I watch. I still clearly remember the thought flooding my brain.

"I'm so glad that Barbara is here this year, so it isn't happening to me."

As an adult, I can look back and realize that our grade 1 and 2 teacher was a very troubled woman who took her frustrations from home out on all of us. Living with an alcoholic husband who would disappear for months at a time must have been extremely stressful for her. We, in the classroom, experienced that stress on a daily basis.

As I look back, I have various memories of those years, but cannot at any time offer a complete picture of my life in grades one and two. Instead, there are only fragments. I find it interesting that I have no actual memory of the woman beating me. And yet, if she didn't, why would I have this other memory?

This also happens with my memories of my relationship with Mr. J. As a very young child (preschool, I believe), he would approach me and say things to me that distressed me very much. I didn't understand these things he was saying, but I did know they were wrong, and I knew I had to protect myself from him. His approaches continued on throughout the years and I developed strong patterns of behavior to counteract them, which still affect me to this day. I find it especially fascinating that I realized at such an early age that I was dealing with a dirty old man and that I needed to protect myself from him, especially when I heard he was arrested years later for sexually fondling young girls at the schoolyard in his own community.

However, when I go back into my memory, there is absolutely no way I can remember the details of what the man said or did that upset me so. I remember what he looked like. I remember his crippled wife. I remember the many comments I heard about how good he was at caring for her. I distinctly remember the feelings of fear, disgust and the need for caution. But I don't remember at all exactly what he said, except for one occasion when I was in junior high school and he approached me at a track meet and told me that he had been dreaming about me. This can hardly be considered a criminal statement. As a legal witness, I would be at a total loss and yet I am sure his behavior was the same towards me as it had been to the other young girls. However, my response was different. I didn't accept his gifts, go off with him alone, or allow him to touch me. Instead I fled and in fleeing I erased the memory of what I was fleeing from.

"False memory syndrome" came to the forefront in the 1980's and 1990's as many people who were in therapy began to "remember" incidents of abuse as children. Many of these "memories" resulted in charges against the people who were involved. These people, in turn, denied that the situation had ever happened. In some cases, the memories were recanted by the people who claimed to have "remembered". They stated that their therapist had led them to create the memory through suggestions that abuse had occurred. This led to a lot of confusion in the area of repressed memories.

In your search for self, it is very important that you take false memory syndrome seriously. It is possible to create false memories through your imagination. Take all suggestions and advice cautiously. Examine everything closely. Admit that there may be things you do not remember or understand and that this is okay. Forcing yourself to "remember" may lead to the creation of memories of a past that did not happen.

Be aware that remembering actual details from the past is not what is important in the search of self. Coming to a clear understanding of your reactions does not mean you have to relive the past in any way at all. The important factor is to understand that the current reaction you are using may be in response to something from the past rather than the present moment. Figuring out if you are responding to the past (chronic anxiety) or the present moment (acute anxiety) is your job. Then you can decide whether you want to continue with this reaction or replace it with something more effective. I know that my response of withdrawal in crowded community and church environments is based directly on my past experience with Mr. J. When I find myself using this reaction I have to ask myself just what I am withdrawing from so I can decide whether I want to continue doing it or not. Sometimes it is the past, and I can make the effort to interact with others in a different way. At other times, it is in response to something in the present moment such as my recent reaction to a specific used car salesman recently who kept touching me as he tried to make his sale. Then I can continue to withdraw in order to protect myself without any feelings of guilt or shame.

Professionals who push people to deal with the trauma of their past before they are ready may do more damage than good, as the self may not yet be ready to deal with these issues. Repression of memory happens for a reason. The self must be protected from these memories in order to survive as a whole. Digging into the past without regard for this reality may either create more trauma for the individual or a situation in which false memory syndrome may come into effect as the self continues to protect itself from what truly happened. This doesn't mean that the original trauma is necessarily worse than what can come up through false memory syndrome, but that the self, unable to cope with whatever happened when he/she was young, continues to need the protection. Fiction, of any kind, is easier to deal with. False memory syndrome leads to new beliefs about oneself that do absolutely no good on this journey as they are as false as the memories on which they are based.

This happened to one of my clients. After the birth of her daughter, she began to partake in extreme behaviors that made absolutely no sense to her. She went to a psychologist who diagnosed her with post partum depression. Time passed. Medication was administered. The behaviors continued. The psychologist suggested that this woman had been sexually abused by her father. The woman had a hard time believing this could be true, but nothing else made sense to her. As both her parents were deceased, she had no one to confirm or deny the suggestion. The woman tried to remember what had occurred between her and her father with the help of the therapist.

After a while the woman moved to the city where I was working. The behaviors continued and her husband insisted she find another therapist. Somehow, she ended up with me. When they came into the therapy room, they claimed that they needed to deal with the incest by her father. By this time she was convinced it had happened in spite of the fact that she could not remember it.

As I listened to her story, I was struck by the difference in the behavioral patterns of each of her parents as she described them. I tentatively asked a question: "Do you feel that you are going to hurt your little girl in some way?" The woman started trembling and turned white. These words released something in her body. We didn't know what it was at the time, but there was definitely a physical change in that moment.

Over the years that we worked together, this woman discovered she had indeed experienced sexual abuse when she was very young, but that it happened at the hands of a maternal uncle, not her father, and that her mother was aware of what had happened. The memories returned to her through regression. This was a multi-generational pattern of behavior that had been transmitted through her mother's family for generations. Bringing it out into the open has allowed the young woman to ensure that the pattern is broken and that her daughter is safe.

Repressed memories are released through two different experiences. A person may reach the point of not having enough energy to keep holding them in. This typically happens as a person nears middle age and may involve regression, which will be discussed in the following paragraphs. A person may also experience sensory input that matches what has happened in the past, which then triggers the breakthrough from the unconscious to the conscious memory. This is common with children who have witnessed murder and repressed it as we saw in the case study at the end of chapter one.

Regression is the defense mechanism in which one retreats to an earlier developmental level involving more childish responses and usually a lower level of aspiration. In many ways most people have a tendency to regress back into behavior patterns that worked well for them when they were living at home when they visit their parents. These adult children then accuse their parents of treating them like children. What they don't understand is that their unconscious reactions to certain stimuli are triggered by their presence in an environment of the past. Once they recognize that they are in charge of their own reactions and make a conscious choice to react differently these behaviors can be controlled. However, as long as one blames someone else for their personal reaction, nothing will change.

It is important to realize that the level of anxiety one is dealing with will affect the level of regression one experiences. Times of high anxiety will result in a tendency to react in the automatic ways we learned as very young children. This does not mean that we will stay there, or that we have a problem. It only means that the level of anxiety is HIGH. Reducing the level of anxiety will allow us to return to a state in which we have more options in our reactions.

This is one mistake that is constantly being made in the field of autism. Many treatment programs are based on reducing what are called inappropriate behaviors without any understanding of the role these behaviors play in the lives of people with autism. During periods when things are calm, the behaviors may decrease and at times may even appear to have been eliminated. Positive reinforcement for the reduction of certain behaviors may appear to be successful as the person with autism develops other coping skills to deal with the anxiety level they are currently at. During times of low anxiety, this is possible. The person with autism may develop a number of different and apparently "more appropriate" ways of reacting and interacting. However, high anxiety will limit these choices and it may appear that the child or adult has "regressed" back to his old behaviors. This typically happens during puberty, a time when the growth that is occurring in the body and the brain causes everyone high anxiety. For those within the autism spectrum, who experience life at an extreme, puberty is much more difficult than it is for more typical young people. As these teenagers resort to using coping skills and calming behaviors from their early childhood, the assumption is made that they have "regressed" and that everything that has been taught over the years is lost. It has all been a waste of effort! But this is not true. When the anxiety decreases, the other reactions will be accessible. However, this misunderstanding by parents and professionals does little to decrease the level of anxiety.

A more serious form of regression happens when the body no longer has the energy to continue to hold repressed memories in the unconscious. As these memories slip back into the conscious area of the brain, the person regresses back into their childhood where the trauma first occurred. They will react at whatever age they were when the abuse occurred. Voices will become higher. Vocabulary will be limited to that of a small child. Facial expressions and body movements will be childlike. The person's body appears to change physically to the point that it may be hard to recognize them. Their behavior may not make any sense in the current moment as they relive the trauma that happened to them in the past. They are not consciously aware of the present, or of what is happening to them. They will respond to anyone who is interacting with them as if that person is part of the past. After a regression of this type has taken place, the person may have regained the experience or parts of the experience in their conscious memory. Regressions of this type, as long as they are not pushed, release only as much information at a time as the self can safely handle. Be cautious of any treatment modality that would push someone to remember. The memories are hidden to protect.

The above are only a short list of examples of the defense mechanisms that we as human beings engage in to decrease the impact of anxiety on our mind. They are the most common ones I have come in contact with. The human mind is incredibly flexible and can come up with many more so you personally may use others that are not documented here. Hopefully these examples will give you an idea of what is possible so that you can begin to recognize the coping skills you are using. Only then can you make a conscious choice of whether you want to continue using them or replace them with something else, or even better, bring the anxiety out into the open so that you don't have to rely on coping skills.

The truth of the matter is that it often feels far more comfortable to use coping skills to deaden one's response to anxiety than it does to face acute anxiety head on, out in the open, or to make the effort to reduce one's dependence on chronic anxiety. This is because it has become part of the 'self' on the level of the mind. This level can be changed, of course, but it is resistant to change because change is uncomfortable. It is also difficult to change because it is the level which is closest to the spirit. Coping skills become defined as needs that have to be filled: "I need a shot of cocaine," "I need a to play solitaire on the computer," "I need to deny." There is no "need." There is no illness as is suggested in the medical community. There is no "addiction". There is a habitual reaction which has solidified **its** place in the level of your mind. It is only your own personal method of reducing discomfort to **a** manageable level.

This doesn't mean the body adjusts easily to existing without the particular chemical (nicotine, alcohol, high level of endorphins, etc.) or behavior on which it has become dependent. There will be a physical reaction that makes one feel even more discomfort when this chemical is low or no longer in the system. The urge to replace the chemical becomes almost impossible to resist. It also doesn't mean that some of the withdrawal reactions won't become as bad as or worse than the anxiety they were dispelling in the first place. The threat of their absence becomes as anxiety provoking as anything else one has ever faced. It doesn't mean the discomfort for the chemical release one is experiencing isn't very real in the present moment. It just means that the self, as such, does not actually need require the chemicals or other coping skills to exist. In fact, the true self would be realized to a greater degree if these coping skills were not being utilized.

PUTTING IT INTO PRACTICE

The mind is the storehouse of our past. In it we find everything that has happened to us throughout our journey on this earth. It is the source of our reactions to everything that happens to us. These reactions determine who we are as a person, both on the inside and on the outside. When we are working at the level of the mind, we are more concerned about what is happening within, but if we change anything at the level of the mind we will also experience an impact on the social and material levels of self.

Step one in the journey to self at the mind level is to figure out your own individual responses to heightened levels of anxiety. You will have different responses for different situations. You need to know all of them. This is done by stepping back and watching yourself as you react to all of the different varieties of stress you experience. Do you shut down and cut yourself off from the world?

Do you automatically reach for a biochemical release through food, alcohol, cigarettes, or drugs? Do you build up your level of endorphins through exercise or repetitive behaviors? Do you focus on helping others? Do you go shopping? Do you triangulate someone else into the situation? Do you become quieter, or louder? Do you become apologetic or sarcastic? Do you retreat into fantasy? Do you attack others, either verbally or physically? Do you run away? Your reactions will be unique for you as an individual. There will be different reactions for the levels of intensity of anxiety. As you begin to recognize your responses you can begin to note what specific events or feelings trigger each response, and what level each response represents.

If you do not feel you can do this on your own, you can incorporate others into your search for yourself. You might want to ask close friends or family members how they see your behavior when you are stressed. You might want to go to a therapist and work this through. You might want to join a group who are dealing with the same types of stress as you so that you can see how others are reacting differently and thus reveal how you react yourself. You will want to look closely at your family, especially your parents, or those people who cared for you on a daily basis when you were a very young child. Through them you will find your strongest responses to stress: those that appear automatically when you are totally overwhelmed.

Once you have figured out your responses, the next step is to bring the anxiety out into the open as soon as you feel the response occurring. If you are the type of person who uses food as a coping skill and you find yourself heading to the fridge and reaching for the ice cream, you must stop and figure out exactly why you were feeling stressed before you headed towards the kitchen. You must consider exactly what is going on in the moment that has brought you to this point. This isn't something that is going to happen automatically. It is something one must develop as a new pattern of behavior. At first, **you** may well have finished the ice cream before it even occurs to you to consider your action as a sign of anxiety. You may have spewed out all of your frustration with a coworker to a friend long before you realize that you are triangulating again. This is okay. It is part of the learning process. It is part of the journey to self. You cannot expect perfection. As you learn the new responses, the automatic responses will change, your dependence on the old behavior will decrease, but you must be kind to yourself. If you aren't, you may place barriers in your way that will make the journey more difficult. Be patient. Be loving. Be kind to yourself. The process cannot be stopped completely. Change is inevitable. Your spirit will not give up.

Once the anxiety is in the open, you must decide what you are going to do with it. A major step is determining whether the stress you are experiencing is chronic or acute. As we have learned, acute anxiety is that which is real in the present moment. My bills need paying. My child is sick. I have been fired. I don't have any food in the cupboard. I am grieving the death of my father. These are all situations that need a specific answer in the moment. These situations have to be dealt with in some way or another. Using a coping skill is not usually a very effective way of dealing with them and may often make the problem more severe over time but it is a typical response, especially if the solution to the problem leads to change of self. Putting the problem out in the open, in front of everyone in your life, is more effective than resorting to coping skills. This may not make the problem go away, but will give you the opportunity to develop a concrete plan of action. It may provide you with more time to work out a resolution to your dilemma. It may provide you with solutions you haven't considered trying or options you weren't aware of that are shared by those to whom you have shared your problem. It may provide someone else the opportunity to give to you. It is true that it is more blessed to give than receive and that most of us feel more comfortable in the role of the giver. However, no one can be blessed through giving if there are not those who are willing to receive. We all must receive at some point or other.

One of the fallacies we may have been taught is that we must be strong, silent and indomitable in order to be a success in life. This fallacy is based on the theories of individualism, theories that claim that each of us is an entity to itself. Theories that claim we can succeed all by ourselves. Theories that suggest we are weak and pitiful if we do not succeed. The American Dream is based directly on this fallacy. It leads directly to a sense of shame and failure during times of acute anxiety which, in turn, leads to a heightened level of anxiety. It appears that using a coping skill such as denial to deal with the acute anxiety is more effective than being honest about what is happening to us because it allows us to evade the feelings of shame and failure we would face if we disclosed the truth. Life doesn't work well that way. Yes, coping skills can and will deaden feelings for a time and perhaps allow us to avoid facing the consequences of our situation in the short term, but the reality is that we are then faced with even higher levels of acute anxiety in the long term. We just don't have enough energy for all of that.

The fallacy that we should be able to do it all ourselves is based directly on the premise that we start off as equals and have an equal chance to survive and to succeed. The recent knowledge of how our brains are constructed through experience negates this premise. It might be an acceptable assumption if every one of our children were exposed to the 'best' mankind can offer from the day of conception, but we know that isn't happening. It isn't happening much of the time because of those who have the power and control and refuse to share anything with others, as much as failure on the part of those who go without. But as long as we hang on to this premise we can feel free to point our fingers at others and mock them for their efforts rather than taking the responsibility of reaching out a helping hand in the midst of their struggle. In doing so, we close ourselves to the reality of their spiritual journey, which in turn makes us deny our own. The whole world suffers the consequences.

So, putting your acute anxiety out into the open and then dealing with it is the only effective way to solve your problems. It will take time and effort to get into the habit of doing this, but once you do, life becomes so much easier. The energy you were using to cover up the truth and to employ the coping skill of choice is now available to face the present moment. Your spirit can guide you, if you listen. Life becomes so much easier.

The other type of anxiety you may be dealing with is chronic anxiety. This anxiety is that which is not happening in the present moment but is happening in our minds due to past experience or worries about the future. Much of this chronic anxiety comes directly through reminders of traumatic incidents that happened to us in the past. Many of these memories are locked in our unconscious but we still respond to the stimulus automatically with the protective patterns of behavior we developed as children. My tendency to sabotage myself after I had told someone what I wanted, and the discomfort I felt when I had my back to the door during public gatherings are two examples of behaviors that I used automatically throughout the years without any conscious idea of why I was responding as I was. I had to take the time to explore my past to discover the source of the anxiety. Once I realized that these behaviors were direct responses to my grade one and two teacher and the dirty old man, I could let them go. This did not happen overnight. The discomfort I felt when these feelings from the past were triggered was hard to ignore. I had to allow myself to feel uncomfortable in order to learn new responses. This took years.

In the midst of this, one can decide whether wants to dwell on the pain of the past in the present moment or not. One can decide whether one wants to continue to react with the protective measures developed in the past, in the present moment. We do have freedom of choice when it comes to these responses. The dirty old man of my past is dead and buried. I can continue to choose to stand facing the door in public situations and guard myself from his presence or not. If I do, I will be living in a state of chronic anxiety, based directly on past experience. If I do, I will be using my energy to protect myself, not to enjoy the present moment interacting with others. If I do, I will be handing control of my life over to him. That is the choice. At this point in time I usually choose to tell myself that he is dead and gone, and move about the room easily, without any reaction from the past. However, on those days in which I am at a high level of acute anxiety, for any other reason, I choose to face the door. It's easier that way, and it's okay, because it is who I am.

One of the saddest fears many display in our current times is a fear of appearing weak. Many people believe that revealing an aspect of the experience of anxiety indicates that one can be considered a "lesser being" in our society. In order to protect what we assume to be our level of self-esteem, we put on the big act. Secrets are kept, chemicals are ingested, relationships are strained, all in the need to appear strong and independent. The self suffers in so many different ways: physically, mentally, emotionally, spiritually and socially.

The lack of understanding about the force of anxiety in our lives, the impact of constant change on the self, and the importance of coping skills to deal with discomfort have led to a situation in which only certain levels of response have become acceptable. A situation in which people are considered either normal or abnormal based on their responses. A situation where coping skills are labeled as inappropriate behaviors or mental illnesses. A situation in which we are divided into a hierarchy of functioning: those who are successful in covering up their pain and discomfort in ways that the rest of us feel comfortable with and those who are not. A situation in which the former group either takes responsibility for looking after the latter, or looks down on them because of their failure to conform.

This occurs in the midst of not working with a level playing field. The actual experience of a child during the first six years of life is crucial in giving that child the foundation of self that they will have to deal with for the rest of their lives. The actual experiences of each person as they travel this journey will create the level of responses one needs. One's actual experiences will allow for the development of whatever reactions one chooses. It's all based on one's actual experience, experience that happens without choice, without planning. Experience, through which one has very little control and yet creates the self that one becomes. The labeling of those who are considered lesser, allows us to assume that there are people who are normal, and who are freely living their lives without help, in the midst of others who so desperately need to be corrected. It's not that simple.

My father was a smoker. He smoked throughout all of my childhood, my teen years and most of my adult years. I could have followed in his pattern had I so chosen, but I didn't and there is a reason for that. We lived in a two-story farmhouse. The top story of the house contained the children's bedrooms. One night as I lay in bed with my sister, we heard a strange noise. It sounded like a monster coming up the stairway. The slow careful steps were combined with a horrendous rasping noise as the monster struggled for breath. We clung to each other in fear, hidden completely under the quilt. The monster drew closer and closer and suddenly appeared in the doorway of our bedroom. It was our father, who rarely had any reason to come up those stairs, and who could not breathe normally when he did so, because of the damage the smoking had done to his lungs. I never forgot the sound of that night. I never wanted that for myself and I was fully cognizant that his noisy breathing was a direct result of smoking. And so I never had the inclination to try it. My brother chose the opposite. He started smoking as a teenager. He may have slept through our experience. He may have perceived my father's behavior as something to emulate. I don't know and it's not my responsibility to figure it out. That's his journey, but I do know that smoking was not defined as a negative experience for him until he tried to quit as an adult.

I come from a family of teetotalers. I don't know why my paternal grandparents were so against alcohol, but they were. In fact they were so set against it that they refused to grow malt barely because they didn't want to make a living on someone else's pain. That's quite a stand to take! One that I am pretty sure I may do differently, if I were ever faced with that choice. Their beliefs meant that I grew up in a home in which I was not exposed to family members who were using alcohol as their coping skill. It meant that my father didn't have an alcoholic drink until he was in his sixties. The experience from my maternal side of the family is different. I have no idea who the drinkers were or how much any of them drank before I was born, but I do know it was part of their experience.

However, it came to a swift end through the accidental death of one of my cousins. Again, my life was free of those who used alcohol as a coping skill. I wasn't in control of any of this, but I am who I am because it happened.

This doesn't mean that I didn't develop coping skills of my own. It doesn't mean that my coping skills were any better or worse than those that are used by anyone else. They are the ones that fit me in my individual body, in the midst of my individual experience. The same goes for you. It also doesn't mean that my skills were better or worse than anyone else's when it comes to the breakdown of the physical body. The use of all types of coping skills is destructive over time. And that's why it is so important for each of us to figure exactly what coping skills we are using, what we are using them for, and how we can stop relying on them. Life should be lived, should be celebrated, should be experienced fully without the need to deaden the pain and discomfort.

I came from a family where I was safe. Completely and totally safe. The negative influences that affected my development came from the community: the dirty old man in the church and the abusive grade one and two teacher. At home I never experienced abuse in any form, neglect in any way, any reason to fear. This isn't true for many and I am so thankful I have had the opportunity to live the life as a child that I did. My early life included examples of hard work, of conscientious effort, of strong morals, of community involvement, of respect for our fellow men, of love and unconditional acceptance. It was a gift. An incredible gift. So what right do I have to look down on anyone else, especially those who experienced the opposite as children? What right do I have to place myself above anyone because I don't need to use as an extreme level of coping skills. I don't have the same pain to deal with. I don't have the same discomfort. I don't have the same fear.

The journey of self is a solitary, individual journey in which one must come to a realization of who one actually is, and how one has become this person. Understanding the power of anxiety in one's life and the recognition of one's own individual coping skills is an important step in that journey. Only then can you make the effort to change and to succeed. This understanding and recognition can then take you to the next level of the self: the social self, a place where we meet our fellow men head on and where we face the importance of being interconnected with other human beings in this world. Their stories will be different. Their spirits will have their own separate reason for being. Their minds, complete with their conscious and unconscious reactions, will be totally unique. Hopefully through coming to a clear understanding of your self, you can also come to a place where you can respect and accept each and every other human being, in spite of their differences. They have as much right to be their 'self' as you do to be you.

Living in Pain: A Case Study

He was the youngest in a family of families. A family in which the pattern of child-bearing had been spread out over the years so that it almost seemed as if there were three distinctly different families in all. His older sisters were already married and bearing their own children when he was conceived, and so he was uncle to children who were older than himself. In the middle of the family, just eleven years above him was his older brother, the only other boy in the family. And then there was his little sister, who was born two years before he was, the two of them after-thoughts, it seemed, of his parents' relationship.

They lived in a community surrounded by the members of his mother's family and this boy was loved by all. His father was the outsider, born and raised in a far off community, sent to this town on a job by his employers. He shared his gifts and abilities freely with those around him, but he never reached the point where he truly felt at home.

The child was two when disaster struck. His only brother was suddenly, tragically killed in an accident. His parents reeled from the grief, blaming themselves and each other for his demise. The father couldn't face the pain on his own and returned to his birthplace. The mother struggled on, a strong woman who took care of herself by keeping her feelings locked deep inside. The little boy grew up, unaware of how the grief was tearing his mother to pieces and with little knowledge or memory of the man who had fathered him.

He wanted to be loved and accepted. He needed to be loved and accepted. But the holes developed within, holes that were there, not because he wanted them, not because he had created them, but because they just were. The hole of his father's absence. The hole of his mother's absence, caused directly by her grief which decreased her ability to interact with him. The hole of the loss of his brother. He experienced the pain of these holes. He couldn't explain where it came from. He didn't have anyone to share it with. He buried it deep within himself.

He developed a habit of being the carefree one. The one who could laugh and play tricks on others. The one who always had a good story to tell. The one who could party all night, dancing with every girl in the community until the wee hours of the morning. The one who was hiding his pain. He had his nephews and nieces as best friends; his sisters, more like aunts; and his grandmother, solemn and old, to strengthen him, to be with him. But it wasn't quite enough. He didn't know why. The pain didn't go away.

He left the community to see if he could find peace somewhere else. He met a young woman who captured his heart. She welcomed him into her life, into her arms, and for a while it seemed as if he had found what he was looking for. But the pain didn't go away. The holes were never filled. And to make it even worse, her father rejected him completely, never welcoming him into their family, not even accepting his children as grandchildren. New holes appeared. The pain deepened.

He was a hard worker. He was a good provider. He was an incredible man. But he didn't know how to be a father. He had never experienced what it was like to have a father so he didn't know how to be one to his children. He tried to interact with them as he did with others: carefree, laughing and joking, in the midst of hiding his pain.

He discovered that alcohol could dull the pain. Make it go away for a while. Make him stop feeling so empty. He turned to it often. His carefree nature attracted many others who were also dulling their pain through alcohol. He began to spend more time with them in the bar than at home.

When he drank too much his nature changed. The laughter was gone. The pain took over. A rage exploded within him. He could no longer hold his feelings in. He became vicious and angry. He was strong. He was quick. He had wrestled as a youth. He became known as a fighter. He turned on his wife. He turned on his children. He turned on his friends.

The years passed and each member of his family dealt with his behavior in their own individual ways. His wife became isolated in order to protect herself from his drunken rages. Some of his children perceived his drunkenness as a weakness to be abhorred and rejected and turned their backs on the family unit. Others needed a father so much that they joined in with his behavior, each in turn fighting the long-term effects of alcohol abuse. Still others married a spouse who had the same behavior patterns, following closely in their mother's footsteps.

He's getting older. The truth is coming out. As family members, whose lives were much less stressful than his, age, they are pulling the family together. Researching the family tree. Documenting the stories. Discovering their own roots. Sharing these discoveries with each other, with his children. And as the children learn, they realize their father is someone far different than they once assumed.

Nothing that happened to this man was done on purpose. Nothing that happened to him was done out of spite of any kind. Everything was tied to pain. The pain of an accidental death. The pain that tore a family apart and was never dealt with out in the open. The pain that continues to be played out in the different reactions of family members, over 80 years after the original loss happened. He was never a "drunk." He was never a failure as a father. He was never an alcoholic. He was a man in pain. A human being living his life in the best way he knew in the circumstances in which he was placed. And that's how it is for all of us.

Chapter 7
The Development of the Social Self

No one else is a failed attempt at being us,
they are each their own unique self.

ANONYMOUS

CURIOSITY KILLED THE CAT AND IT'S GOING TO KILL YOU TOO. THIS IS A PHRASE I REMEMber hearing, over and over again, as a young child. I suspect it was an apt description of my behavior, as I certainly was curious about everything that was going on around me and constantly paid attention to or explored situations that had nothing to do with me. The adults were likely trying to tell me that I had no business being so snoopy but I never understood their meaning. I just absorbed the feeling that being curious was something to be ashamed about. This didn't hinder my interest in the world. I continued to explore anything and everything. But my self-esteem did take a beating and I began to hide my interest in the world so that no one could "put me down".

One day we went to visit my Aunt Christine, who lived in a small town near our farm. As farmers, we lived without running water and used an outhouse as our toilet. Visiting Aunt Christine was a novelty because she had all of the conveniences of the time in her house. I was likely about four at the time of this particular visit and I used her modern bathroom with a great deal of trepidation and excitement. The door locked. I could indulge in my curiosity without anyone knowing. I had never had access to a flushing toilet like this before and I wanted to figure out exactly how it worked. I carefully removed the things from the back cover of the tank and lifted it off, peering inside to see if it would tell me how this toilet worked. The sight that met my eyes was repulsive, and just as I looked in at it, someone knocked on the door. I quickly replaced the lid, the doily, and the crocheted doll whose skirt hid the extra toilet paper roll, and called out "I'm almost done" to whomever was behind the door.

As we drove home that evening I thought about the glimpse I had had of the contents of the toilet tank and surmised that what I had seen was a conglomeration of poop, toilet paper and pee much like that in the pail of the chemical toilet we had in the basement of our house during the winter.

I decided that somehow flushing the toilet sent all the waste up into the tank, where it would stay until someone would move it on --- just how, I wasn't sure. It seemed a strange way to do things, but who was I to question progress. Due to the "curiosity killed the cat" attitude of everyone around me, I couldn't come out and ask about a toilet of all things and so I puzzled over these details for years.

In time, of course, I had the opportunity to check out the tank of another toilet. This time, all I found was clean water, what looked like a lopsided rubber ball and some levers. I began to realize that the toilet worked the opposite of what I had first surmised and this clean water went down into the toilet after one flushed. Although it was more logical, it certainly made that first view questionable. I knew that it was full of unmentionable things. It was gross. And yet, how could it be, if this is how a toilet worked?

Throughout the years this puzzle came back to me and I would find myself in different situations, checking out the tank of the toilet, just in case I could find a reason for what I believed I had seen. And every time, all that met my eyes was the clean water. The years sped by, elementary school, jr. high, high school, college and finally marriage and my own home and still no answer. Hundreds of toilets checked. None like the first one.

And then came 1982. I was 33 years old and living in the same town as my aunt. By this time, I had just about given up checking toilet tanks and had convinced myself that what I believed I had seen was a figment of my imagination. We had recently moved into this home. One day, our toilet stopped working and as the Mother, I had to figure out exactly how to fix it. I lifted off the lid of the tank and to my surprise I was back in the past, looking at same sight I had seen, so many years ago. But this time I was able to take the time to investigate it fully. No, it was not the poop, etc. that I had envisioned when I was four, but instead a variety of molds and fungi in a multitude of dark slimy colours that were floating and growing in the toilet tank. I realized that we were connected to one of the "old" water wells in the town, in much the same way my aunt had been so many years before. The water had a high content of sulphur and other minerals. Obviously, although it was deemed "safe" for drinking, it also allowed this type of growth, if water was left standing. My puzzle was solved and, in the midst of that understanding, I realized for the first time how much the phrase "curiosity killed the cat" had held me back throughout the years. Curiosity was never going to kill me. It was something I should be proud of, something to celebrate

The social self, as described in the first chapter of this book, is made up of the view of the self held by every person who knows us. Each person in our lives contributes their view to this level and often these views may vary greatly from one person to the next. The views of those who see us close to our lifeline are the people with whom we are the most comfortable. Those whose view is far from the lifeline are hard to live with as they sap us of our energy. We have two choices when dealing with these people: either to attempt to live within their view, which takes an awful lot of energy and moves us away from fulfilling our full potential, or to reject their view and live in constant conflict with them. In order to preserve our energy, we must come to a point where we cut ourselves off emotionally from them. The importance of the particular person in one's life as well as our own feelings of self worth will determine which choice we make.

The more people who have a positive social image of us we have in our life, the stronger we will be as individuals. The more people we have in our life who have a social view of us that is close to, or matches, our life line, the easier it will be for us to accept who we are, to get to know ourselves as we are created to be, and to focus on our strengths and our abilities to reach our full potential. The more people we have in our life who focus on the negatives, and who try to "fix" us to make us "acceptable" in order to fit a certain "societal pattern," the harder it will be for us to get to know ourselves and to achieve our full potential.

This view is developed from the very moment of our conception. The attitude of our parents towards our presence in our mother's womb can affect us before birth. Is she happy and excited about our presence in her life, or is she concerned, overwhelmed by anxiety in other aspects of her life, or even unwilling or unable to welcome us as a child to love? Is our father there, sharing her joy with her, speaking to us in anticipation, listening to our heartbeat and watching us kick, or is he oblivious to our presence or totally uninterested in the fact that we exist? The baby can feel all this through the chemistry of the mother and it will affect them for the rest of their life.

Various factors will impact the view others have of us after our birth. Although I am sure that the "curiosity killed the cat" comment didn't occur in my presence when I was an infant, the stories I hear about that time do indicate the view people had of me. My swift arrival, which took place before the doctor could arrive at the hospital, or the nurse had the opportunity to change into her uniform, meant that her good wool suit was doused in birthing fluids. There was a determination in my cry that set me apart from every other baby in the hospital and my early development had me walking at nine months and climbing up on anything and everything I could find. Mom had to keep the chairs up on the table when no one was sitting on them in order to protect me. There is a story from my baby-sitter who bathed me and dressed me up in a white dress, only to find me sitting in a pan of motor oil which my father had just drained from the car; stories of getting lost in a wheat field, of being run over by a wagon, of being bitten by our dog. Obviously I wasn't an easy child to raise and yet, as a preschooler I was allowed to be the child I was. This is indicated through the celebration the true Gail, still clear and strong that day I rode home during threshing and saw the future as documented in the chapter on change.

Things got worse when I started school and became the "problem child" of the year in my grade one classroom. The message from my teacher was very clear. I was totally unacceptable as I was and so I was in trouble all the time. When you are with someone who is using double blinds to control you, nothing you do will be right. I remember sitting in my desk frozen in fear because I couldn't find my pencil. I knew I was going to get in trouble because I couldn't do my work, but I also knew

I would get in trouble if I put my hand up to tell the teacher I couldn't find my pencil. There was absolutely no way to do things right. There was no way to stay out of trouble.

In the midst of this, my older sister, who was in second grade, in the same classroom, was the teacher's pet, and no matter what she did, she could do no wrong. So not only was my view of my self affected, my relationship with this sister has also been strained. As the teacher compared my lack of effort to her achievements, I gradually chose not to make any effort at all. I didn't want to be like her. I wanted to be celebrated for myself, not someone else.

I started school as a five year old. At that point in time, every one who was six on September 1st automatically became a grade one student. However, any children who turned six between September 1st and December 31st of that year had a chance to start grade one, if their parents so chose. These children were given an IQ test to determine if they were ready for school. I remember going to the high school building to write the test, on adult sized furniture, sitting on a chair with my legs dangling. I remember the other children who took part, some who would join me in grade one and others who would wait to start school the next year, based on the results of this test. I even remember some of the questions: drawing a leg on a table and a tail on a dog. I have never been given the actual results of this test, other than being allowed to start school at five, but it affected me throughout all my years at school as teachers would scream at me, "With your IQ, you should get 100% on every exam!" This didn't help much as I resisted their message with every ounce of determination I had. There was no way at all they were going to make me be like my sister.

I might have passed the intelligence test with flying colours, but I lacked the social skills I needed to fit in with the other children. It was a small school, so every year our classroom had two different grades in it. On the even years I was okay because the close friends that I finally accumulated were with me in the classroom, even if we were in different grades. The odd years were horrendous as I felt like there was something seriously wrong with me because I wanted to be with the "babies". It took a number of years, likely in my mid teens, for me to realize there was nothing wrong with me, that my response was logical, because the girls who were my friends were far closer to me in age than those in my grade. By then it didn't help much as I was now separated from these friends as we moved to a larger school, which only had one grade in each classroom. I struggled along, coping with all of this the best I could, and sharing none of it with anyone, in direct response to how one reacts in the Scandinavian culture. How much better it would have been to talk about it openly as a child. But this is not how my people did things.

In the long run, the view of the teachers became a positive element in my life, though it took a long time to develop. As an adult, there is no way anyone can make me feel like I am dumb or that I am not capable of something. In direct contrast, a friend who was treated the opposite by his teachers, accepts the label of stupidity, automatically, even at times when the person he is with has not even thought about something like that. This friend is colour blind and thus is not able to differentiate between such colours as red, green and brown, some of the first information we are taught as children. Instead of recognizing his problem, the teachers would make him stand up in the front of the classroom, holding up his work as a demonstration of how to do things wrong. Whenever he would tell his parents that his teachers had called him stupid, they would reply, "They sure got that right, didn't they?" This erroneous view in his social self is almost impossible to change. We have to stop doing this to our children.

The views of my teachers were passed on to the students I spent my life with in the classroom. I was a very sensitive, shy, smart, feisty, determined child who was given the message that none of these attributes was acceptable. As I work as a consultant in classrooms today, I so often see the same thing happening to far too many children. I don't know if teachers realize what incredible power they wield over these precious selves and how long the messages that they share with these children will last. I'm hoping that things are getting better, but I don't know that they are. Every time I see a teacher put a child down in the presence of their peers I feel a chill. I am fully aware of the long term impact this can have on the social self of that child in so many different ways. Of course, the particular child is likely experiencing a totally different life style than I was, and the impact on them will be very different, but I know that we must be very careful.

My loss of self esteem also escalated as I dealt with the advances of the dirty old man who would approach me during functions at our church and in our community on my own. As I have said before, I don't know where I got the sense not to listen to what this man said, not to go off alone with him, not to accept the gifts he offered, but even so, his impact on my sense of self was devastating. With the simplicity of a child I rationalized that the presence of this man in the church, accompanied by his crippled wife, meant that he was a good man. Thus there must be something wrong with me to have him approaching me in this manner. Although the revulsion I felt led to my reaction of flight, which kept me safe from his further advances, it also made me feel very negative about myself. There had to be something wrong with me for this to happen. I had to hide it from everyone and I did until I was an adult.

By the time I graduated from high school I was already locked into using coping skills to deal with the social self I had developed over the years. Although I may have appeared to be doing okay on the outside, passing my courses, playing basketball, editing the school newspaper, singing in our youth choir at church and so on, I was a complete mess. I spent the majority of my time retreating into fantasy through books or day dreams in order to feel any sense of security. As other teens spent their time interacting with each other I was all alone, creating a world in which I was welcomed by everyone. I was ripe for the next step in my life.

THE TRUE SELF VERSUS THE PSEUDO SELF

The pain was excruciating I reached up and gently ran my fingertips against the bruised reddened surface of my cheek, my mind curiously far away from my body. Thoughts of how men could ever choose go into a boxing ring, knowing that they would suffer in this way, flashed through my mind. For that is what my face had been the night before: my husband's punching bag. And this morning, it wore the scars.

I gave my head a shake in an attempt to force myself to concentrate on my present situation. As I gazed at the reflected image of my two blackened eyes and swollen spit lip, I wondered how on earth I was going to be able to deal with my life looking like this. He had made sure the children were up, had their breakfast and were off to school so they didn't have to see me, but they would be home for lunch in a couple of hours. There was no way I would be able to cover up this mess.

A knock sounded on my door and I turned unconsciously and opened it. My father stood on the steps. In horror we gazed at each other, our eyes filling with tears, my hands lifting in supplication. I tried to speak, but the words wouldn't come. He turned away abruptly and strode off to his truck. Wearily, I closed the door and sank down onto a nearby chair, trying to figure out what I was going to do next.

Yes, I was a battered woman. For 24 years of my life, I lived in a marriage in which my husband went into periodic rages in which he either beat me or destroyed the room we were in. At one point he almost succeeded in strangling me before our 16-year-old son rushed into the room and dragged him off me. This is not something I am proud of or ashamed of. Although the tendency of mankind is to keep such abuse quiet, one cannot fully accept and understand one's 'self' without stating what actually is, or at this point in my life was. Because, like the thumb sucking I gave up as a child, this abuse is a part of my past so it exists within my 'self' in my mind as a memory, not in my present social self as a current way of relating with others. If I cannot put it out into the open to release the anxiety it creates, it will simmer below the surface creating all sorts of physical and emotional problems. If I don't admit that it happened, I cannot determine the impact that it has on my unconscious reactions in the present moment. We have to face the whole picture to see the whole self.

If you look at this situation through my 'self' you see one picture: the picture of a woman who is being abused by her husband. As a wife I experienced something that I had not even dreamed possible as a child. Life in my family of origin was very stable and secure and centered around the home, the church and the community. Although money was scarce, I had never felt deprived in any way. I had never seen my father show any type of aggression to anyone. I had no idea what it meant to have one's parents coming home drunk because mine didn't touch liquor. As I look back at my early years of marriage, I realize that I had never considered that families might be any different from my own. I had no way to know how to react to this type of behavior. I adapted as well as I could, all the time not quite believing that it was happening.

The journey towards an understanding of one's self provides us with the ability to understand the behaviors of those around us. Although I am certainly not advocating that spousal abuse is acceptable or that it should be ignored, or considered appropriate in any sense, my journey to self has led me to the point where I see the above scene in a completely different light. By focusing on my husband's model of self rather than my own, his reactions began to make sense, in spite of the pain that they caused. His reactions were as firmly based on his past, his beliefs and his needs as mine were and are. In other words, we must look at this scene not as a woman being abused by a man, but instead as a man reacting at a limbic system level with the response of fight due to his current level of anxiety which has totally overwhelmed him.

As a young, naive teen, I entered marriage with expectations based completely on my childhood home and having very little self-esteem, a direct result of the lack of acceptance of my true self throughout my years in school. My husband grew up in a totally different world, of which I was unaware at the time. He described his childhood and I accepted what he said because it matched what I already knew about families in general. I had no idea that his major coping skill was also to create a fantasy world in order to deal with the pain and the terror of his past. I kept my fantasies to myself. His were all out in the open, but they were as much fiction as mine were.

In direct contrast to my life, this man grew up in a state of deprivation with an alcoholic, abusive and incestuous father. He, too, lived in a community surrounded by extended kin, but his grand-father's will, which deprived all but one of his daughters of the expected inheritance, meant that his experience of extended family was one of rejection, jealousy and bickering. When he was nine, his father vanished. The family struggled on in extreme poverty until he was 13. At that time his mother had a nervous breakdown and he and his siblings were put into Catholic orphanages. This new home should have been a refuge, a place to heal and to grow. Instead it was a hell-hole of depravity where sexual and physical abuse reigned supreme.

I knew little of this when I first got married. Like most families who live with these extreme behaviors, all of the information noted in the last paragraph was secret, unspoken, hidden in the dark regions of his mind. He described a past to me, which he now admits he gleaned from families he had seen on TV, because there was no way that he could admit the truth. As time passed, I knew that there was something different, something I couldn't quite place my finger on. I knew our relationship was not like that of my parents or my friends. My discomfort was based directly on his anger, his jealousy and the physical abuse, which he blamed directly on me. As the years went by and certain things happened that couldn't be explained in any other way than exposing the truth, I gradually got to know his real story. It took 20 years for the biggest secret to come out into the open. It took another ten to piece this all together.

For 24 years I lived in a marriage in which the social view of my spouse was as far way from my lifeline as possible. My husband's view of me, based on his childhood experience, his beliefs of marriage, of women, of commitment and his own behavior determined that I, as his wife, would cheat on him with other men. The abandonment he had experienced at the hands of first his father, and then later his mother, meant that he couldn't trust anyone. His greatest fear, based directly on his past, was that I would leave him and he would be alone again. The threat of the possibility of abandonment ruled our lives.

Our relationship was one in which jealousy dominated all of our interactions. This jealousy appeared within the first weeks in which we knew each other, and continues on even today. As person who had grown up in a totally different world, I responded to him in a totally different manner. When one looks closely at our relationship, I was as far off the mark as he was with my social image of him. Although I can only look at this experience through my own eyes, I expect that it was as difficult for him to meet my social view of him as it was for me to live with his.

As the wife of a jealous husband, I learned to adapt my behavior in order to protect our relationship as best as I could, in much the same way I had learned to adapt to the presence of the dirty old man in my childhood. One New Year's Eve we attended a dance where we came across one of my schoolmates and his wife. Roger and I had attended school together for 12 years and as the tallest in the class had often been paired together for a variety of reasons throughout the years. We both played basketball and traveled with the teams on the same buses. By the time we graduated, we were two of a group of six who had been together the last 12 years of our lives. Throughout this time neither of us had ever expressed any romantic interest in each other. He was almost like a brother.

So, that night, in my mind, Roger certainly wasn't a threat of any kind. However, in my husband's mind, he was competition for my love. When Roger kissed me in the melee after the clock struck 12:00 the battle was on. Within seconds, I saw the look of rage on my husband's face and I knew that I was in trouble. Nothing I said about Roger made a difference. The wall of ice came up, and my husband was no longer listening. Our celebration of the New Year was over and the joy of the evening was completely wiped out. That wall of ice stayed in place for over a month. I learned my lesson. I never again reacted with ease with any man from my past. I generally either avoided them completely or was so aloof around them that they didn't speak to me. This went so far to the extreme that I didn't even acknowledge the presence of another of my male schoolmates who lived on the same city block as I did for a few years when my sons were little.

Over time, I learned to adapt more and more. The way I walked, the way I looked at another person, the words I used or didn't use, the clothes I wore and so on were met with disapproval and were either changed or given up to meet his standards. I quickly learned to approach only women when he was with me and never mention the fact a male had served me in a store or a gas station, no matter how interesting I thought the story. These adaptations kept me safe most of the time, but it wasn't a fail proof system. Sometimes, I forgot, or assumed this person would be safe for some reason that made sense to me, but not to him. One evening we spent some time with a young man who had been in grade ten when I was in grade twelve. Since he was younger than I, I assumed that he was safe. I had been the skip of our high school curling team and he shared his appreciation of me with my husband because he claimed that I was the person who had taught him how to curl. This revelation ended in a severe beating when we got back to our house. At other times, I wasn't dealing with reality, but with whatever was happening in his imagination in the moment. At those times nothing I did made a difference other than putting up with either the violence that ensued or the wall of ice that could go on for weeks.

During all those years, I did what I had to do, with no idea of the impact that it was having on my self, on my energy level and on my physical body. I went from being a person who could eat anything I wanted to developing a whole list of allergies which grew longer, the longer I stayed with him. I experienced back pains so severe that I had to roll out of bed onto the floor in the morning and then pull myself up slowly against the wall as it was impossible for me to go to a sitting position from a lying one. Doctors couldn't find anything specific wrong with me and prescribed pain medication as a treatment, which did little to curb the pain. Over the years another pain developed in the region of my lower rib cage, an ache that never went away completely and grew significantly worse whenever we, as a couple, had to deal with other people. In 1992, when I finally made the decision that I could no longer put up with his behavior, it felt as if a sword had been pulled out of my lower chest. These pains were gone, never to return in the same way.

In the years that followed, my family insisted that I deal with my ex-husband in social settings. In the beginning I reacted with trepidation and fear, overcome with the anxiety that I again would have the sword thrust back into me. Later my reactions grew more extreme as I totally refused to adapt at all to his presence and insisted that the family make him take responsibility for his own behavior instead of expecting me to be the one to adapt. As I look back over those years, I am sorry that I caused my family such upheaval, but I know that I had to do it in order to protect my fragile sense of self. At this point I am actually back to being willing to adapt in order to be in his presence so that my sons can have both their parents in the same space for special occasions. My sense of self is safe as I am fully aware of what adaptations are needed and why they are brought into play.

I expect that my social view of my husband also made an impact on his life, but I hesitate to write much about it because that was his journey in life, not mine. I do know that throughout the years we were together infidelity on his part was the furthest thing from my mind, because I believed he was like me, and that he was committed to our marriage. As I look back over our marriage at this point, I am amazed that I was so blind to what was happening right under my nose. The stories he told, which often changed from one telling to the next. The situations he got involved in, which only pointed in one direction if I really thought about them. The places I found him. The people

I found him with. I ignored them all. When friends and acquaintances approached me with details after I left, I wondered how on earth I could have been so blind. But why not? It was just another part of my adaptation.

The more I learn about the self, the more I realize how my relationship with my first husband was doomed to fail. From the first night we met, he lied about his past and his present. Fabricating the truth was the survival skill he had learned very well as a child in his family of origin. It was the skill he used to protect himself, and no one can fault him for that, considering what he had experienced. But it was also a skill that formed a impenetrable wall and made having a meaningful relationship with him impossible for anyone.

By the time I left him, fear, pain and anger had replaced any positive feelings that I had for him. For many years I carried a heavy load of guilt. How could I have had children with a man I didn't love? This question has changed as I learn more about the self. It evolved into "How can anyone love a person one does not know?" Due to the amount of fabrication in his life, I never had the chance to get to know the real man at all. There are as many good things about him as there are negative, but what do they mean? Is the real man the one who beat his wife and cut his children out of his life for months on end or is he the hard worker who leaves a perfect job, and then comes home to draw cartoon strips for his sons and grandsons? The truth is that he is both of these and so much more. But who is the true man? In the midst of all the coping skills he depends on, can anyone ever really reach his true self? Does anyone know him? Does he even know himself?

The passage of time allows feelings to move on to new levels. The fear, the pain, the anger subsided. For a while there were no feelings at all in conjunction with him. It was safer not to feel anything. But that didn't last either. Now as I look at my sons and recognize certain elements of their father in their features, I am swept back in time and can feel the love we shared. It was there. My life wasn't a lie. I did love him, in spite of everything. There is a sense of healing in that knowledge.

As mentioned earlier, when we are dealing with people who have a false image of us as an individual, we have two choices. We can either adapt to meet their viewpoint and spend our time living as a pseudo self, or we can insist on being true to our own self. This is not possible until we know exactly who that 'self' is. In the same way that our mind is created through the experiences that we live throughout our life, our social self is also created through experience. The process of discovering exactly who one is is a process in which one weeds out the true self, as found on our life line, from all the other pseudo selves we have created to meet the expectations of those with whom we interact.

The pseudo selves we portray to the world begin to be formed as soon as we are born. The reactions of our families and the labels they put upon us begin to form the social self immediately. "She is such a quiet child." "He's a real fighter." "What a cry baby." Some of these labels may be very close to describing the true self. Others may be far off the mark, having more to do with the dreams and expectations that the parents had of their unborn child than the actual personality of the child that is born. I have watched the development of one boy over time described as being tough and a fighter from the very first week of his life. When you really get to know this child you discover that there is nothing in his make-up that can define him as a fighter. In fact, he is a child who has incredible abilities as a peacemaker and yet some family members continue to define him in the opposite way, whenever they speak of him. In response he has become known as a troublemaker in school as he tries to live up to the label that was given him. Making the effort to recognize the labels and the roles that were assigned to you by your family and your community allows you to determine whether you want to hang on to them or not. Are they pseudo, or are they true?

Other parts of our pseudo selves are formed by the expectations that are placed on us as children. Families in which "Children should been seen and not heard" produce children who do not speak up for themselves. Families in which excellence in education is valued may produce children who are high achievers, or children who become anorexic or bulimic because of the frustration caused by trying to meet expectations they are incapable of achieving. Parents who were frustrated by their lack of opportunity as children may foist their dreams on their children, pushing them to become sports stars, entertainers, or enter a profession that fits the true self of the parent far more than that of the child. Other parents who have experienced success in their life may insist that their children carry on their work without any thought of whether the child is interested or has abilities in that area. None of these expectations have a sense of malice or a sense of failure or insufficiency behind them. In fact they are usually held with the best interest of the child in mind. However, it does mean the person lives as a pseudo self and is unable to meet their full potential because so much energy is going into creating a self that is not on their life line.

The community also puts each of us into roles in which we may or may not fit well. The strongest pseudo selves that are used by the community are called stereotypes. Stereotypes can be based on any specific factor that would differentiate one group of people from another such as race, culture, gender, place of residence, ability, disability, educational level or employment status. Although most stereotypes appear to be used for minority groups, one must realize that we all are affected by them in different ways. As white, Anglo-Saxon males in the school system, one might expect that my sons would have the highest level of expectations placed on them, but I discovered that this was not so. I grew up in a family in which one was expected to do well at school and always assumed that I would attend university as an adult. These expectations were supported by everyone I was in contact with. I raised my children with the same level of expectation, but discovered that they were not treated that way by the schools they attended. When my oldest son was in high school, I chose to return to university and finish the degree I had begun before his birth. In a letter written to me at that time, he expressed his appreciation for my efforts, because he claimed it had changed the attitude of his teachers towards him. These teachers, who were measuring our family as that of a tradesman and a stay at home mother, had no idea who I was as a person, nor that I had a university education.

Their expectations for my sons were based directly on the levels of attainment they thought we as parents had reached. How many other children are treated this way? Thankfully my children all went on a post secondary education of some sort in spite of the expectations they faced in the school system, but some of them are not using this education at this point. Perhaps their view of their selves was affected by the school system in much the same way mine was.

The closer we stick to life in a group that is the same as we are, the easier it is to accept the stereotypes we have of others. The more we step out into the world and take the opportunities we have to get to know others who are different from us, the more we realize that the stereotypical pictures we carry in our minds of a group do not fit the individuals within that group. Each human being in this world is a totally unique person because of how we develop over time. Once we accept this and learn to celebrate our differences we are free to interact with others on their life line and have them do the same for us. We are free to shed the stereotypical views that other may have of us and walk away from those we have of other people. Living on the life line begins with the recognition of the impact of change and anxiety on the self. If we understand that stepping out in the world as a true self is going to feel uncomfortable and expect it to be such, we can relax and feel that discomfort without heightened anxiety. If we understand the impact that anxiety has on us as an individual, then we can measure our current level of anxiety by our reactions, and relax with the knowledge that this doesn't mean there is something wrong with us, but rather that we are coping with the discomfort of change. The message doesn't have to be one of guilt, of shame, of failure or of illness. We are okay.

The more we focus on the stereotypical responses of others as a negative force in our lives, the more we choose to live at a pseudo level, rather than as a true self. This is evidenced by the leaders whose choices in life have led to effective change in society such as Dr. Martin Luther King, Jr. and Mahatma Ghandi. Instead of focusing their efforts on what was wrong, they concentrated on the positive changes that needed to happen. And change occurred. Individuals and groups who concentrate on the negative aspects of the stereotypes rather than on positive factors do not achieve these results. This is because these individuals and groups are working from the pseudo self not their true self as King and Ghandi chose to do. Each of us, as an individual on our journey of life, can learn from these examples. By taking the responsibility of figuring out our true self and moving away from living within a pseudo self, we have the power to instigate the changes we want. By staying in the role of the psuedo self, we give that power to those who hold the stereotype of us in their social view. We do have the choice.

A clear example of this is experienced by celebrities who have social selves that are so much bigger than the rest of us. Their position in this world puts them in a place in which their lives become fodder for the masses as so many of us want to have a connection of some sort with them in order to feel better about ourselves. Much of the information shared via newspapers, magazines and television may be based directly on that individual, though we will not be able to know this for certain, because we do not actually have a personal connection with them. We must remember that all of this information has a monetary value connected to it. It's pulled together to sell whatever product we find it in, and thus is suspect. This is certainly true of the headlines of the tabloids that expose shocking revelations about different celebrities month after month. Those who are written about have a choice whether to react to these stories and allow the pseudo self created by the tabloids to have power in their lives, or to ignore them and continue living on their life line. This isn't easy as the social self contains those views whether we want them to or not. It makes life as a celebrity much more difficult than it should be and may create heightened levels of anxiety, which directly results in their need to resort to using coping skills.

Through the lives of celebrities we can learn the importance of living on our life line. Celebrities who have come to the realization that fame is something that happens outside one's spirit, not within, are celebrities who are able to cope well with the increased size of their social self. They fully realize that they are being measured in the world by only a portion of themselves, that which is exposed by the reason that they become a celebrity: their job, their role in society, their specific ability that makes them stand out from others. Their ability to be measured at an individual level may be lost in the midst of a social self consisting of the views of so many people. I think it is very easy to come up with examples of people who have suffered because of this limited picture of themselves in the midst of an overwhelming social self. Celebrities who have willingly shared the reality of their lives with us and who are accepted on their life line, blossom in the midst of their fame. Celebrities who are living as pseudo selves, either trying to live up to a social view of others, or attempting to cover up their weaknesses, are those who are caught up in the midst of surviving via of coping skills. In time this facade collapses in one way or another.

The negative view that society holds of our coping skills, equating them with weakness, failure, or mental illness means that the typical response to their use is shame and an attempt to hide from the world. Hiding these reactions means moving into a pseudo self, which means that one needs to use more energy to carry on, and thus lives in a heightened state of anxiety. This, of course, then increases the need to use our coping skills. These responses become cyclical over time and may cycle out of control, especially if we are unaware of the process, as most of us are.

Living on the life line means that we must squarely face who we are as humans and accept the good as well as the bad. We must accept that the coping skills we use are a part of us, not something to be a ashamed of and hidden away, but reactions that will occur in times of high anxiety. Any effort that we make to cover up or hide these reactions will move us to living as a pseudo self. Personally I have to face the fact that I may act like an ostrich, hiding away from the world and ignoring things that should be taken care of in some situations of anxiety and that I will eat to cover up my emotional pain in others. I have to accept the fact that I may end up in a position in which I am screaming at another person again in the future. I am not a perfect person and I never will be. No one else is perfect either, and I must become tolerant of their reactions in the same way that I am tolerant of my own. Life is not easy. Life does not always seem to be fair. This is okay. This is why we have coping skills. Once all of this is understood and out in the open, life becomes much easier. There will still be trials and tribulations for each of us to bear, but we can face them squarely without shame or guilt. Allowing ourselves to feel the anxiety and use whatever coping skill we need in the present moment will help us face anything.

Once we accept our own coping skills and the importance they play in our lives, we must move on and do the same for all of the other people that surround us. We cannot ignore the fact that our view of them is a part of their social self and will have a negative or positive impact on them in the same way that their view of us affects us. If we hold a false view of them, we are forcing them to live as a pseudo self. If we can accept them as they truly are, we allow them to live on their life line; to celebrate their true self and aid them in achieving their full potential.

This is especially clear when one works in the field of autism where the focus of treatment has been, and still continues to be in some places, to "normalize" the child with autism and make him indistinguishable from his typical peers. A letter from a father who is involved in this type of treatment explains it this way:

> I understand what you are saying and I agree. My wife and I have provided my son with autism, an ABA program for 4 1/2 years now. We started with more of a Lovaas style with DTT and then gradually began to incorporate NET more and more. But our program would probably not be considered an ABA program by "purists". Our quality of note taking by our therapists varied often. Many times the notes were narrative, rather than any sort of trial by trial recording. What made it work is:
>
> 1. we had a video system that recorded therapy in progress
>
> 2. My wife stayed home and was in charge of his program full time. So she constantly was aware of what was working and what was not. What he had mastered and what he needed to still work on.
>
> We did not always concentrate on what was the "cause" of his behavior and deal with that. We did try to do this though when we could determine what it was. Often it WAS rather just teaching him how to appropriately behave in learning environments like a classroom or play group. So we are not "ABA experts", BUT our son has progressed TREMENDOUSLY.
>
> He is functional, which was our primary goal, and he is approaching, to the observation of an average lay person, indistinguishable from other kids. So I am comfortable that we have

*done the right thing with him using ABA (DTT and NET) to treat his Autism. You can
read about him and what we have done at a web site I have created with another parent.* J. P. R.

Although this parent, and many like him claim to "know" what they are doing, and believe that
they are acting in the best interest of their child, time will show what an incredible mistake they
have made. As these children become adults they begin to search for their true selves. Once they
discover others within the autism spectrum, people who react to the world in much the same way
they do, they describe their response as having a huge weight lifted off their shoulders. They spend
their time looking for others who can make sense of their lives and write books on their experiences
with very revealing titles : *Pretending to be Normal, A Real Person, Life and Depression, A Journey
with Asperger's'* and *I Don't Want to Be Inside Me Anymore.* As Thomas McKean states in his
autobiography *Light on the Horizon:*

> *"Parents, please be careful in the way you raise your children. You never know when one of
> them may grow up to write a book about you."*

As an autism consultant, I meet many of these children when they reach their teens. They have
been taught all their lives to "fit" into a particular pattern, but during the changes of puberty, they
hit a wall, as they have no clue who they are as an individual, and why their body is reacting the
way it is. They also have now come to a point in their life in which social interactions are taking
precedence, in the midst of a body they don't understand and have difficulty controlling. This leads
directly to inappropriate or ineffective social reactions, which then may lead to teasing, bullying
or avoidance by other teens who are also in the midst of social angst. This, in turn, leads directly to
a severe loss of self-esteem. Most of them suffer from depression, which is not helped by the many
antidepressants available. In fact, most of these medications only make things worse.

My treatment of these teenagers consists of teaching them how people within the autism spectrum
differ from those who do not have it, and how these differences impact their lives on a daily basis.
We focus on a personal history that was based on the need to protect oneself from the impact of
the stimulation coming in from the environment, which meant that they didn't learn all the social
lessons as preschoolers, as their peers did. It's not that they "can't" do it, it's that they had more
important issues to deal with at the time. We focus on how their own body is unique and how they
can learn to read their reactions in different situations in order to protect themselves from overload
and to cope effectively in any environment. Only then are they free to reach their full potential.

The people on the autism spectrum who come to me for therapy are not always in their teens.
Sometimes they are in their twenties, their thirties or forties. The oldest actually reached seventy
before he began the journey of discovering who he really is. But their stories are all the same:
feelings of being left out, of not knowing how to respond, of rejection and frustration, of shame and

loneliness. My office is often the very first place in their lives where they have felt unconditional acceptance and respect. A place where no one has tried to change them into someone they are not. A place where any behavior is totally acceptable, as we recognize it as a coping skill for the stress they are experiencing, not something that is inappropriate. This immediately lowers their anxiety level, and the behaviors decrease on their own. Our groups are unique because they are a gathering together of people who respond much like one another in an atmosphere in which no one is trying to fix them. Caregivers who attend are struck by the fact that the autistic behaviors, which they see everywhere else, are no longer being exhibited. In fact the comment has been made more than once that no one would realize these people had autism if they just happened to walk in the door. They all appear 'normal'. But, of course, they're not. We haven't 'cured' autism. The behaviors will return when needed in other situations in order to calm the body. We have just provided an environment in which the anxiety level can remain low so that the behaviors are not required. The basis of this environment is full unconditional acceptance of each individual exactly as they are This unconditional acceptance of our true self on the social self level is what each and every one of us needs the most from every person with whom we interact. This unconditional acceptance is what allows us to reach our full potential, for until we are free to be exactly who we are with the people in our lives, we are limited in what we are able to accomplish. However, it's often not something we do experience in life as most people develop an image of us based directly on their own beliefs and experiences, rather than who we are as unique individuals. This is why it is so important for each of us to take responsibility for our journey of self, rather than relying on the rest of the world to paint the picture of how we choose to live.

Discovering the fungus in the toilet was the beginning of my rejection of the pseudo self I had lived in for so many years and my current celebration of my true self. This is a process that didn't happen overnight. It has taken many years to come to the point I am at today. It is a process of change that I expect will go on for the rest of my life. Hopefully this book will help others to understand and move forward at a much faster pace than I did. However, be patient with yourself. It does take time and that's okay.

Once I had begun to celebrate my sense of curiosity, I was able to react positively to a social view of me that claimed I was intelligent. Instead of rejecting that view, I clung to it and took the step of returning to university and finishing my degree. I went out into the work world where I learned that I was proficient and capable, finding solutions to problems that no one else had developed. I ended up working with people who are on the autism spectrum and discovered my passion in life: a passion that is far from anything I had ever dreamed of. As you have read throughout this book, different revelations through experience and through education led to changes in my understanding and acceptance of myself, which in turn led to major changes in my life and in my behavior. At present I am married to my second husband, have a good relationship with all of my children and work in a field that excites me and fills me with great joy and contentment. I have written two books on autism, which are sold throughout the world and which make a very positive difference in the lives of those on the spectrum. It's an incredible feeling.

Discovering your true self is a journey which takes time and effort because you have to sift through all of the social selves that you are presented with to discover which are true and which are pseudo. A good beginning on this trip is to concentrate on the positive and discard all that is negative. The true self is always a positive force, not a negative one. Another step is to take the time to listen carefully to your own intuition, instead of the voices of those who surround you. This is the voice of your spirit, the voice of the true self. A third step is to let go of the need to control your life and let it happen. You have no idea where it might take you. The final step **is** to learn to recognize the coping skills you typically use in times of social stress to discover whether the person you are portraying to others in the moment represents you as a true or a pseudo self. How can they know you if you do not allow them to see the real person you are?

Living as the true self is living in a state of joy and contentment, which is very difficult to describe, but you will know when you are there. It's a place in which you can accept yourself totally, and celebrate exactly who you are, instead of hanging on to shame and guilt and other negative feelings of the past. It's a place where you can look at others with love and compassion, comfortable with their differences and without the need to make them react or be like you. It's a place where you can speak up clearly and confidently, sharing your beliefs with others without feeling threatened by the fact that they may not believe the same. It's a place where you can recapture the honesty and openness of the newborn and celebrate the simple joys of creation. It's an incredible place to be. I only wish it hadn't taken me so long to get here.

Once you get to the point of understanding, accepting and living as your true self, you will find that you don't always stay there. Reactions based on the past may lead us back into living as a pseudo self as it is more comfortable if that is where we have spent most of our lives. When this happens, don't despair. Remember the pendulum effect in the process of change and be patient with yourself. Once you have felt the contentment of living as a true self, you will return. The longer you live at this level the easier it is to stay there. Be prepared. Times of anxiety, of any kind, may send you back to using coping skills that you don't really want to use anymore. Environments from the past may send you back. Sensory input that matches that which you experienced in the past may send you back. The expectations of others may send you back. Relax and be aware. It's okay. You haven't lost yourself. You are just being human.

Recognizing the importance of the true self versus the pseudo self for our own 'self' allows us to begin to also recognize the pseudo selves that we carry of others. Our definitions of the world we carry in our minds are more closely linked to the spirit than to reality. In other words, we prefer to see people in their best light and create an ideal image of them. For example: a mother is supposed to be loving and kind. One's family is supposed to be functional. One's teacher should share information that is dependable and useful. When this doesn't happen we may create false pictures of others, pictures that are based on the ideal, not on the actual person we are dealing with. When they fail to live up to the ideal, we get angry and resentful. We often take their negative reactions personally because the ideal person would not act like that. We have set up an impossible situation.

In the same way that we have to accept our selves, we have to open up and accept others as their true selves. This is the true gift that we can give anyone: the opportunity and the acceptance to be who they are. Since our view of everyone we meet becomes a part of their self, it is our responsibility to ensure that this view is accurate. No one in this world is perfect. No one in this world lives at the level of our ideals. We are all struggling through life with the burdens that we have accumulated over time. When we can understand and accept that about ourselves as well as about others, we give everyone the freedom to reach their full potential. If we don't make that effort, we are forcing them to live as a pseudo self.

NECESSARY COMPONENTS OF THE SOCIAL SELF

The social self is made up of the view of every person who has knowledge of us on this earth. The creation of this self happens over time through the people we are in contact with. The significance of each view varies according to the importance of the person in our life in the present moment. At conception, our mother has the most significance as it is her womb that is our residence and the choices she makes with her body will impact our development. After birth each member of our immediate family takes precedence over others in the community. Through these people we will experience the input that will lead to the development of our brain as preschoolers. The number of people in our immediate family and the make-up of this family will vary from person to person. The impact of each of these people will vary depending on the amount of time spent with each person and the interactions we have with them. Immediate families usually consist of the people that live in the same home as the child, but in our current society, will also include any one who is acting as a caregiver of the child. Mothers are generally considered to have the greatest impact because of the time and effort that they put into the child, but this is not always the case, especially if we are dealing with working mothers. Baby-sitters also play a major role.

As we grow and develop, our social self shifts to fit the people who influence our lives the most on a day-to-day basis. For some time, the social view of our teachers becomes uppermost in our development as so much time is spent in their presence and they have so much control over the experiences we have each day. Peers replace our parents as role models and best friends become a major support. As adults these are replaced by our bosses and the people we work with. A significant other usually takes precedence over any one else for a time, and their place shifts slightly as we add children to the mix. Each of us has a different variety of social views that are the most important to us. There are no rules. There is no right way. What happens happens, and this is okay. It's how we can use this information to understand our 'self' that is important.

However, there are a number of important factors that we cannot ignore if we are to truly understand the model of self. In the chapter on change we discussed how holes develop in the social self when we lose someone through death whose view was once in our self. These holes are painful and use energy to heal. The healing of the holes happens through the process of grief. The amount of energy that the healing of each of these holes takes is dependent on the level of importance of that social view to your self.

There are certain people in our lives who are so important that we must have their view of us to exist as a whole person. If this view is missing, a hole develops in the social self which will not heal over, no matter how long we live. Our biological parents are an example of this factor. These permanent holes formed in the social self are demonstrated most clearly in children who were adopted at birth or in children who do not have any contact at all with one or both of their biological parents. These people describe the pain of not knowing who they are, of feeling like they don't belong, of not being a whole person. Although there will always be circumstances in which children will not have access to their biological parents, we must be very careful to ensure that this happens as little as possible. These children will survive, but their lives will be more difficult because of these holes. The amount of energy they have available to succeed will be lower than that of children who know their parents, as they have to use energy to deal with the hole in the self. The impact of anxiety will be higher because of this decrease in energy. They will be more dependent on coping skills than the rest of us. Is this okay?

There is one very interesting group of children these days who experience this hole in themselves. They are the children of women who decided that they wanted to have a child, on their own, without the interaction of a man, for a variety of different reasons. As scientific knowledge of reproduction increased, this became possible through the use of sperm banks and artificial insemination. Many of these children are now in their teens or older and they are demanding that they have contact with their biological fathers. Fathers who had no thought at all of the children who would be produced from the sperm they either sold or donated to the sperm banks. Fathers who never dreamed how many children may be possible through this action. Fathers who had no intention of taking any responsibility for the children who bear their genes.

As adults we have to start making the effort to ensure that this doesn't happen, unless absolutely necessary, to any more children. It's not that you cannot survive without knowledge of your biological parents, but it makes the lives of these children so much more difficult and painful with this hole or holes in their social selves. Most of the reasons for this development are based directly on selfishness on the part of the parent: individuals of both genders who want to enjoy sex without taking the responsibility for the reproduction that occurs, women who want to have the role of mother without making the effort to establish or sustain a relationship with the father, individuals who want to parent in the midst of insisting on a sexual union that has nothing to do with the reproduction of children. This doesn't mean that there is anything wrong with enjoying sex, choosing the single life or being a homosexual. It's when you are bringing a child, another spirit, into the picture without any thought or consideration of their 'self' over time, that it becomes questionable.

Other examples which may lead to the development of these holes are those developed in the parents who gave up their children for one reason or another, and those of siblings with whom one has never had any contact. The presence of these holes and the pain that is felt because of them demonstrate the importance of our immediate biological family as an aspect of our self. If it is missing, we are not whole.

Filling these holes takes place through contact with the person that the hole represents. It's that simple, and yet in our society, it's also that difficult. The opening of adoption records so that adopted children have the opportunity to contact their biological parents as adults is a step in the right direction. The new forms of adoption in which the biological parents and their extended families have contact with the adopted child throughout their life is even a bigger and better step. Recognizing the importance of interaction with family members to the self and allowing a child access to all of their biological family is the most important thing we can do. A child can NEVER have too many people loving them. Our relationships with our children are not a competition. Feeling threatened by another's interaction with your child is an indication that you are living off your life line. The only people that should be kept away from a child are those who might sexually assault the child or harm the child in some way. The crazy thing is that these people are often the people we don't have the courage to say no to. Our whole society suffers.

Other people are important to include in our view, even though their absence may not result in a hole in the self. I believe that grandparents are extremely important to children because of the impact they have on the true self of the child. Grandparents are in a unique position with grandchildren because they have the same love for the child as the parents, but they are not responsible for the development of the child in same way that the parents are. This gives grandparents the opportunity to love the child unconditionally without the anxiety of making certain that this child turns out okay as an adult. The grandparents aren't stuck with the child, but can take them home and drop them off without any guilt when they are tired or overwhelmed or wish to do something else so they don't have to expose the children to their coping skills. Parents don't have that opportunity most of the time. Grandparents are also usually more mature by the time they take on this role, and have gone through the process of discovering themselves and recognizing and accepting themselves much more than their offspring. This gives them the opportunity to relax and go with the flow as things aren't measured in black and white anymore.

In an ideal world, each of us would have four grandparents who would be an integral part of our life, celebrating the true self with us on a continuous basis either in person or through other contacts such as the telephone or e-mail. However, this isn't always possible. We don't live in an ideal world. My maternal grandmother died when I was about a year and a half old, so I never had the opportunity to develop memories with her. My paternal grandmother was locked into keeping the secret of her birth so that none of us got to truly know her and vice versa. Neither of them had the opportunity or ability to celebrate who I was as an individual with me. Many current grandparents are in similar situations. Perhaps they are so overwhelmed with anxiety that they only have enough energy to use on their coping skills. Perhaps they have had to assume the role of the parent of the child, as the real parent is either unable or unwilling to do the parenting that is necessary. Perhaps they are stuck in a family in which emotional withdrawal is the major coping skill and their children have left the family unit and do not keep in contact. Perhaps the break-up of a marriage means that one set of grandparents no longer has any access to the children. This list can go on and on. Sadly it is the children who lose out in the long run. As an individual on your journey, you can ensure that this doesn't happen in your family. Celebrate our little ones and share with them the joy of being true to themselves.

Another very significant group is our whole family of origin. These are the people who are the most like us when compared to all the other people in the world, for they share the same genes that we carry in our bodies. They are our connection to the culture we are part of and transmit the unspoken rules of the family and the culture to each of us. The intergenerational transmission of patterns of behavior **is** carried through the family of origin, whether we are aware of it or not. As we noted before, these patterns continue, even when there is no contact with this family. Actual contact with our family of origin varies from one family to another, from one individual to another. This contact may be very positive or negative, depending on how the family is functioning. Coping skills will be developed in the child, and carried on through one's adult years dependent on the modeling that happens through this family. Shared experience forms similar connections in the brain over time.

No one in your family of origin is going to be exactly like you, but in this group you are going to find the bits and pieces, here and there, which gathered together form the whole person that you are. This is what our daughter discovered at the family reunion we attended as she exclaimed "I have never been in a room in my whole life, where so many people have exactly the same nose as I do." Although this group, as her paternal grandmother's family, was only one quarter of her genetic make-up, she was able to discover certain things about herself that fit within this family. The joy of laughter, the sense of love and togetherness, the canned milk served with the coffee and, of course, her nose. It became a safe place for her because of those similarities. It gave her an opportunity to enjoy her body, because it was so much like the other bodies in the room. It also gave her the impetus to connect with other parts of her family so that she could find more of herself

You may not like everyone in your family of origin, and that is okay. This family is where we need to learn about others so that we can understand and accept ourselves. Much of what we find uncomfortable in someone else is a part of ourselves that we either haven't accepted or is a reason for our choice to live as a pseudo self. Discomfort may also be connected to the pain of the past, which will affect your anxiety level in the present, if it has yet to be dealt with. This pain may be carried on for decades and even centuries without closure in many families. Unless you have contact with your family of origin, you will not know where the pain originates, but it still will affect you. Much of this pain may be covered with denial and kept secret. It will have power to continue to hurt every family member until it is released. Bringing it out into the open is often all that is necessary to dispel it. This cannot happen without the knowledge of where it came from in the first place.

Anyone who is cut off from their family of origin is, in fact, cut off from themselves. I do realize that there are many different reasons why people choose to leave their family of origin and not return, but one is not going to be able to really come to a full understanding of oneself when one is cut off from this primary group. Making the effort to reunite with these people may take a lot of energy. It will mean putting the anxiety out into the open, which will be very uncomfortable for everyone involved. It may mean breaking patterns of behavior that have been in existence for generations. It may mean bowing your head and asking forgiveness for the way you have treated others. It may put you back into a situation that is very frightening to you because of what happened to you as a child. However, you are not a child any longer. You are an adult. The choice of response is yours and yours alone. Reaching out to the family may be a very uncomfortable choice, but it is necessary if you are going to feel totally free to be yourself.

Reaching out to your family does not mean that you are suddenly going to have these people accept you on your life line. If they are people who are stuck living life within their coping skills they will likely not be able to change to meet your needs in your time. However, by reaching out to your family, you can take a major step on the journey to self by recognizing the patterns in your family and deciphering what is real and what is a coping skill. This is an important beginning. You can also initiate the process of change in your family by being the one individual who is able to accept others as they are, unconditionally. This is not about changing them. It's about accepting them. The effort you make may begin a process of change throughout your family that is almost impossible to imagine.

The social level of your self is built first through your immediate family, then through your extended family, and finally through the community at large. The community includes your place of residence, your particular culture, and your race. It then extends on to the whole world. Being cut off from any portion of the social self is a clear indication of pain for some reason or other. The coping skill that is being used to control this pain is emotional isolation, usually accompanied by rationalization which provides a rational argument to continue the isolation. Many of us are hanging on to a pain from the past without having any clue where it comes from. How many wars are being fought today that have pain in the past at the root of the conflict? If you are cut off from any part of your social self, examining your past for the source of this pain may be a positive first step in allowing yourself access to your whole social self.

THE IMPORTANCE OF MENTORS

In the midst of this, what do we do if we don't have people in our family available who celebrate our unique spirits and allow us to be our true seelves? Relax, we are not alone. We are surrounded by a whole world of people who may fill the role of either mentors or kindred spirits to help us on our journey. Good mentors are those who have reached the point of living on their life line most of the time (one can never expect perfection) and who understand and accept themselves, freeing themselves to also be accepting of others. An individual who can find a mentor who clicks with them is truly blessed. Special mentors in my past included Uncle Olaf, a bachelor in our church, who spent a lot of time with our youth group and who was not related to me in any way. Uncle Olaf was love in our life. He accepted each of us as an individual and loved us unconditionally. A sign in his home spoke of this love and acceptance: *a stranger is only a friend you have yet to meet*. I still think of Uncle Olaf every time I see that phrase. I only hope that I can share love with others in the same way he shared so willingly with me and with all the rest of us as teenagers.

Another mentor that I treasure was my teacher in grade eight. Ingeborg Johnson was a very gentle, kind, intelligent woman who loved to learn and who loved to share this love of learning with each and every one of us as students. She never raised her voice. She never put anyone down. She rattled off epic poems from memory, poems that I still remember to this day. Her love of learning broke through the resistance I had developed over the years at school. It didn't mean that I became a perfect student but it meant that I began to enjoy the fact that I was able to learn quickly and easily. I started to make an effort to excel, at least in the areas that interested me in the moment. Memorization became a joy in the midst of a challenge and I focused my efforts on learning the material she shared with me. Although I didn't realize it at the time, Mrs. Johnson was responsible for exposing parts of the true Gail in the midst of a educational setting where I had learned to keep her closely under wraps. Although she only taught me in grade eight, Mrs. Johnson was part of my life right up until her death. She taught down the hall when I was in high school and used me as a supervisor of her class at times. We visited back and forth in each other's homes when I was first married. And finally, I sat at her bedside and wept with her as she shared the frustration of losing the ability to speak coherently, a direct result of the brain tumor that finally took her from me. I so was blessed to have her in my life. I hope that everyone can share such a relationship.

Mentors can make such a difference in a child's life. The unconditional acceptance of only one person can wipe away the negative images on the screen of the social self, erasing so much damage and allowing the true spirit to shine through. Many of the adults with autism who are succeeding in our world point to one person who made the difference in their lives and set them free to be themselves. Teachers, friends, grandparents, neighbours and parents have all held the role as that one person who made a difference for these people.

Each of us has the opportunity to be mentors. In fact, I believe each of us has a responsibility to reach out and to mentor those around us to all who need to experience unconditional acceptance. And that means everyone in the whole world. All that we need to do is to celebrate the uniqueness of each person we interact with. The opportunities will present themselves to us to make a huge difference in the lives of others if we are open to them.

Kindred Spirits

The last group of people who have a unique impact on one's social self are one's kindred spirits. All of us have kindred spirits, people who are on almost the same or a very similar life line as we are. We usually feel very comfortable with these people when we first meet them. This is because they are not a threat in any way as they are so closely connected to us. They look at us through eyes that are much the same as our own.

Kindred spirits can also be used to discover who we really are. When we are living in the midst of denial they may be the most difficult people to be with, as they force us to look at ourselves in a way that no one else has the power to accomplish. The discomfort we are feeling in that moment is a direct result of not living on our life line. We may tend to avoid them so that we do not have to face our true feelings. We may tend to avoid them in order to stay within a pseudo self. If you truly want to find your true self, you must be willing to face these feelings of discomfort and spend time with these people.

How do your recognize them? If you know someone that you wish desperately to be like, you are likely connecting with them at a spiritual level because they are kindred spirits. If you have had a close connection with someone in the past, especially when you were children, and it is now difficult to keep up, it is likely that you are kindred spirits and that one or both of you are living as pseudo selves.

Kindred spirits can be found anywhere. They don't have to have a genetic connection with you. They don't have to be the same gender as you. They don't have to be of the same race or the same culture. They don't have to be of the same age. They can be anyone. I have been blessed to have contact with several kindred spirits throughout my life. Our connection was difficult to explain until I began to understand the importance of the model of the self. These people, who appear so different from me in so many ways, are like me at the spiritual level. It's an absolute joy to be with them.

I wouldn't have the opportunity to know many of these people if I insisted on staying in the tight little boxes of my community, my religion, my culture, my educational standing and so on. I met them because I am willing to open myself to all sorts of experiences and environments. I met them because I don't see differences as something to be afraid of, or something to avoid, but instead as something to seek out and enjoy. Perhaps this is because of my level of curiosity. I don't know, but I do know the kindred spirits in my life give me a connection to my spirit that nothing else does. I hope that you, too, are blessed with their presence in your life.

COPING SKILLS ON THE SOCIAL LEVEL

As we move on to the coping skills that are used at the level of the social self, it is important to realize that we are not talking about anything that is "separate" in any way. The mind, body and social selves are all interconnected. Anxiety affects all levels, and all levels are impacted by the various coping skills that are used. Some of these skills may resemble those that are used in the mind. The reason that we separate them into different categories is so you can recognize how they are used and how they impact the self at the different levels.

Coping skills on the social level are used to project the image of self to others that we wish they would hold of us and to allow that view to continue in spite of what is happening in the present. Usually these skills are necessary when one is projecting a pseudo self to others instead of allowing oneself to be their true or solid self. Coping skills on the social level decrease anxiety due to interactions and relationships with others rather than with ourselves at the level of the mind, or with our possessions on the material level of self.

Triangulation

Triangulation is the most common example of a social coping skill, one which all of us likely engage in during our lives at some point. Triangulation involves three different people and is used to decrease the level of anxiety between two of these people. Triangles take place in every type of social interaction in this world and have both negative and positive functions in relationships. They are positive in that they are very effective in reducing anxiety in the present moment. They are negative if used to the point that the source of the anxiety is never revealed or dealt with in any way.

A mother and a daughter have a disagreement about the type of clothing the daughter should be wearing to school. The daughter walks out on her mother and goes to meet her friend at the mall. There she pours out all her frustrations and anger at her mother on her friend. The friend sympathizes with the daughter, who now feels supported and understood. Her anxiety level diminishes. The daughter has triangulated her friend into her relationship with her mother.

In the meantime, the father comes home from work. The mother pours out her frustration and anger with her daughter to him. The father tells the mother that he understands and that he will take care of the situation. Mother's anxiety decreases. She has successfully triangulated her husband into her relationship with her daughter.

The daughter returns to the home feeling better because of the conversation with her friend. The mother greets her calmly because she has handed the problem on to her husband. If he takes the role of the listener and ignores the whole situation, their home will be calm and the family members will likely be able to interact well because the number of reactions available has increased, due to the lowered level of anxiety. Perhaps mother and daughter can compromise on the clothing at this point. Perhaps the mother will not say anything about what her daughter is wearing, or the daughter can wave off her comments without a reaction because she "knows" she is right. In this case triangulation has had a positive impact on the family in the moment.

If the father reacts differently, everything will change. The daughter returns to the home. The father greets her and chastises her for treating her mother with disrespect. He then goes on to tell her that she is not allowed to wear certain items of clothing as determined by her parents. The daughter's level of anxiety rises again and she runs to her room screaming in frustration and slams the door.

At this point the mother may step into the picture again and turn on the father for being so mean to their daughter. Now she has triangulated herself into the relationship between her husband and child. She may then go to the child's room and either get angry with her for her response to the father's words, or sympathize with her for his cruelty. As you can well imagine, both these reactions are going to have a negative impact on family life.

Be aware that in spite of the positive or negative outcomes, the original disagreement has not been resolved in either situation. This is what makes triangulation so destructive to our relationships with others and to our self as a whole. If we cannot face an issue with one person without bringing in another person, we are not being true to our self. We use up precious energy every time we do this.

My family is one in which triangulation is a common coping skill chosen to reduce anxiety. Most of the time it is used in the short term to deal with new or unusual situations that we haven't faced before. When my father was slowly losing his abilities to walk and to talk, my mother would phone us to share her frustration. When we, as daughters, were concerned about our mother after father's death, we would connect with each other to talk things over, before confronting her directly. When I was concerned about my children over the years I would often air those concerns with Mom before I dealt with my children. The anxiety was decreased and in a short time, the issues could be resolved.

However, other triangles have gone on for years and have not been as positive. In 1972, my younger sister got married. My oldest son was designated as the ring bearer, to accompany the flower girl, a niece of the groom, down the aisle. They were both three at the time. We were aware that these children were very young for the roles they were to play, but both of them were very special to the bride and groom and they wanted them to be part of the celebration. Throughout the preparations for the wedding and even on the night of the rehearsal my son was willing and eager to do his best.

When the big day arrived, he was dressed in his suit, a miniature copy of that of the groom. We went to the church where we came face to face with the flower girl, a tiny model of the bride. As soon as he saw her, he rebelled and refused to enter the church. He spent the whole wedding sitting out on the front steps of the church with his father. His explanation was simple and to the point: There was no way he was going to marry that girl. He didn't even know her!

The wedding went off without any other glitches, and no one seemed too upset about what my son had done. In fact, most of us who had heard his explanation thought it was rather cute. However, the social presentation my mother had so carefully groomed had been ruined in her eyes. She kept her mouth shut until everyone had left and then attacked my husband with fury, claiming that he had been responsible for our son's behavior. We were sitting in the car, about to leave for home. My husband reacted as only he could, slamming his fist through the windshield of the car.

My mother realized she had gone too far, and offered to speak with him privately to apologize. They went into the basement of her home and talked for hours. When they emerged they had formed a triangle so strong that it still affects everything that happens around me. Family therapist Ronald Richardson speaks of the three corners of the triangle as persecutor, victim and rescuer.[19] In this triangle I became the persecutor, my husband the victim and my mother the rescuer.

Throughout the years, I recognized that this triangle played a big role in the relationship I had with my mother. I could never say anything at all against my husband in her presence without her coming to his defense, always citing the fact that he had it so rough when he was a child and that he needed special consideration. It got to the point that I became silent, rather than speaking out and being harassed. Gradually I withdrew, never realizing that this triangle was continuing on without me.

Twenty years later my eyes were opened. It was Christmas. In the midst of my turmoil of trying to live up to the year-long business commitment we had signed as a couple, I had reached a decision. I would only stay with him to the end of June I had shared the decision with him. Naturally, this weighed very heavily on his mind and although he was trying to change in positive ways, the rage and insecurity he felt inside took over more often than not. Bedtime was especially difficult. Night after night we went without sleep as he tried to convince me that I was in the wrong and that I needed to stay at his side for the rest of our lives.

We arrived at my parents' home to celebrate Christmas with the whole family, and were sleeping in the basement when this pattern of behavior started up again. As he got more and more upset, I realized I was not safe and that I would have to leave. I got up to find a motel to stay in. Hearing the commotion, my parents joined in the fray, trying to convince me to stay. As I tried to explain what was happening, my mother suddenly began to support my husband's position by outlining a number of different accusations he had made about my infidelity throughout the years. I was in total shock. I had never done anything of the sort, and yet, here was my mother listing off the

---

19 Ronald Richardson, (1995), *Family Ties that Bind*. Vancouver, B.C.: Self Counsel Press, pp.67-69.

details of these sexual encounters that I was supposed to have taken part in. Stunned I returned to my bed. The next morning I left and found a motel where I spent the rest of the season in hiding. It was definitely my Christmas from Hell.

Throughout the next year the relationship with my mother continued to cause turmoil. I left my husband and had very little contact with him, but I was constantly being accused by my mother of doing this, that or the other to hurt him. He was using her to get to me, and it worked. Every time anything came up, he would phone her to complain. Nothing that he was telling her was the whole truth, but he used enough of the specific details to make it sound like the truth and that he was the victim. Then she would call me crying, telling me what a terrible person I was and how I had to stop doing all these things that were hurting him. This continued on for almost a full year. I began to think I was going crazy and that I would have to cut myself off from everyone I loved in order to protect myself. In time, mother began to see what kind of a man he really was and how he was manipulating her. We began to talk openly about what was happening. She admitted that from the time of their conversation in the basement after the wedding, he had approached her with detailed descriptions of affairs I was supposedly having. Since I said nothing, and since she was raised to believe that people did not lie all the time, how could she do anything but believe him?

This triangle still exists today, though it is certainly much weaker than it used to be. For some time my mother was the one who kept me up on where my ex-husband was, what he was doing and how he was interacting with my sons. In time this changed, too, as he cut himself off from her, due to her lack of support. In the rare times we are all together, one can still see their connection with each other. I don't mind any more. They fill a need in each other's lives that is good for them. I concentrate on building my relationship directly with my mother. That's what is important to me

The most severe form of triangulation is adultery. When couples experience anxiety and choose to use coping skills to decrease it, rather than dealing with it openly, the end result may be adultery. Since we learn our coping skills from our family of origin, the tendency to triangulate may or may not be as significant a factor for one partner in a relationship as another. As the anxiety level increases one or both members of the relationship may find it easier to go out and find someone else to interact with either at a courtship or sexual level than to actually face the anxiety with one's partner head on. This is especially true if the partner is also using denial as their coping skill. It's easier to use one's own coping skill for each of them than face the discomfort of challenging their anxiety head on. One triangulates while the other denies.

Adultery is destructive because of the importance of all of the levels of the self. Although the message of society may be that sexual unions only happen at the material level through the body, they actually impact every level of the self: material, social, mind and spirit. We all know this, deep within, once we have committed ourselves to another person. Two do become one. Adultery brings another self into that union. The guilt and shame that we feel is very real. This leads to heightened levels of anxiety, which in turn leads on to the use of more coping skills. The situations spiral out of control.

Adultery is also destructive because of all the different selves that can become involved in this situation. As I learned through my divorce, our split did not only affect the selves of my ex-husband and me, but also every self that was connected to us in any way, especially those of our children and our immediate family. The heightened levels of anxiety and the increased levels of energy needed to keep an affair going affect everyone who is connected to the three in the triangle, especially the children. Not only are they living with the impact of the adultery in the present moment, they are also learning the coping skills they will use in the future, and may carry on this reaction as an intergenerational pattern of behavior.

The coping skill of triangulation is not just about cheating on your husband or wife. Triangulation occurs every time you take an issue you are having with another person to someone else. Triangulation occurs every time you let a job or a possession affect your relationship with another person. We do it all the time. I fully believe that it is impossible for us as humans not to triangulate in some way or another. The ideal triangle in this world is one that includes our creator. If we went to God with all our anxiety, triangulating him into the relationship we have with someone, instead of bringing in another person, all relationships may be much smoother.

Emotional Isolation

The second major coping skill that affects the social level of self is a direct result of one of the defense mechanism of the mind. Emotional isolation as described in the last chapter is a defense mechanism in which a person withdraws into passivity to protect the self from being emotionally hurt. If you do not allow yourself to feel anything, nothing will hurt you.

For 24 years my ex-husband used emotional isolation as a defense mechanism in our relationship. For 24 years he would retreat behind what I called a "wall of ice" and stay there for days on end. I never really knew what would trigger it. I never knew what would bring him out of it. It was something that I could not control in any way at all. And, although I did not understand why at the time, it was something that was far more devastating to me as a person than any type of physical assault that I experienced. I didn't understand why it had such an impact until I first saw James's Model of Self.

One of the first times I experienced "the wall of ice" was shortly after we were married. We had watched a movie together. In the movie, the actress, who was built a lot like me and was blonde and blue eyed like me, was raped by several young men. It was a very sad story, which showed the lengths of depravity that people can go to if they so choose. During the movie, my husband retreated into emotional isolation as he projected what was happening to the girl on screen to me. At this point in time, I do realize that he was doing this to avoid dealing with the pain of his past, but at the time, it didn't make any sense at all to me because I did not know of that past. He did not touch me or speak to me for over two weeks. It was as if I didn't even exist. This pattern of behavior was repeated time and again throughout our marriage and I felt absolutely lost every time it happened. Only after I discovered the Model of Self did I realize that this was indeed what had happened. Part of me had ceased to exist every time he retreated behind the wall.

As a therapist, I have had the opportunity to see this "wall of ice" through the eyes of children. Clients have shared stories of living with the same type of reaction, either from their father or their mother, who would disappear for days on end behind the wall. These clients claim they lost not only their father in this process, but also their mother, who wasn't "there" for the children because all of her energy was concentrated on trying to get through to the father; trying to keep him happy and bring him back from beyond the wall. The children were overwhelmed by the lack of love from either parent, especially the mother, when this wall is in place. They were able to recognize why the father was gone. Their mother was not as easy to explain and so they were far more devastated by the loss of her love.

Emotional isolation has a severe impact on relationships because of our level of social self. Since this level is made up of the view of your self that another person holds of you, each time that person retreats into emotional isolation, he or she effectively wipes their view of you out of your social self. A hole is created where that view should be. This hole has the same impact on the self as if the person had died. It is gone. You grieve. You adjust. And then the person relents and decides to open themselves up to you again. Their view reappears on your social self, which has to adjust again to its new form. When you are dealing with someone who uses emotional isolation as a common defense mechanism this self doesn't last. Every time the person decides to retreat into emotional isolation again, you lose that part of your social self. You are on a roller coaster of feelings as your self is in constant upheaval. The more involved this person is in your life, the greater the impact. The anxiety you face with all of this change is often overwhelming. The amount of energy you expend makes continuing the relationship questionable.

I lost the social view of my husband every time he went behind the "wall of ice." My children lost so much more for they became orphans for a time. Emotional isolation is a coping skill that is based directly on dealing with the pain of the past. Although it may appear to be useful in the moment, the long-term effects are horrendous, to the individual, to the family, to all of society.

The final result of emotional isolation will be emotional cutoff. This happens when the person you are isolating yourself from comes to the decision to no longer interact with you at all in order to protect themselves from your actions. Emotional cutoff may happen gradually over time, or abruptly as a person decides to no longer have anything more to do with the other. Again a hole will appear in the social self, but this time it is for good, unless the relationship is renewed in some way or another.

Over and Under Functioning

The defense mechanisms of under functioning and over functioning are mechanisms in which one person either takes over the responsibilities of another person, or hands responsibility of themselves to someone else. A current term used in the psychological community for this mechanism is enabling. Although this term is usually used to describe a dysfunctional system, we must realize that it, like all of the reactions we use as coping skills, has a positive impact in decreasing the level of anxiety in one's life, making it functional in its own way.

People who over function step over the boundaries of the self and into those of others, taking over the responsibilities of the person or persons. Over functioning appears, at times, to be a "good" thing as the person who is engaging in it is most often regarded as giving, caring and selfless in the midst of rationalizing that the other person needs their input in order to survive. Usually behind this rationalization lies the truth: people who over function usually do not think that they themselves are worthy of being looked after. Over functioning is their attempt to cover up their own low level of self worth. Instead of looking after themselves, as they should, they spend their time and effort looking after others. With all of their energy being expended on others over time, their own 'self' begins to break down, usually at a physical and/or mental level.

Under functioning is the direct opposite of over functioning, but it has the same result over time. A person who is under functioning is one who is not taking full responsibility for themselves and allows another person or group to take over the responsibility of maintaining one's 'self'. There are many different ways to under function and people may do all or only one of them. You may expect others to provide you with the necessities of life. You may refuse to control your own reactions and expect another to do so. You may let others make decisions for you. You may not assert your rights, your beliefs, and so on. The pattern of under functioning, like all of our reactions, is usually learned over time, either through direct experience in one's childhood or through the intergenerational transmission process.

Over functioning and under functioning go hand in hand. You need a person or group who are willing to over function in order for under functioning to take place. My first husband and I were clear examples of how this process works. In the midst of his not appearing to have the ability to control his rage, I accepted the responsibility of doing it for him by adapting my behavior. This was not fair to him, to myself or to our children. He was the one responsible for controlling himself, no matter how difficult it was. He was also the one who was responsible for sharing the truth with me, which would have led to a decrease in anxiety and a decrease in the need to control the rage. By taking over the responsibility of controlling the rage, I created a situation in which he was able to keep his secret. I have to take as much responsibility for assuming my role as the over functioning member of the family as he does of under functioning.

The processes of over functioning and under functioning happen at a societal level as well as an individual level and are as damaging over the long term to those that are involved. One example of this type of over functioning is putting labels on certain people and then limiting the responsibility they are expected to take in their lives based directly on that label. In the past, political systems were run by the males in many places in the world, as females were considered too inferior to have the vote. Certain people were not 'educated' because it was believed to be a waste of time and effort. Psychiatric labels led to institutionalization, robbing hundreds of thousands of the right to be part of the community at large. The color of one's skin meant segregation. All these decisions led to one group of people taking over responsibilities of other groups. Although we might like to think that most of these decisions are part of our past, the over functioning of one group of people over another continues to go on. Our elderly are now the ones who are forced out of the community and their families to be looked after in specialized homes. The disabled become pawns in a society which only regards them as useful in the jobs they provide others, not in their own right. Minority groups of all sorts continue to be left out in many different ways.

As in individual interactions, the process of over functioning by one person or group is always accompanied by under functioning by another person or group. Groups who have managed to pull themselves out of this situation, are those who have taken the situation into their own hands and demanded change. The people of India, under the leadership of Ghandi took their independence back from the British. African Americans, under the leadership of Dr. Martin Luther King, Jr. and others broke through the barriers of segregation. The people on the spectrum of autism are speaking up for themselves and their voice is getting louder and louder. Groups that wait for others to allow them to take charge will never make it. Groups that stand with their hands out, waiting for others to fill their needs will never make it. Groups that expect others to take responsibility for the past, no matter how horrendous it might have been, rather than concentrating on the present will never make it.

Any adult who takes the responsibility of another adult is over functioning, no matter if he is doing it as an individual or as part of a group. Any adult who allows someone else to take responsibility for a portion of his/her life that he/she is capable of looking after is under functioning, no matter if it is as an individual or as part of a group. The direct result of using this coping skill, either over or under functioning, is the loss of the full potential by both persons, or at a societal level, by both groups. Although there are many people who may need our help in different ways, it is very important to ensure that they retain responsibility for everything they can. No one is here on this earth to be "taken care of" by the rest of us. No one is here on this earth to be completely self-sufficient. We all need each other, and we all have gifts that we are responsible to share with others. If we take over the lives of anyone else, we rob them of the opportunity to share their gifts with us. If we regard anyone else as inferior to us, we will not be open to the gifts they have to share. If we become the "caregivers," we will not have the energy to care for ourselves, and it is our self that will be damaged. We must be careful.

Compensation

The last defense mechanism that I want to focus on at a social level is compensation. Freud defined compensation as the mechanism by which one covers up a weakness by emphasizing one's desirable traits. By focusing on the positive, we can pretend that that we are worth more and sadly, that is the message we are given from the time we are little children. However, when we are unable to accept all of ourselves as okay and cover up pieces of ourselves, hiding behind the facade of a pseudo self, we don't let the people in our lives see the true self, and thus their views of our social self can never form the true picture of us. We are forced to live in a pseudo world by our own reactions.

An extreme form of compensation is bullying. Through this reaction we use the imperfections of others instead of our own to emphasize our own positive traits, convincing ourselves that we are better than they are. Again this is a direct result of not being willing to own up to and face our own imperfection. By concentrating on another, instead of ourselves, we take the lens off us. The anxiety that is caused in our bodies by our unwillingness to face our weaknesses means that we try to deny them completely. Most of these weaknesses are not real, but are the direct result of living as a pseudo self. The discomfort is caused by our unwillingness to change ourselves. The higher the level of this discomfort, the more extreme our "bullying" reaction will be.

Bullying occurs every time a person hides, or attempts to hide their own weaknesses by attacking those of another. Although there is a tendency for our society to view bullying as something that happens in school playgrounds, it is actually a problem that is rife throughout the interactions of all people here on earth. Whenever the self feels threatened by its actions and reactions and turns these negative feelings onto another person, one is bullying that person.

At this point in time, there is a concerted effort, especially in schools, to wipe out bullying. We cannot do this until we truly understand what bullying is and how it is used to decrease the anxiety in the bully. By recognizing bullying as a coping skill, we immediately take the power away from the action. By recognizing the power of the pseudo self --- that is, the mistake of children being given the message that they are not and never will be acceptable as themselves, but rather need to meet the expectations of others --- we can allow our children to be free to be themselves. All of our infants live on their life line. We move them to being pseudo selves as they grow by fearing differences, by focusing on competition, by defining certain things, certain attributes, certain abilities and certain people as being better than others. There is no "better." We are all the same, in the midst of having different attributes, different abilities and different ways of being. All of these differences are necessary for the human race to survive on this earth. They are gifts, not imperfections. They need to be celebrated.

This is the true secret for defeating bullying. The celebration of the true self of each and every human being on this earth, the unconditional acceptance of differences, the anticipation of allowing each of us to achieve our full potential. What a dream! The only thing that is standing in its way is for each of us to move to the point where we are living directly on our life line. By taking responsibility for ourselves we can gradually move the whole world in that direction.

The use of coping skills at a social level such as triangulation, over and under functioning and compensating affects us as negatively as a self as those of the mind do. The energy that we are using to "cope" is wasted and no longer available to share our full potential with the world. The energy that we use to carry on the facade of a pseudo self is wasted and no longer available to share our full potential with the world. This lack of energy leads directly to the breakdown of the self in a physical and psychological way over time. It is so much more effective to live on one's life line and to allow others to live on theirs.

THE POWER OF A SMILE: A CASE STUDY

The first time I saw him he was standing outside of our local grocery store, selling the street newspaper, which allows homeless people some dignity as they try to pull together enough money to exist from one day to the next. He was dirty and disheveled and I averted my eyes as I walked past him, as I do with so many who are in this position. I didn't have the extra change in my pocket to share with him in the moment and thus I preferred not to acknowledge his presence in any way. I caught the flash of a dazzling smile as I passed, which pulled my eyes to his face. It was difficult to ignore the smile. I apologized for my lack of money. He told me it was okay and wished me a good day with another smile.

I saw him often after that, standing there, selling his papers and talking to the many different customers as they came out of the store. Sometimes I had change, other times I could only say hello and wish him well, but his smile and demeanor never changed. It stayed the same no matter how much I was able to give him. It felt good to receive it from him.

And then one day, there came an abrupt change. He was clean. He was polished. He was shocking, in bright black hair and black clothes, so different from what he had worn before. I asked what happened and he told me that a hairdresser, who worked in the mall, had told him to come in for a free haircut. This led to the decision to dye his hair. She had been so intrigued by his smile that she had offered her services to him for nothing. Someone else heard what she had done, and turned up with new clothes for him to wear. He looked like a different person all together. But the smile was the same.

Then came the day that he told me he wouldn't be there any more. Another customer had been pulled in by that smile in the same way I had been, and had offered him a full time job. He wouldn't need to stand on the street selling his papers any longer. He would be back in the work force. He was looking forward to becoming a contributing member of our society again. I wished him well and missed him for a time.

One day he reappeared and I asked him what had happened. He told me that he loved the job, but it had irritated an old injury in his back and the pain made it impossible for him to continue doing it. This made me look at him with different eyes. This was not a bum standing on the corner selling newspapers. This was a man who had a history, who had a reason for living as he did, who was doing the best he could in the circumstances in which he was placed. I wanted to know more.

We have made several appointments to share lunch sometime so that I could share more of his story with you in this book, but it hasn't worked out for us, for one reason or another. Perhaps it's not meant to be. He's not in front of the store so much these days, and he tells me it is because he is now contributing to the newspaper and makes some of his money that way. He also has different spots in the city where he chooses to sell his papers.

At this point the smile continues to be shared with those who are lucky enough to come across this man in their daily journeys through our city. It's an incredible smile. One you can't ignore. It leaves me, at least, longing for more. Obviously I am not the only one who is affected by this smile. As I work on this book I wonder about this man's purpose on this earth. Is this what he is here for? Is his smile the gift that he has been given to share? Does he need to be in the position that he is in to be able to share it in the most productive way? Is the purpose in life, for some, as simple as this? I don't know, but I do know that his smile took me to places I wouldn't have thought possible as I journey on. I interact with others differently because of it. I continue to celebrate it, whenever I have the chance to share it with him. We interact with each other easily and joyfully both in person and in my memory. I don't have much money to share with him. I can't give him a job. I don't want to take responsibility for one moment of his life. And yet, I truly believe that we are interacting at the level that God has created for each of us. All because of that smile.

CHAPTER EIGHT
THE DEVELOPMENT OF THE MATERIAL SELF

At the end of life we will not be judged by how many diplomas we have received, how much money we have made, how many great things we have done. We will be judged by "I was hungry and you gave me to eat, I was naked and you clothed me, I was homeless and you took me in." Hungry not only for bread - but hungry for love. Naked not only for clothing - but naked of human dignity and respect. Homeless not only for want of a room of bricks - but homeless because of rejection

MOTHER TERESA, 1983

THE CHINA IS PILED NEATLY ON A DISPLAY TABLE. THERE ARE PLATES AND PLATTERS, teacups and saucers and special serving dishes. My eyes light up with pleasure. I have been searching for these pieces for many years and here they are, right in front of me. Should I buy them, or leave them for someone else who is also collecting this particular pattern?

"It's a sad story," the salesman tells me. A story of decisions made for a child, of years of gift giving and finally of pain. It was supposed to be a good thing in the beginning, but it didn't work out that way. And so now, the china awaits a new home.

She was born in 1967, the centennial year of our country, a special child. An only daughter for a couple who had struggled hard through the years and who did not expect to have any children. But here she was. They were determined to give her everything that they had not been able to have for themselves.

They settled on the china because it represented the year of her birth in the midst of also being a symbol of the 100th anniversary of the country they had fought to call home. Centennial Rose: a special pattern to commemorate the special occasions of their little one, a limited edition, which would ensure that the china kept its value over time.

The first piece was bought the day they brought her home from the hospital, the day they welcomed her into their home. The regal tray took its place in the china cabinet beside the other bits and pieces of glassware they had accumulated throughout their lives since arriving in this country. These bits and pieces symbolized all their family had lost as the second World War decimated their lives and their homeland. This new piece of china, a symbol of their love for their daughter, held a special place of honor. It represented all their hopes and dreams for this child. It represented the life style that their parents had lost and that they now envisioned for her in the future.

The other pieces came later, gradually, throughout the years: a full place setting for every birthday, the teapot and serving pieces over the years at Christmas, a Bristol mug to celebrate the passing into a new grade at school. They were all hers, but she wasn't actually allowed to touch them. She would unwrap them carefully with her mother by her side, hand them to her mother who then took them and placed them gently for show. Over the years this collection gradually took over the whole china cabinet and the rest of the glassware was relegated to the kitchen cabinets.

It was easy to purchase them for the first ten years, as you could go into any shop that sold fine china and pick out any piece you wanted. Then, as a limited edition, the company stopped producing them. One had to make the effort to check out a lot of different stores to find the last available remnants of place settings and individual pieces. No longer could they follow a set pattern of gift giving, but could only present whatever pieces they were able to procure. But they persevered, and the pieces of china continued to appear as gifts all through her teens.

She left home in her mid-twenties after finishing university and obtaining a job in a legal firm. The china was carefully packed and transported to her new home. She decided to have a formal dinner to celebrate her new status with a small group of friends and family members. Her parents arrived early and were aghast when they saw that their daughter had laid out the china on the dining table. "What do you think you are doing?" they cried out in anguish. "You can't use this china for eating! It's much too valuable for that." As her mother carefully stacked up the pieces and returned them to the china cabinet, the daughter dutifully followed her mother's lead, taking out the everyday dishes for her guests.

The china remained unused in the china cabinet. Each Christmas and birthday another piece would appear as a gift, now scrounged from flea markets and antique stores, the only place that one could buy it. The pattern from the past continued. The daughter would carefully unwrap the present, thank each of her parents for the piece and then place it in the cabinet with the rest of the collection. She thought about using it when her parents weren't present but worried that they might find out somehow. They were getting older and their health wasn't good. It wasn't worth the trouble it would cause.

In time her parents passed on and the daughter decided that she was finally free to use the china. She took it all out and carefully washed each piece, trying to anticipate the joy of sharing it with friends. But she found that she couldn't do it. There was no pleasure in laying it out on the table, only extreme discomfort, and so she returned it to the china cabinet. And then, finally deciding that she didn't want to deal with the pain it evoked any longer, she brought it to this store to sell.

I share this story of a china collection as it symbolizes so many powerful factors in the development of our material self that we rarely think about, but that form this level of 'self' in ways that impact our lives every day. As we learned in the first chapter, the material self is made up of everything we call our own: the things we buy, the roles we take on, the clothes we wear, the food we eat, and the bodies we live in. Although we may like to think that these things are freely chosen by us as individuals, we must admit that they, like everything else about the self, develop over time through the experiences we have throughout our lives. Much of the material self is determined by others: our parents, our community, our economic standing, our location in the world, in much the same way that this china set came into the life of this woman. Much of the material self is controlled by others in the same way that these parents controlled the use of their daughter's china. And even more so, much of the pleasure and satisfaction we get from our material self develops though the reactions of others and the actual experiences we have had over time. In other words, even though all of these different factors of the material self may appear to be separate from us, they do become a part of our actual self through our experience here on earth.

Defining and understanding our material self clearly gives us the opportunity to make decisions about what we have in our material self: what we want to keep, what is most important for us to focus on, and what we would like to walk away from. Living on one's life line is not about not having a material self, but instead creating one that allows us to reach our full potential. Because the material self is so large, we will not focus on all of the different factors that comprise it, but on the level as a whole.

There are four different tools one can use to measure if something in the material self fits on one's life line. These are the impact of our beliefs and values, energy output, the pseudo self, and the use of our individual coping skills. We can use each or all of these to clearly understand how different aspects of the material level are currently influencing our ability to live up to our full potential. This gives us the opportunity to choose what factors we want to keep, and those we want to change. We can take charge of the actual form of our material self, but we can't do so without making an effort to understand and take responsibility for it.

Tools for Measuring the Impact of the Material Level

Beliefs or Values

The beliefs and values that we have stored within our minds are unique and individual to each of us based on our own personal experience in this world. These beliefs come directly to us through our families, through our communities, through our cultures and through our personal experiences. Many of our beliefs are unspoken, and yet understood and accepted so deeply that we don't even know we are acting on them. Others are right out there in the open, all around us as spoken or unspoken messages we are receiving on a day-to-day basis from our families or the society we live in. These beliefs will determine what we choose to have in our material self. It is important to figure out what one believes in order to make the best choices at this level.

If we believe that we can only be successful with a perfect body, we will either spend all our energy trying to achieve it, or on coping skills dealing with the sense of failure we have about ourselves because we don't have that perfect form. If we believe that the medical, pharmaceutical and commercial interests are focused on a profit margin, instead of the best interests of humanity, we will stop accepting what they hand over to us without thought and begin to take full responsibility for the choices of what we are putting in our bodies. If we believe that our value in the world is measured by the amount of dollars we have or the possessions we own, we will focus our efforts on the acquisition of material goods and not reach our full potential. If we believe that certain jobs, levels of education, places of residence or roles make some people better than others, we will never be able to give unconditional acceptance to ourselves or to anyone else in this world. This keeps us from living on our life line. The material self must be regarded as a tool to an end, not the end itself. Our beliefs will determine whether we are able to reach that end.

One of the biggest fallacies we live with as human beings is that there is not enough money to do the things we want to do, things we know we should do. There's not enough money to ensure that everyone in the world has their needs met. In other words, there is not enough money to go around to allow each person to reach their full potential. It's a message we hear all the time. And it's such a lie. Because this isn't about money. It has never been about money, and it never will be about money. This lie keeps so many of us from even trying.

First of all, we must consider exactly what money is. In the beginning there was no money. People survived by finding the things they needed in their environment: food, drink and shelter. Those who were able to access these material goods survived. Those who did not died. Our world is an incredible place and provides for our needs in so many different ways. Humans were successful in providing for themselves in all sorts of different environments in all sorts of different ways. The differences between us began to develop.

Human beings are very flexible and adaptable and they began to realize that they could be more successful in gathering the things they need to survive by focusing on one need and sharing it with each other instead of having each person concentrate on their own needs. Barter of the material goods became the method of commerce. In time money was created in order to simplify the bartering process. Although this is a very simple explanation of our history, it is enough for us to understand where money originated.

In the past there were times in which we had a shortage of products based on our ability to access these products. The people who had more than they needed began to gain power because of what they had. This led to a hierarchy of power based on what people owned. Those who focused on the acquisition of more goods gradually gained more power. Those who were content to live without, or who were unable to acquire more for any number of reasons, lost power. Groups of people joined together to control the power over both land and products. They developed currency in order to organize themselves. These groups became countries. Governing bodies were developed. These governing bodies were in control of the currency that was created. This system basically stayed in place until the end of World War I. At that point the currency in the world was based directly on a gold standard: the amount of gold that was held in the treasuries of each country. There was a limit to the amount of currency that could be created because of the limited amount of available gold in the world. This, in turn, limited our possibilities. Many people believe that this is what our money is based on today, but they are wrong. International agreements after World War I changed everything.

At this point countries continue to create the currency that we use, but they are no longer in charge of how much money the world actually has. Banks have been given the right to create money through loans. This has created situations in which people, companies and even countries owe billions and trillions of dollars to the banks. Many people fear the level of this debt. This fear can be used for control of others. But we don't have to fear it if we understand what has happened. Let's bring this anxiety out into the open.

A fable of the past tells of a woman who was able to spin gold from straw, an incredible feat when the monetary basis in the world was the gold standard. The reality of our time is even more fantastic: our money is now being created out of thin air. If you understand how this happens, the current debt load in the world begins to make sense. It also reduces our level of fear concerning this debt. Sadly, there are a lot of people in the world who do not want the ordinary person to understand this, but we must make the effort if we are going to reach our full potential.

So, this is how it happens. I am going to use figures in this example, but I want you to understand that these figures are not necessarily those being used by specific banks. Although the World Bank has the most control over this situation, not all agreements are the same. Some banks may have their own specific figures to base their contracts on. Different countries may use different figures in working with their banks. I have not made the effort to make certain that these figures are correct in any way. They are only an example of how the process happens. I hope that no one gets stuck on the accuracy of this example based on your specific experience and understanding of economics. You probably know more than I do. This is okay. It's the theory, not the exact details, that are important.

You have $1000 that you want to keep safe. You deposit it in the bank. This gives the bank the basis to lend money to another person. The amount of money they are allowed to loan out, based on your $1000 suddenly becomes the equivalent of $5000. It's not that your money will go to the other person, but that the bank now has the right to loan out $5000 to someone else based on your deposit if they so choose. The money that is loaned is not real. Most of the time it exists only as numbers that move from one account to another in the bank's books. However, when the loan is repaid, the money becomes real. Actual currency is used to repay the loan. Numbers written on a piece of paper have now become money. On top of this, we also have the creation of interest, which is the extra money that the lender has to pay for the right to use the original $5000. With this kind of system in place, the amount of money that can and has been created is limitless. That's why banks are able to continue making vast profits year after year without fail. It's also why debt loads are able to increase without the whole economic system collapsing. So it's not about money

The facade of the importance of money in our lives breaks down when we look at how we actually distribute the money in this world. How much do we choose to use to educate our children in comparison to how much we are willing to spend on our coping skills such as fantasy? Any society willing to spend millions of dollars for one man to play a game such as basketball while some of its children go hungry is a society that doesn't have a problem with money. The lack of money is only an excuse. How long are we going to accept this?

When people live at the material level of self, money becomes all-important. We move from worshipping our creator to worshipping money and we are content to allow all sorts of horrors to take place because of this worship. Those in charge of the economic situation in the world do not want you to know about this. They want you to believe the fallacy that there is not enough money. They want you to accept the situations that continue because of this lack of money. This gives them a power based directly on chronic anxiety, not reality. If you believe the fallacy you are disempowered. If you don't have money and you believe that you need money to make a difference, you won't try to change things. If you believe the fallacy and you have money, you will do anything to hang on to it. Your beliefs about money will keep you in your place.

Money is definitely part of our material self. The amount of money we have makes a huge difference in how we live, but it is not how we reach our full potential. In fact, the love of money or the pursuit of money is the main force that can keep us living at the material level rather than moving on to that of the spiritual self. We can easily become so wound up in protecting our wealth, spending our wealth and accumulating more wealth that we do not even consider moving to a higher level of self. Or we can become so envious of those who have wealth that we go without instead of moving on.

Those who have a lot of money have a very serious position in our world when it comes to reaching their full potential because they have the most to give up if they don't worship it. How will they spend it? How much energy will they devote to it? How can they share it with others in a way that will make a difference in the world? How can they live without feeling guilty? Without having to use their coping skills to cover up these feelings of guilt?

The economic situation of our world is a situation that not many of us pay any attention to, much less understand clearly, in the midst of dealing with it every day of our lives. The assumption that certain people are worth X amount of money while others are worth twice as much, or even more is accepted without thought. The assumption that some can have far too much, while others don't have enough to survive, doesn't lead to any concern. We accept the hierarchy of economic power, a hierarchy that often doesn't make any logical sense at all. The classes of the past, based on family connections have now been replaced by economic status. What will replace them in the future?

This is not about living without. In fact, living without is the furthest thing from my mind. It's about living with the best that is important to you as a person, in the midst of knowing that what you have will require you to expend energy. We cannot exist without material goods. The advancements we have made throughout the centuries have led us to a point where we can have more than we ever have had been before. These material goods enrich our lives in so many different ways, easing our workload, adding beauty and comfort to our days, providing connections to each other and to our past, and giving each of us the opportunity to share ourselves with those we care about in different ways. If we cut ourselves off from our material self, we lose as much as if we cut ourselves off from each other or from our spirit.

The production of material goods and the commerce that allows us to share goods with each other may be the unique purpose of so many different people on this world. The contributions at the material level of so many different people have made such an impact on our world. The inventions of people like Thomas Edison, The Wright Brothers, Alexander Graham Bell, and Henry Ford make positive contributions to our lives every day, but these are only the big names. There are countless others who have added their own small piece to the picture that we take for granted without any thought or gratitude to the person who came up with the idea in the first place. We need food. We need clothing. We need shelter to survive. Vehicles, machines, and appliances all make this survival easier. If we walk away from the material world, we walk away from the people who produce them, distribute them and do the upkeep on them. Much of the "stuff" in our world may seem superfluous and unnecessary, but it also may play its part bringing someone joy, allowing someone to be creative, or letting a certain person reach his full potential, so it's all important. We can't measure this impact for others and it is not our responsibility to decide what is, or what is not, to be. It is far better to accept the material world that fits us as an individual, to measure the impact of choices we are making ourselves and celebrate that which we have in our own way, to listen to our inner voice and follow its lead.

Measuring the impact of our choices happens at two levels, that of the self, and that of humanity, which returns us directly back to the fallacy of not enough money. This fallacy leads to a competition based on greed. Instead of measuring people on their abilities and what they can share with the world, we base their worth on profit margin. This concern of profit margins has led to the creation of corporations that are growing bigger and bigger all the time by joining together, or buying each other out in a desperate attempt to increase the "profit margin" with little concern of how this will affect humanity. Countless people are caught up in a variety of jobs, which take all of their time and energy, just to increase the profit margin of a corporation. We are like hamsters, running in circles on a wheel in a cage, with no thought of why we are doing what we are doing or what impact this has on other people. Asking yourself exactly what you are working for and how it is improving your own life and the lives of everyone on this earth is an important step on your journey to self. The world we live in right now doesn't have to stay this way. The choices we each make as an individual will be the impetus for change.

The lack of importance of a profit margin is best demonstrated during times of disaster. No matter where a natural disaster occurs, the rest of the world steps in to provide help in whatever way it can. These are the times when we have the opportunity to experience the best that mankind has to offer. In these moments, it's never about money, although a lot of people try to make it seem that way. It's about trained manpower. It's about building materials. It's about obtaining the necessities of survival: shelter, food and clean water. It's about mechanical and technical power. It's about sharing the energy one has with those who have lost everything for the moment. It's not about a profit margin. And yet when we return to our ordinary lives, we tend to forget and move back to that which really isn't very important.

In the midst of all this we live in an incredible time. I can get on a plane and fly across the country or all the way to Europe or Asia in one day. When I get there, I can take out a simple piece of plastic and have a brand new car turned over to me to use as long as I want. This piece of plastic will also provide me a place to sleep that is equal to, and usually even more opulent than, that which I live with at home. A room that is cleaned by another and that I can move in and out of at will. I eat meals that are prepared for me by chefs. I can enjoy any type of entertainment that I want. Or, if I so choose, I can stay home and do none of this. I can shop in a local grocery store and buy foods that have been flown in fresh, from every corner of the world. I can access the top entertainers in the world, on my computer, my television set, my stereo or I-pod, or even in a local theaters or concert halls. I can clothe myself in the latest styles via shopping malls or the Internet, or choose to wear the same clothes, day after day, year after year because of my washer and dryer. Our medical knowledge is at a point where almost any medical problem can be solved. Our technical advances have taken us to the moon and back and can have me instantly in contact with a friend who is on the opposite side of the world in any number of different ways. The possibilities in our lives are endless. The reality is that there is no way I can access all of the possibilities open to me because of a lack of energy and time. I have to be selective. So does everyone else. But it's not because of money or profit margin, even if that is what we all believe.

The journey to where we are as human beings and the choices we now have has taken centuries. Throughout time, the possibilities open to certain people have been restricted by other people in a variety of different ways: through class, through religion, through education and through economic standing. When the labor force began to fight for their rights through the union movement in the late 1900's, the upper class tried to restrict these changes based on a fear that there wouldn't be enough goods to meet their needs if we allowed the working class the same privileges. Over a hundred years has passed. We have not run out of goods. It's difficult to imagine how much stuff this world actually has. There is no shortage.

When I was in high school, we were warned that the population of the world was too large and that we needed to take control of it, if we were to survive. They warned us of food shortages, which would lead to starvation and famine. The number of people in the world continues to rise as the ability of humans to adapt has continued. We are not starving. In fact, most of us are suffering from the opposite problem. We have too much. The famine that is experienced in the world today is not due to a lack of food, but an unwillingness to make the effort to share with those who have less. This is not about money. This is about the will to be true to ourselves, to be true to the rest of humanity, to be true to our creator. We have to stop making excuses.

Then what is it about? It's about fear: the fear that I will go without if I allow you to have. This may have been true in the past but we have to realize that we live in a much different world than that of our ancestors. We have to realize the world has become a place in which we are in touch with every other human being on earth and have access to everything. The decisions we are making are not those that result in our going without, but that result directly in the threat of terrorism we are currently facing. Our need to keep everything for ourselves means that millions of others are going without. The children that are raised in this situation are ripe for indoctrination into groups that promise to punish us for our greed. We can't ignore the global responsibility of this situation any longer. We have to wake up and admit that we are as much of the problem as anyone else.

Our focus on keeping everything for ourselves leads to a situation in which much of our energy is being used for the acquisition of more material goods. Everything on the material level uses energy of one kind or another. We use monetary energy based directly on biological energy to buy that which we own. This leads to the necessity of providing shelter and organization to keep on top of all of the stuff we have acquired. Things need to be kept up, or discarded and replaced by something else, in order for the self to avoid the discomfort of loss. Things need to be protected. We can go on and on. All of this takes energy.

A basic law of nature is that energy cannot be either created or destroyed. It can only be changed. This means that we are not losing anything or gaining anything when we use energy. Our earth is capable of sustaining us. Take a moment to consider the reality of that statement. We constantly get the message that we are going to run out, or we are going to change things so significantly that we will destroy the earth. This is the message of people who believe that human beings are powerful. It is a fallacy. It is a message of fear. We are safe from the stupidity of humanity. The power of nature, the power of our world, the power of our creator, is far beyond ours.

I learned this message back in the 1980's when I attended an international film festival at our local university. One of the films focused on the nuclear bomb tests that took place near the Bikini Islands in the early 1950's. These tests were conducted by the American government to determine the long-term impact of a nuclear blast on the earth. The film focused on the fact that the government had undertaken these tests without warning the inhabitants of the islands. After the bombs exploded, the atomic dust settled on the beaches. The people woke up to find their world buried in a white powder, which they assumed was snow, never having actually being exposed to real snow. They played in it for days.

It wasn't snow. It was nuclear fallout, which led to a lot of different problems for some of the people involved. The film claimed that the US government was avoiding taking responsibility for what had happened to the people on Bikini Island. It was a typical doom and gloom story, trying to make us feel sorry for someone else.

I watched this movie in absolute awe, not because of what had happened to the people, but because of what hadn't happened. All my life I had believed in the devastation of a nuclear bomb. I had been told that everything would be destroyed and that everyone who was not killed by the actual blast would die from radiation poisoning in a short time. I had been taught that the land would be decimated and would not be productive for generations. And here, in front of my eyes, was the proof that none of this was true. Yes, there was a direct impact on some of the people of the island over time, and note that I say "some" not "all," which is what I thought should have happened. The film I was watching was made about 30 years after the original blasts occurred. These people played in the nuclear fallout. They should be dead. Their island should be barren wasteland for decades or even centuries. It wasn't. The land was continuing to provide for these people as it had throughout history.

Not everyone was affected by the fallout, contrary to what I had been taught. Those who were pregnant either miscarried or bore babies that were deformed in some ways. Some of the people developed cancer as the years passed. Some of the children had genetic problems as adults, either being unable to reproduce or having children born with deformities. And yes, this wasn't fair. The US government had made a choice to do something that dramatically impacted the lives of these people. But not everyone was affected. Some lived much the same lives they would have if this hadn't happened. They were not all changed by the fallout. And those who were affected survived. Yes, their lives were different, but they weren't lost. Life on the island continued. This world is tougher than anything man can conceive or do.

If we take the law of energy to heart, we can begin to live in a way where we share the world's resources with everyone instead of hoarding them for ourselves. We can focus on what we can do to ensure that we make the best choices. The importance of oxygen is an example. We get the oxygen we breathe through the plants that grow around us. It is a symbiotic relationship. If we insist on destroying all the plants, especially the trees, and even more so, the vast tracks of forests that are so vital to this process here on earth, we will create a situation in which there is no longer enough oxygen for us to breathe. If this happens our bodies will suffer. We may die. It is the direct consequence of our actions. But then the trees will grow again. They do have this ability, and the earth will continue on without us. Look at any space that has been left without human input for some time. Nature takes it back again. Like so many other situations on our earth this is an easily avoided problem, either by not cutting all the trees or by replanting the forests. Why don't we do this? Because we don't have the money? No. Because we don't have the will. We are so busy worshipping a small profit in the present moment, living at the level of the material self, that we ignore the big picture. We are so indoctrinated with the fear of not enough money that we do not demand the changes necessary to protect the forests. We become so involved in all of the insignificant details of our material 'self' that we ignore our earth, one of the most important pieces of the material self for each and every one of us.

The same is true with the recycling of all of the different metals and other materials that we throw out every day. The garbage dumps of this world are absolutely unbelievable. We are treating far too much of our resources as trash, something to dispose of in our pursuit of a profit margin. The human tendency to ignore the whole picture is so evident when we look at our garbage dumps. Thankfully we are not dependent on human law. It's the natural laws that are in control. These materials are not gone for good. We are not that powerful. Energy can neither be created nor destroyed. It can only be changed. When we need it, we will learn this lesson, and this material will be there waiting to be mined. Again, it's not about money. It's about the will to put out the effort to access these materials. It's about giving up on the lie.

Reaching our full potential is not about worrying about money. It's about letting go of that worry. It's about not allowing ourselves or others to use money as an excuse. Once we make this paradigm shift we can have the freedom to take on any challenge. To do what has to be done without worrying about how we are going to pay for it. And it happens. Some how, in ways that we can't predict in advance, it happens. By letting go, we release our spiritual power. It makes our journey here through life unbelievable. How sad that so many never get to experience this freedom.

In 1988 I began working in the field of autism and realized how little I knew. As I worked with these people I recognized the sensory connection that often leads to their extreme reactions. I went out into the world to learn about this sensory difference from autism experts of the time and discovered that no one had really paid any attention to it, at that point, and that no one considered it to be very significant. But I knew, deep down inside that I was on the right track. I started to collect the words of those on the spectrum. They confirmed my beliefs. I developed a method of care based on this information and tried it out first on a 17-year-old who was in desperate circumstances --- head banging almost every day, all day. His family was at a breaking point. He destroyed three rooms in the local hospital when they tried to hospitalize him, so they refused to keep him there.

There was no place for him to go. He came into my life, into my home, and in a short time we had made big differences for him. No, we didn't cure autism, but we made it possible for him to stop head banging; for him to start showing us who he truly was as a person; for him to start taking part in day-to-day life in a meaningful manner. In time his family took him back as they now felt capable of caring for him. I never saw him again.

This led on to other children, other families, and I chose to teach them what I did rather than hanging on to it myself. This isn't something I can own. I received it as a gift from those on the autism spectrum and I pass it on to others to share with those who are impacted by autism. I got in contact with families from around the world. A mother in England shared her research on the connection of autism with endorphins with me as I shared what I had learned about the sensory system with her. She heard about a conference in England where she thought we should present our findings. I offered to write it up and let her present for me, but she didn't feel she could do it justice. Instead, she got in contact with the conference organizers, who offered to pay my expenses if I would attend. I did and my theory on the sensory connection to autism was presented to the world for the first time.

Some of the people at the conference were very excited about the work I was doing and wanted to find a way to share it with the people they were working with. They suggested that I write a book on what I was doing. Writing a book had been a dream for me since I was a child, but I certainly hadn't ever thought of it being on something like autism. I did know that I had to find a way to share what I was doing, and a book made sense. The problem was not writing it. Much was already written in the reports that I was handing out to the families I was working with. The problem was how to get it published. I didn't have a clue how to achieve this end.

I went back to Alberta and contacted every publisher in the province asking if they would be interested in publishing this type of book. It was a rather naive way of doing things, but it got results. I got a lot of rejection letters, but there was one glimmer of hope. The University of Calgary Press said they were interested, as long as the book contained scientific research. Again, this was not a problem for me as I had already included a lot of information directly from scientific research of different kinds, and was interested in adding more. I agreed to work with the University Press and was assigned an editor. I arranged my life so that it was possible for me to earn a living in the midst of taking time to write and I bought a computer. My first book was on its way.

Two years later the book was complete, in spite of all of the chaos that had been going on in my life. The editor and I worked well together, making sure that it flowed as it should and that it fairly represented the scientific research I was quoting. When I turned in the completed chapters for their final editing, he gave me a new assignment: to contact everyone I was quoting in the book to get letters of permission to quote. It looked like a sure thing.

And then, we had an election in our province and our new premier decided to change the way the government was funding the universities. The funding for the University Press disappeared overnight. My book was in limbo. This is where letting go and letting God becomes so important. I could have thrown up my hands up in despair. I could have challenged the University Press and demanded that they live up to our agreement. I could have gone out and searched for another publisher. Instead I continued to do my job, getting the letters of permission from the other authors and their publishers.

One of the publishers wrote me two letters. One gave me permission to quote. The other indicated an interest in the book if I was interested in them. In the end, everything worked out far beyond my dreams. The owner of this publishing company was the past president of the Autism Society of America so he had real connections with the autism community, not only all over the United States, but also the whole world. Because of Future Horizons, my name became known and the book has been sold all over the world, making a difference in the lives of so many. Had it been published by the University Press, it likely would be sitting on a shelf collecting dust at this point. Instead it is making a difference in the world. Not worrying about my lack of money, not worrying about my lack of knowledge of the publishing industry, not worrying about the end result let me achieve something I had dreamed about. This can happen for you too if you give up worrying about money; if you give up believing the lie. There is enough for all of us.

I am not the only person who has discovered that letting go allows you to get to places you never thought possible on your own. Most of the ordinary people who are making millions with simple ideas or interventions are people who learned this lesson. By sharing their "gift" with the world, they receive in return. When letting go is combined with the knowledge that energy cannot be created or destroyed, but only changed, and that the earth can sustain us if we so let it, each of us can have the power to reach our full potential.

Energy

Our journey through life is dependent on energy. Much of the energy we expend is either dependent on what is included in our material self or not available because of how we focus that energy on the material self. This energy comes in many different forms: the physical energy of our bodies, derived from the food we eat, the air we breathe and the water or other liquids we drink; the biological energy we create through movement, which can be used to change the environments we live in, in an incredible variety of ways; the monetary energy of the wages we earn for the work we do; the creative energy of our thoughts and ideas and the way we put them into action in the world around us; the emotional energy of the feelings we share with those with whom we come in contact.

Each of us has energy to use, each day of our lives. The amount of energy we will be able to access is totally dependent on how and where we choose to spend this energy. The ability to reach one's full potential is also dependent on these choices. If all of your energy is focused on staying alive, there is little left for anything else. If all of your energy is focused on obtaining material goods or putting monetary energy aside for the future, the social and mind levels of the self will suffer. If all of your energy is going towards coping with anxiety, it's not available for obtaining material possessions. This is not about an all or nothing situation. It's about spending your energy as wisely as possible and discovering ways to have more of it available. This does not always happen in the ways our world currently stresses.

The real secret to increasing your energy level is often letting go and letting God, rather than striving harder or hoarding more. Many of us have to make a major paradigm shift to reach this end. We may have to let go of the values and beliefs we have accumulated throughout our lifetime. We have to learn to accept our automatic reactions so that we can make the effort to choose to make new ones when necessary. We have to take the time to stop and listen to our spirit, rather than paying attention to the many voices in the world around us. As we have already discovered, all of this leads to change, which is difficult, anxiety producing and thus also requires more energy. We need a good reason to make that effort, so will likely not do it until we fully understand the different levels of the self and the value and effort that each of us, as an individual person, is willing to put into them.

Most of us go through life without thinking about how we are expending the energy we have. We move through the different steps of our journey, growing up, getting an education, finding a mate, starting our first job, working on a career, buying a home, creating a family and so on. None of these steps is frivolous or unnecessary. They are the foundation on which we are able to base our efforts as we work to achieve our purpose here on earth. We cannot work towards a purpose without having a method of survival in place. The level at which we provide for our own needs and the needs of those we are responsible for depends on the level of effort that we have put into these different steps. However, we can also get caught up in one or another of these levels without realizing we are stuck. We may be so concerned about earning enough money to get by one day after another that we are stuck in a job we hate because it does not allow us to share our special abilities and talents with the world. We may focus so much on achieving another step in a career that we become oblivious to the negative impact our efforts are having on the world in one way or another. We may acquire all sorts of possessions which we claim make us feel better about ourselves, only to discover that all of our energy is going towards paying for them and worrying about them, instead of interacting with others.

Life on earth today is like a big jigsaw puzzle with billions of pieces, each representing a person. In order for our world to go on, these pieces have to fit together, interlocking with each other, each contributing its own specific energy in its own way. We cannot eliminate any one without having an impact on the whole. We cannot determine that any one is surplus, unnecessary, or unsuitable for our picture. We all have our place, no matter how insignificant it might seem in the moment.

This doesn't mean that everyone is partaking to their full potential in the present moment, but that every contribution adds to the picture in some way or another which allows the rest of us to choose a positive or negative reaction. As I learned from the Titanic story of my grandfather, and so many other instances in my life, a positive response is always an option, no matter how negative the original input. God can use us to turn evil into good. Anything and everything that happens can be used **as a** lesson either in how to do things, or not do things. How each of us chooses to focus the energy we have been given will determine the level of achievement as a species. At this point, the tendency to respond to threat with violence at an international level may give us the feeling that there is no path to peace, but this is wrong. History is clear, when we move away from the negative to the positive great things can happen. One by one, we can begin to make that journey, changing ourselves and in time changing the whole world.

As you make your journey, you must measure the amount of energy you are currently expending on the various aspects of your material self and decide whether you want to continue on in the same fashion or make the effort to do things differently. In the past, much of my energy was focused on safety and accommodation, leaving little excess for material goods. Once I left that situation, I had energy for so many other things. The reality of my past meant that I focused on the education I had gone without, because of the choices I made when I was young, and the reacquisition of all sorts of property I had given up through the divorce. Over time we discovered we had too much stuff crammed into too little space and organization became a priority. Writing this book means I put aside earning a living much of the time and wonder if it will be worth the effort. Is anyone going to want to read it? At the present time we are also considering the value of buying our own home so we spend time and energy talking to real estate agents, viewing property and discussing the issue. In the midst of this activity, questions swirl around me: is a home of our own a good way to invest our energy or am I only hanging on to an intergenerational pattern of behavior? My family is living in Canada because of our belief of owning one's own piece of land. During my first marriage we bought our first house when we were still too young to legally own property because of that belief. Now as renters, we are uncomfortable. This is not how we do things through our family belief system, in the midst of knowing that this is easier in so many different ways. Are we content to let our landlord have the role of a property owner while we concentrate on other things? As with everything in this book, there are few right and wrong answers. It's all a matter of juggling what is the most important in the present moment for me as an individual. However, if we don't make the effort to examine where our energy is going, it will be used automatically, often in ways we don't want.

You may want to use the model of self to measure the amount of energy you are expending on various elements of the material self. As we learned in the first chapter, the amount of the various kinds the energy being expended may be indicated by the amount of space that the aspect is taking up in each of the levels of the self. The importance that this aspect holds for you as an individual is measured by how close the aspect is placed toward the inner edges of each level. The size and placement of the aspect should be relatively the same at each level if it is working well for you. And of course, the closer this aspect is placed in regards to your true self, the closer you place it to the life line. Preferably, certain aspects will fill all four of these conditions. This is how you know whether you are meeting your goals or not. If that which is taking most of your energy is the most important at all of your levels of self and is close to your life line, you are on track. If that which is taking most of your energy is as far away from your life line as possible and on the outer edge of your levels of self, you might want to question how you are living. The satisfaction and contentment of reaching your full potential will not be possible without change. You must make the decisions of how that change will occur.

Pseudo Self

The third tool that can be used to measure the impact of the material self is the recognition of the pseudo selves we tend to claim as our own. Many of the aspects of the material self are clear indications of the habit of living as a pseudo self. Anything we own, anything we wear, anything we do because of the social view of others is an indication that we are living as a pseudo self. This doesn't mean we don't own things, wear clothes and do things as our true selves. It's about recognizing why we are making the choices that we make, and how these choices fit on our life line.

As a baby boomer I grew up during a time when there were certain clothes that were in style and no one wore anything else. This is why we can dress like the fifties and everyone immediately knows exactly what we are doing. The poodle skirts, the saddle shoes, the black jackets and white tee-shirts with the slicked back hair. We put them on and step back into the past, even if it is a past we never experienced. We pretend that these outfits represent a whole decade, but they really don't. Poodle skirts would only have been in style for one year. Each year it was something new, and each year we followed the dictates of the year and dressed alike: border prints, reversible skirts, shifts, mini skirts, hot pants, bell bottoms, and so on, as the years went by. The effort it took and the money we spent to be exactly the same is remarkable when seen from the viewpoint of today.

Things have changed a lot when it comes to the clothes we wear. Although we still have the yearly fashion shows that claim to be leading the way, and although we still have people who will be happy to tell you what's "in style", the variety in our wardrobes today speaks more of who we are as an individual than ever before. This doesn't mean we still can't get caught up in wearing clothes in order to fit into a certain group, to be acceptable in the eyes of a certain person, or to present a certain picture to the world that seems to be important to us in the moment. The fact that this happens doesn't always mean we are living as a pseudo self, but it may be a clear indication that we are.

When we look at our wardrobes we have to ask the questions of why certain items are what we choose to wear. Is it because it is comfortable? Is it because it looks good on us? Is it because of how we feel when we wear it? Beautiful? Confident? Outstanding? Or perhaps hidden? Unnoticeable? Untouchable? The answers to these questions will be as individual to each of us as the items themselves. There are no right or wrong answers. The answers you get will speak to your inner self. They will give you a picture of who you are and where you are living when it comes to your life line.

We can look at every other aspect of the material self in much the same way. Do you hold the job you hold because of the joy and satisfaction you get from it, or does it have more to do with the social view that others have of it? What about your house; its size, its style, its location, its decor? Is your home decorated like something you have seen in a magazine or does it display items you love that let the world know exactly who you are? The vehicles you drive, the clubs you belong to, the associations you support, the activities you partake in, the people you spend your time with. This list can go on and on. All of these will indicate whether you are living on your life line or if you are living as a pseudo self.

The easiest way to measure this is to watch how you respond to the aspects of the material self. If your first thought about things is "What will others think about this?" or "How impressed will other people be with this?" you are living as a pseudo self on the material level. If your first reactions are of joy, excitement or contentment you are finding the material things that expresses your true self. Only you know your own response.

Coping Skills

The fourth way we can measure the impact of our material self is to pay attention to the amount of anxiety we are experiencing, as revealed through our use of coping skills. When we have made the effort to recognize our individual coping skills and to understand the level of anxiety they are used for: we can use this information to understand how the various aspects of the material self are affecting our level of anxiety.

The first and foremost aspect of the material self for each of us is our physical body. It comes to us in birth. We lose it in death. It is the container in which the world recognizes us as an individual self, though it certainly does not contain all of the self. We have absolutely no power at all over the particular body we have. We must accept what we are born with. It grows and it changes throughout our life span, again with very little control on our part. Although there are some modifications that are possible, some activities that might make a small difference, and some choices that may make it work better, basically the exact construction of our body is out of our hands. The coping skills that we use impact our body more than any other part of the self.

There are a few human beings in our world who may have a body that is considered a perfect example of what a body should be. Interestingly this model of "perfection" varies across different cultures and throughout different ages and yet we all talk about the current view of perfection as being something that is worth paying attention to. Instead of celebrating the wonders of our bodies from the time we are little children we are often given the message that they are not good enough because of this view of perfection. That we don't "measure up" to some unrealistic standard such as the emancipated appearance of the model Twiggy in the late 1960's when I was a teen. From the time we are little we are told that we are too short, too tall, too skinny, too round, too dark, too light, too curly, or too straight and so on. It seems that whatever we are just isn't good enough, no matter what it is. The advent of digital photography with the ability to alter any photograph is creating an even more unrealistic picture of this "perfection," a perfection that is truly unattainable by any living human being. And yet the energy of many is spent either trying to attain an "ideal" or having to use one's individual coping skills to deal with the feelings of frustration, shame and failure of not being able to meet these standards. This is a total waste of our energy.

The journey to one's true self includes the acceptance of the body that one has been blessed with, and an effort to fully accept and understand its own unique qualities. In the midst of accepting oneself, one also can then come to the realization that there is no way to live in the skin of another person and truly understand things from their perspective. My interactions in this world are based completely on a body that is my height, my weight, my skin colour, my level of sensitivity and so on, which may make these interactions different from those of any other individual. Sometimes these factors are beneficial, and other times they may lead to frustration. The reality is that all of us have to deal with parts of our bodies that bring us joy, and parts that are not so convenient. At times these parts may indeed be the same thing. As a tall person I have always been able to reach things on the top shelf and found success as a basketball player. However, I have also had problems with my height as it was hard to find slacks with legs long enough for me throughout the years. One has to take the good with the bad.

We are each born with a body that is capable of achieving our full potential on this earth, whatever it may be. This in spite of the fact that not all bodies are whole. In the same way that any experience in our life can either result in something good or in something negative depending on what one focuses on, a body that is not whole can still survive and does not have to keep anyone from reaching their full potential. A body may also be born with everything in place and working well, and then fail through illness or accidents at some point in life. Again, this is not a reason for a person to give up on reaching their full potential. The body is at the material level. We can continue on and make a positive impact on this world in spite of what has happened to our bodies. Often a loss at the body level opens the eyes of the person involved and lets them tap into their true potential in a way that one might have not achieved had their body stayed whole. This was probably best demonstrated by Christopher Reeve who lost so much in his riding accident and yet continued on to make a huge difference for others from his wheelchair.

People who are living on their life line are people who have realized that it is not the body we live in that we need to focus our attention on to reach our full potential. They accept the bodies they live in, and they understand the importance of keeping those bodies healthy and strong, but beyond that, their energy goes elsewhere. They may also understand how one's appearance can affect one's level of self esteem, so will put in the effort to look good, but it is not the most important focus of their lives.

Our bodies bear the brunt of the coping skills we use. For me, the use of food to dull any emotional reaction over the years has led directly to a weight problem. Other coping skills destroy in other ways. Alcohol leads directly to the breakdown of brain cells over time and the destruction of the liver. Smoking affects the lungs and the heart. Unexpressed emotions are stored throughout the body and may lead to cancer. Decreasing one's level of anxiety through the coping skills of the mind uses an incredible amount of energy, which is then not available for the immune system to protect the body. Your responsibility on your journey to self is to figure out how to protect your own body. This is the container that your spirit will dwell in until you die. It is worth taking care of.

The last few years have led to an explosion of knowledge about my body that far surpasses what I knew before. This may have something to do with the process of aging, during which one begins to have difficulties with their body that one hasn't had before. It also might have had something to do with the breakdown of my body as it dealt with the level of stress and anxiety I was exposed to over time and the impact of the coping skills I was using to deal with the amount of stress I was experiencing. As I neared my forties my throat began to have a variety of different problems. Breathing was no longer silent and effortless, but sounded raspy and horrible. I began to react to certain foods with either the swelling of the throat tissue or the production of thick phlegm, which threatened to choke me. I had sleeping problems due to my inability to breathe well. Doctors couldn't explain what was going on and issued me an epidermal needle to keep with me at all times. Allergy tests proved inconclusive and frustrating as they indicated I was reacting to chocolate and shellfish, in the midst of my knowing full well that it was citrus type products, especially the peel of the lemon that brought on the worst symptoms. This, at a time when lemon was freely added to water in restaurants throughout the continent, often without any warning to the diner. During the time of the highest level of stress, my back began to ache, to the point that I could not get up out of my bed in the morning or bend down and pick up anything from the floor. I learned to roll out of bed onto the floor and then crawl up the wall slowly in order to stand. This pain immobilized me for months. Again the doctors couldn't find anything wrong and the treatments they offered had little impact on the pain level. Finally it subsided in much the same way it began, without warning, without an apparent reason.

Leaving my marriage led to a slight alleviation of these symptoms. I was now safe from the rage of my husband which led to a decrease in my stress level, but I was now also facing all the major changes in my self that were a direct result of my decisions to leave. So my anxiety level remained high and many of theses symptoms continued, while others got worse. It was easy for me to define them as a result of aging, but I knew that I couldn't continue allowing my body to deteriorate at this rate if

I was going to enjoy my old age at all. As the world of autism began to focus in on the gastrointestinal and immune systems of people on the spectrum, I became aware of different products that were supposed to help symptoms such as mine. These included MSM (methylsulfonylmethane), vitamin C, cod liver oil, and omega threes. They made a difference but I still needed more.

My education about the immune system first started with my work in the field of autism where we are beginning to realize that many of the problems for people within the spectrum begin through a suppressed or overactive immune system. I came in contact with a food supplement called Immune 26 as a treatment that appears to help some children and adults with autism. I started taking it myself in August of 2002 to find out if it was effective. By September I knew that massive changes for the better were occurring in my body. At this point I know this product has totally changed the course of my life.

Immune 26 was developed by Dupont as an attempt to come up with a medicine that might replace the vaccination process. The development of the immune system in humans and in other species was studied to see how specific immune systems develop over time. As humans, our immune system comes directly through that of our mothers and takes a long time to develop. The first immune information is shared by our mothers while we are in the womb. This is supplemented after birth through her milk. This is the same for all mammals. In direct contrast, other species only have one shot to share immune information with their offspring. For example, when a bird lays an egg, all of the information must be in that egg in order for the chick to have access to it. This is the only opportunity the adult bird has to share this vital information with its offspring. The scientists at Dupont created a product that uses this information. Chickens are exposed to illnesses that impact human beings. They develop an immunity to these illnesses. The immune information is passed on to the chick in the egg as antibodies and immune cofactors. When we eat the eggs, our bodies access this information in exactly the same way that we received immunity through our mother's milk. Immune 26 balances our immune system so that we are able to deal with the various germs we encounter in a natural manner.

In the spring of 1967, I graduated from high school and entered a community college in a nearby city. I moved into a dormitory and immediately got sicker than I had ever been in my life. My throat was so sore that I couldn't eat or drink. I spent my time sucking on lozenges and falling asleep without warning, even in classes. It was certainly not the life of a typical 17-year-old university student. The actual details of that time are sketchy in my memory because I was so sick, but I know I did try to soldier on, going to classes and attending the extracurricular events in the midst of my illness. In time I went home for a weekend where my parents immediately took me to our doctor, one of the few visits I had had to his office since my birth. After he examined me, he angrily rebuked me for not taking care of myself. According to him I had contacted strep throat and was in very serious condition. He prescribed antibiotics, which I took. The strep throat appeared to have been defeated.

Thirty-five years later, after a month on Immune 26, I woke up to discover that I had strep throat again. The body remembers the specific pain. I was very busy at the time and decided I would have to book a visit with my doctor the next day. I didn't have the chance. The next morning I was so sick I could barely get out of bed, but in the midst of feeling so weak and so sleepy I also felt an incredible strength. It felt like armies were marching through my body, doing the work they were meant to do. I put off calling the doctor until the next day.

That day I awoke without a trace of the strep throat. No pain, no fatigue, no weakness. I felt fine. In time I learned that it was even better than that. Not only was the strep throat gone, but so were all my breathing problems, my allergic reactions and the two lumps that I had had on each side of my neck all those years. In the coming weeks and months I felt better than I had felt for years. I was sleeping soundly again. People couldn't hear me when I breathed. I could eat anything without a reaction. I began losing weight without trying.

I took Immune 26 as a daily supplement for almost a full year. If I was in the presence of colds or other sources of infection. I upped the daily amount in order to protect myself. I was never sick. At this point in time I no longer take Immune 26 on a daily basis, but boost my system before I work with families or travel on airplanes. In the past an airplane trip could wipe me out for ten or more days after my return home. Now there is no reaction at all to travel. It's an incredible way to live.

Dupont spent millions of dollars on research on Immune 26. They discovered that it helped in all sorts of different conditions including heart problems, cancer, chronic fatigue syndrome, Crohn's, arthritis, and so on. One of the unexpected discoveries was the positive impact it had on depression. However, one must realize that the positive impact is not a "cure" for any of these conditions, but a reaction that occurs because the immune system is working more effectively. Thus, when Dupont approached the FDA with this product, they were told that it cannot be marketed as a "medicine" as such, but can only be sold as a food supplement. Since food supplements are not considered to be the money-makers that medicines are, and the focus of Dupont is the profit margin, they chose to set this product aside. It wasn't worth developing, in their eyes, in spite of the positive impact it had on the human body. Dollars are worth far more than people's lives. However, the scientists who had developed this product over the years continued to have faith in it. They bought out the rights from Dupont and now sell it through a company called Legacy for Life.

As I experienced the positive impact of immune 26 on my life, I began to really think about how important our immune system is to our bodies and how little attention we pay to this process. I also began to look at my beliefs about the medical system, my body, and the steps I was willing to take to keep myself and my family healthy. I realized that there has been a major shift over time away from allowing the body to look after itself, towards a reliance on doctors and medicine that actually suppress the immune system over time. The immune system uses fever to fight the invasion of germs in our body. Our habit of reaching for a pain-killer every time we have a fever stops the immune system from doing its job. The antibiotics we shovel into our bodies destroy not only the bacteria they are fighting but also all sorts of other bacteria that play a positive role in the function of our bodies. The presence of strep throat in my body after 35 years may indicate that antibiotics don't actually wipe out the bacteria, but allow them to go into a dormant stage. There is a lot to think about.

As the journey of life goes on, I continue to learn more about the body and how to keep it healthy. In March of 2005, I came across a system of providing energetic medicine that has opened my eyes far beyond what I ever dreamed possible. The Scio (named after the Greek word for knowledge) was developed by Dr. Bill Nelson, a physicist who once worked at NASA and decided to take the knowledge of quantum physics he had learned there to create something that would help mankind. After several treatments on this machine I chose to buy one myself and become certified as a bio-feedback therapist. Most of my energy is now spent working with this machine with all sorts of people including those on the autism spectrum.

One of our major responsibilities here on earth is to take care of the body we dwell in. In order to do this well, each of us must measure one's values and beliefs to make the choices that work for oneself. Understanding the power of the dollar in our society is very important in measuring the personal significance of the messages that one gets about the food we eat and the medical care we access. The commercial preparation of food is determined by a profit margin, not whether it is good for us. The medical community is controlled by pharmaceutical companies that are mainly interested in making money, which means that keeping you sick is more profitable than health.

There is no set diet that works for everyone. When we look around the world and consider the diversity of menus that people exist on and have existed on for thousands of years, it is apparent that we, as a human species, are able to grow and develop on a variety of different diets. Some will help us stay healthy and age without difficulty. Others, such as those based on flavor enhancers such as sugar, salt or MSG, do more harm than good. Each of us has to take the responsibility to figure out what we believe, where these beliefs originated, and what we are going to do with them to look after our bodies in a way that best fits us as an individual. At present I am on a journey to find what works for me with my particular body. You have to make the effort to find your own solutions for yourself. These will be impacted by your beliefs and you will also have to make the effort to determine whether you want to keep maintain them or not.

The first step of figuring out what impact the material self is having on your need to use coping skills is, of course, to figure out exactly which skills you personally use as an individual. We use different skills for different types of anxiety. As I have mentioned before, eating has always been a major skill for me, as I deadened my emotional reactions with food, but material goods are not about emotions for me. They may certainly have an emotional context for others based on their individual experience in life. The country superstar Shania Twain talks about the importance of having a well-stocked larder in order to feel safe. This is a direct reaction to the lack of food she had as a child. Other people attempt to use shopping to numb their emotional responses. This is common for children who did not experience unconditional acceptance when they were very young. Each of us has our own story.

When it comes to material goods, I find that I have different reactions. Money problems lead to what I call my ostrich reaction, of putting my head symbolically in the sand, ignoring things in hopes that they will go away. The solution to this situation appears simple. Put the anxiety out in the open. Admit you have a problem. But it's not easy for me. It takes incredible effort to break out of that pattern and admit the truth to myself. And then even more to speak up about it to another person, even my husband. But it's so much easier to live once I do. A load is lifted off my shoulders, even if the situation isn't resolved. Having it out in the open makes the difference. Of course, the next step is to make the decisions that ensure I won't be in the same situation again. Letting go and letting God does not mean that I am not responsible for using my resources efficiently. But God will provide in very unique ways if you turn yourself over to him.

When my children were little, we went through a period of severe financial stress as my husband dealt with the uncertainty of consistent employment due to a slump in construction where we were living. He ended up taking a position out of town with an employer he really didn't trust, in order to keep ahead of our bills, leaving me at home to juggle what we had as I looked after our two young sons. Our lack of trust in this employer proved accurate. By the end of the summer, my husband came home without earning anything. He ended up taking a job at a local sawmill, in order to make a living. He enjoyed this work, but I knew we were in trouble. Our monthly bills were more than his paycheque each month, and we still had everything to catch up on that gone unpaid while we waited for him come home. Each month we were slipping further and further behind. I was eight months pregnant so didn't have any way of contributing to the situation. There was no way we were going to make it. Every day I was steeped in worry. We were experiencing acute anxiety at its highest level.

My husband was at work when the letter came. It was about a bursary that I had accepted as a student, which was to be paid back through employment once I had finished university. Since I hadn't completed my courses, I couldn't be employed and so they wanted the full amount of the bursary back at once. The letter stated that I had a month to clear this up in full or they would take me to court. I read it in absolute horror. We weren't making it as we were. There was absolutely nothing left to put towards the bursary. I had reached the end of my rope. I sank to my knees and cried out to God for an answer, for a release from the problem we faced.

Across town my husband leaned over the machine he was working at. A moving piece of machinery caught his glove and pulled him into the machine, crushing his hand and lower arm between two rollers. He screamed out in excruciating pain. A friend quickly reached over turned off the machine. An ambulance was called. He was rushed off to the hospital.

What an answer to prayer! In many ways one might look at this story in horror, but this accident provided the perfect release from the monetary stress that we needed. Since the accident happened at work, it was covered by workman's compensation, which meant my husband continued to earn his wages. All of our financial commitments were covered by disability insurance, so our bills were paid. A phone call to the county describing what had happened to my husband was enough to put the payment on the bursary on hold without the threat of litigation. We had the time and space to take control of our financial situation. In time, this accident led to a move to another city for rehabilitation, which lead to employment back in the construction field and paycheques that not only covered our needs but allowed us to catch up with past debts.

God arranged everything perfectly. A surgeon, who specialized in the reconstruction of bodies that had experienced this level of trauma, was visiting our local hospital on the day of the accident. He was walking through the lobby on his way to the airport when the ambulance with my husband pulled up at the hospital entrance. Instead of flying home, this surgeon went straight into surgery and rebuilt my husband's hand and arm so that one cannot tell that it was ever damaged. The only difficulty he has had with it in the years since this happened is that it must be protected in cold weather because of the metal inside which replaced the bones that were crushed beyond repair. The damage to the body was taken care of. Through this experience, I learned to let go of financial control of my life.

This doesn't mean that I can spend money without thought. This doesn't mean that I am not responsible for the decisions I am making. This doesn't mean that I don't have to make the effort to earn a living. It does mean that I can live without worrying about money. It means that I know God can and will provide for me, and each of you. That I can depend on his wisdom, which is so much deeper than mine. That I don't have to go out and search for work, it will come to me. That I can take the time to write this book, knowing I will be taken care of. That I can live in the present, instead of worrying about the future. It's an incredible place to be.

Owning too much stuff leads to chaos in my life. I prefer a home in which everything has a place and everything is in its place. My tendency to put the needs of others before my own means that I deal with social interactions, especially at a family level, by neglecting my own needs. So when the family is involved I concentrate my energy on them, rather than making certain that things are in their own place. The more family involvement, the more difficult it is to live in my home. The more things are out of place, the more energy I expend on trying to find what I need, which in turn leads to a breakdown in social interaction. Solving the problem means setting aside a day or more for myself, during which I concentrate my time on making sure that everything has its own place and making the effort to put everything into that place. This is a gift I give myself. Once I am organized, I have much more energy for everything else.

Figuring out your own coping skills and then pinpointing what is triggering the reaction will allow you to understand exactly what you need to do to lower your anxiety. For some it may mean cutting up your credit cards so that you are not tempted to spend more of your monetary energy than you take in, creating high levels of anxiety when it comes time to pay your bills. For some it may mean getting rid of a lot of the excess that you have filled your life with. Everything we own at a material level takes energy. The less we own, the more energy we have, once our needs for survival are met. This is demonstrated very clearly on the television shows that focus on organizing one's life such as Clean Sweep where couples come to the point where they are completely swamped with too much stuff. For some it may mean giving up the dream of a big house which is taking all your extra energy to heat, to clean, to keep up, and moving to a space that will shelter you without exhausting you. For some it may mean quitting a job that is draining you of your energy because it does not fit on your life line, either by not allowing you to use the talents and abilities that you have been gifted with or by not contributing positively to our world. There are many jobs out there that are demeaning to humanity, either because they negatively affect society as a whole, or because they are destructive to the potential of one or more human beings on this earth. Other jobs are a problem because they force you to live as a pseudo self due to the social interactions in that particular workplace. You can recognize if your job keeps you off your life line by the amount of coping skills you are using to get through each day. If you have to smoke, if you reach for a drink, if you are eating far more than your body needs, you might want to consider what you are doing to earn a living. Since the material self is so large, this list could go on and on. You are the one who has to make the effort to recognize how you are living at the material level and determine if it is worth making the effort to change or not.

COPING SKILLS AT THE MATERIAL LEVEL

The coping skills we use to decrease anxiety can happen at the material level as well as the other levels of the self. These skills may incorporate any of the different factors within the material self and range from changing the chemical make-up of the body to becoming a shopaholic, trying to fill an emotional emptiness with things, or focusing all of one's energy in a specific role such as mothering or climbing the ladder of your career so that you have no time for anything else. All of them will decrease the level of anxiety in their own way for each of us as an individual. All of them are also destructive to the self in one way or another over the long term.

The most common coping skills we use at the material level are used to decrease anxiety via the body. These coping skills are based on changing the biochemical make-up in the brain, which dulls the level of stress we are feeling. As I have mentioned before, these coping skills include the ingestion of food, drugs, and other substances such as caffeine, alcohol and nicotine and the use of behaviors that result in the production of endorphins in the body, our natural painkillers.

The different chemical components of these substances work directly in the brain to help the body dull the impact of the anxiety by changing the way we feel. Since anxiety is inevitable, these substances can and do become addictive. The more often the body is impacted by the biochemical, the more it creates a situation in which the presence of the chemical in the brain is the status quo. Since the 'self' resists the discomfort of change, the body reaches a state in which it depends on the ingestion or production of the substance to feel safe and normal. The use of the chemicals moves from a situation in which we are depending on them to decrease anxiety from one source or another in our lives, to a situation in which we are trying to avoid the discomfort of change, by keeping the level of biochemicals stable. The longer we allow ourselves to use or produce the chemicals, the more our body "needs" them in order to feel normal and the stronger the reaction of discomfort we experience when we try to stop using them. This doesn't mean that the self actually needs the chemicals to survive, but that it appears to, because of the level of discomfort experienced when one's self is going without them.

This is a situation in which the psychiatric and psychological communities have again chosen to move a natural human response from the level of a coping skill to that of an illness. Obesity, alcoholism and drug addiction are defined as illnesses in an attempt to move people away from a state of shame and failure due to their dependence on these behaviors. This creates a new dependence, one based on medical care. It's not a healthy place to be either. Since most of their treatments come in the form of a medication, we have only substituted one type of chemical dependency for another. Is this what we really want to do?

Acknowledging the impact of anxiety on the self and the use of biochemical means to decrease this anxiety allows us to take care of the situation as an individual and move beyond the use of coping skills to reach our full potential. It allows us to recognize the need to cope in times of high anxiety and provides the opportunity to rationally choose a response rather than reacting automatically. The process of stopping the automatic response of using coping skills that affect the biochemical make-up of the body is not an easy process. You will go through withdrawal as your body adjusts to the change in your biochemical make-up. You will experience the pendulum process of change in which you react to the discomfort you are facing. You will often face a lot of pressure from others who do not want you to change because you will also be changing their self in some way. You may not only have to give up the substance that you have been depending on to reduce your anxiety, but also the people you do it with, and the environments you do it in, for a time, and perhaps, for some, forever. It's a tough road, but it is definitely worth it in the end.

The use of repetitive and stereotypic behaviors and other activities such as strenuous exercise are also biochemical coping skills, as they result in the production of endorphins, the natural painkillers of the body. A simple example of how this works is our automatic reaction to the pain of a paper cut on the tip of the finger. As soon as we feel the pain, we shake our finger. This repetitive movement creates the endorphins, which in turn dull the pain.

Repetitive behaviors are our instinctive responses to pain and anxiety and are necessary for our survival. We know this because they are the coping skills that are used by newborn babies. They are also the skills that we share automatically with our infants when we try to calm them. We rock them, we pace back and forth with them, we pat them, we sing repetitious songs to them and now, in our modern age, we may give them a pacifier or take them for a drive in the car where the consistent sound and motion relaxes their bodies so that they can sleep. Repetitive behaviors to reduce anxiety are also used by animals. In fact, we first learned about the existence and power of endorphins when scientists studied the biochemical effects of pacing on the brains of caged animals. The importance of these endorphins for protection of the self is indicated by the fact that the highest levels are found at the throat in both humans and animals. Predators go for the throat when they kill. The location of these endorphin-producing cells allows the body **to** dull the pain of that experience.

Repetitive behaviors come in many different forms. Some of them, like rocking, pacing, twirling one's hair, tapping a pencil and so on, are recognized as reactions to anxiety. Others, such as chewing gum, become such a common element in our daily lives that we pay little attention to the impact they have on reducing stress on our bodies. Still others are useful actions because they produce something in the midst of the repetition. Anyone who has had the opportunity to milk a cow on a regular basis understands the calming effect of that rhythmic action. Knitting, crocheting, kneading bread dough, and whittling are all examples of repetitive behaviors that calm us in the midst of production. Other repetitive behaviors play a role as creative or physical activities in our lives such as dance, tai chi and jogging. All of these activities have the same result in the long run. They produce endorphins, which in turn decrease our feelings of anxiety.

The individual use of these behaviors varies from one person to another. The level of sensitivity of one's body will determine the use and the level of intensity of these behaviors. The environment and experience one is engaged in, in the present moment, will also determine their use. People who are highly sensitive will need to use them at a higher level than those who are not so sensitive. The repetitive behaviors used by those on the autism spectrum are not any different than those used by the rest of us other than in their intensity and quantity because of the level of anxiety their bodies are experiencing.

Repetitive behaviors are also used to deal with the level of stress caused by boredom. The human brain needs to be engaged. If it is not engaged, it needs to be calmed. Although this is likely most easily recognized in the behavior of caged zoo animals, it is also a common response in such places as airport terminals as humans deal with long waits of layovers and flight delays. Our response to boredom is not limited to such places, as repetitive behaviors fill our time and calm our brains in all sorts of situations and ways. As with everything else, our individual reaction to boredom varies from one person to another, as do the repetitive responses we choose to react with. There is no right or wrong as each person reacts in the way that fits their individual needs and make-up.

One of the fascinating factors one comes across when studying the use of these repetitive behaviors is how negatively most of them are viewed by our society. Our discomfort with anxiety is revealed very clearly by the labels we put on people using repetitive behaviors and our negative reaction to our children's use of them. We teach them that these actions are inappropriate without providing anything as a replacement to decrease the anxiety. We mock them and chastise them when they use such behaviors. We even resort to biochemical means in our attempts to get rid of the behaviors. The question we have to ask is why. The answer is clear. We do not want to face our own anxiety. We do not want to face the anxiety of our children. We do want to face the anxiety of others. It is easier to block it out and pretend it doesn't exist than to openly acknowledge the anxiety and do something about it. By rejecting our natural response to anxiety, we can pretend it doesn't exist. It's a dangerous road to follow.

This negative reaction to the use of repetitive behaviors over time has led to the situation in which very few people have any idea of the impact they have on our lives. Instead of individually understanding and using these behaviors to protect ourselves, we berate ourselves for weakness and put down others when they are used. We cannot live without coping skills of some type or other, so we replace them with those that do so much more damage to us over time, such as drinking, smoking or overeating. What's more, we have no clue what happens to us when presented with repetitive stimulation and put ourselves in danger without being aware of the consequences. Research from Australia has revealed that truck drivers who drive for long periods of time are affected by the hum of the motor and constant movement of their seat. The brain gradually shuts down because of the repetitive input and the driver's ability to respond quickly is compromised, putting all of us in danger on our highways

Video and computer games are one way we currently use repetitive behavior to calm one's body without any understanding of what we are doing. The repetition of sensory input in these games creates endorphins that dull the feelings in the brain, in much the same way as any other repetitive behavior. The video terminals now used in casinos are a dramatic example of how one group of people is using our dependence on repetition to destroy other human beings as they become conditioned to the feelings that the repetition of these games provides the body. Even more terrifying for me is the impact that these types of games are having on our little children as they focus more and more of their time and energy on Game Boy, X-box, Nintendo and so on. These games become as addictive as any other of the biochemicals we ingest, because of the production of endorphins that allow us to not to feel the pain and anxiety that life brings us. The body is uncomfortable when it goes for a time without the production of endorphins, produced by these games. The child or adult reaches a point in which he or she must continue to play the games in order to feel normal. There are thousands of people of all ages who are so locked into these games at this point that they are totally oblivious to anyone or anything else in the world. When it comes to the self as a whole, this is not a good place to be.

In the midst of this we also have created a world in which certain repetitive behaviors are considered not merely acceptable but preferable. Exercise regimes that use repetition create endorphins in much the same way as rocking and pacing. Jogging is only an extreme of pacing. Although these behaviors appear to be a positive choice as a repetitive behavior, they can be destructive to the body if they are used as a means to decrease anxiety. Anorexia nervosa is the direct result of becoming addicted to the endorphins produced by exercise, which in turn dull feelings of hunger. People have starved themselves to the point of death in this way.

Another way that the power of repetitive behavior is used without a clear understanding is through the use of mantras during meditation. Repeating a word or phrase either aloud or in one's mind creates the endorphins in much the same way that repeating an action does. These endorphins dull our anxiety so that we feel more comfortable. Certain people claim that the use of these mantras will connect us to our spirit, but they are mistaken. Instead they allow us to decrease our reaction to the anxiety we are facing in our lives so we feel better. This does not mean that the anxiety itself is decreased, but that our response feels different. Using mantras in meditation is better for the body, of course, than the ingestion of chemicals, but it is no different than any other repetitive behavior. It too can become addictive over time.

In the midst of all of this caution, we must be fully aware that repetition and the production of endorphins is the natural way of reducing anxiety in our bodies. We need to not only acknowledge the use of repetition as a method of calming ourselves, but also learn how to use them most efficiently. Although the most effective way to deal with anxiety is to put it out into the open and deal with it directly, there are times when this is impossible. During such times, repetition is likely the most preferable coping skill to use because it is our natural form of protection. Each of us must take responsibility for determining what works best for us as an individual in the particular moment instead of basing our reactions on what we have learned in the past.

The most extreme example of the use of endorphins to relieve one's pain and anxiety is the use of physical pain to dull emotional pain. When the body is hurt in any way, it produces endorphins to block the pain of the injury. The emotional pain and the anxiety the person is experiencing in the moment is also dulled by these endorphins. Any assault to the skin through pinching, biting, or cutting, though physically painful in the moment, totally wipes out the feelings of emotional pain one is experiencing. Self-injurious behavior, as this is called by the psychological community, is a common response for those on the autism spectrum who are in situations in which they are totally misunderstood by those who are caring for them. Sadly, once those on the spectrum have learned how effective self-injurious behaviors can be to reduce one's pain, they become a habitual response to all stress and anxiety. We must make the effort to understand and protect these children so they never have to reach this point.

Self-injurious behaviors are used by all sorts of people. Sadly, this response is reaching epidemic proportions for our North American teenagers at this point in time. Cutting was demonstrated through a teen cult movie a couple of years ago as a means to relieve emotional pain. This demonstration consisted of cutting the skin on the wrist or arm with a sharp knife or razor. The cuts do not have to be long or deep to be effective to block out the emotional pain one is feeling. The use of cutting spread to internet sites which focus on this practice, teaching more and more of our teenagers, who are stuck in a world in which their parents are so immersed in their own coping skills that they are not there for their children, to use cutting as a release of their emotional pain. Working with these teenagers, as clients, is difficult as they talk about how easy it is to cut and how free they feel once the endorphins wash through their bodies. The temptation to escape from the emotional pain in their lives is often too hard to resist.

As with everything else, the behavior of cutting is not the problem, but only an indication of an underlying problem. Being a teenager is not easy. The massive production of grey brain matter during puberty creates a situation in which the teenager no longer has the same connections to their brain and to their body as they did before. This results in a dramatic loss of the self which is neither understood accepted by our society at large. We choose to blame the teenagers for their behavior rather than helping them cope in this new reality. We choose to believe that they can do it all on their own, without guidance, not realizing that children who are eight, nine, or ten are likely far more in control of their lives than anyone from 11 through 15 years of age. We mass more and more of them all together in one small space, called schools, purely for financial reasons based directly on the myth that there is not enough money, where they turn on each other to mask their pain. We ignore the reality of coping skills as a way to decrease anxiety and laugh off their interest in alcohol, cigarettes and drugs as a natural teenage response, not the reaction to unnatural levels of anxiety: reactions that may well enslave them for the rest of their lives.

Signs that your child is cutting are easy to see, if you are paying attention. Recurrent small scratches on the skin may be the result of cutting. They may be explained as scratches from a cat, or someone's fingernails, but if you see them more than once, you might want to pay attention. The insistence on wearing full-length sleeves may also be an indication that one is covering up the scars. The sites your child is visiting on the Internet may also be cause for concern. Children who are hurting do not need their privacy. They need their lives to be out in the open for their own protection. But, of course, this is not going to happen if you are modeling secrecy and denial to them through your own coping skills.

The psychological community has reacted to the upsurge in cutting to an extreme, in much the same way they do other coping skills. If you are a parent who is worried about a child who is cutting, be aware that focusing on the behavior will not help. Your child needs your unconditional love and acceptance at this point, not your condemnation or labels of mental disability. Your child needs to understand clearly the changes that he or she is experiencing in the brain and body. Your child needs to know that every teenager is dealing with this discomfort in their own way and suffering as much as they are, in spite of what might appear differently. Your child needs to know exactly what coping skills are and how they impact the body so they can choose whether they want to use them or not. Your child needs to know they will come through this okay. That it is not easy. That these are not the "best" years of their lives. That they will not only survive but will most likely look back at these years and be proud of how they survived. Your child needs to know they can depend on you for love, unconditional acceptance and guidance, in a time in which they desperately need that guidance. It is okay. It will be okay.

Most of all your child needs the freedom to bring all of this into the open. To have the freedom to share their fears and anxieties with others. To have the freedom to make mistakes, and not to be made fun of. To have the adults in their world protecting them from the bullying that goes on at this age, not adding to it. To learn how to bring anxiety out into the open to dispel it through role models and through their own experience. If we can give them that gift, they will not have to rely on coping skills to get through each day. And even more so, they will not pass these coping skills on to the next generation.

Once we understand that changes in the biochemical make-up in our brains and bodies are effective in relieving our anxiety, we can learn different ways to use this information to relieve anxiety in as safe a way as possible. One of the most unique adaptations I have discovered is a perfume that is based on the pheromones that our skin gives off when we feel good about ourselves. As with everything else in my life, it comes with an incredible story, a story that came into my life in a strange way, and thus was something I felt might be worth paying attention to. A magazine was delivered to my office. I do not have a subscription to this magazine and had no idea why it came in the mail. I decided that it might have a message for me and so I looked through it before I tossed it in the trash. This was a good decision and this is the story.

Once upon a time there was a scientist who was working in a university laboratory somewhere in the world in the early 1960's. This scientist had decided to focus on the properties of skin cells and had gone to a nearby hospital where he collected these cells off the inside of casts that had been discarded after they had protected broken arms and legs. He kept these skin cells in flasks in the lab.

One day this man came to work to discover that everyone in the lab was acting strangely. The other scientists were typical scientists, usually totally involved in their work, paying little attention to one another. On this day they were talking to each other, sharing jokes and pictures of their families. At lunch they all ate together in their lunchroom, instead of sitting alone at their desks eating their sandwiches. They even got out the cards and played games before returning to their work. The original scientist looked at this scene in absolute amazement. What had happened? It didn't make sense, and yet, these new behaviors continued on throughout the day.

That night, as he was leaving the lab, he noticed that someone had removed the corks from his flasks of skin cells. He put them back in place and went home. The next day, the scientists had all returned to normal and no one ever mentioned that day again.

Years later this scientist was reading a journal in which an article described how another research group had isolated the pheromones that our skin gives off when we feel good about ourselves. As he read the article, he remembered that day in the lab and realized it might have been the open flasks that led to the strange reactions of his coworkers. He immediately went out and placed a patent on the chemical basis of the pheromones and then developed a perfume that contains these pheromones. This perfume is called REALM.

As I read this story I, too, was thinking about other things. I work with people who supposedly suffer from an impairment in social interaction. The stereotype of the typical scientist is that they are antisocial. If their behavior changed when the flasks were open, perhaps this perfume would help the people I work with. I saved up my dollars to buy a bottle to try out my own experiments.

The first person I tried it with was a 17-year-old who was coming to my office on a weekly basis in an attempt to relieve his anxiety. His main coping skill is rocking his body, and when he was there he would rock almost constantly. Since I do not worry about coping skills, I allowed him to rock as much as he needed. This meant he felt very safe with me.

I told him the story of the scientist and then showed him the bottle of perfume. I asked him to sniff it to make sure that it was safe for his body and then went on to ask him if he would like to try it on his arm. Throughout this whole process he rocked constantly. He held out his wrist and I sprayed a quick blast of perfume on it. Amazingly, the rocking stopped instantly. It did not start up again throughout the two hours he was with me. When I asked him if he felt any different, he replied "no". But his body was certainly reacting differently. We experimented with the perfume for the following weeks, not using it every other visit and then trying it again. When he had the perfume, he did not rock. When he did not have it, he rocked. The only time this changed was when the rocking was for feeling good about something such as winning a game. Then the perfume had no impact at all. The rocking continued in spite of the perfume.

Since that first experiment, many other people on the autism spectrum have tried REALM with positive results. The perfume appears to calm the body in ways that are amazing. I think what is happening is that the pheromones in the perfume trick the mind to believe that the body is feeling good about itself, which in turn allows the body to appear to feel good about itself, which in turn allows us, who are looking at the body, to react in a positive manner to the individual, who no longer appears to be anxious and socially inept. Our comfort level, in turn, impacts the person with autism and they can interact with us in a more normal manner. However, it hasn't been effective for everyone, especially those who have problems with a high acuity of the olfactory system. Pheromones have no noticeable scent, so this perfume has had another scent added to make it marketable. The anxiety caused by the odor of the perfume is higher than the power of the perfume to help the person. At this point a lighter scent of REALM has also been released, which has made it useful for more of my clients. The extremely sensitive people likely need the pheromones without any scent at all.

As with everything else in this book, REALM is not only for those on the autism spectrum; it's for everyone. It promises to make you feel good about yourself and it lives up to that promise. Think about that uplifting feeling you experience when you are with a person who feels good about themselves. It's like that. You feel better about yourself when you are with someone who is feeling good about themselves. I believe this is because of the pheromones that they are exuding. REALM does the same thing for you. It provides those same pheromones that convince your brain that you are feeling good, which in turn raises your spirits. What an adaptation for life: something that provides your body with the chemical messages in a safe and exciting new way. It's worth trying when you are feeling low: maybe your job isn't going as you want it to, maybe you don't feel loved by anyone, or maybe you are feeling a little depressed.

Another type of coping skill used at the material level is the acquisition of "stuff". Shopaholics use the acquisition of stuff to decrease their level of anxiety in the same way that alcoholics use alcohol, drug addicts use their particular drug of choice and overeaters use food. These people buy more and more and more in an attempt to feel good about themselves. It doesn't work, because the true self is never lived on the material level. It also leads to a lot of other problems that are connected to paying for the stuff or having enough energy to cope with all the stuff. Sadly, instead of dealing with these factors, the person who shops to feel good about themselves usually ends up heading out for more stuff, which increases the level of anxiety over time. Coping with anxiety is all about cycles, cycles that spiral upwards as long as the anxiety is not dealt with, no matter what level of self your coping skills impact. This is as true on the material level of self as it is at the level of the mind and the social self. The use of coping skills tells you so much about yourself. Take time to pay attention to them.

A third type of coping skill that is used at the material level is triangulation, much like the triangulation which happens at a social level, but in which one triangles something at the material level, such as one's job, one's hobby, one's role or one's stuff into a relationship with another person. In these cases a person may use their work to avoid confronting the anxiety they are facing with another person. They may retreat into a hobby rather than engage in social interactions. A woman may focus completely on housework to cover up her lack of sexual interest in her husband or the pain of his lack of interest in her. Again the variations of these responses are innumerable.

A type of triangulation can also be used as a response between different areas of the material self. A person may immerse themselves in their work to avoid a role they don't want to face such as taking on the responsibility as the adult child of an ailing parent, or lose themselves in a hobby such as gardening to avoid the reality of paying their bills. None of these reactions are necessarily negative but become a problem if the original anxiety is never dealt with. As with all other coping skills, they are useful in reducing stress and anxiety in the moment and are destructive only if the anxiety is never resolved.

PUTTING YOUR MATERIAL SELF ON YOUR LIFE LINE

There are a lot of parts of the material self that we have missed talking about in this chapter. This is not because they are not important, but that there are so many, one could write volumes about their impact on the whole self. I am hoping you can take what I have shared here and extend it to cover all of the other aspects of the material self.

Many changes occur throughout our lives in the realm of our material self and the whole self is affected by each change in positive or negative ways. The importance we individually place on various facets of the material self determines the intensity of stress and emotional upheaval that happens when changes occur. Examples of traumatic changes to the material self which happen throughout one's life journey and will cause upheaval include puberty, menopause, the death of a loved one, the birth of a child or grandchild, the loss of a home to fire, the crash of the stock market or the loss of one's job. Each of these will cause us discomfort. Each of them will be resisted. Each of them will result in the use of coping skills. Some of them will result in one having to go through the grief process. This is okay. It's what life is all about.

Although the material self is the outer ring of the self, it does not mean we can live without it. Everything in the material self is as connected to the spirit in the same way as that which we find in the social self and the mind. As we move towards our life line we can choose to keep that which truly represents us, in the midst of clearing away that which does not. This includes all that we own, the clothes we wear, the food we eat, the homes we live in, the jobs we do, the roles we hold and the communities and activities we choose to partake in.

Some of the china that I found that day in the antique shop is now sitting in my china cabinet. I don't know why that pattern affects me as it does, but every time I look at a piece or hold it in my hands I feel a thrill. It is a true gift in my life. I started collecting this china pattern when I was in high school. I didn't get very much of it because of the life I was living. The few pieces I had, like those of the girl that had these, went unused, not because I didn't want to use them, but because I didn't have enough pieces for a meal. As I have on moved in my journey, I have come to the point where I not only can afford to buy this china, but feel important enough to deserve it.

Finding it isn't easy. Pieces appear occasionally in the antique shops that we visit and we have picked up what we could when we found them. We had the reached the point where we could set a table for four and celebrated that achievement by using them on our wedding anniversary.

I began to hear the voice deep inside the day the china appeared in the antique store where I found it. The voice was telling me that I had to go to Mildred's Antiques. It didn't say why. We were considering buying oak bookcases at the time and I thought that this message might have something to do with them. I waited a week before I responded to the voice and took the time to visit the store. As I walked around, my eyes searched for bookcases that would meet our needs. They weren't there. I came around the corner and saw the table piled with china. I knew then what the voice was telling me.

Although I was tempted, I didn't buy it all, but concentrated on the pieces I could add to what I already owned so that I could actually use it for dinner parties. I now have enough dinner plates to serve my whole family at once. This is exciting for me. This china won't sit unused in the cabinet as it did in the past. It will be an active part of my life. That's what the material self is for. I hope you find the same joy in what you have in your material self.

Case Study

She grew up in poverty and suffered neglect and abuse at the hands of family members. She was on the verge of becoming a juvenile delinquent when fate intervened. Her mother decided that she couldn't handle her any longer and shipped her off to live with her father. In his home, she finally experienced the love and unconditional acceptance that every child on this planet so desperately needs. She has gone on to become one of the richest women on the earth.

Across the country, a young girl, who loved to cook with her father, grew up. When she was an adult, he passed away and she decided to share their passion with the world. She opened a restaurant where she shared the delicious recipes her father had developed with her customers. Those who ate this food appreciated her efforts, but there were not enough of them to pay all the bills. After four years of struggle, this woman was about to give up her dream.

And then, in a way that can happen for all of us, a door opened. On the last day the restaurant was to be open, this woman got an order to supply sandwiches for a simple business meeting. As she made this food she could have given up in despair and thrown in whatever, just to get the job over with. It was the last day; it wasn't going to make any difference in her ability to succeed. She may as well have refused to do the order or handed it on to someone else. But she didn't. She put every bit of care and love in those sandwiches as she did into all the meals she served in her restaurant. She did her absolute best.

The simple business meeting was not all that simple. Among those in attendance was the rich lady mentioned above who had the material goods to actually make a difference in the lives of others. When she ate the sandwiches, she declared them to be the best she had ever eaten. She was told of the plight of the restaurant owner and quickly made the decision to help out. With this help, the restaurant stayed open and woman was able to continue to share her passion with the world.

This story exemplifies how all of us are to work at a material level. If we have, we can share. We don't have to take. We don't have to own more. We can allow others the joy of reaching their full potential in the midst of reaching our own. A typical business scenario based on the accumulation of material goods would have the rich buying the recipe from the poor in order to increase their profit margin on the back of this woman's potential. It isn't necessary, but it happens every day in so many different ways. It's so good to see that the opposite can happen.

We all know the rich woman through her television talk show, The Oprah Winfrey Show, as the number one talk show in the world. It was watched by an estimated 30 million viewers a week in the United States and is broadcast internationally in 110 countries. This means that Oprah likely has one of the biggest social selves in the world. She carries this burden with a style and presence that is an example for all of us.

Oprah could be included as a case study in this book as an example of how to travel the journey to self at all levels: in spite of difficulties, in spite of a childhood that was definitely not perfect, in spite of her position in an industry in which public opinion makes it difficult to stay true to oneself. She has openly shared her coping skill of overeating with us all without shame, allowing us the freedom to do the same. She broke through the walls of secrecy surrounding childhood sexual abuse by sharing her own story, and the stories of so many others, thus demonstrating how to ease the power of anxiety in one's life. She followed her spiritual path from the pain of childhood, through one door after another, and shares her appreciation of those who opened those doors for her with us all. She focuses on our ability to dream and celebrates the accomplishment of those dreams with us. She shows us how to do things right: to love one another, to celebrate each other's talents and abilities, to read, to share, to listen to one's intuition, to learn from one's mistakes, to be open and honest. And in the midst of all this, she admits that she isn't perfect. Her journey isn't over. Who knows what other gifts will be revealed in the coming years. In the meantime, we experience a positive role model through her life that we can emulate, no matter how much we have suffered in the past. Her success, in spite of her pain, shows us the way.

Chapter Nine
Connecting with the Spirit

Is that all there is, is that all there is?
If that's all there is my friends, then let's keep dancing
Let's break out the booze and have a ball
If that's all there is.

PEGGY LEE

WE WERE WALKING HOME TOGETHER FROM A NEW YEAR'S EVE PARTY. IT HAD BEEN A good night as parties go. The food was tasty and plentiful. The company was cheerful. The band was upbeat and talented. We had eaten, conversed and danced the night away to our hearts' content. And now, in the wee hours of the morning, we were heading home to start another year. As the snow crunched beneath our feet, the sky above erupted in colour. Vivid reds, greens, blues, whites and yellows danced before our upturned faces, the most incredible display of Northern Lights I have ever witnessed. As I stood there in that dark night, watching the sky above me, I thought about the party we had just attended and the year that had just begun, the beauty of the night, and then deep inside the words of the song above rang through my mind. *"Is that all there is?"*

This feeling was a constant companion throughout the years that I lived my life with my first husband. Throughout the years I raised my children. Years that should have been filled with happiness, laughter, contentment and the joy of meeting a challenge, but instead I experienced the nagging reminder time and again that, no matter what was happening to me, I was missing out on something. Something very important. Something crucial to life itself. And I was.

Although this thought was with me often, I never mentioned it to anyone. I never quite knew what to do with it. At times I blamed myself for not being satisfied with what life had to offer. I blamed myself for not getting things right. But nothing I did seemed to help. I looked to my marriage, my children, my home, my family, an education, a job, a healthy body, and still I wasn't happy. This was because the answer did not lie in the world around me, but deep within. My spirit was crying out in the wilderness of my self, trying to get my attention. Trying to get me to move to living on my life line. Trying to show me how important it was to be true to myself.

I was in my thirties before I began to change. I had wasted a good portion of time on this earth, living as a pseudo self, escaping the reality of my days through coping skills and destroying my body in the process. No, I was not resorting to drowning my sorrows in liquor as is suggested in the song, but I was hiding behind a wall of fat created by the food I was eating to numb my feelings. My life journey focused on striving to get through each day instead of achieving anything.

Throughout these years, I thought I was in touch with my spirit. I was a Christian. I had accepted Christ as my personal savior. I attended church and studied the Bible. I was totally aware of the fruits of the Holy Spirit and used them regularly. I lived what most people would call a good life, not because I was necessarily a good person, but because I didn't have the desire to do anything bad. And yet, in the midst of all this, I wasn't in touch with my own spirit. I might have been in contact with my creator, but I was wasting his most precious gift: my self.

This message of dissatisfaction from my spirit also came to me through recurrent dreams that I didn't understand. They all involved a house: a house I had acquired in different ways, as a gift, as an inheritance, through purchase, or at times one of the houses I had lived in, in the past. No matter how I acquired the house, its state was still the same. In the beginning of the dream the house was ugly and derelict from the outside, and stayed the same as I entered the door and went from room to room. But then something changed. There came a point when there were more rooms than one would anticipate, looking at the exterior of the house. These were secret rooms to which only I knew the passage. Once within them, the house became more and more luxurious, of unbelievable beauty and quality. The space and the beauty went on and on until I woke up.

When I went back to college in my mid thirties, I attended a psychology class in which our professor asked us to share a recurring dream. I shared this one with our group and the students all speculated as to what it could mean. Nothing they said clicked with me. Then the professor offered her explanation. She told me that I was the house and that all of the beauty I was experiencing in the dream was the beauty of my inner self. This beauty was being hidden from the world by the life I was currently living. Only I had the power to reveal this beauty to the world. Thus began my real journey to self, a journey in which I am attempting to share that beauty with others. It has taken a long time.

Although I have learned many different lessons over the years, the last dozen years have been a real eye opener. The model of the self has opened my eyes to so many different things, but most of all it has allowed me to truly get in touch with my own spirit. It started with a meditation exercise during my Master's program where we were to visualize a journey. I found myself getting off a train at a deserted railway station in the middle of the desert. As I stepped off the wooden platform I realized I was totally and completely alone in an alien land. A sense of peace and calm came over me and I realized for the first time in my life that I was all right, exactly as I was. I was safe, no matter where I was. I didn't need anyone else. I didn't need to fit in any mold. I didn't need to change in order to succeed. I could just be Gail, and that was okay.

This led to a freedom I hadn't experienced since I was a small child. This led to a celebration of life that has continued on, every day since. A celebration of the simple joys in life. A celebration of the incredible vastness of our world and everything that is in it. A celebration of the beauty of creation. A celebration of who I am as a person, without any barriers. A celebration of each person I meet for their own unique role on earth. The more I allow myself to be me, the more I shine through. The more I am me, the more joy I experience. The sense of dissatisfaction is completely gone. Not because I found something outside that filled my needs, but because I went within and found myself. Not because I did anything incredible, but because I accepted the reality that it was okay to be me. That acceptance led me to the point where I was not only living on my life line, but also closely connected to my spirit.

THE SPIRIT

The most important level of self is that of your spirit. Your spirit is what connects you to your creator. Your spirit is what connects you to the rest of mankind. Your spirit is what connects you directly to the world we live in. Your spirit has the knowledge of who you are as an individual and what your journey on this world should be. It recognizes the forces of good and evil and knows the importance of honoring our creator, taking care of our world, and loving ourselves and others. It cries out with longing from deep within when you are not meeting its needs. It will fill you with a joy and a sense of peace beyond description when you are. I know this because I have experienced both the longing and the joy and peace myself. My hope is that this book may help you take the opportunity to access that same level of feeling.

Your own personal journey to this point may not have been one in which this spirit was either acknowledged or focused on. This is okay. Denial of the spiritual force within is one of mankind's strongest coping skills. If you worship the dollar, the economic decisions you make may depend on the absence of recognition of the spirit in yourself or in others to allow you to do what you do. If you worship pleasure, the denial of the spirit may be how you convince yourself that your rights to access pleasure are far more important than the rights of anyone else. If you live at the level of a pseudo self, you may choose to ignore the spirit as you convince yourself that you are better than anyone else who does not live like you, in order to block the discomfort you feel. If you live in the midst of a family who are completely dependent on the use of coping skills, you may have never even contemplated the importance of the spirit, as all of the energy in your family has been going elsewhere. If you live in a family hurt deeply in the past, the concept of the spirit may have been given up as a direct result of the pain that was being experienced. Denial of the spirit is a common coping skill. This doesn't mean the spirit doesn't exist. It just means that somehow, somewhere you did not get the opportunity to get to know your spirit. It is never too late.

Some of you may have always known you have spirit, but you may not have been taught exactly what that means. You may have assumed it's something that doesn't matter much until you die. You may have assumed it has religious connotations that are only important when you are at church. You may have assumed it is limited in power in much the same way that you are limited in your own individual ways. You may have heard how powerful it is and how well connected it is to the whole. You may have been trying to connect with it over the years but have not figured out how. You may have been connected all along and know exactly what I am talking about. Each of us is different. Each of us has a different journey. Again, this is okay.

Your spirit has been with you all through your life. You may not have been paying any attention to it, for whatever reason you, yourself, hold. This is okay if this is where you want to stay, but denying your spirit will limit your ability to reach your full potential. It will be the barrier that impedes you on your own individual journey. Ignoring your spirit will reduce the level of joy and peace you can experience throughout life. You will go without. Those you love will be impacted by your choice in turn and will also have limits placed on their journeys. This isn't something to be taken lightly. Yes, you can choose to continue to ignore your spirit, but in doing so, you will also ignore your self.

The first step to reaching your spirit is as simple as acknowledging its presence, admitting to yourself and to your world that you have a spirit. We all know this as young children, but it is taken away from us over the years through the experiences we have in this world. Acknowledging your spirit opens you up to its voice so that you can begin to find your life line. You don't need to know what this line is when you start. It will become clear to you over time. Once you have opened yourself up to your spirit you can move on to discover how the rest of the levels of your self are meeting its needs or squandering its energy. The next step in this journey is to allow yourself to truly open up to the emotions you are experiencing.

EMOTIONAL HEALING

Our emotions are how the spirit expresses itself through our mind and body. The spirit is able to deal with any level of emotion, without a problem, because it never changes. The other levels of self, (the mind, social self and material self), which are open to change, block us from experiencing strong emotions. The intensity of emotions can be uncomfortable. Discomfort is a sign of change. The self protects itself from change by using the coping skills to decrease the level of discomfort. Strong emotions are suppressed and stored in the mind rather than expressed in order to avoid the discomfort. We lose our connection to our spirit. This is a process that happens over time.

Our spirit has endless power. It can deal with any emotion that comes along, no matter how strong or how uncomfortable it feels. Suppressing these emotions is far more destructive than allowing ourselves to feel them. We know this as infants and as small children, but we are taught otherwise over time. We gradually learn to suppress our emotional reactions to make our mind, our social self and our material self comfortable. We also learn to suppress our emotions to protect the feelings of others. We store these unexpressed emotions in the cells of our bodies. They gradually block the flow of energy through our body which is expressed through the physical and psychological breakdown of our mind and body over time. Allowing oneself to actually feel one's emotion in the present and to release the emotions of the past is a major step in the journey to self.

You are totally capable of feeling and dealing with every emotion to its highest level of intensity without danger. The hardest part of this process is breaking through the resistance to feeling that you have built up over the years. Emotions cannot hurt us, no matter how strong they are, no matter how uncomfortable they feel. Giving your self the permission to feel them is the first step. Taking the time and the effort to do so is the next.

There are two kinds of emotions. Those that are real and are necessary for us to deal with the acute anxiety we face in our lives come directly through the spirit. These are the emotions of joy, love, kindness, peace, generosity, grief, fear and righteous anger. The other emotions that we tend to use are those that are fictional in much the same way as chronic anxiety is fictional, as they are based directly on what we make up in our imagination. These emotions are based in the mind. Examples of these emotions include jealousy, envy, greed, and hatred. Fear is a real emotion because it protects the self from that which can destroy it. However, fear can also become an emotion of the mind when it is focused on chronic anxiety, not reality. The same is true for anger.

Opening ourselves to our emotions is a two-step journey based on the past and the present. One step is to learn to allow ourselves to feel what we feel fully in the moment. The other is to revisit one's past in order to release those feelings that are stored. It really doesn't matter which you do first. Like any other change you attempt, it will not happen all at once but will be a process that one gets better at over time.

Facing the past and allowing ourselves to feel the trauma we have experienced is not an easy step. Our first tendency is to protect ourselves from the pain and we do this through the use of coping skills. The mind stores the memories of trauma in such a way that they are hard to access in order to protect us from the pain. Our minds also store the various coping skills we use to suppress these emotions and put them into practice automatically with little input on our part. Opening ourselves up means we have to move from an automatic response to a rational way of reacting. This is a big change. Change is most difficult at the level of the mind. This means that facing the past will be difficult.

The social level of self is also affected by our emotions and our tendency to cover up that which we are feeling. We are been taught not to express our strong emotions because other people, who are suppressing their own emotions, feel uncomfortable when we express ours. In an attempt to present a social view that others feel comfortable with, we move to a pseudo self. We are rewarded by those around us, who react positively to our lack of emotion. Facing our past means moving back from the pseudo self to one's life line. This requires change. As we have learned, change at more than one level of self causes more discomfort. We are working at two levels: the mind and the social self. Facing one's past becomes even more difficult. It is not only possible, but also necessary if you are going to reach your full potential.

There are some therapists who claim that one can "let go" of the pain, if one allows oneself to feel it enough. I don't believe this is true, though I may be wrong. There are many different situations in life that are so painful that the actual pain will never go away. This is okay. We must honor that pain, not ignore it, nor dismiss it. These are the true lessons in life: to respect the pain in order to ensure that no one else has to endure the same thing in the future. However, we have gotten so far away from respecting pain that we don't seem to care any more. Far, far too many children of our world grow up without love, without safety, without respect. The damage they are experiencing is mind boggling if we take the time to think about it, but we don't care. We would rather stay secure in our own static position than make any effort to make things different.

Pain makes us feel uncomfortable. This is okay. We can deal with the discomfort. Once we acknowledge it and allow ourselves to feel it, we are okay. If we let it go completely, we forget the destruction it causes and allow the evil to continue in the future. The real problem with pain is that we are unwilling to face it at all and choose to use coping skills to either dull it, or to block it out completely. The process of "letting go" of the pain is often a process in which we are using coping skills such as isolation and compartmentalization to protect ourselves from feeling the pain. This leads to physical and psychological breakdown over time. It is not the pain itself that destroys. In fact it is the pain that protects us when we allow ourselves to feel it. Destruction comes through the fear of facing emotional pain and acknowledging that pain not only to each of us as a self, but also to society as a whole.

The tears and the pain of those who have been hurt as children must be allowed to be shared openly in our world. It is we, as a whole society, who cannot face our own discomfort with emotional feelings, who should be ashamed. The tears of the abused and neglected are a clear message to the world that we must make the effort to put an end to this evil. They are not something to be ashamed of.

I know it is hard but it is possible to feel the pain without being overwhelmed by fear or the need for protection. It is possible to live without feeling the pain all of the time, once you have allowed yourself to fully feel it. It is possible to heal the hole of loss. It is possible to live in the joy of the present moment. This is the true gift of the spirit: to be able to face reality with strength, with courage, with patience, no matter what happens; in spite of the pain, in spite of the discomfort. As adults we are all free to do this.

There are two factors that one must not only know about but also trust absolutely to develop new responses to emotional feelings. The first is to recognize clearly that the trauma you experienced or the issue you faced in the past is in the memory, not in the present moment, so it has no power to hurt you in the here and now. It may feel like it is going to destroy you as you let go and let yourself feel, but it won't. It didn't in the past. You survived. It cannot do anything at all in the present because it is not in the present. This doesn't mean that I believe we must spend a lot of our time wallowing in the pain of the past. It takes far too much time and energy to do that. It also means that you can't expect to change your coping skills if you are still in acute danger in the present. There are times and circumstances in which you may have to begin at a material and social level before you can truly make a difference. But for most of us, the pain we have to deal with is that of the past. Each of us carries our own burdens throughout life. You know which ones are affecting you personally.

The second factor you must also trust is that your spirit is strong enough to deal with any emotion that occurs. For it is. The spirit is dependent on the mind and the body to exist in this world. It will never put you in a situation that will hurt either the mind or the body, and it will never express an emotion that is too strong for either one. Using coping skills to suppress emotions over time is far more damaging than allowing oneself to actually feel one's emotions. However, it is these coping skills that allow us to survive in the moment. We are safe, no matter what happens.

Facing the trauma of the past is not about actually reliving the trauma in the present, but rather revisiting it in the mind so that one can feel the actual emotions one should have felt instead of suppressing them through any type of coping skill. These situations in our past became traumatic because we were not able to express our real emotions or to share them with someone else because this would have made the situation even more dangerous. A child cannot be honest about how they feel about their abusive, neglectful parent, either to the parent themselves or to anyone else, because of the threat that they may lose that parent, which will cause devastation in the social level of self. A child cannot be honest about the loss of their parent's love and affection after the death of a sibling, because there is no way that they can allow themselves to bring their parent more grief. I could not be honest about my grade one teacher because I would have suffered even more punishment at her hands had I been open about the effect she was having on me and others. I could not be honest about my relationship with my husband and keep my home and family intact.

Reliving the trauma becomes a process of allowing oneself to actually "feel" the emotions that one has not expressed in the past. One will not only have to face the actual emotions, but also the fear that accompanies allowing oneself to fear them. The level of difficulty will depend on your own experiences and so will be different for every person in the world. Again, this is not an easy step, because we did not have the ability to protect ourselves when the incident first happened to us, so our coping skills are what kept us safe. It is not easy to give them up.

I don't know exactly what anyone else has to deal with so I can only share my experience. I do know that my past is different than others. I do know that many children have experienced far worse than I. I do know that their fear and their emotional reactions will be much different than mine. I do know that this takes time, no matter who says otherwise. I do know that it is much easier once you have connected with your spirit, but that connection is not a magic key that erases everything from the past at once. I do know that you will be okay, if you trust your spirit. I humbly offer my experience as an example of what can happen.

For 24 years I lived in an abusive marriage in which I had very little knowledge or understanding of what was actually going on. From **my** current vantage point, it all makes sense, and I am fully aware that what I was dealing with were the coping skills of my husband, who had such a different childhood from mine. In the midst of these coping skills, I was not safe, and yet I had to continue living not only for myself, but also for my children. How did I do this? I became numb. I suppressed all of my feelings to the point that I didn't feel anything. It was the only way I could get through it and stay alive.

This numbness allowed for other things that might not appear to make sense. It allowed me to stay in a relationship when I knew it was not safe. It allowed me to concentrate on the positives, not the negatives, when I talked, or wrote, about my life. It allowed me to stand tall in my home and in my community, so that no one guessed my truth. But all this time, all those years, I felt as though I had a huge sword stabbed through my body, just below the ribs. This sword held the pain inside. It didn't let it out, though occasionally something would bump up against it and remind me how incredibly awful it was. But these feelings didn't last. I cut them off as I did all others and remained numb.

This numbness remained with me for some time after I left. Again it kept me safe in the early years in its own way, but gradually it slipped away and finally was gone for good. I am not numb anymore. I don't know if I could make myself numb if I had to. I do know I don't want to. I enjoy feeling and experiencing life to the fullest. And believe me, it is the fullest. In the past I felt very little. For a number of years I felt extremes. In time this too passed, and my emotions evened out.

The first thing that happened was the sword was removed. This left a gaping hole of pain, which has taken years to heal, pain that had me crying for up to a week at a time, unable to move, tied in knots. The slightest thing would set off the pain. I couldn't stop it. I was rejected when I tried to share it with anyone. Their discomfort with my heightened level of emotion led to a defensive reaction on their part. And so I had to work it out alone. This is not something to be afraid of. One's spirit is strong enough to bear it.

One night everything changed. I was lying in bed in my apartment and the couple below started fighting. As the battle raged on through the night, I lay there and listened and realized that this is what I had walked away from. How many nights had I gone without sleep as my husband ranted and raged? How many nights had I had to defend myself from his attacks, both verbal and physical? How many nights had I cried like the woman below me was now crying? As I stepped back into the trauma through their experience, I was so thankful that this environment was over, for good, for me. What an incredible feeling of gratitude and peace!

Of course, this wasn't the end of the pain, but now pain and joy began to alternate. The next step was to experience vivid flashbacks that put me right back into my past in my mind, which allowed me to feel the experience with all of my emotions. These flashbacks would totally drain me of energy for days on end, but they also allowed me to achieve peace with my past. During this period, all of my emotional feelings were felt to the extreme, which meant that a lot of people were very uncomfortable with me. As the flashbacks faded away, the extreme emotions gradually leveled out. I moved away from dealing with the pain to forgiving myself and others. It was a gradual change At this point I live in joy most of the time. It's a good place to be.

This doesn't mean I have totally stopped using coping skills to deal with emotions. It means that I live in a home in which it is safe for me to express my emotions most of the time. But there are still times when I don't know what to do with them. I live in a big city that is situated in the midst of some of the best farm land in the world. Rapid expansion is putting more and more of this land under pavement and concrete for residential subdivisions. Every time I see another piece of land going under construction I am filled with a sadness that reaches my very core. I know we are making a mistake. I know we cannot waste this type of resource without facing the consequences of these choices in the future. I know we are not treating our home, the planet earth, with the respect that we should, but I also know that I don't have the answer or the power to affect change on this level. So I allow myself to feel the emotions, to acknowledge their presence, and then set them aside for a time. If you are not able to do this, you may be tapping into your purpose here on earth. The inability to ignore a situation may well be a message that it is your job to do something about the situation.

Every time we return to the scene of trauma in the past, we are going to have to use a lot of energy to deal with the pain of what has happened. This energy will not be available for anything else in the moment. The level of pain will depend completely on the situation itself. Situations like my experience on the verandah of my grandmother's house, which led to my feelings of being on the outside, will take far less energy than something like being raped as a small child or being involved in the death of someone. Some situations may be able to be explained and let go of. They will be based on chronic anxiety and once one has brought the chronic anxiety out into the open, one can realize that the pain never actually existed. Others won't be that easy. The spirit mourns. The mind adjusts. The social and material levels expand, contract and shift. Change will occur. All of this takes a lot of energy. The spirit is strong, but the self will still go into protective mode if it is pushed too far. We must be tender and loving to ourselves as we deal with the trauma of the past. We must be tender and loving with others as they deal with the trauma of their past. Change is difficult. The anxiety level they experience because of this change will produce to stronger anxiety reactions. We must be patient. We must be kind. We are using our energy to heal.

Learning to allow yourself to feel in the moment requires a lot of effort, as you must break the habit of relying on coping skills to cover up your feelings. You have to monitor all of your reactions in order to ensure that you are not habitually storing the feelings again, either to protect yourself, or to protect others. I still live in a family in which the rage of childhood sexual abuse continues to haunt us all. My sons must choose between their parents at times in order to protect themselves and their children from this rage. Although I fully understand why this is happening, it still hurts deeply to be the one who is excluded. Allowing myself to feel that pain, and acknowledging those feelings to my children isn't easy. However, the amazing part of this journey is how deep the feelings can be in a moment and yet how one feels completely washed clean once one has allowed oneself to feel them, and shared them openly with others. No longer do these feelings feel like acid, eating away at my self. Within minutes I am calm, content and filled with a peace that passes all understanding. This is what living at the spiritual level is all about.

THE ACT OF LISTENING

Listening to our own personal spirit and fulfilling its needs is our ultimate task here on earth. This task is fundamentally different for each and every one of us. Our spirits speak to us with a voice that is known as intuition. We may choose to listen to that voice or to ignore it. If we listen, it will guide us on our journey, protect us from danger, and help us reach our full potential. The more we listen to the voice and respond to it, the more it tells us, and the further along in our journey we go. It can't lead us if we don't listen. If we ignore it, we will suffer the consequences in many different ways including unhappiness, dissatisfaction, anger, and physical or psychological aliments. They are all direct consequences of not living on your life line; of not reaching your full potential; of not meeting the needs of your spirit.

Listening and responding to your spirit is again not something that happens without effort. It is a choice we all face on our journey through life and we must make the effort to choose. Although we are all connected closely to our spirits as infants, our experiences in life may build a wall that is difficult to break through. The size and the shape of that wall will be different for each of us, but we all have issues to deal with. As the different levels of self develop over time, the discomfort of change restricts our ability to react. We move away from responding with the freedom of the spirit to that which fits in with the confines of our family, our community, our culture. We begin to react in fear rather than trust. We begin to concentrate on protecting ourselves and controlling our lives instead of relying on God. The spiritual connection we once had may become blurred or appear to disappear completely. We have to make the effort to keep it open, but no one tells us this is necessary.

Our creator has given us all free will. The gift of free will gives us the responsibility of our journey in life. This isn't something we can do without thought or effort. This isn't something we can hand on to another to take care of for us. This is our personal responsibility as a human being on this planet. Each of us must face the truth and make the choice whether to connect with our spirit and follow its lead or ignore it. However, this gift of free will is impacted by the free will of others, through what has happened before we are born. In turn, our decisions will impact those who follow us. As the Bible states: the sins of the fathers are visited unto the children to the third and fourth generation[20]. This isn't a statement of punishment. It is the natural law of the development of the self. In the midst of being an individual self, we are all interconnected with each other, through the past, in the present and for the future. The decisions and reactions of others will impact us and create the actual self we become. Our decisions and reactions will influence others. We are individuals in the midst of a whole.

I can't tell you what your voice is saying to you. Mine has told me to take a job I didn't I apply for, to open myself to the love that was waiting, to get involved in some things and to step back from others, to reach out and to retreat to wait patiently. I spent a lot of my life living far from my life line. When I finally decided to make the effort to change, I experienced a freedom that I didn't believe was possible for anyone. If I listen to the voice of my spirit, doors open without much effort on my part. When I try to take control and do things my own way, the doors close. The more I listen to the voice, the more joy I feel, the higher satisfaction of life I experience, the stronger connection I have with God, with others and with all of creation. The more I listen to the voice and respond, the more I hear it. The same can happen to you.

Our voice speaks to us in many different ways. On a rare occasion I have heard an actual voice, but most of the time the message comes in other ways. I have had the unsettled feeling deep in my stomach that something is wrong. I have had recurring, persistent thoughts about something that didn't make sense to me but when I follow through on them I discover their meaning. I have faced a wall in a variety of ways that I now realize is a clear indication that I am going the wrong direction. I have felt the aha moment as I listened to the words of others, which opened up new avenues of thought and action. I have listened to the messages that arrive through recurring dreams. I have used family members, friends, teachers, religious leaders, therapists, celebrities, strangers, clients and children as my teachers. I have sat in stillness and listened. I have spent hours on my knees in prayer. I have heard the messages clearly, while on the move, hiking in solitude through the beauty of this world. I'm not claiming that I get it right all the time, but that I am trying and it is worth the effort.

The important lessons of life that we need to learn come in all sorts of different ways. I believe that my first contact with my spirit came through the church where I grew up: a church in which I was taught about my creator; a church in which I was taught that the greatest law **is** to love the Lord

20 Exodus 20:5

253

your God with all your heart, with all your mind, with all your soul and your neighbor as yourself; a church that stressed that salvation is achieved through grace as a gift, based directly on the death of Jesus on the cross, not as something that we earn in any way; a church in which I learned first hand about the imperfection of man. As a young child I often observed the actions of the elders as contrary to that which I was being taught and wondered at my ability to differentiate between the good and the bad. This was a church where I put God on hold for a time as a teenager, as I wanted to live before I turned my life over to him; a church through which he called and he called and he called, through the Word, through the music, through the actions of others, through the joy of those who had surrendered their lives until I finally responded and got the first glimpse of what it means to live at the level of the spirit. But this was only the first step of a journey that I have traveled on for years and one that still continues.

I learned about the power of faith when my husband hurt his hand at work and all of our financial concerns were taken care of. I learned the powerful lesson of forgiveness while sitting in a bar with my mother-in-law where I suddenly realized that she was doing and had been doing the best she could with the knowledge she had at the time all through the years. I learned about the intensity of love standing outside my apartment building looking down through a window on a couple who were ignoring our efforts to catch their attention. It was very late at night. We had taken our young sons to a drive-in movie where they had slept in the back of the station wagon while we enjoyed a night out. When we arrived home we discovered that our new apartment manager had chosen to lock all of the exterior doors. No one had told him that none of us had keys that actually worked in these doors. And so there we were, at 3 in the morning, with four very tired little boys dressed in their pajamas, locked out of our home.

The couple in the downstairs apartment were still up, sitting in their living room, watching television. We knew that they typically kept to themselves, but we thought it would be easier for them to come up and open the door than for us to wake the new manager. And so we rang their bell. We tapped on their window. We called out to them. They chose to ignore us. As I looked down at them through the uncurtained window, I was overwhelmed with a feeling of love that was far beyond anything I had ever felt before. I couldn't be angry. I couldn't be frustrated. I just loved them. I knew I wasn't doing this by myself but that had truly I tapped into the love of God, the love of our spirits. And then I turned and did what I had to do for my sons. I woke the manager. Once you have experienced that level of love, you don't forget it.

Other lessons come in other ways. When my sons were young they left the television on one afternoon. This gave me the opportunity to watch a special on the scientist Immanuel Velikovsky. This show led me to his books, which I devoured one by one, which in turn opened my eyes to so many new and different ways of thinking about our world. Velikovsky was a Russian scientist who was also a Jew. At a certain point in his life he spent a year in Israel studying the Jewish scriptures.

When he came to the story of Joshua, where it states that the sun stood still for a whole day[21], he faced a dilemma. As a Jew he believed that the words captured the actual events that had happened that day. As a scientist he was totally aware of the consequences of what he was reading. If the sun stood still, it was not the sun that had stopped moving, but the earth. And if the earth stopped moving, the whole planet would be affected in a number of catastrophic ways. He set out to determine if he could find the evidence that would prove the story true. This led to a whole new way of looking at the history of the Jews and of our whole world. He published his findings, which were in direct conflict with many of the theories held by other scientists of the time. Instead of acceptance, he faced criticism and rejection. His books were banned.

One part of his theory centered on the make-up of the planet Venus. He claimed that Venus was made up of certain chemicals. The rest of the scientific community believed it was made up of something else and used this as an example of how wrong he was. When the first space probes reached Venus, they found that Velikovsky was right while the other scientists were mistaken. This led to a renewed interest in his theories, which led to the ban being lifted on the publication of his books and the television show I watched. However, most of his wisdom continues to be ignored and untapped because it doesn't fit into the status quo.

Velikovsky taught me to understand how we accept that which we are taught and how we can be confined by those teachings; how to recognize the difference between real science based on logic and natural laws, and that which is based on the social view of self, where the view of others is more important than actual facts; how to question what we are presented with in a calm and logical manner; how to trust that which we truly know and to search out the answers when we are not sure. All of these lessons seemed to be of little importance to a young stay-at-home mother of preschoolers. They are invaluable in my work in the field of autism.

Much of what I have learned over the years would have been missed had I not been open to accepting to new and different thoughts and ideas. If one wants to truly connect with one's spirit, one must be willing to step out of the confines of one's development and open one's self to the whole world. In opening yourself to the world, you allow yourself to truly connect with your inner self, with your creator, with others, and become a meaningful part of the whole picture. No one individual out there has "the answer" for everyone else. We all share pieces of the picture. One piece may be the key that clears the way for you as an individual while being totally meaningless to the person next to you. There isn't a single formula and there isn't a specific route.

Your spirit is calling to you, every minute of every day of your life. I don't know exactly how you are experiencing that call, but it is happening. You may be in the habit of turning it off. You may be scared of responding. You may be afraid of giving up control. You may not think it is important. You may not want to face the reality of change. Your spirit will continue to call, for as long as it has

---

21 Joshua 10:13-14, The Holy Bible

to. When you take the time and make the effort to respond, you will know what it feels like to truly come home to yourself. You will discover a joy that is beyond belief. You will experience the peace that passes all understanding. You will learn how your life makes sense. You will find out that you are love; that we all are love and this is our main purpose here on earth. It raises our journey of life to another level.

Once we have learned to listen, we can solve all sorts of problems just by asking for the answer. I am driving down the highway thinking about a school project I am in the midst of. We are to work with some type of group therapy as part of our assignments during my Master's Program in family therapy. A local autism society has offered to advertise sessions for parents of children with autism for me for this project. My inner voice tells me that I should have a co-facilitator for this group. As I drive along I think about each of the students in my class, wondering who might be able to fill this role. Honey comes to mind as the best candidate for the position. I don't know why, but I decide that I will follow my intuition. I will offer this position to her.

Honey is from Australia. I don't know much about her at present, other than she is married and has two sons. She is a warm, loving, happy person who gets along with all of us so she would be good to work with. But this group is to focus on autism. Will she be of any use to these specific parents with their unique concerns?

When I approach Honey, she shares something with me that I was totally unaware of. When students get their bachelors degree in Australia, they must do research and write a dissertation on this research in order to graduate. Honey's research focused on the parents of children with autism. Of all of my fellow students, she was the best candidate for co-facilitator. I had no knowledge of this, but my spirit knew. Had I not been in the habit of consulting and listening to my spirit, I likely would not have even thought of asking Honey to join me.

This type of situation is repeated over and over again for me. I have a problem. I put the question out into the open. I listen for the answer. The answer comes, clearly, without explanation, and often doesn't make sense to me in the moment, but when I follow through on it, I find that it is the perfect response. The Bible states: ask and you shall be given, seek and ye shall find, knock and the door will be opened. Our Creator stands ready to fulfill our needs perfectly. There isn't anything that can't be solved. Once we connect with our spirit we can have it all.

CONNECTING WITH OTHERS

The more I listen, the more guidance I receive. In time, I learned that my spirit not only talks to me directly, but also gives me messages for others. Some of these messages I understand. Others make absolutely no sense to me at all, but are meaningful to the person I am to share it with. It was difficult for me to share these messages in the past because I was taught to mind my own business as a child. So when I was driving down the road with a mother and her children, I hesitated in sharing the message that had come to me: "Your family is the most important thing in your life in this moment. Treasure it." But the message was strong and I was learning to go with my intuition, so I told her, "I don't know what this means, but I am feeling like I have to say this to you," and I did. Months later she thanked me for speaking to her, admitting that she was in the midst of thinking about leaving her husband for another man. My words allowed her to concentrate on her children, and on making her family a top priority in her life. When she started doing that, the other man faded into the background and she discovered that it wasn't her husband who was neglecting her as much as she had gotten into the habit of looking elsewhere for love and satisfaction. This family is still together.

Over the years, I have gotten into the habit of sharing all the messages that I receive for others. I always start out with "I don't know what this means," because even if I think I know, I might be totally wrong, judging their situation through my definitions of life, rather than theirs. I also do not tell them what to do with what I am saying. I just put it out there for them to decide how to respond. "I don't know what this means but I feel like I need to tell you that a company you are involved with is questionable in some way". "I don't know what this means, but I am feeling that you need to go to the doctor." "I don't know what this means, but I am concerned about your son. You may want to touch base with him."

As I have shared these lessons with others, I have realized that one's spirit is not only crying out to one's self, but is also connected with all of the other spirits in the world. My journey on this earth is not only for myself, but is also a gift to others. Sharing this journey with others is a major part of the journey itself.

We knew this in the past, as the journeys of life were handed down from one generation to another through the spoken word. The oral tradition is a tradition based directly on lives that were lived and lessons that were learned. The focus on individualism through the past 100 years has attempted to destroy this connection. No longer do we share our lives. In fact, in most instances, we are prevented from sharing, through laws of confidentiality based directly on the coping skills of denial and secrecy. We claim that these laws protect people, but they do not. They destroy.

A child who has been raped by an adult is not at all protected by confidentiality. Only the rapist is. The child needs this "secret" to be out in the open. The child needs to be able to freely talk about what has happened in order to release the pain. The child needs to be able to name names and to point fingers and say "shame on you." Anything less gives the message that the child is at fault in some way or another and coping skills will take over their life as they deal with the pain, the shame and the sense of guilt.   Confidentiality is one of the ways we are successful in keeping a pseudo self alive. A man who has tested positive for HIV is not protected by keeping his medical records confidential. The temptation to lie about his condition is too strong when he needs some type of sexual release. This puts another in danger. It also allows him to stay in denial and go without treatment. The devastation of this illness is allowed to spread across the whole world through our dependence on confidentiality.

Demands for privacy are another way we attempt to protect ourselves when we are not living on our life lines. We claim that this privacy is a right, when all it does is allow us to continue living a lie. Living as a true self means living with nothing to hide, nothing we are ashamed to share openly with anyone else. Only those who are doing something they want to kept hidden and secret, because it reveals a reality about themselves they are not proud of, need privacy. When cameras were installed in a school for troubled youth, it was the teachers who demanded that it was an invasion of their privacy. Why? Because the cameras revealed that the teachers' behaviors instigated the students' negative responses. They didn't want to take responsibility for their own actions. They wanted to keep on insisting it was the children who were the problem. The "right" of privacy is a ruse used to hide from the world, to hide from one's own self. It doesn't work.

The fear mongers of the world convince us that we need confidentiality in order to be protected in a financial way. What would companies do with the information if it wasn't kept confidential? Would they insure us? Would they charge higher premiums? Would they deny us our rights? When we fall into the trap of "there is not enough money", these concerns are very real. But when we turn our lives over to our spirits, it doesn't seem to matter any more. There really isn't anything worth hiding. The energy needed to keep things confidential can be used so much more effectively some other way.

We have all heard the saying: the truth will set you free. This is a message that comes directly through our spirits. The truth cannot hurt you. Yes, it may make you face up to the consequences of your actions, which may not be the most comfortable thing to do, but in doing so, you and the people you love are protected. If you want a measure of how well you are living on your life line, ask this question of every move you make: "Can I openly share what I am doing with anyone and everyone in the world?" If the answer is no, you might want to question why you are doing it.

Freely sharing our life journey with others allows them the freedom to find themselves. They, in turn, can be open about what is happening for them. They can begin to make the effort to seek out their own spirit, their own life line, in the midst of living surrounded by other people who may claim it isn't important.. Our stories, combined with the stories of others, allow for a connection with others who have dealt with similar issues, and allow access to solutions to problems that might not otherwise be considered. The stories allow us to give up any shame or sense of failure as we admit we are not perfect, that we are all struggling in our own ways. We can then relinquish our anxiety so we can give up using our coping skills to get through from one day to the next.

Once one is in touch with one's spirit, it is very easy to let go and allow others the freedom to take responsibility for their own life. We must protect our children. We must ensure that they have the strongest foundation possible in their lives, but once they are adults, we must also give them the freedom to truly be themselves. This is true for every adult in this world, no matter what conditions they faced in the past; no matter what difficulties they face in the present. We can stand by them or walk with them and share their journey, but it is not our responsibility to take over that journey. We can offer to share our energy with them in they may need that energy, but it is not our place to take over any portion of their life for them. As soon as we insist that we can take care of things better than they, we are relinquishing our own 'self' as well as standing in the way of allowing them to reach their full potential. It's not always easy to step back, especially if you have been taught to care for others all of your life, and are focused at the level of the social self, but it is necessary. The joy of living at a spiritual level is that it not only makes sense but it is easy to do. It is the gift you freely give to others.

The primary purpose of each spirit in this world is to love. To love our creator. To love each other. To love ourselves. Once one is living at a spiritual level, one finds it easy to love. Much of what goes on in our world at a human level becomes unbearable because of that love. Much of what goes on in our world at a natural level begins to make more sense as one recognizes the way that love is created through the experience of loving. Loving another means accepting them as an equal, no matter how different they are from you. Loving another means allowing them to live on their life line, in much the same way that you are living on yours. Loving another means unconditional acceptance of that which you like, and of that which you are not so comfortable with. Loving each other means opening your heart, mind and spirit to the pain and suffering in the world. By reaching out to others we are able to discover the rewards and obligations of deeply feeling what life has to offer.

In order to be successful in love, we must realize that love is not only a noun, which describes a feeling, but also a verb, which is an action towards another. We all get into trouble when we concentrate on love as a feeling. If we wait until we feel the "love" we have for someone, we will never get there. If we wait for others to "love" us, we will never get there. If we concentrate on our feelings, we will likely discover that there are far more reasons to dislike someone than to like them. But when we act in love towards them, no matter how we feel, we will discover that we can find reasons to like them. By concentrating on the actions of love and acting as if we love others, by doing them a good turn, we will find that we have less reasons to dislike them. The energy we have committed to this act will give us the impetus to continue to act in love. Gradually the feelings of love will evolve through our actions. We have to act first to develop them.

Loving others begins with loving oneself. The law of love states that you must love the Lord your God with all your heart, with all your soul and with all your might and your neighbor as yourself. You cannot love another until you love yourself. This is a difficult reaction for many, especially those who were raised in a spirit of criticism and failure as children. Although we are all born loving ourselves, the experiences we have as children develop our mind through the connections in the brain, to change us into something else. It's not an easy journey to begin to love yourself if you were given the message that you were totally unlovable as a child, but you can, and must, overcome it if you are to reach your full potential as an adult. It will mean recognizing the automatic reactions you use towards yourself which indicate the lack of love. It will mean replacing the words of constant criticism you faced as a child, found in your inner tape recorder, with words of love and acceptance. It will mean taking responsibility for meeting your own needs and desires, instead of relying on someone else to do it, and in doing so, perpetuating the feelings of being unloved. It will mean looking for love from within, instead of from others. You will find it, because it is part of your spirit, the spirit that is always the same. Once you reach life at a spiritual level, you will find the power to love yourself and to love others, for this is where it originates

Loving your self and loving others, in the long run, is the total acceptance of the self as it is. It is knowing I am okay as I am. It is knowing that each and every other person on this earth is okay as they are. It's not about judging anyone. It's not about changing anyone. It's not about fixing anyone. It is about accepting everyone else as okay as they are. Not as the pseudo self they portray to the world, but as the person they really are. It's a celebration of life, a celebration of ability and even more so, a celebration of the differences that give each of us our own purpose in this world.

Loving yourself and others depends on the acceptance of coping skills as natural factors for survival. It's about accepting your own responsibly to figure out those that are the best for you in the situation in which you find yourself and then to respond accordingly, in the midst of recognizing and accepting that others may well depend on something completely different. It's about knowing that one will have to use more skills during times of high anxiety and change, and that this is okay. It's also about knowing that you will automatically resort to those coping skills developed in earliest childhood at the times of extreme anxiety, in spite of the effort you have made to create new ones, and that this okay. You are who you are. They are who they are. This is okay.

LIVING WITHIN THE NATURAL LAWS

Living at a spiritual level allows us to live at the level of the natural laws of the universe, rather than focusing on material gain or social norms. We will no longer concentrate on defending our individual "rights" as a person or as a family, a race, a community or a culture, but recognize that we are all one people. Whenever we violate the rights of one person, we have violated the rights of all. These rights are defined by the decision of one's conscience or intuition in the moment, rather than the rigid laws created by mankind. Different responses are required in different circumstances. Our responses will be based on the universal principles of justice that we know within. They will be self-centered, for our first responsibility on this earth is to ourselves, but they also will respect the rights and dignity of all human beings as individual selves.

To be true to the universal principles one must feel oneself as a part of the cosmic direction in a way that transcends social norms. Right is defined by the decision of conscience in accord with self-chosen ethical principles that are logical, universal and consistent. The heart of these universal principles are those of justice, reciprocity, equality of human rights, and respect for the dignity of human beings as individual persons, as well as a total respect for the world we live in. In other words, the human who is living at their full potential is one who is able to accept being a small part of a whole universe and fully live within that acceptance.

Acceptance of being part of the whole universe means that we accept and live within the laws of the universe without fear or need to control. Humans are only a small and insignificant part of a huge picture that is completely out of our hands. This is okay. If we live within the rules of the universe, more typically called the laws of science, we will be okay. If we insist on ignoring those rules and try to control everything ourselves, we will have to face the consequences.

A major part of this acceptance is being able to accept the unknown part of life. We don't need to unravel all of the profound mysteries of God, human nature and the natural world. We must recognize and accept that there are other dimensions to life than those we can measure. We might never have all the answers. We can live comfortably without them. We can face obstacles, doubt and paradox, fully knowing that God is present in this world and that we are going to be all right.

Some of the most basic laws of the universe are outlined throughout this book. We, as a self, are much bigger than our body, our mind, or our spirit. This self develops over time and is constantly evolving. We are closely connected to the universe we live in and to every other self in this world. Change causes discomfort to the self and so is resisted, but it is inevitable. Change leads to anxiety. The experience of loss leads to a process of grief, which takes time to go through and must be felt in order to be completed. Anxiety is decreased typically through the use of a variety of coping skills, which we learned as children, though it is more effective to bring it out into the open and live in the present moment. There are times when we cannot access this response as well as our automatic ones. Forgiveness of ourselves and others is the healing balm to each self. It makes us okay

Each of us has a different model of self. Some of us choose to concentrate our energies on our material level so that it completely dwarfs the other levels. Others focus on their social level, concentrating all of their time and energy on their relationship with one person or a lot of different people. Still others centre in on their mind or their spirit. There is no single way that is correct in building a model of the self. However, reaching one's full potential may be elevated or hindered by the model that we choose to live in.

Only you can decide the self you want be. Since the self is developed through what has happened to us throughout our lives and the choices that we make based on those experiences, we can all make different choices along the way. Creating a model of self that fits on our life line is the true goal of each spirit here on earth. This model will vary from one person to another. This is okay.

Some of us are able to reach the point of living on our life line easily because of the family we grew up in and all of the acceptance and love they gave us as children. Some of us do it in spite of the family or circumstances that we grew up in, that we are forced to reject. Some of us become who we are because we went without, without a family, without positive role models, without possessions, and we are determined to live differently as adults. In the midst of this journey we must face each of these realities head on and choose who we really want to be. We can despair and wait for others to take over and fix us, or fix things up for us. We can wallow in resentment toward those who didn't do what they should have. We can steep ourselves in envy of those who have what we desire. We can choose to step outside ourselves to avoid the pain for a moment and view ourselves from the viewpoint of a benevolent stranger to determine who we really are. We can pick ourselves up, carry the pain for a while, listening, helping, and allowing time to help us heal. Some of these responses will be effective. Others will place barriers in our way. Only you can decide the actual steps that you need to take for yourself. It is your journey and you are in charge.

SUPREMELY BEING: A CASE STUDY

She sat in the Pioneer Courthouse Square in Portland, Oregon each day, all day, for nearly six months. She sat quietly, cross-legged, looking out over the square. Good posture, bad clothes. A thin woolen coat over a turquoise dress. Hiking socks and Tevas. When it rained, an anorak, and when it poured a transparent poncho. If asked to talk, she'd flip the blanket off her knees and onto the cold stone, so one could sit beside her.

When asked what she was doing, she replied, "unifying the cosmos" or "centering the universe." If you asked her age, she replied, "All time is now." If asked her name she simply stated, "I am that I am," echoing God's quip to Moses in the Book of Exodus. She claimed that she lives "wherever", and that "finding food is not a problem. Food is energy, just like everything else". She claimed she's spiritual rather than religious. "I'm not telling anyone what to do. I'm simply stating the truth and if they choose to experience it, that's up to them. The ultimate truth: that we are all one; that love is all there is." People are friendly to her, she said, "because they're reflections of me, as is everyone."

This role model of living at a spiritual level is most important for the impact that she had on other people. Over the course of the day dozens of people came up and talked to her. They shared their food with her and sometimes brought her clothes and blankets, which she gave to homeless people. She'd stand to hug a friend. She greeted people by nodding and saying "Namaste," the Hindu greeting that she said roughly translates as "the divine in me recognizes the divine in you."

One woman stopped to talk with her every day. She claimed that she found her presence a great comfort. She described the woman this way: "She wishes for nothing, she won't take money, she is a saint, she is God, she is goodness in our community, and I hope that our community recognizes that without judgment. She is God to me, and that's enough for me. She opens her heart to everyone who passes by. She's a beautiful soul. Very happy."

A young homeless man explained why he chose to sit behind her in the square: "We're living in a world with no connections between each other. People want to know they're seen, so they come here and stare at each other." Another friend claimed that visitors go into confession mode when they are with her. A man explained, "We all have religion, this is a test for them there religious types." He recognized her healing powers and was trying to persuade his brother, an alcoholic, to come and speak with her.

She claimed this is not about her. She describds what people want from her is "Connection. With themselves. With their divine selves."

She disappeared as quietly as she had appeared. One day she was sitting in the square. The next she was gone. No one knows where she went. Most likely on to some other spot to share her spirit quietly and unobtrusively with the world.

This woman is an extreme example of what it means to live as a spiritual self. But living as a spiritual self does not always look like this. Each of us has our own path to follow. And yet, in the midst of our path, we can follow her model, no matter who we are or what we are involved with. Trust that we will be provided for. Be open, non-judgmental and available to all who come into our presence. Accept the reality that it isn't about us, it's about the whole universe. Each of us is only a small piece, with a very close connection to the whole.

CHAPTER TEN
AND IN CONCLUSION........

"Anything less than the best we can be is pure misery."

NOTHING THAT IS WRITTEN IN THIS BOOK IS NEW. NOTHING THAT IS WRITTEN IS UNKNOWN to each and every one of us throughout the world. It is the message that has been shared over and over again by those with wisdom throughout the ages. It is the message of the classics: the novels that continue to inspire us throughout the years; the movies that warm our hearts and bring tears to our eyes; the ballads that are shared from one generation to the next; the art, the music, the poetry, and the drama that holds its appeal in a world that is constantly changing; and the holy scriptures of many different creeds and religions.

I first learned the power of this message when I bought and read a collection of what were termed the "best" short stories of the world. As I read through each story, I found that each theme spoke to me personally, a young mother in Northern Alberta, no matter where the story had originated: Indonesia, China, New York, London, Berlin. I realized, at that point, that there is a powerful connection between each and every human being on this planet, a connection that can unite us, if we make that choice. If we make the effort to celebrate our spiritual core and listen intently to its voice, rather than focusing on the differences that are spread throughout the other levels of the self. If we do the things that we know intuitively are good and right, in the midst of a human world that is telling us otherwise.

For, in spite of the fact that we are all aware of this message and that we all honor this message in our spirits, we don't live it. We don't live it in our homes, where the acquisition of material goods has taken over the time and energy we might otherwise use to develop and sustain positive relationships with our spouses, children and other family members. We don't live it in our educational systems, where differences are mocked and punished instead of celebrated, and where the goal appears to be achieving homogeneity in a world where being the same will destroy us over time. We don't see it in the medical community, where the worship of the almighty dollar has taken over the whole profession through the use of insurance companies and pharmaceutical giants. We don't see it in the economic community, where people are enslaved by multinational corporations, whose only focus is the profit line created by other people who are swamped by overindulgence of the material self. And most of all, we don't see it in the psychological community, a community which claims to be helping in the midst of destroying; where coping skills are defined as illnesses, where children who are desperately crying out for love are given labels of oppositional defiant disorder and then medicated with drugs that haven't even been validated for use on children. No wonder we are in such a mess!

The lessons that the world needs to hear are lessons we have had to learn over and over again throughout human history. The Hopi Indian legends tell of a time when their leaders had to flee the evil that had pervaded their society, a time when the laws of the Great Spirit were ignored and the people had begun to live for material gain, disrupting and destroying the whole society. Children were uncared for. People became enamored with success and self-importance. Many decided that they indeed had created themselves and that spiritual matters had no importance. Does this not resemble much of the world we live in today?

In the 1400s a peacemaker was born to the Hurons. At that time, relations among the humans of the area were horrendous. Savage blood feuds and warfare among all of the nations of the northeast area of America had enveloped all of society in pain. Everyone bore a grudge against someone else. Revenge was paramount, which led to more pain and the need for more revenge. It didn't seem that anyone could escape this endless cycle of violence. Everyone was mentally and physically exhausted in much the same way, I am certain, as I was, living as an abused wife, and in the same way that so many in our world are exhausted today.

Deganawidah was born to an outcast of the tribe and grew up recognizing the warfare as nothing more than the quarreling of little children. Over time he developed what was called the Great Law of Peace, which spread throughout the territory and finally led to the creation of the confederacy of nations that united the Iroquois, the Hurons, the Onondagas, the Mohawks, the Senecas, the Algonquins and other smaller bands in the area. Peace was achieved, not through fighting, but through love and acceptance of difference. Benjamin Franklin's theories of government were directly influenced by Deganawidah's ideas and in turn were implemented in the creation of the government of the United States.

I could go on and on with examples such as this from history, but I think we know the truth. Fighting only leads to pain, and results in more fighting. Love, on the other hand, results in more love. This is the message of people of our time who reached the point of living on their life line: of Ghandi, of Mother Theresa and of Dr. Martin Luther King, Jr. It is the message of the prophets, prophets who are found in every race, every culture and every religion in this world. It is the message our elders learned on the battlefields of the first and second World Wars. It is the lesson we are learning as we watch the scenes of pain and destruction come to us from Iraq and other volatile places in the world where fighting continues to be the reaction of choice. It is impossible to "fight" for world peace and to expect it to result in peace. All it results in is more fighting.

If we can turn our energies away from fighting, away from the need for power and control, away from the acquisition of more and more material goods, towards love, we can and we will make a difference for the future. What we have learned from this book, through the model of self, is that it's not going to be an easy journey because it means we must face change and change is uncomfortable. It's not going to be an easy journey because we are going to have to break habits and resist using the patterns of behavior that happen automatically. It is going to be a journey in which we must squarely face ourselves to accept these automatic patterns of behavior and expect them to happen when we are faced with anxiety. It's going to be a journey in which anxiety must be brought out into the open, something that none of us are used to doing or are comfortable doing. We may assume that it makes us look weak but it is the only way we will become strong. It's a journey in which differences must be accepted and celebrated instead of defined as a threat. It's a journey in which forgiveness must be paramount: forgiveness of ourselves, forgiveness of others.

Can it happen? Yes, I believe that it can, but it is going to take a lot of courage and a lot of energy. I see that it is already in progress in so many different ways. The anxiety of my grandmother, as an illegitimate child, is no longer a major problem to be faced in most parts of the world. The battles for the acceptance of gender difference, of skin colour, of sexual orientation, of disability have been openly discussed and are being addressed. We haven't found perfect solutions to all problems, but changes have occurred and are continuing to happen each day. There is hope.

There is something stirring in the spiritual vacuum of society. People are brave enough to admit they are empty. People are searching for answers. People are recognizing that life has a purpose and are trying to discover their own. There is an openness happening in the religious bodies of the world. Groups are admitting that mistakes have been made in the past and continue to be made in the present. There is a growing acceptance of the fact we all worshipping the same creator, in different ways and with different names. There is an acceptance that we need to learn to work together in peace and harmony, instead of conflict.

I am part of the baby boomer generation: a unique group of people who were born after the Second World War. We are unique in many different ways, for we are the children of parents who fought for freedom of the whole world, parents who knew the experience of working together as team and of going without having grown up through the depression. Parents who were determined to create something new and different for their offspring. We were also unique in our numbers for suddenly we had a demographic group that outnumbered every other age group of its time. There were more children than adults when we were young. There were more teenagers when we reached that age and we burst out into the world and united with each other in a way that had never happened before or since. We continued to hold this unique position of power as young adults, as parents, and now as people facing the specter of aging together, simply because there are more of us.

This is a situation that didn't happen through chance or planning. It was a direct result of many different factors: the wars, the losses that occurred through the fighting and through the depression, the advanced level of medical knowledge which lowered the childhood death rate throughout the world, the advanced level of technical knowledge which connected us to each other through radios, telephones, television, and finally the computer and an Internet that makes it possible for us to instantly interact with anyone on the globe, whenever we choose.

The baby boomers have reached the point where they are ready to truly examine their lives and find their true potential in this world. It's been a rocky ride over the years, as people searched for the answers in their own ways, without knowing exactly what they were looking for and how they would recognize it when they found it. Anyone who lived through the turbulence of the sixties, when the power of the world was being held in the hands of teenagers, whose brains weren't completely formed, understands clearly what I am talking about. As we, as a group, advance toward our final maturity, it is time for us to take our position as the wise women and men of the world, and to make the effort to ensure that a massive paradigm shift occurs throughout society: a paradigm shift that will allow the wars to end, that will allow us all to live in peace and prosperity, that will allow our little children to grow up in a world without pain.

How do we do this? We must accept the fact that we are all individual selves that are completely and totally interconnected with every other person on this planet. We must accept that we are a spiritual force with a mission on this earth, a mission that we are missing out on because we have allowed ourselves to become stuck on the material and social levels of self, rather than focusing on the spiritual self. We must accept the fact that our primary purpose on earth is to love: to love our creator, to love each other and to love ourselves. When, and if, we do this, we will all achieve our full potential here on earth in ways that are far beyond our wildest dreams.

Each of us will have a different purpose in the midst of being this emissary of love. I can't tell you what your purpose is, but your spirit will guide you, if you make the effort to stop and listen. The more willing you are to do this, the more incredible your life becomes.

I know that one of my purposes on this earth was to make the voices of those with autism audible to the whole world. I am only one small piece of that part of the puzzle. I work in conjunction with incredible people who are spread throughout all the corners of this earth: people in Australia, England, Norway, Russia, South America, United States, Canada and every other country in the world. Some of these people I am thrilled to know personally. Others are only a name connected to a theory or a treatment modality. And then there are many more who are only an address on the Internet. Together we are making a difference in ways that touch the very core of my being. We still have a long way to go.

I could be content to continue in that purpose only, but as the years passed, and as the knowledge grew, I came to the realization that this is not just about autism any more than anything else in this world is just about one thing. Everything is connected, and my work in the field of autism is only a stepping-stone to the work that must be done with everyone in the world. In this same way, the work you are doing, in your own way, in your own corner of the world, is connected to us all, whether it is teaching a child, digging a hole, sharing a song, or baking a pie.

Letting go of the constraints of the world to follow one's intuition is not always an easy journey. As I have shared throughout this book, my journey has been one in which I have had to break away from everything that I held most dear to my heart, but in doing so I have retained all that I thought for a time I had lost. I am able to celebrate with a level of joy that is so far beyond anything I had dreamed of when I was stuck back in that world, so far away from my current life, that I can hardly believe it. A person who is living in fear must concentrate on safety, not love. A person, who is living in the midst of a social image that does not match the true self, is a person whose energy is being drained, which leads to depression. A person who is hiding away from the reality of what has happened to them, or in their family, is using their energy for secrecy. A person who has not dealt with the pain of loss is unable to give love because their energy is being drowned out by that pain. One has to make the effort to change in order to be free to be the person they were meant to be. It isn't easy. It causes a lot of stress and anxiety. But it definitely is worth the effort.

One spring I had the opportunity to be sitting in a cabin on an isolated lake in Pennsylvania, in total solitude. It was a private cabin, on a private lake. An old cabin, which had been part of a family for generations and which bore the traces of that family history proudly. In this peaceful retreat from the world, I was able to relax completely and restore my body and mind from the stress of overwork and too much change due to my travel itinerary.

As I sat on the dock and looked out over those calm waters, I marveled at the powers that had brought me to this spot, and provided me with this opportunity for healing. It was a family cabin. There was absolutely no way that I could have wrangled myself an invitation on my own. I didn't even know the people who owned the cabin. There is absolutely no way that I could have spent any amount of money to buy my presence at this cabin. It was not for sale. I was only there because of my connections in the autism world: my connections to a family who knew the family who owned the cabin and were able to arrange for my time there; my connections to people who looked at me and realized how exhausted I was, and who were willing and able to change their plans to give me this gift of solitude. This is what happens when we let go. This is what happens when we are emissaries of love in this world. This would not have been possible had I insisted on hanging on to my old way of life, had I resisted the changes that had to occur, had I not listened to my intuition and let go of the control of my life.

This is the gift that I wish for each and every one of you as you continue your search for self. Go in love and serve the world.

LIVING ON YOUR LIFE LINE: A SUMMARY

God grant me the serenity to accept the things I cannot change,
the courage to change the things I can,
and the wisdom to know the difference.

THE SPIRIT

- Acknowledge that you have a spirit.
- Listen and respond to your inner voice.
- Take ownership of your feelings. Don't blame them on anyone else.
- Celebrate your true feelings and allow yourself to feel them.
- Let go and let God. Stop living in fear.
- Share your journey with others.
- Acknowledge that change will bring discomfort, but face it anyway.

THE MIND

- Determine your own reactions to the different levels of anxiety and use them to measure how much anxiety you are feeling.
- Differentiate between acute and chronic anxiety.
- Diminish acute anxiety by bringing it out into the open and dealing with it.
- Diminish chronic anxiety by exposing it as a figment of your imagination and choosing to live in the present moment.
- Define your own belief system and recognize how your beliefs affect your reactions. Decide whether you want to hang on to each belief or discard it, one by one. Acknowledge the grief process for any belief you discard.
- Examine your past to understand the source of your reactions.
- Bring the unspoken rules of your culture out into the open so you know when you are responding to them
- Get in touch with your family of origin so you can recognize the intergenerational patterns of behavior that may affect you.
- Move away from reacting unconsciously to acting rationally. Give up reactions you do not want to use anymore and work to replace them with something else.

- Be aware that you will resort to the reactions you first learned as a child in times of high anxiety. Acknowledge that this is who you are as a person, and be gentle with yourself.
- Acknowledge the coping skills you use and make a rational decision whether you want to use them or not in the present moment. Forgive yourself when you slip back. Keep trying.
- Give yourself time to change.
- Be aware that change at the level of the mind is going to be the most uncomfortable and most difficult.
- Respect the pendulum effect in the process of change.
- Recognize the importance of the development of the brain both in yourself and in others, especially our future generations.

THE SOCIAL SELF

- Love yourself, and love your fellow men.
- Use your spirit and your beliefs to determine your life line not the reactions of other people.
- Measure how you interact with others in regards to your life line: is this your real self, or a pseudo self?
- Acknowledge the pseudo selves you have a tendency to use and rationally make the decision when to use them or not.
- Acknowledge the grief process you will experience when and if you give up a pseudo self.
- Forgive others for your experiences in the past.
- Forgive yourself for what happened in the past.
- Stop trying to change anyone but yourself.
- Stop taking anything that anyone else does personally.
- Respect the unique feelings and experiences of others as being different from your own at the same time as being as significant in this world.
- Acknowledge the coping skills that others are using and recognize that these are directly due to anxiety. Bring that anxiety out into the open, not to fix anyone else, but to diffuse the power of the anxiety.
- Get to know others so you can interact with them on their life line, instead of reacting with them at the level of a pseudo self. Acknowledge their experience and their pain as being different from yours.
- Reach your own full potential so you can model the process for others rather than concentrating on fixing them
- Take responsibility only for which you are responsible. Don't apologize for that which you do not own.

THE MATERIAL SELF

- Get to know your own body as it is. Celebrate it. Love it. Take care of it. Make use of its abilities. Respect its limitations. Treat it like the precious gift it is. Make the effort to have it look as good as possible.

- Let go of using coping skills in order to protect this body from physical or psychological distress over time.

- Look at each of the material possessions you have or you are acquiring and determine if they are what you really need. Are they worth the energy that they will take: in the present moment and throughout the years to come? Do they let the world know you as the person you truly are or do they make the world see you as a pseudo self? Do they add to your life or distract from reaching your full potential? Make rational choices of how much "stuff" you need in this life.

- Create a home which demonstrates who you are as a person, not one that meets the current fads or competes with your neighbors. Invite people over so they get to know that part of your self. Break bread together.

- Look at all of the roles that you hold. Are you meeting your full potential in each of these roles in the way that your spirit leads? Do they allow you to live on your life line or are they forcing you to be a pseudo self? How much of your energy is going to each role? Do you want to hang on to them or reject them?

- Do the best job you can do, any time that you do anything. There is no job that needs doing that is unimportant or demeaning. It's the quality of effort you put out that determines your worth, not the actual job, or the money you receive for it.

- Measure your employment by how it fits on your life line and what kind of an impact it is having on society as a whole. There are many kinds of employment out there not worth doing. The sooner we give them up, the better our world will be. Listen to your spirit when it comes to employment and then, when you decide to do something, do the very best that you can do.

- Celebrate your individual talents and abilities and share them with others. Be prepared to pay others for those you don't have.

- Give up on the fallacy that there is not enough money. Let go.

- Acknowledge the process of grief in everything you let go of at the material level of self.

NOURISHING THE SELF

- Step out of your "I don't do...." box and embrace life. Concentrate on the positives rather than the negatives.

- Engage in random acts of kindness as a gift to yourself and to others.

- Grow something.....whether it be pets, plants or children.

- Create something......... sing, dance, paint, cook, whatever

- Spend some time in nature each day if possible. Choose a lifestyle which makes this possible.

- Make the effort to visit the high energy spaces of the earth as often as you can to replenish yourself: mountains, old forests, the ocean,

- Visit places where life is celebrated: farmer's markets, festivals, parades, concerts and so on, and celebrate.

- Do unto others that which you want them to do unto you. If you do good, you can expect it in return, if your do evil the same happens; the evil will to return to you. You are in control!!

- Use traditions from the past or create your own to create a sense of consistency in your life.

- Be willing to receive as well as to give. This gives others the chance to give.

- Laugh. Search out that which is funny in your day to day life. Laugh long, laugh loud and laugh often. Laugh with others, not at them.

- Respect the power of change in your life

    - The 'self' is in a constant state of change.

    - Change is uncomfortable and is thus resisted.

    - Loss produces "holes" in the self, which must heal.

    - The healing of these "holes' occurs through the process of grief.

    - The process of grief includes the reactions of denial and isolation, sadness, bargaining, anger, guilt, depression, acceptance and hope. These must be experienced and allowed to be felt in order for one to move on.

    - Accept that once loss has occurred, the grief process will reappear from time to time when one is reminded of what one has lost.

    - Live in a state of forgiveness, of your self and of others.